D1550522

INNOVATION CAPITAL

INNOVATION CAPITAL

CAPITAL

HOW TO COMPETE
—AND WIN—
LIKE THE WORLD'S MOST
INNOVATIVE LEADERS

JEFF DYER
NATHAN FURR
CURTIS LEFRANDT

HARVARD BUSINESS REVIEW PRESS
BOSTON, MASSACHUSETTS

Library of Congress Cataloging-in-Publication Data

Names: Dyer, Jeffrey H., author. | Furr, Nathan R., author. | Lefrandt, Curtis T., author.
Title: Innovation capital : how to compete—and win—like the world's most innovative leaders / Jeffrey Dyer, Nathan Furr, Curtis Lefrandt.
Description: Harvard Business Review Press : Boston, Massachusetts, 2019.
Identifiers: LCCN 2018052385 | ISBN 9781633696525 (hardcover)
Subjects: LCSH: Success in business. | Capital. | Leadership. | Business networks. | Technological innovations.
Classification: LCC HF5386 .D985 2019 | DDC 658.4/063—dc23
LC record available at https://lccn.loc.gov/2018052385

ISBN: 978-1-63369-652-5
eISBN: 978-1-63369-653-2

CONTENTS

1

Innovation Capital

The Capacity to Win
Resources to Innovate

This book is about a critical but underappreciated ingredient for successful innovation: how innovators win support to turn their ideas into reality. Although this ability may sound simple, for the innovators we studied, it was a subtle, multifaceted art at the very heart of their success.

The book is about innovation, but it's not about getting new ideas. Despite the importance of good ideas, innovators need something more than just a good idea to succeed. Nor is the book about innovation processes, such as customer engagement, design thinking, and lean startup. Despite the potential of these processes to ensure customer value, innovators still need resources to succeed. Nor do we explain how to create an innovation culture in this book. Even if leaders know how to create such a culture but lack the support to turn their innovation into reality, they will fail.

In saying this, we are in no way downplaying the importance of creativity, understanding customer jobs to be done, prototyping using minimum viable products, or organizational culture. These concepts are vital to success. But they have been covered in other books on innovation, including our own books, *The Innovator's DNA* (which teaches you how to get creative ideas) and *The Innovator's Method* (which teaches you how to test and validate those ideas with customers).

But no other books have discussed this secret ingredient that separates non-innovators (with good ideas) from successful innovators (who win the support needed to turn their ideas into reality). This book is written to open the black box of that secret ingredient and answer the question, *How can you win the support needed from bosses, colleagues, partners, and investors to bring your idea to life?*

All aspiring innovators, whether they are working alone or in an organization, must overcome the *innovator's paradox* if they want to succeed. What is the innovator's paradox? Quite simply, the more novel, radical, or risky your idea, the greater the challenge you will face acquiring the resources you need to turn your idea into reality. Although we all say we want more-radical ideas because they are likely to have a greater impact, when it comes to getting the means to pursue radical ideas, the greater the risk and uncertainty, the more skittish potential supporters (investors, bosses, partners, etc.) become. Before jumping in, most supporters want the idea to be proven or at least want the uncertainty reduced in some meaningful way.

But how can you prove that an idea can work if you lack the resources to start developing it? You need resources to make innovative concepts succeed. Even the leanest of the lean startups need some resources to test out their ideas. Most truly big ideas need a lot more.

Your capacity to overcome the innovator's paradox—to secure the necessary means to turn novel and risky ideas into reality—is key to innovation leadership. We've all seen leaders who excel at winning backing for their ideas. But this ability isn't simply due to charisma, luck, or some other undefinable quality. Their capacity to inspire advocates and benefactors is a science and an art that generates something they have that others do not: *innovation capital*.

Innovation Capital: The Ability to Win Resources for Your Ideas

Over the last several years, we have had the chance to learn from dozens of Fortune 500 executives, dozens of innovation teams and startups, and exclusive interviews with some of the world's most innovative leaders, including Jeff Bezos (Amazon), Elon Musk (Tesla, SpaceX), Marc Benioff (Salesforce), Shantanu Narayen (Adobe), Indra Nooyi (PepsiCo), Mark Parker (Nike), and Jeff Weiner (LinkedIn), and many others. We discovered that the ability to win support for ideas is about much more than simply pitching effectively. It is an entire set of skills tied to leadership, influence, social capital, and relationship management. In short, innovative leaders build a body of skills that generate innovation capital: the ability to compete for—and win—the resources needed for innovation to flourish.

Innovation capital isn't tangible, like money or equipment. It is an intangible force, like political capital, that helps you assemble the means to implement your ideas. It comes from who you are (innovation-specific human capital), who you know (innovation-specific social capital), and what you are known for (innovation-specific reputation capital). It gets multiplied by what we call

FIGURE 1-1

Where innovation capital comes from

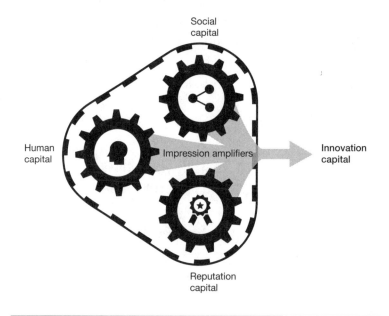

impression amplifiers—actions that get attention and credibility for you and your ideas (see figure 1-1).

Innovation capital lies at the heart of your ability to convince resource holders to support your ideas. You have to earn and develop innovation capital by practicing specific behaviors and leveraging the right activities at the right time. People aren't born with innovation capital; they must build it. And it's far more critical to innovation than most of us realize (see the sidebar "Who This Book Is For").

The importance of innovation capital first dawned on us when we were interviewing one of the world's most innovative leaders, Marc Benioff, chairman and co-CEO of Salesforce. When discussing his own success as an effective leader of innovation, Benioff emphasized that his ability to champion innovations at

The Components of Innovation Capital

HUMAN CAPITAL: forward-thinking, creative problem solving, and persuasion abilities

SOCIAL CAPITAL: social connections with those who have valuable resources

REPUTATION CAPITAL: a track record and reputation for innovation

IMPRESSION AMPLIFIERS: actions that generate attention and credibility for you and your ideas

INNOVATION CAPITAL: the capacity to win the resources needed for innovation to flourish

Salesforce has increased over time—because he has developed his innovation capital:

> My ability to generate innovations for Salesforce has basically built up over time. Over twenty years, I've built up what we might call *innovation capital* that I can spend to try new things—to change the organization, change the products, change what needs to be changed. Whoever comes in and is the next CEO is not going to have as much innovation capital. They're going to have to accrue that on their own . . . They're going to have to earn it by being an innovative leader. That's the only way you can get innovation capital.

Benioff understands that as he has improved his innovation leadership skills (who he is), widened and deepened his social connections both inside and outside Salesforce (who he knows), and advanced his reputation as an innovative leader (what he is known for), he has increased his innovation capital. This type of capital has increased his capacity to influence others to support and join his innovation initiatives.

Innovation capital explains why Elon Musk was able to raise over $1 billion to enter one of the most historically unattractive (unprofitable) industries in the world (automobiles). It explains why he can simply mention *hyperloop*, an idea that has been around since the early 1900s, and interest in the idea suddenly explodes as financial backers step in to fund a company and ultimately to seed a new transportation industry (figure 1-2). Innovation capital also explains why talented people rush to work at the companies Musk has founded and why SpaceX president

FIGURE 1-2

Hyperloop awareness: the Musk innovation capital effect

Elon Musk first mentioned his idea of hyperloop technology in July 2012 (see arrow). Hyperloop technology has been hypothesized, in various forms, since the nineteenth century.

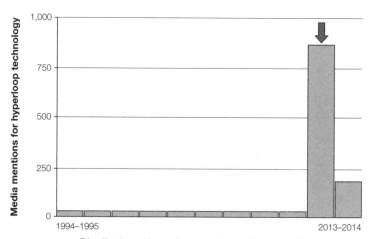

Note: Media mentions are from Factiva database of most popular business sources, 1994–2014.

Who This Book Is For

In our research, consulting, and teaching, many people involved with innovation have repeatedly told us how discouraged they are when their new idea never sees the light of day. Many corporate innovation teams, startup entrepreneurs, and other innovation leaders simply feel unable to win the capital, talent, technical support, or other necessary resources to move forward. We have written this book for people like them and for anyone else who wants to become a more effective leader of innovation, no matter the person's position or project. We wrote this book both for aspiring corporate leaders who need support from bosses and peers across the enterprise for their ideas and for entrepreneurs who need to find investors and collaborators.

In this book, we draw on our research with both managers and entrepreneurs. Because we are writing to these two camps, we include examples of individuals inside organizations as well as entrepreneurs. While the context is somewhat different, the strategies are very similar, and there are critical lessons to be borrowed from each group. Moreover, although we studied the leaders with the greatest innovation capital—people like Bezos or Musk—and we weave in lessons from one-on-one interviews with these legends, most of us are not going to be the next Bezos. So instead we interpret what is relevant from their actions to more typical innovators, and we weave in examples of how more-representative leaders and entrepreneurs have used these same lessons to build innovation capital.

Because our ultimate goal in writing this book is to help you learn how to become an effective leader of innovation—to successfully secure the resources you need to nurture your ideas and

(*continued*)

launch new initiatives—we have included practical advice, tools, and tips in every chapter. To support and augment these tips, we have developed a free set of digital tools designed to help you develop your innovation capital. You can find these resources at www.innovatorsdna.com/innovation-capital.

We wish you the very best of luck as you embark on your innovation journey, and we look forward to hearing about your adventures!

Gwynne Shotwell has said, "We rarely lose a candidate." And finally, Musk's innovation capital explains why twenty-two million people follow his every tweet. With this level of innovation capital, he can assemble the resources necessary to convert novel ideas into transformative realities.

The Power of Innovation Capital

Before we introduce our insights about how to build innovation capital, let's consider the dangers of overlooking the importance of innovation capital. These dangers are best illustrated by the battle between two great inventors: Thomas Edison and Nikola Tesla.

Both Edison and Tesla were considered great inventors. Edison was known more as a practical inventor who produced inventions largely through trial and error. Lacking sophisticated training in mathematics or engineering, Edison instead applied a famous work ethic to produce new ideas through brute trial and error, arguing that invention (or, to use his word, genius) is "one percent inspiration and ninety-nine percent perspiration." He is credited with inventing the phonograph, the motion picture camera, the alkaline battery, and, most importantly, the electric light bulb and the accompanying distribution system for electric power.

By contrast, Tesla grew up in Europe and showed early signs of genius. His ability to perform integral calculus in his head led his tutors to think he was cheating. He attended Joanneum Polytechnic in Graz, Austria, one of the world's best technical institutions. After his studies, Tesla briefly worked with Edison early in his career. Although he admired Edison's work ethic, Tesla had an opinion about Edison's approach: "His method was inefficient in the extreme . . . I was almost sorry to witness his doings, knowing that just a little theory and calculation would have saved him ninety percent of the labor. But he had a veritable contempt for book learning and mathematical knowledge, trusting himself entirely to his inventor's instinct and practical American sense."[1]

Tesla's genius and education led him to develop the foundations for electric induction motors, wireless telegraphy, radios, neon lamps, and remote control. In fact, his inventions in three-phase electric power and alternating current eventually enabled the global distribution of electricity as we know it.

However, although Tesla's ideas arguably were more brilliant, he was unable to commercialize his ideas. He died virtually penniless in a hotel room in New York.[2] In stark contrast, Edison died wealthy in his New Jersey mansion having won the Congressional Medal of Honor and having his birthday, February 11, designated as National Inventor's Day. If Tesla's ideas ultimately had more impact, then why was Edison so much more successful?

One part of the answer is certainly the lessons taught by earlier studies of innovation. For example, Edison learned early in life that inventions are only valuable if someone is willing to pay for them. At the age of twenty, he invented a device that counted the votes in the US House of Representatives in only a minute or two—saving both time and money. But no one would buy it.

It turns out that legislators didn't want the voting to be made quicker and more efficient, as the process in place allowed for filibustering and politicking. His first invention taught him an important lesson. "Anything that won't sell, I don't want to invent," he said. "Its sale is proof of utility, and utility is success."[3]

But another underappreciated factor contributing to differences in Edison's and Tesla's success was Edison's ability to win backers, collaborators, and attention for his ideas—his ability to build and leverage innovation capital to turn his ideas into reality. For example, Edison worked purposefully to fashion an image of himself as a hardworking, hands-on inventor (in addition to his constant reference to hard work, he even once reportedly smeared soot on his hands and face before an interview to bolster that reputation).[4] He also worked hard to build his social capital with other talented inventors, but also with wealthy families and financiers like J. P. Morgan, the Vanderbilts, and the Rockefellers. As a result, Edison attracted talented associates like Swiss-born machinist John Kruesi and an English master mechanic, Charles Batchelor. Then when Edison developed a commercially viable light bulb, he was able to convince Morgan to advance him $30,000 for the Edison Electric Light Company. When the company began installing electricity in homes, Morgan's home in New York was one of the first to get electricity. The electrification of the financier's home generated further attention for Edison's invention.

But his connections with people and actions to get attention for his ideas weren't accidents; they were practiced habits that the inventor repeated over and over. For example, the morning that his lab developed a working phonograph, Edison took it to New York to the office of the editor of the *Scientific American*. "I said I had something to show him," Edison said. "He asked what it was. I told him I had a machine that would record and reproduce the human voice. I set up the machine and recited 'Mary had a little lamb.' Then I reproduced it so that it could be heard all over the room. They kept me at it until the crowd got so great Mr. Beach [the editor] was afraid the floor would collapse."[5] This demonstration led *Scientific American* staff to take up the cause of his invention, writing about it in newspapers worldwide throughout the next week. He also promoted the phonograph—and all his other inventions—by creating a list of "applications" (what we would call *use cases* today) for it. Phonograph "applications" included reproducing music, making phonographic books, recording teaching lectures, and taking dictation.

By contrast, although Tesla was a brilliant inventor who developed technologies that have shaped our modern world, he lacked Edison's skills at building and employing innovation capital. For example, after he developed his ideas for an induction motor that ran on alternating current (AC), Tesla tried unsuccessfully for several years to raise funds to commercialize it. He spoke of his frustration: "The utter failure of my attempts to raise capital for development was a major disappointment."[6] During this period, Tesla developed patents for other useful inventions, such as arc lights and dynamos. But he struggled to find the means to commercialize these ideas until B. A. Vail and Robert Lane approached him with the proposal of forming an arc light company. When Tesla agreed, Vail secured a contract for lighting the streets of his hometown, Rahway, New Jersey. The company installed moonlight white arc lamps around the city, and when the electrification of Rahway was completed, *Electrical Review* featured it on the front page of its August 1886 issue. Tesla was optimistic. He believed that once the lighting of Rahway was complete, his company could get on with the serious business of producing AC induction motors and huge electrical grids. But Vail and Lane had other plans. They maneuvered to dismiss Tesla from the company. And because Tesla lacked the innovation capital to fight them or to restart on his own, he found himself ousted. "It was the hardest blow I ever received," Tesla said. "I was forced out of the company, losing not only all my interest but my reputation as engineer and inventor."[7]

But Tesla didn't give up. He persisted with his AC induction motor technology and eventually published a groundbreaking paper—"A New System of Alternate Current Motors and Transformers." This work helped him win the financial backing to start the Tesla Electric Light Company—with an eye toward commercializing his AC induction motor technology. But despite Tesla's inventive ideas, the company was unable to assemble the resources needed to commercialize the technology.

Tesla was a visionary and was even described by Edison as someone whose "ideas are magnificent."[8] But he was simply unable to attract the right talent and financial resources to successfully commercialize his ideas. Some have suggested that his personality traits were a contributing factor. He was reclusive and kept rigid habits (he worked each day from 9 a.m. to 6 p.m., ate dinner at the same restaurant each night, and had to be served by the same waiter). Tesla's partners eventually sold Tesla Electric Light Company's patents to George Westinghouse, CEO of the Westinghouse Electric Company. The involvement of Westinghouse is one of the only reasons we know of Tesla today. According to one Tesla biography, "Tesla was a visionary. But without the backing of the great entrepreneur and gifted engineer George Westinghouse, Tesla's revolutionary inventions would probably have come to nothing."[9]

Ultimately, Edison's commercial victories over Tesla were due not to the superior quality of Edison's ideas but to differences in the men's innovation capital. Although Tesla deserved better, his lack of innovation capital hindered his efforts to attract the talent and backing to commercialize his ideas. As a result, he died poor and faded from history until recently, when his invention, the AC motor, and his name became the heart of Tesla Motors.

Building Innovation Capital: Lessons from Innovative Leaders

Creativity is not enough. The Tesla versus Edison comparison illustrates the difference between a great inventor and a great innovative leader. Apple cofounders Steve "Woz" Wozniak and Steve Jobs offer another illustration. Wozniak was a great inventor (and even built solid innovation capital), but Jobs had the ability to lead innovation in a way that Wozniak could not. Edison and Jobs had a broader skill set than did Tesla and Wozniak, and these skills allowed them to recruit talent, secure financial resources, develop desirable products, and gain attention for themselves and their projects.

Over the last two decades, our research on innovation and our work with hundreds of individual innovators has unpacked many of the better-known lessons about creativity, ideation, and innovation processes. But when we peeled apart stories like Edison versus Tesla, and Jobs versus Wozniak, we repeatedly saw something else that had been missing: innovation capital. To better understand innovation capital, we conducted in-depth research and interviews with the world's most innovative leaders and those who work with them. We ranked these leaders for *Forbes* using proxies of their innovation capital (see the appendix for our ranking methodology).[10] We then studied and conducted exclusive interviews with many of the top twenty-five leaders (table 1-1): CEOs Bezos, Musk, Benioff, Nooyi (PepsiCo), Parker (Nike), Weiner (LinkedIn), Narayen (Adobe), Satya Nadella (Microsoft), Scott Cook and Brad Smith (Intuit), Len Schleifer and George Yancopoulos (Regeneron), Arne Sorenson (Marriott International), and Scott Stephenson (Verisk Analytics).

In addition to these innovation outliers, we interviewed other successful leaders—other large-company CEOs and startup

TABLE 1-1

Top twenty-five most innovative leaders worldwide, 2018

| Leader and rank | Company | VALUE CREATION | | INNOVATION |
		Three-year market value creation (in $ billions)	Three-year stock market gains (%)	Company innovation premium (%)
1. Jeff Bezos	Amazon, Inc.	$450	366%	71.5%
2. Elon Musk	Tesla Motors, Inc.	48	819	75.3
3. Mark Zuckerberg	Facebook, Inc.	376	563	61.8
4. Timothy Cook	Apple, Inc.	369	123	11.6
5. Satya Nadella	Microsoft Corp.	278	84	31.6
6. Marc Benioff	Salesforce, Inc.	50	143	80.7
7. Shantanu Narayen	Adobe Systems, Inc.	68	365	64.4
8. Reed Hastings	Netflix, Inc.	78	1,351	72.2
9. Jeff Weiner	LinkedIn Corp.	16	96	60.0
10. Larry Page and Sergey Brin	Alphabet, Inc.	491	197	33.9
11. Arne Sorenson	Marriott International, Inc.	38	264	53.7
12. Robert Iger	Disney (Walt) Co.	74	116	26.2
13. James Whitehurst	Red Hat, Inc.	11	127	56.1
14. Jeffrey Leiden	Vertex Pharmaceuticals, Inc.	29	258	58.2
15. Jean-Jacques Bienaime	BioMarin Pharmaceutical, Inc.	9	81	63.6
16. Mark Parker	Nike, Inc.	45	142	34.6
17. Stephen Easterbrook	McDonald's Corp.	29	46	25.8
18. Michael Mahoney	Boston Scientific Corp.	26	333	41.7
19. Scott Cook and Brad Smith	Intuit, Inc.	23	165	45.6
20. Indra Nooyi	PepsiCo, Inc.	65	75	38.5
21. Len Schleifer and George Yancopoulos	Regeneron Pharmaceuticals	23	120	39.5
22. Scott Stephenson	Verisk Analytics, Inc.	5	46	50.6
23. Jeffery Yabuki	Fiserv, Inc.	17	232	37.0
24. Steven Collis	AmerisourceBergen Corp.	10	113	47.4
25. Muhtar Kent	The Coca-Cola Company	33	27	42.8

Note: For a detailed description of our methodology, see Jeff Dyer, Nathan Furr, and Mike Hendron, "How We Rank the Most Innovative Leaders," *Forbes*, September 4, 2018, https://www.forbes.com/sites/nathanfurrjeffdyer/2018/09/04/how-we-rank-the-worlds-most-innovative-leaders/#49de93aa1139.

entrepreneurs—who, from a wide variety of industries, had achieved some success in building innovation capital for themselves and their organizations. We assembled historical case studies like the Edison-Tesla example above. And we interviewed dozens of up-and-comers—individuals who aren't yet in senior or visible positions but who are building their innovation capital in a variety of companies and industries. The up-and-comers include startup entrepreneurs, corporate entrepreneurs, mid-level managers, and even recent college or MBA graduates looking for their first job. In other words, we studied ordinary folks like you and us—people starting to build their innovation capital and learning how to be successful leaders.

We combine the insights from this research—the innovation outliers, the successful leaders, the historical case studies, and the up-and-comers—spreading examples of each throughout the book, to help you understand how to build your innovation capital, no matter your position or project. These insights are critical for leaders or managers in business, entrepreneurs and change agents, artists and designers, scientists and inventors, or anyone else who has an idea and needs to win support to make it real.

The Components of Innovation Capital

So what convinces people to support an idea, whether the support be their time (e.g., joining your project), money, endorsement, or any other backing to help you and your idea? As we described, our research suggests that people and organizations will be influenced primarily by three interrelated innovation-specific factors:

- Human capital: who you are as a leader of innovation

- Social capital: who you know with expertise and resources

- Reputation capital: what you've done to warrant a reputation for innovation

The effect of these three types of capital can be multiplied by *impression amplifiers* that help you gain attention and credibility for your ideas.

How exactly are potential supporters influenced by these factors? In academia, we use what we call a *simultaneous equation model* to describe how these factors work together.[11] Sponsors are simultaneously weighing all these factors together: whether you have the innovation skills as a leader to pull this off (who you are as a leader of innovation), whether you are well connected with others who will need to support your project (who you know with resources or expertise), and whether you have a track record and reputation for innovation success (what you are known for). Potential sponsors may weigh each of these factors somewhat differently, but they consider all these parts of your innovation capital to decide whether to support you and your ideas.

These combined parts work together like gears in an engine (which is why we have depicted figure 1-1 as a set of gears). As you get each gear moving, it can have a flywheel effect. The *flywheel effect*, first coined by management expert Jim Collins, refers to the process of getting a huge flywheel (say, a massive 5,000-pound metal disk) into motion. Initially, attempts to move the flywheel produce almost no movement—it is almost impossible to imagine the flywheel at speed. Then, slowly, the wheel gathers speed, and suddenly the momentum of the flywheel kicks in your favor. You push no harder than during the first rotation, but the flywheel goes faster and faster. Each turn builds on the work done earlier, compounding your investment of effort. Eventually, the huge, heavy disk flies forward, with almost unstoppable momentum. The innovation-capital engine—with its three gears and the lubricant of impression amplifiers—can propel a person's innovation capital in a similar way.

This analogy is relevant because building your innovation capital starts with small steps that can eventually have big outcomes. Innovation capital outliers—leaders like Bezos and Musk, who are numbers one and two in our ranking—didn't start out being that different from the rest of us. They accumulated their innovation capital through small steps and then got momentum from the flywheel cycle. Today they have more good ideas to champion because more people bring good ideas to them; they develop more social connections because of their reputation—people want to know them. And because they have access to a greater number of good ideas and more social connections, they can build their reputation for innovation by launching more innovations. These components are interrelated in a positive way—more of one component leads to more of another (academics call this relationship *mutual causality*, but you might just think of these components as positively reinforcing each other).[12] Resource holders simultaneously consider all three components when deciding to give someone their time or resources for an innovation project. So let's examine how you can get your innovation capital flywheel started. We'll begin with a brief description of the three components and the impression amplifiers.

Human Capital: Who You Are as a Leader of Innovation

Not surprisingly your knowledge and skills—your human capital—will play a critical role in building innovation capital. Although who you are has many dimensions, three abilities play a greater role in building innovation capital: forward thinking, creative problem solving, and persuasion. (Creativity obviously plays a role in innovation capital, but we focus on the role of creative problem solving because creativity has the greatest impact on an individual's innovation capital when applied to problem solving rather than random idea generation.) For example, the first skill that helps you build innovation-specific human capital is what we call forward thinking—or the ability to engage in mental time travel to envision future opportunities before others do. It partly explains why Satya Nadella (number five on our innovative leaders list), a graduate from a mid-tier computer science school, rose from one of tens of thousands of entry-level engineers to become CEO of Microsoft. Nadella attributes his rise in part to his forward thinking. When he joined Microsoft, he believed that the company's future would be in the cloud and artificial intelligence rather than in the cash cow businesses of the day, such as Microsoft Windows or Microsoft Office. So initially he worked as a Windows NT (server operating system) evangelist, led Bing (Microsoft's search engine) and eventually joined the server and tools business (forerunner of the cloud) and developed expertise in areas that he believed would be critical to Microsoft's future success. This forward-focused approach required betting on, and building expertise with, the cloud technologies that would shape the future *before* it arrived.

But it isn't just recognized leaders like Nadella who engage in forward thinking to build their innovation capital. Mary Lombardo, an executive at United Technologies Corporation (UTC) used forward thinking to help both herself and her company build innovation capital and prepare for the future. She realized that UTC's industry would undergo major changes in the 2020s and that, to prosper, the company needed to better understand both the market (demand) and the technological uncertainties facing the company. So she proposed that the company create "scout" positions to provide insights into the market and technological uncertainties facing the company. Company leaders were persuaded by her arguments, and scout positions were created to provide information to help the leadership team better understand how markets and technologies were changing. Lombardo was recognized for her forward thinking and rewarded with greater responsibility within UTC's innovation function—including having the scouts report to her. Lombardo told us, "I've had people on my team tell me, 'You're thinking about things it takes people two years to catch up to.'"

In addition to mental time travel, the leaders we studied built their innovation capital through creative problem solving (including so-called first-principles problem solving) to pursue those opportunities and by cultivating their ability to persuade others to join them on the journey. We will return to these skills and how you can develop them in chapter 2.

Social Capital: Who You Know with Expertise and Resources

It may come as little surprise that your social connections—your social capital—can help build your innovation capital. But what may surprise you is that your strong social ties matter less than your ability to facilitate connections and relationships with weak social ties. We will introduce a social concept called the *Dunbar number* in chapter 3 and explain the limits of your strong social connections. Successful leaders of innovation excel at networking through weak social ties to get the resources they need. We also examine which characteristics, or categories, of people are most valuable to have in your network. The world's most innovative leaders focus largely on networking with five types of people: (1) innovators and entrepreneurs, (2) organization leaders, (3) financial benefactors, (4) influencers, and (5) customers. Individuals from these five categories bring very different, but valuable, resources to innovation projects.

As an example of how to bring resources to a project through social connections, consider how Gavin Christensen, a young venture capitalist with aspirations to run his own venture fund, built his innovation-specific social capital. Christensen was fortunate to secure an associate position at a venture-capital fund. But he was a long way from running his own fund. He knew that his connections would be important in his becoming a partner or starting his own fund. So with the buy-in of the partners of the firm, he led the creation of an award program within the local venture fund ecosystem. The awards would recognize the top innovators and entrepreneurs and, in an award ceremony, would bring them together to build community. Inside the firm, this program was seen as extra work that was helpful, but not strategic or high visibility to promotion inside the firm. However, the award program was well received and supported within the ecosystem. Fundamentally, people enjoy recognition, particularly the recognition of their peers. Recipients prized this validation because it included an element of peer evaluation and approval. But more importantly, it created a way for Christensen to build relationships with all the top investors and innovators in the region.

When he later went to launch an innovative seed fund, these relationships proved crucial in securing the capital he needed to launch the new fund. As Christensen recalls, "Getting started as an investor is hard. Being the first institutional seed investor in the Rocky Mountain region during the Great Recession added extra degrees of difficulty. How do you get smart people to trust you with millions of dollars of their money to invest when you are in your early thirties? You give them something first. Fundamentally, venture capital is an intangible good. Because I knew all the innovative people in the area and many had a positive relationship with me, it really helped to get the ball rolling, and the recognition program was part of that."

We examine in more depth how to access and build relationships with individuals across these categories in chapter 3.

Reputation Capital: What You've Done to Warrant a Reputation for Innovation

Your reputation for innovation—built from your visible track record for innovation—also makes up an important part of your innovation capital. Although at first it may seem a bit of a chicken-and-egg problem (how do you develop a reputation as a successful innovator without the resources to develop this reputation?), there are several pathways to building a reputation for innovation.

First, the most valuable thing you can do is to be a founder— but that doesn't mean you need to be an entrepreneur. Innovators find a way to have an impact, whether that means starting a company or simply launching an initiative. For example, Indra Nooyi, chairman and former CEO at PepsiCo and number twenty on our list, traces some of her innovation capital back to her efforts to identify the key global megatrends affecting PepsiCo's business. She founded a MegaTrends group to identify the trends and propose moves the company needed to make to navigate them successfully. Similarly, Kate O'Keeffe, an executive at Cisco, attributes much of her reputation for innovation to her founding of Cisco Hyper-Innovation Living Labs (CHILL)—a process for innovating with suppliers, customers, and partners. CHILL was cool enough that it was even written about in *Harvard Business Review*—and naturally this attention bolstered O'Keeffe's reputation as an innovator. It doesn't matter whether you are the founder of a new process to recruit and hire the best people, a new way to reach potential customers, or a new process to reduce defects and improve quality. But be a founder.

You can also build a reputation for innovation by taking on challenging, and visible, assignments or by associating with prestigious individuals or entities in a way that allows you to "borrow" from their reputation. Alternatively, you can build a reputation for innovation by demonstrating strategic judgment or a track record of making the hard calls about where to allocate resources for future growth. A final way to build your brand as an innovator is to exhibit scrappiness, or a dogged spirit that enables you to get a lot done with few resources. Over time, your reputation for scrappiness can build your track record as an innovator. We examine in more detail how to build your reputation for innovation in chapter 4.

Gaining Attention and Credibility through Impression Amplifiers

Even if you currently don't have much innovation capital, there are still things you can do to win buy-in for your innovative idea or project. Our study of innovative leaders revealed that they are masters of persuasion, and they consciously use seven specific techniques to manage the impressions of others. We call these techniques impression amplifiers. We define impression amplifiers as observable actions you can take to get attention and support for your ideas. More specifically, they can be used to sell your idea by making it understandable and appealing or to demonstrate that others believe in and support your idea. Research in esoteric-sounding areas like symbolic management and impression management show that impression amplifiers work as powerful forms of persuasion. Perhaps most importantly, they are techniques that anyone can use starting today.

For example, Marc Andreessen and Jim Clark were cofounders of Netscape (the web browser), a company that had a huge initial public offering (IPO) of $2.9 billion in 1995. Before they were eventually beat by Microsoft's strategy of bundling Internet Explorer with Windows, Netscape was the technology company star of its time. Although Clark was the legendary founder behind Silicon Graphics and the brainchild of Netscape, today Andreessen has far greater innovation capital and is much better known. Why? Impression amplifiers. Although both men had strong human capital, the Netscape team worked strategically to leverage impression amplifiers to present Andreessen as the kid prodigy behind Netscape. For months the PR team worked to promote Andreessen, and their coup de grâce came when they landed a cover photo on *Time* magazine, portraying Andreessen, barefoot and sitting on a throne, and labeled "the barefoot genius." The team's tactics worked brilliantly, winning attention and credibility for both Andreessen and Netscape. Andreessen's story illustrates but one of seven impression amplifiers that innovators use to win support for their ideas. We'll expand on these amplifiers in chapters 5 and 6.

Although Andreessen's story may make these techniques seem out of reach (most of us won't be profiled in *Time* magazine), they are actually much more within reach than you realize. For example, Brad Jones, when he was an executive at ANZ Bank in Australia, used broadcasting and committing (another amplifier) to win support for a controversial mobile money platform business, Wing Money, just before the financial crisis of 2008. To win attention and support for his internal venture, Jones reached out through his social network to the head of corporate social responsibility, told her about Wing Money, which serves the underbanked in Cambodia, and convinced her to write about the project in the annual report. This brought valuable attention and legitimacy to the venture. He also applied for, and received, a grant from the government of Australia, which created an irreversible company commitment to the project. Later, when the financial crisis set in and all projects were being cut, Jones' efforts saved Wing Money, a business that has gone on to be very successful today.

Although there are many tactics that can be used to persuade someone to support a course of action, most fall within seven impression amplifier categories: broadcasting, signaling, storytelling, materializing, committing, comparing, and creating scarcity (FOMO). Each impression amplifier works because it is governed by a fundamental psychological principle that influences human behavior and gives the tactics their power. Impression amplifiers are examined in detail in chapters 5 and 6.

Igniting the Virtuous Cycle of Innovation Leadership

Our examination of the world's most innovative leaders revealed an interesting leadership pattern that is used by many leaders with innovation capital. We call it the virtuous cycle of innovation leadership. The cycle begins by identifying a lofty vision that attracts others to the project. The vision should create an exciting or inspiring emotional connection. The lofty vision attracts better talent, which produces better products and customer experiences, which attract a larger customer base, which builds a stronger brand, which in turn attracts the best talent. And so on. The cycle repeats.

Musk (number two on our list) has initiated this virtuous cycle at Tesla, starting with a lofty mission to "create sustainable transportation" and to "reduce carbon emissions" (but also building cars that are beautiful and *fast*). He has started a virtuous cycle at SpaceX with his ambitious concept of traveling to Mars to build a colony that could one day potentially save the human race. And he has created a lofty vision on a smaller scale with products like the Tesla Powerwall, the battery pack that Musk says may "change the fundamental energy structure of the world."

But it's not just famous leaders like Musk who set a virtuous cycle in motion. Sterling Anderson, former head of Tesla Autopilot, is doing the same thing at Aurora Innovation, a startup focused on providing a full-stack autopilot solution for major automakers like Volkswagen and Hyundai. Anderson left Tesla to cofound Aurora with Chris Urmson, former head of autonomous driving at Google. Together they have painted a vision of being the "Intel inside" company for autonomous driving. They are targeting the passenger economy, estimated to be worth $800 billion by 2035 and $7 trillion by 2050, according to a 2017 study by UK data research firm Strategy Analytics. Using a lofty vision and their own innovation capital, Anderson and Urmson are attracting top engineers (according to a *Fortune* article).[13] They are hoping to ignite the same cycle that has worked for Musk and many others. We examine innovation leadership and the virtuous cycle of innovation leadership in chapter 7.

Innovation Capital Matters for Companies, Too

Our research also reveals that innovation capital matters for companies much more than most leaders realize. Stakeholders give companies that build a reputation for innovation more resources and leeway to grow by doing new things. For example, Amazon has a reputation for innovation whereas Walmart has a reputation for efficiency (as measured by the number of media articles in major business news sources that describe the companies as innovative or efficient). We studied the S&P 500 firms to determine which firms had a reputation for innovation—and whether that reputation influenced the firm's market value. Specifically, we looked at a company's market value multiple. (Calculate market value multiple by dividing the company's market value by the book value of a company's assets; the greater the multiple, the more investors see value being created beyond the book value

FIGURE 1-3

Market value multiple associated with a reputation for innovation

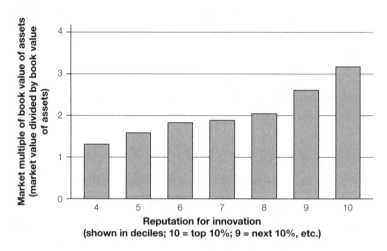

Source: Compustat financial data and Factiva news articles.

Note: N = 1,930; 361 S&P 500 firms from 2000 to 2014; excludes firms in regulated industries as well as firms with zero (null) values for reputation for innovation. "Reputation for innovation" is measured as business media articles describing the company as innovative.

of the company's assets.) We found that a company's reputation for innovation matters—in a big way. Companies with a strong reputation for innovation (in the top 10 percent) achieved market value multiples that were almost three times higher than firms at or below the fiftieth percentile (figure 1-3).

In the case of Amazon versus Walmart, Amazon's market multiple was over 5 times the book value of its assets, whereas Walmart's was only 1.5 times the book value of its assets. Not surprisingly, Amazon's media reputation for innovation was ten times greater than Walmart's between 2013 and 2018. Amazon's reputation for innovation has allowed the company to continue to obtain support from investors and stakeholders while launching dozens of new products and services, often outside its retail business, even as it delivered low or negative profits. In contrast,

Walmart has been punished by investors for pursuing innovation over efficiency. Indeed, when Walmart announced in 2015 that it would cut profits to reinvest in store improvements and innovation, the stock price collapsed nearly 30 percent while the CEO was speaking.

The takeaway is that a reputation for innovation—at the individual or organizational level—helps you obtain resources and gives you the freedom to experiment and try new things. It has a real impact on a company's market value.[14]

Our research sheds light on how well-known companies like Amazon and Tesla—and even lesser-known companies like the ING Group and Monster Beverage—have built innovation capital. Our research also reveals how companies that historically had low innovation capital, like Walmart, can build their innovation capital. We describe how companies build innovation capital in chapter 8.

Building Your Innovation Capital

Our goal with this book is to help you build your innovation capital. We describe the techniques we have learned from both the world's great innovators and everyday innovators. To help you evaluate the strength of your innovation-specific human capital, social capital, and reputation capital, we also provide assessments for you to complete at the end of chapters 2 through 4. We have structured the book to help you answer questions you may have about how to build and use your own innovation capital, and we offer advice and tips on how to take it to the next level. For example, the book will help you answer the following questions:

- What skills are most likely to convince others that I have what it takes to successfully lead an innovation project? (chapter 2)

- What problem-solving process should I use to increase the probability of developing a breakthrough (disruptive) solution? (chapter 2)

- How do I create a so-called reality distortion field to persuade others to join or support my innovation projects? (chapter 2)

- How do I network effectively to get resources from the right people for my ideas or projects? Who are the right people to target? (chapter 3)

- How do I get noticed at my organization and build a personal innovation brand? (chapter 4)

- How do I convince my boss, my colleague, an angel investor, or a venture capitalist that my idea has merit? (chapters 5 and 6)

- What does it mean to provide visionary leadership? How do I do that? (chapter 7)

- How can my organization build a reputation for innovation to attract customers, employees, investors, and other key stakeholders? (chapter 8)

- How can I get support from key stakeholders to pursue innovation initiatives in an organization that lacks innovation capital and then build the organization's reputation for innovation? (chapter 8)

As you build your innovation capital, you will become more valuable to your company. As more people in your company develop their innovation capital, your company's reputation for innovation—your company's innovation capital—will also rise. Our research shows that the most valuable reputation that any individual or organization can have is that of innovator.[15]

A reputation for innovation carries more prestige, more status, more value than does any other label. You may not be persuaded yet, but perhaps the most important next step in your career is to build your innovation capital. Our research suggests that for most business professionals, this step is critical in becoming an effective leader. Indeed, in today's world, successful leadership is all about being a successful leader of innovation. So read on. Our book will teach you how to build and use your innovation capital so that you can be a rising leadership star.

2

Who You Are

(and What You Can Do to Improve)

Not surprisingly, innovation capital begins with your innovation skills, or your innovation-specific *human capital*. Surprisingly, the skills that go into building innovation capital are more specific and actionable than you might imagine. It isn't nearly enough to just be creative or think big if you want to be a leader of innovation.

In our research on the world's most innovative leaders, we asked them what personal skills have been most important both to their success as innovative leaders and to their ability to win support for their ideas. We also talked to people who worked with these leaders and asked what skills they thought were most important to their leaders' success. We wanted to know why others wanted to join the innovative leaders' teams and why people were willing to give these teams money and other resources for their ventures.

The respondents mentioned a few skills over and over. Before we discuss these skills, we should acknowledge that natural abilities and intelligence (e.g., general intelligence [IQ] or emotional quotient [EQ]) or personality traits (e.g., openness to new experience, extroversion) provide the building blocks of skill or capability. But opportunity and practice (effort) are what make someone capable of achieving a certain level of performance. For example, someone may have natural musical intelligence, but without the requisite opportunity and practice, the person might never deliver a great musical performance. Likewise, someone may have creative intelligence, but without practice or opportunity, he or she might never become an inventor (see the sidebar "What's the Difference between Natural Abilities, Natural Intelligence, Personality Traits, and Skills?").

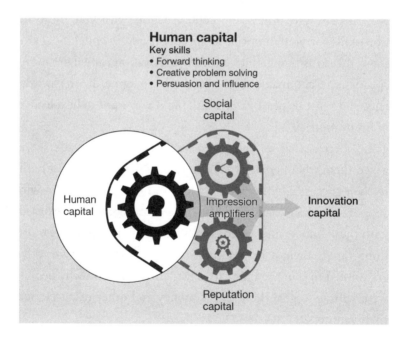

Human Capital Skills That Build Innovation Capital

FORWARD THINKING: the ability to see and understand trends in customers or technologies and to envision what will be important—and valuable—before others do

CREATIVE PROBLEM SOLVING: the ability to solve ambiguous or complex problems creatively using the five discovery skills, a first-principles approach, or all of these techniques

PERSUASION: the ability to promote your ideas by connecting with others in a confident and compelling way that convinces them to support you and your innovation project

As we interviewed and studied the world's most innovative leaders and what they did to succeed as champions of innovation, three skills stood out:

- Forward thinking: the capability to engage in mental time travel—to see and understand trends in customers or technologies and to envision what will be important before others do. This capability builds on natural creative intelligence and an openness to new experience and is critical for nailing the first job of an innovative leader: finding an opportunity, a vision, for creating value.

- Creative problem solving: the ability to solve ambiguous or complex problems in a creative way. Jeff Bezos (number one on our innovative leader list) calls it being a "self-reliant problem solver." LinkedIn CEO Jeff Weiner (number nine on our list) calls it "resourcefulness." But the bottom line is that if you are going to pursue a vision of

What's the Difference between Natural Abilities, Natural Intelligence, Personality Traits, and Skills?

Since late in the 20th century, researchers in education and psychology have identified a broad set of natural abilities and personality traits that are the building blocks of who we are—and what we do well. By *abilities*, we are referring to characteristics, such as people's natural intelligence. Psychologists have empirically validated at least seven types of intelligence. Some people are "smart," as measured by IQ; these folks can memorize facts and figures, can solve math problems, and are good at structured problem solving. Some have good interpersonal skills, as measured by a high emotional quotient (EQ), or the ability to read, and respond appropriately to, others' emotions. Some people are creative—divergent thinkers who generate novel ideas. Some have the gift of gab, or linguistic intelligence; they can articulate ideas in a way that connects with an audience. Some have the ability to visualize objects in 3-D—using what is called visual-spatial intelligence—to understand how things work (an especially valuable skill for architects, mechanics, designers, and engineers). Still others are athletic (kinesthetic intelligence), while others possess musical intelligence. (Kinesthetic and musical intelligence are primarily valuable in specialized fields of music, entertainment, and athletics.)

Beyond all these types of intelligence, we also differ in our *personality traits*, which are defined as relatively stable patterns of thoughts, feelings, and behaviors. Our personality traits include the "big five":

- Extroversion (or introversion)

- Agreeableness (or disagreeableness)

- Openness to new experiences (or not)

- Conscientiousness (e.g., being organized and detail oriented) (or not)

- Being emotional or neurotic (or not)

More recently, proactivity, or assertiveness, has also gained support as a personality trait.

As we studied the world's most innovative leaders, we conducted assessments, whenever possible, to identify elements of their abilities and personality traits that were particularly important to their success as a leader of innovation. We should acknowledge that these leaders all had high IQs, at least according to their performance on standardized tests (e.g., SAT/ACT), on which a high score would open doors to some of the world's finest educational institutions. But there are throngs of high-IQ folks who lack the chops to be great innovative leaders. So let's just acknowledge that to become a great leader of innovation, you must meet some IQ threshold. However, this level of natural general intelligence need not have been reflected in good grades in school. Some of the world's great innovators struggled in school.

In addition to having a high IQ, those who took our assessment scored higher on creative intelligence (reflected in a propensity to engage in questioning, observing, networking, and experimenting) than did typical organization leaders. Most, especially those who advanced through the ranks at large organizations, also had emotional intelligence; they were good at reading people. Finally, they scored extraordinarily high on the personality traits of proactivity and openness to new experience. These were important building blocks to the skills of forward thinking, creative problem solving, and persuasion. These are labeled as human capital skills because even though your natural abilities and personality traits influence their development, they can—and should—be

(continued)

developed and improved through practiced effort. We observed successful innovative leaders constantly engaging in practiced effort to improve their skills at forward thinking, solving thorny problems creatively, and persuading others to join their projects.

the future and do something novel, you will need to solve complex problems creatively. This skill relies on proactivity as well as general and creative intelligence.

- Persuasion: the ability to connect with others in a way that convinces them to support you and your innovation project. Sometimes called a reality distortion field, or even charisma, persuasiveness allows you to draw others to you and relate to them in a way that encourages them to pursue an innovative project. This skill builds largely on self-confidence (boldness), extroversion, and emotional intelligence.

These three human-capital skills are critical to effective innovation leadership and building innovation capital. In the following sections, we describe each of these capabilities and how to develop them yourself.

Forward Thinking: Mental Time Travel

In chapter 1, we briefly introduced the role of forward thinking in Satya Nadella's rise to become one of the most innovative leaders in the world. Let us examine his transformation in greater detail. In the summer of 1988, when Satya Nadella walked off the plane at the Milwaukee, Wisconsin, airport to start his master's degree in computer science at the University of Wisconsin–Milwaukee, there was little evidence to predict that Nadella would someday become the CEO of Microsoft. The University of Wisconsin program was excellent, but it didn't offer the prestige that would have come with a Stanford or an MIT degree. Moreover, four years later, when Nadella joined Microsoft, he was one of hundreds of software engineers that the company had hired that year. How could Nadella stand out?

When he joined Microsoft, the action—and profits—were centered on the company's premier consumer products, Microsoft Windows and Microsoft Office. But that's not where Nadella chose to work. As he looked to the future—ten, fifteen years ahead—he believed that the next wave of technologies that were going to be critical to Microsoft's future success were in the areas of cloud computing and artificial intelligence. So he avoided the cash cows and accepted a role as an evangelist for Microsoft NT (operating system for workstations and servers)—a risky career move, since it was outside the fast track for promotion in the company. This eventually led to an assignment leading Microsoft's foray into search engine technology with Bing. He then chose to work in the server and tools business (the forerunner of Microsoft's cloud computing business). While his colleagues were winning big bonuses and advancements in the consumer products business, these other businesses were seen as relatively low prestige, not the place to be if you wanted to rise in the ranks of Microsoft. But Nadella believed that these emerging technologies had great potential to deliver customer value in the future. He set to work and learned everything he could about these technologies.

Nadella distinguished himself during the next eighteen years at Microsoft as a hardworking, persistent learner—someone with emerging expertise in online services and cloud service technologies. "In 2008, I moved to lead engineering for Bing, and other online services, one of Microsoft's first businesses born in the cloud," Nadella told us. "We knew we weren't just building a search engine—we were building the foundational technologies that would fuel Microsoft's future. In spite of having grown up building distributed systems in the client-server era, this new assignment helped me learn about web scale distributed systems and applied machine learning. And so when I moved to run our enterprise business in 2011, I knew that the fundamentals of this business would need to go through a sea change."

Nadella was rewarded for his forward thinking by being asked to take over Microsoft's fledgling cloud business in 2011. At the time, Microsoft's cloud revenues could easily be counted in the millions of dollars, not the billions like Amazon Web Services. "I had to convince my team to shift focus from the big server and tools business that paid everyone's salary to the tiny cloud business with almost no revenue," Nadella said. "Their attitude was one of frustration—they were making all this money and now this little squeaky thing called the cloud came along and they didn't want to bother with it."[1] When Microsoft CEO Steve Ballmer offered Nadella the job to lead the cloud business, the CEO said, "You should think about it though. This might be your last job at Microsoft, because if you fail there is no parachute. You may just crash with it."[2]

Nadella was able to see the importance—and potential—of the cloud before others at Microsoft saw it. So he pressed on, leading a transformation of the company's server business from client services to cloud infrastructure and services. He also pushed to bring Microsoft's database, Windows server, and developer tools to its Azure cloud. Within two years Microsoft's cloud business was generating revenues in the billions, and total revenue from the cloud business—including the larger server tools business—had jumped from $16 billion to more than $20 billion. Nadella's expertise in these important new technologies, and his success in demonstrating that they were critical to Microsoft's future, distinguished him from others who were vying to replace Ballmer as CEO in February 2014.

What Forward Thinking Is and Why It Is Important

Nadella is what we call a *forward thinker*. He engages in mental time travel to imagine the future. This practice is a choice and a habit. By trying to envision the future, innovative leaders can see what else is possible in their industry and then place smart bets, often risky bets, on the technologies or activities that could be transformative.

How do they become forward thinkers? They start by positioning themselves to learn and develop expertise in the technologies and trends that will shape the future of their companies and industries. Of course, these leaders won't always be right, but if they engage in informed future thinking, they increase their chances of being right more often. "A leader," Nadella said, "must see external opportunities and the internal capability and culture—and all the connections among them—and respond to them *before they become obvious parts of the conventional wisdom*. It's an art form, not a science. And a leader will not always get it right. But the batting average for how well a leader does this is going to define his or her longevity in business."[3]

Elon Musk offers another great example of a forward-thinking mind. Musk is so forward-thinking that he is imagining the day when we need a space colony on Mars to prevent extinction of the human race from an asteroid or some other cosmic event. He is also on a mission to create a world run mostly by sustainable energy. Musk's brother Kimbal describes him: "He's able to see things more clearly in a way that no one else I know of can understand. There's a thing in chess where you can see 12 moves ahead if you're a grandmaster. And in any particular situation, Elon can see things 12 moves ahead."[4] Bezos is another leader who is very forward-thinking—especially from the customer's point of view. Andrew Jassy, CEO of Amazon Web Services, has worked with Bezos for twenty-one years. He gave us his take on Bezos's approach: "Jeff is very good at looking around corners to see what's next. Even when Amazon was just an online bookstore, Jeff was adamant that we not cement our brand as a bookseller. He had us looking into all sorts of different products and markets where he believed we could provide a better customer experience. He has great empathy for the customer and just seems to know what they will want."

Great leaders of innovation, like Nadella, Musk, and Bezos look to the future to understand what customers will want next, and they investigate emerging technologies to understand new ways of offering value. But it's not just famous people who do this. Kyle Nel, the former head of innovation at Lowe's, displayed forward thinking as he helped the company think about the future of retailing. "What holds big companies back is that they often just can't imagine what they could do," Nel told us. "You have to help people imagine what the future could be." To do this, Nel brought in a panel of science-fiction writers to help a normally conservative executive team imagine how they could take advantage of augmented reality, robotics, and other technologies to transform the future of retail. The science-fiction writers created "speculative organizational fiction," in which they imagined how new technologies could transform retailing. These stories helped Lowe's executives imagine how the world could be different and helped them suspend their disbelief long enough to do something meaningful about it.[5]

As a result, Lowe's deployed robots in stores that were taking inventory, created some of the first 3-D printing services, created exosuits (external robotic skeletons) that help workers do their jobs, and sold the first augmented-reality phone for remodeling in stores (the phone sold out in four days with no advertising). Largely because of Nel's forward thinking, Lowe's rose to number one in retail innovation on the *Forbes* Most Admired Companies list and number one in augmented reality on *Fast Company's* Most Innovative Companies list.[6]

Finally, forward thinking doesn't have to be just about breakthrough technologies and sweeping futuristic changes. When Steve Easterbrook (seventeenth on our top innovative leaders list) took over as CEO of McDonald's in 2015, same-store sales had been declining for almost two years amid a more general brick-and-mortar retail Armageddon. To address the problem, Easterbrook decided to imagine how to improve the customer experience, using whatever tools possible. Easterbrook asked, Can technology enable us to offer an entirely different experience where customers can order how they like, what they like, pay the way that suits them, and then be served in a manner that suits them? To do so, he introduced the "Experience of the Future" concept, which includes new store prototypes, customer-forward tech platforms like the mobile order and pay app, and a mobile delivery partnership with Uber Eats. McDonald's new stores feature self-ordering kiosks and tablets that give customers more choice in their in-store experience. You can now sit down, order, and have your food delivered to you. The mobile order and pay app offers easy ordering from the comfort of customers' smartphones. Customers can automatically order their "favorite" meal and then pick up their food at the counter, in the drive thru, or through a new curbside pickup option. The at-home delivery partnership with Uber Eats, meanwhile, has been a hit with customers. Today, customers can get their meal delivered at home from more than 11,500 restaurants in twenty-one countries. While these changes aren't particularly radical, they offer a better customer experience than competitors can offer. These moves, among others, have propelled same-store sales growth from negative 1 percent in 2014 to positive 6 percent in 2017 while the stock price has gone from $95 to $165.

Advice on Becoming a Forward Thinker

Are you a forward thinker? How much time do you spend each week thinking about how our world is changing—and predicting how those changes will affect the things you care about? Forward thinkers try to answer the following types of questions:

- What will customers or other people want next?

- What trends are shaping the world over the next few years?

- What will emerging technologies enable us to do that we couldn't before?

Bombard Yourself with Customer and Technology Trends

One way to piece together answers to the questions asked above is to bombard yourself with information about (1) what customers and other people are consuming and (2) what new startups are offering. You want to get a sense of where things are headed.

As an example of how leaders watch trends to get a sense of the future, former PepsiCo CEO Indra Nooyi developed a Mega-Trends document to identify significant trends and technologies that would influence PepsiCo's business. Nooyi (number twenty on our top innovative leaders list) had become CEO of PepsiCo just in time for the global financial meltdown in 2008. The company she inherited was laden with a portfolio full of soda and salty snacks at a time when consumers were shifting toward more nutritious options. But despite an environment of declining soda consumption, Nooyi has doubled PepsiCo's stock price during her tenure. How?

Nooyi identified trends toward more nutritious and more sustainable products early, and she transformed PepsiCo's product portfolio accordingly. In fact, in 2006 the company's Fun for You portfolio (e.g., Pepsi, Mountain Dew, Doritos) was about

70 percent larger than their Good for You (e.g., Quaker, Tropi-
cana, Aquafina) and Better for You (e.g., Pepsi Zero Sugar, Baked
Lay's, SunChips) portfolios combined, but by the end of 2017,
they were nearly equal in size. She told us she credits her focus
on MegaTrends and firsthand observations of customers as being critical to her own forward-thinking capability and PepsiCo's
success:

> I'm in the marketplace all the time looking at stores and
> eating places to see what's going on there. I look to my
> kids, to millennials, to see what their habits are. And to the
> edgy communities and where the edgy communities are
> going. Whether it's San Francisco, or Seattle, or Oregon
> or Boston or New York, these are all lead markets. And in
> many ways, what happens there—not in the big grocery
> stores, but in the warehouses converted to stores, the farm-
> ers' markets, the Brooklyn or SoHo shops—tells you a lot
> about where the edges are becoming more mainstream.
>
> So if you keep following the edges and watch what the
> youngsters are doing, it gives you a pretty good idea of
> what's coming. And we have to have an open mind. Believe
> me, there are times when I see my kids doing things, and I
> go, "What is wrong with you? Why can't you do things like
> we did it?" And the typical answer is, "Mom, get a life. This
> is how things are happening today." Then you go, "Oh my
> God, the world is changing."

In addition to watching lead customers, you can also watch the
frontier of startup innovation. It's easier than you might think
to familiarize yourself with what fast-moving startups are doing:
simply start reading. Check out websites such as VentureBeat
.com, Crunchbase.com, and PitchBook.com, or read up on the
companies in most-innovative lists or fastest-growing lists, such

as the *Inc.* 100, to identify the edge of innovation and what is getting traction. As you observe, ask yourself, What new value propositions are being offered? With what new technologies? Asking these questions can give you a sense of what entrepreneurs see as opportunities.

But it isn't just about the products and services the startups are supplying. The startups and fastest-growing companies are also shaping demand. They are setting customer expectations about what is possible and desirable in the future. By watching the emergence and rapid growth of Uber and Airbnb, you might have predicted the emergence of other, similar peer-to-peer sharing-economy business models, from recreational vehicles (RVshare.com) to storage (Neighbor.com), flowers (BloomThat), and grocery delivery (Instacart). Understanding the strategies, business models, and technologies behind the fastest-growing startups each year can often provide a window into the future as you look for patterns and trends.

Finally, read . . . *a lot*. Most of the world's most innovative leaders, including Bezos, Nadella, and Nooyi, are voracious readers. They ingest books and other reading material at a staggering rate—perhaps one or two books per week. "I read like a crazy person. I read everything," Nooyi says. "I read books. I read abstracts. If somebody's read something, I tell them to tell me what that book said. If I don't understand something, I'm always digging deep, going to school on it, questioning."

Devote Time to Mental Time Travel—Preferably with Others

Mental time travel takes time. So you have to regularly devote focused time to synthesize and take stock of what you know. Microsoft founder Bill Gates would regularly take one or two weeks each year to step away from work and read articles, books, product proposals, and technical papers sent to him by Microsoft employees and other leading thinkers. This break eventually became labeled Think Week and was a key technique that Gates used to regularly engage in forward thinking. He would occasionally emerge from Think Week with an important perspective on the future and would share it with company leaders and employees. In fact, in 1995, he wrote an insightful memo at the end of Think Week: "The Internet Tidal Wave," which foreshadowed how the internet would influence Microsoft and business in general.[7]

Beyond taking time on your own to think deeply about the future, you can benefit by doing it with others. Research shows that forecasting is even more effective as a group activity. Teams do a better job of forecasting the future because there is greater breadth of knowledge and teams are less susceptible to cognitive biases (more on this in the next tip). Gates ended up expanding Think Week to the top fifty to one hundred leaders and technologists at Microsoft so that they could collectively think deeply about the future. Likewise, Indra Nooyi updated her MegaTrends document every two years to make sure it was evergreen.

As an interesting aside, the insights from this process of forward thinking are deeply valued by the rest of the organization. Key stakeholders in the PepsiCo community would wait impatiently to learn what's coming next. Nooyi says, "I can't tell you how many people call me and say, 'Indra, can you just give us a peek under the tent as to the next megatrend?'"

Cognitive Flexibility: Recognize the Need to Change

Our research shows that one key to successful forward thinking is cognitive flexibility, or the ability to see different perspectives and change your viewpoint, or mental framework, accordingly. One of us (Nathan) studied cognitive flexibility in his dissertation at Stanford years ago while examining the factors that allowed entrepreneurs to successfully change (pivot) as they created new businesses. He was intrigued by how many times successful entrepreneurs had to pivot, often making dramatic changes, during their journey to success. For example, the founders of PayPal pivoted several times before they discovered the business model that eventually made them successful.

The research suggested that part of maintaining cognitive flexibility is avoiding the cognitive biases that lead you to get stuck in your own perspective. For example, *confirmation bias* is the tendency to look for, or interpret, information that confirms your preconceptions or point of view (and to ignore or dismiss conflicting information). Surprisingly, Nathan's research suggests that expertise actually accentuates rather than ameliorates these biases, causing leaders to persist too long down a blind alley.

What can you do to combat your cognitive inflexibility? For starters, recognize up front that you don't know it all. This is what Tom Kelley, cofounder of IDEO, called an "attitude of wisdom." An attitude of wisdom involves "a healthy balance between confidence in what you know and distrusting what you know just enough that keeps you thirsty for more knowledge."[8]

Bezos understands this principle and has adopted a leadership tenet at Amazon to address it. "Amazon leaders are right, a lot. They have strong judgment and good instincts. They seek diverse perspectives and *work to disconfirm their beliefs*." One of the keys to being "right, a lot" is to actively work to disconfirm your beliefs.[9]

Research shows that leaders who develop cognitive flexibility surround themselves with people from a broad range of industry and experiential backgrounds; these people help the leaders see things in new ways. Mentally flexible leaders have an attitude of learning; they are always looking for a beginner's mindset to solve problems, even problems they had already solved themselves.

Finally, the best way to predict the future is to create it. Rather than simply wait for the future to play out, the innovative leaders we studied took an active stance in creating the future—which leads us to our next human capital skill.

Creative Problem Solving

Bezos had a problem. As a twelve-year-old, he desperately wanted a new device called the Infinity Cube. The Infinity Cube was a set of small motorized mirrors that reflected off one another, so that it felt like looking into infinity. Bezos was fascinated by the gadget. But it was too expensive. Most kids his age would have gone without or would have begged for the money until someone relented. But not Bezos. Instead, he carefully examined the components of the cube and then bought the mirrors and other parts and, without any instructions to follow, he constructed his own version of the Infinity Cube. Bezos credits the annual summers on his grandparents' farm for helping him become, in his words, "a problem-solving self-reliant":

> A huge influence on me was my creative grandfather who was a rancher in South Texas. I spent my summers on his ranch starting at age four. I really gained confidence in my creative ability by helping my grandfather fix things on his ranch. He was extremely self-reliant. He built his own fences, he laid his own pipeline, he would build his own barns. He was really focused on problem solving, and he had an optimism that he could solve problems even in areas, like veterinary work, where he had no training. He often didn't have the money to fix things, so we'd have to improvise. One time I helped him fix a Caterpillar tractor

using nothing but a three-foot-high stack of mail-order manuals. You learn that when one way doesn't work, you have to regroup and try another approach.

Being a creative, self-reliant problem solver has characterized Bezos and his brand of leadership throughout his career. When he realized that online retailing had unique fulfillment problems that other retailers hadn't solved, he had Amazon build those capabilities internally. When Amazon needed a cloud infrastructure to support its retail operations, it built those capabilities internally (and then offered these services to other companies via Amazon Web Services). When Bezos saw an opportunity to offer an electronic reader (the Kindle)—a software-embedded device with which Amazon had no prior capabilities or experience—he led the effort to build these devices at Amazon.

While Amazon leveraged internally built software capabilities to launch Amazon Web Services, such was not the case with the Kindle, the company's first foray into hardware. Amazon was then essentially a software and fulfillment company. Building devices would require the development of a new set of capabilities that would put the company in direct competition with companies like Apple and Samsung. Jeff Wilke, CEO of Amazon's retail operations, remembers that at the board meeting where Amazon's leaders discussed whether to make the Kindle, he protested to the board: "I spoke up and said, 'I don't agree. I think we're likely to miss our planned delivery date. Our yields are gonna be too low. We're gonna underproduce. We're gonna frustrate customers. Hardware's hard. We're a software company.' Jeff [Bezos] responded, 'Well, I'm willing to concede that all those things will happen, and I still think that the right vision for our company is to be really good at building hardware. So we need to get started learning.'"

And so they did. Today, Wilke says, "Turns out I was right on everything that I called out, and Jeff [Bezos] was still right to say we should do it . . . We've created a skill set that we can use to invent new things on behalf of customers." Amazon took a big risk leaping into devices, but the company has expanded its self-reliant skills to launch other products and services.

What Creative Problem Solving Is and Why It Is Important

True innovation often requires solving problems that have never been solved before. That's why innovative leaders must excel at creative problem solving. Bezos may be the poster child for being a proactive, creative problem solver but this was a distinguishing characteristic in all of the world's most innovative leaders we studied. Psychologists have identified a trait related to this behavior: *proactivity*, or acting in advance of a future situation to make things happen. But what we witnessed among the top innovative leaders went way beyond proactivity. Many of us have the desire, and perhaps even the will, to be assertive and work hard to make things happen. But many of us also lack the desire and willingness to dive in and master new knowledge—becoming semi-experts in new fields—to lead an effort to solve a complex problem. In addition, we often aren't as creative as we could be in navigating around the obstacles that get in our way.

"You need to have a combination of stubbornness and flexibility," Bezos says. "And even though those two things seem at odds with one another, I don't think they are. Because I think you can be stubborn on your vision but flexible on the details of how you get there. When one approach doesn't work, you circle back around and try another, relentlessly trying different angles until you find something that meets your vision. When I see that in somebody, that shows they have real potential."

Bezos isn't the only leader who looks for creative problem-solving skills in up-and-coming employees. "Resourcefulness is arguably the most important component to successful leadership that we look for at LinkedIn," Weiner says. "At the end of the day, regardless of whether you're in a small startup and you need funding, or you're in a larger company that needs to navigate a corporate environment, you have to have people who are resourceful. Regardless of how challenges present themselves, regardless of how high and how wide the wall, effective leaders are prepared to go above it, around it, or through it in order to get stuff done. When you have people who possess this quality, they become incredibly valuable."

Advice on Becoming a Creative Problem Solver

You can attack problems creatively with a variety of approaches. Two approaches used successfully by top innovative leaders address problems from nearly opposite starting points. One approach, the first-principles method, reduces a problem down to its basic parts and focuses on solving for the constraints. The other approach has you widen your field of knowledge beyond your normal area of expertise. Let's look further at the utility of both these approaches.

Solve Problems Using First Principles

Musk has been instrumental in building three revolutionary multibillion-dollar companies in completely different fields—PayPal (financial services), Tesla Motors (automotive) and SpaceX (aerospace)—and is attempting to launch revolutionary technologies in mass transit (Hyperloop) and mobility infrastructure (Boring). His ability to solve seemingly unsolvable problems is essential to his success and he attributes his problem solving success to *first-principles* thinking. "I operate on the physics approach of analysis by first principles," Musk told us. "The first-principles approach to thinking is where you boil things down to the most fundamental truths in a particular area and then you reason up from there. In most cases, we solve problems by reasoning by analogy, which means copying what other people do, with slight variations." Musk says that we use reasoning by analogy because it is mentally easier than first-principles reasoning—but it is less effective at producing novel solutions.

In lay terms, first-principles thinking—which was first articulated and named by Aristotle—is the practice of identifying what you think is true and then actively questioning every assumption you have about a given problem or scenario.

First-principles thinking helped Regeneron, the New York–based biopharma company, revolutionize how it develops new therapies. Whereas it costs on average $4.3 billion for the average company to develop an approved therapy, Regeneron has been estimated to develop therapies for less than $1 billion per approved therapy, which is 20 percent of the cost of its competitors.[10] How? "We challenge everything," says Regeneron co-founder, president, and chief scientist George Yancopoulos (number twenty-one on our innovative leaders list). "Every concept. Every scientific principle. Nothing is unchallengeable, and you don't take anything for granted. Most of what we believe are facts are not." The next step is to identify the constraints to achieving what you want to achieve and then start with a blank slate and create solutions that might solve those constraints. "We always try to figure out what's limiting in a field. What's the bottleneck?" Yancopoulos says. "Then you look for a game-breaking idea that addresses the limiting factor."

To illustrate how to apply a first-principles process, consider Musk's description of how Tesla approached the problem of the high cost of battery packs for automobiles.

Some people say, "Battery packs are really expensive and that's just the way they will always be . . . Historically, it has cost six hundred dollars per kilowatt hour. It's not going to be much better than that in the future." With first principles, you say, "What are the material constituents of the batteries? What is the spot market value of the material constituents?" It's got cobalt, nickel, aluminum, carbon, some polymers for separation, and a seal can. Break that down on a material basis, and say, "If we bought that on the London Metal Exchange, what would each of those things cost?" It's, like, eighty dollars per kilowatt hour. So, clearly, you just need to think of clever ways to take those materials and combine them into the shape of a battery cell, and you can have batteries that are much, much cheaper than anyone realizes.[11]

Of course, it isn't that easy to "think of clever ways" to combine the materials into a battery cell, but first-principles thinking starts with a blank slate, questions every assumption, and considers a wide variety of options. Here is a three-step process for first-principles problem solving:

First, *identify the problem you want to solve.* For example, in the case of Tesla, the key problems the company needed to solve were reducing the cost of the battery pack (to make it affordable) and increasing the range a car could go on a single charge (to reduce range anxiety). At Regeneron, two big delays in the creation of successful new medicines were the time required to create and breed accurate animal models, a necessary step in ensuring safety before clinical-stage testing in humans, and the time required to develop "fully human" antibody drug candidates that would be accepted in a human immune system.

Second, *break down the problem into its fundamental principles, and list the major constraints to solving this problem.* To illustrate, the main constraint to an affordable battery pack might have been the cost of one or more of the materials. So then you would ask, How could we possibly reduce the cost of that key material? For Tesla, the challenge of creating a lower-cost battery pack had less to do with materials and more to do with the process of combining them into a battery cell at enough scale to reduce the cost (hence the need for the Gigafactory, Tesla's facility to design and build lower-cost lithium batteries at scale). A major constraint to increasing the range of a Tesla from a single electric charge was the weight of the car body. Thus, Tesla became the first automaker to use a lightweight all-aluminum body. At Regeneron, the limiting factor to rapid, successful drug testing was the time required to carefully test, select, and breed for certain genetic qualities in mice to ensure the closest parallels to future human patients. So Regeneron sped up the process by developing a precision technology capable of directly inserting human immune-system genes in mice, eliminating the need for many generations of breeding to accurately model human diseases and produce antibodies that could be safely introduced into humans. These "fully human" mice have allowed Regeneron to more quickly and accurately identify medicines that will work on humans, thereby reducing the cost of each potential new drug. This breakthrough has contributed to a tenfold increase in the company's stock price in the ten years since 2010.

Finally, *create new solutions using a blank-slate approach*. Ask yourself, If I could create any solution I desired, what would that solution be? How would it eliminate the problem or constraint? The point here is to imagine the perfect solution and then consider a wide variety of approaches that might eliminate the greatest bottleneck. At Regeneron, the blank-slate solution was having an animal model respond exactly like a human during early-stage drug testing. Of course, Regeneron needed to figure out how to make this solution a reality, or at least closer to reality.

During this phase, you need to actively engage four behaviors—questioning, observing, networking, and experimenting —as described by one of us (Jeff) and his coauthors in *The Innovator's DNA*.[12] Creative problem solvers excel at *questioning*, constantly challenging the status quo with "why not" questions to turn things upside down. They also frequently ask "what if" questions to envision a different future. They are also intense *observers*, scrutinizing the environment like anthropologists. They get out of their cubicles to carefully watch the world around them—especially customers, products, services, and processes— with a beginner's mindset. These observations give them unique insights into new ways of solving problems. Creative problem solvers also stand out at *networking*, talking with diverse people to spark a new way to solve perplexing problems. These innovators seek to regularly talk with people who don't look, act, or most important, think like them. Finally, they search for new solutions by constantly *experimenting*. They try out new experiences wherever they go. They take apart products or processes to see how things work. And they test their hunches through experiments with pilots and prototypes. These skills have been empirically shown to trigger creative ideas for solving thorny problems.[13]

Become an Expert—Quickly

The more knowledge you possess in more areas, the more problems you can solve. This is especially true when using a first-principles approach. Unfortunately, many of us have developed expertise in only one field (software engineering, information technology [IT], marketing, biotechnology, automobile manufacturing, the food industry, etc.) and we like to stick to our knitting. But the world's most innovative leaders are willing to dive in and develop expertise in new domains if they think doing so will help them solve a problem. For example, Bezos has developed deep expertise in software engineering, robotics, information technology, devices (e.g., Kindle, Alexa) and even rocket technologies (his company Blue Origin competes with SpaceX for space travel). "I've been lucky enough to work with Jeff for a long time now, and I don't know many people who learn at the rate that Jeff does," says Jassy of Amazon Web Services. "If you look at the array and the breadth of activities and disciplines that he interacts with every day, every week, every month, it's incredible. He is an amazing learner."

As an illustration of how one can become an expert quickly, Nooyi told us about one of her most difficult assignments while she was chief financial officer at PepsiCo. During her tenure, she was tasked with overseeing a massive overhaul of PepsiCo's entire IT system. "I was not even an IT person," she told us. "But I said, 'OK, fine. I'm going to have to learn this myself.' So I spent six weeks between Thanksgiving and New Year's becoming a student. I studied everything there was about ERP [enterprise resource planning] systems, what works and what doesn't, data warehousing, the whole thing. I emerged in January as a decent expert on the topic. All of a sudden everyone on the IT team said, 'Wow, this person, once she throws her mind into it, is going to dig deep and then come back and ask us the right questions.' So we all ended up getting to a better place. There were many, many projects like that, where I had to develop new expertise."

Unfortunately, many of us are unwilling or afraid to become a student again—to attempt to master new areas of expertise. But you shouldn't be (especially with all the self-directed learning tools available online). As Musk once commented, "Frankly, I think most people can learn a lot more than they think they can."

Interpersonal Persuasion Skills

In February 1981, Guy L. "Bud" Tribble, a key software developer on the original Macintosh computer, welcomed new employee Andy Hertzfeld by telling him that Apple was scheduled to ship the Macintosh software in just ten months.

"Ten months?" Hertzfeld remarked. "That's impossible."

Rather than argue, Tribble agreed. But then he had to explain to Hertzfeld how Steve Jobs, who was heading the team, had convinced him to try anyway. In retrospect, Tribble described it this way: "The best way to describe the situation is a term from *Star Trek*. Steve Jobs has a reality distortion field." Tribble was referring to a *Star Trek* episode in which the crew finds a planet called Talos, whose inhabitants can generate virtual realities in the minds of other people—or as Tribble later put it, creating "their own new world through sheer mental force." Tribble went on to explain Jobs's ability to use a "reality distortion field" to Hertzfeld: "In Steve's presence, reality is malleable. He can convince anyone of practically anything."

Jobs once used his powers of persuasion to convince Corning CEO Wendell Weeks that Corning could fully develop and produce enough crack-resistant glass (branded as Gorilla Glass) for one million iPhones within six months. Jobs wanted to use glass instead of plastic (the original design) for the iPhone's screen, but at the time, glass cracked too easily. So in early 2007 Jobs flew to Corning, New York, to meet with Weeks to explain his hopes for the screen. The glass had to be durable, and Jobs needed enough of it within six months to be produced for all the iPhones he was planning to sell.

After listening to Jobs, Weeks told him that Gorilla Glass was just a project, not a product; it was still in development and he wasn't set up to produce it. "I'm sorry; we've actually never made it," Weeks said. "We don't have a factory to make it; this was a process we developed, but we never had a manufacturing plan to do it."

On the spot, Jobs placed a large order for Gorilla Glass anyway, repeatedly telling Weeks, "Don't be afraid. You can do this."

Weeks tried to explain that a false sense of confidence would not overcome engineering challenges. "I just sat there and looked at the guy," Weeks recalled. "He kept saying, 'Don't be afraid. You can do this.'"

In the end, Jobs prevailed. Weeks immediately called his LCD screen glass-making plant in Kentucky and said, "Start the process now, and make Gorilla Glass." Corning not only figured out how to make Gorilla Glass in six months, but in the next ten years, it also sold enough of it to cover more than twenty-eight thousand football fields for the iPhone.[14]

Jobs was known for his powers of persuasion—for his ability to get others to believe *his* reality. Indeed, this is an important skill of innovative leaders because they have to convince others to bring their resources to a novel venture that, by definition, is uncertain and risky. So what makes someone like Jobs capable of convincing others that almost anything is possible? And how can you do the same thing?

What Persuasion Is and Why It Is Important

There are many reasons why some people have the power to persuade and others do not. One primary reason is *self-confidence and an aura of success*. Individuals who are charismatic leaders project confidence in themselves. Psychologists call this trait *self-efficacy*, or an individual's belief in his or her innate ability to achieve goals. Persuasive people exude confidence in their ability to make things happen and succeed. We all like to be associated with winners. Persuasive people project an aura of success—in the way they dress, talk, and amplify their symbols of success, such as where they've been to school, where they've worked, and what they've accomplished. (We'll discuss how to build a reputation, and how to amplify it, in chapters 4 through 6). This aura naturally draws others to want to associate with persuasive people.

In addition to bold confidence, persuasive people use their linguistic and logic intelligence to convince others. Some of us are just better with words, for example, and are better at telling a compelling story. Harvard's Howard Gardner refers to this as linguistic intelligence and has demonstrated that we have natural differences on this dimension.[15] Some of us are very comfortable speaking with and persuading others, whereas others are not (think of great orators like Martin Luther King Jr. and John F. Kennedy). In addition, some of us are naturally more gifted at creating logical arguments that influence others to our way of thinking.

Together, these and other interpersonal persuasion skills can be put to good use to create a reality distortion field. The term itself—reality distortion field—is quite relevant to persuasion because *perception is reality*. As sociologists will tell you, the idea of reality is socially constructed. It is what people believe and can be convinced to believe. What if we told you that you can create your own reality distortion field, right now? You have the ability to influence the reality that you project to the world about yourself—and about your projects and ventures. As previously mentioned, we will share later in the book some specific techniques—impression amplifiers—that you can use to persuade and convince others of the reality you want them to see. But above all, you must understand how your personal mindset—your perceptions of yourself and your work projects—can set artificial and limiting boundaries before you even get started. Here are a few examples that may help you understand how perception is, or becomes, reality:

- If you believe that you are not a creative individual, you will not pursue creative activities, and therefore your lack of creativity will be the reality.

- If you are nervous when speaking in public, rest assured that everyone picks up on your lack of ease, and your unpolished speaking skills will be the reality.

- If you are afraid to take a risk and make a bold recommendation about an opportunity you've discovered, you will never stand out or champion a new idea, and your inability to get noticed or get attention will be the reality.

As these examples show, our beliefs about ourselves can become self-fulfilling prophecies. By extension, we each have the ability to influence or inspire our colleagues, but we must persuade ourselves first. Jobs's reality distortion field was a personal refusal to accept limitations that stood in the way of his ideas. This attitude allowed him to convince himself—and others—that any difficulty was surmountable. And using first-principles problem solving with his collaborators, he often achieved the "impossible." You can do the same.

Advice on Building Your Own Reality Distortion Field

Here are a handful of tactics and tools you can use to improve your ability to persuade others. You can find more advice at www.innovatorsdna.com/innovation-capital.

Paint a Vision That Creates Emotional Connection

Think carefully about how you can make your idea exciting and meaningful to create an emotional connection that will persuade others to follow your lead. And it doesn't have to be something as lofty as reducing global warming or putting a colony on Mars.

Nike makes athletic shoes . . . and yet the company's founders, Bill Bowerman and Phil Knight, followed by current CEO Mark Parker, have attracted talent and resources to Nike through its mission "To bring inspiration and innovation to every athlete in the world." The legendary University of Oregon track and field coach Bowerman said, "If you have a body, you are an athlete." Parker (sixteenth on our list) says Nike's focus is to "serve the athlete" and to give these folks the athletic gear and inspiration to "just do it." As a recent example, Matthew Nurse, head of Nike Explore Team Sport Research Lab, and Sandy Bodecker, vice president of special projects, decided to "serve the athlete" by helping one athlete make history by running the marathon in less than two hours (this feat would require a seemingly impossible improvement of three minutes over the world record). They called the project Breaking2, and Bodecker even tattooed 1:59:59 on his wrist to show his commitment. This lofty goal attracted three of the world's top marathoners, plus world-class coaches, nutritionists, physiologists, designers, and engineers to the team—and concluded with Eliud Kipchoge running the fastest time ever recorded: 2:00:05 (more on Breaking2 in chapter 7).

Build Self-Confidence and an Aura of Success

There is a wealth of content written on developing self-confidence, so we won't recap that knowledge here. However, when it comes to innovation, we have found that two elements can consistently lead to the high degree of self-assurance needed to persuade others to join your cause:

- Profound dissatisfaction with the status quo

- Deep-seated conviction of an opportunity (e.g., an insight into a customer need or a new application of a technology) that comes from firsthand, personal experience

Developing both of these perspectives in tandem can give you the assertiveness, motivation, and resilience to persuade others to join you in bringing about real change. And perhaps just as important is doing the homework necessary to know everything possible about the problem you want to solve. If you are prepared, you won't be afraid, and others will sense that.

Develop Your Linguistic and Logic Intelligence

How often do you try to persuade others—at work, at home, or in other social settings—to accept a course of action or point of view? If you consider yourself ineffective at persuading others, then you may need more practice at both the structure of your logic and your verbal delivery. To improve the structure of your arguments, do a deep dive into structured problem solving and logic pyramids (sometimes called *logic trees*). Management consulting firms like Bain & Company and McKinsey & Company have used structured problem-solving pyramids (like Barbara Minto's "pyramid principle"[16]) to teach consultants how to organize a problem and presentation because their success relies on persuading clients through presentations.

At a high level, applying the pyramid principle means simply putting an assertion or a conclusion at the top of the pyramid (e.g., "Coca-Cola should enter the snack foods business"). Next you identify all the supporting arguments, analysis, or data for that main assertion (e.g., Coke should enter the snack foods industry because the snack foods industry has high average profitability and because selling both snack foods and beverages will increase bargaining power over grocery retailers). Then you repeat that process a level down (e.g., identify all the arguments and data to support the assertion that the snack foods industry is profitable). The bottom line is that each assertion that you make must be well supported by subassertions, which must also be well supported by assertions that are mutually exclusive and collectively exhaustive.

Create opportunities at work, at home, and with friends to discuss or debate issues while you practice using pyramid logic. One way to get practice is to take or audit a university business school class that uses the case method, because each case is a debate about a business issue. This will give you practice articulating a convincing point of view.

Conclusion

Our examination of the world's most innovative leaders revealed three personal skills that were critical to their success. The leaders are forward thinkers who see opportunities before others do; they proactively, persistently, and creatively problem solve their way to that future; and they persuade others to join them on the journey. These are challenging skills to develop. But with effort and practice, we can each get better at these skills, which are the foundation of innovation capital. In chapter 3, we examine how you can build social connections with others who can provide the resources you need to launch your innovation projects.

Assess Your Human Capital That Contributes to Innovation Capital

To take the first step in understanding whether you are good at forward thinking, proactive problem solving, and persuading, take the following brief assessment of your innovation capital. See our website www.innovatorsdna.com/innovation-capital for a full version of the assessment and additional resources.

Forward Thinking

Using a scale of 1 to 7, where 1 = strongly disagree; 4 = neither agree nor disagree; 7 = strongly agree, rate the following statements. Be honest in your assessment. In fact, also have those who know you best assess you on these items.

1. I can see what is really important before others do.

2. I actively engage in activities (e.g., observations, reading, conversations) that help me understand the latest customer and technology trends.

3. I regularly take time to think deeply about how changes in customer preferences and emerging new technologies will influence business opportunities.

Add up your score. Here's how to interpret your results:

19–21: You are very strong at forward thinking.

16–18: You are strong at forward thinking.

13–15: You are adequate at forward thinking, but such thinking is unlikely to have a strong impact on your career

Below 13: Your forward thinking will not help your career unless you improve.

(continued)

Creative Problem Solving

1. I have a strong track record of solving difficult (complex) problems.

2. I frequently acquire knowledge and expertise in new domains so that I can more effectively contribute to solving problems.

3. Wherever I have been, I have been a powerful force for removing obstacles that prevent constructive change.

19–21 : Very strong at creative problem solving

16–18: Strong at creative problem solving

13–15: Okay at creative problem solving, but this ability is unlikely to have a strong impact on your career

Below 13: Creative problem solving will not help your career unless you improve

Persuasion

1. I feel that I can inspire others to follow me.

2. I am good at persuading others to see things my way.

3. I am very good with words and can articulate arguments persuasively.

19–21: Very strong at persuading

16–18: Strong at persuading

13–15: Okay at persuading, but this ability is unlikely to have a strong impact on your career

Below 13: Persuading will not help your career unless you improve

3

Who You Know

(and Who to Focus On)

Who is more important to you when you are trying to win resources and support for your ideas: people who know you well, or people who hardly know you at all? Most of us would be tempted to say that the people who know us well are the most important providers of resources to pursue an innovative idea. But there are several problems with this intuition. First, the network of people who know and trust you has severe limits. Have you heard of the Dunbar number? Not many people have a number named after them, but Robin Dunbar, director of the Institute of Cognitive and Evolutionary Anthropology at Oxford University, lays claim to the Dunbar Number. He argues that because of the way our brains have developed over the ages, there are cognitive limits to the number of people with whom we can maintain a meaningful social relationship involving trust and obligation. This limit, baked into the size of our brains and how we process social relationships, is roughly 150 people—the Dunbar number. They are the people that Dunbar describes as those "you would not feel embarrassed about joining uninvited for a drink if you happened to bump into them in a bar."[1]

Although you may think you can stretch this number, according to Dunbar, that's just not possible. As we build close relationships with new people, other people will fall out of our Dunbar network. (Interestingly even on Facebook, the average [median] number of "friends" is just about 200.[2]) If you were to rely only on your Dunbar number for help, how good would your resulting opportunities really be? Unless you somehow have developed close relationships with 150 of the world's richest people, top financiers, top innovators, most clever entrepre-

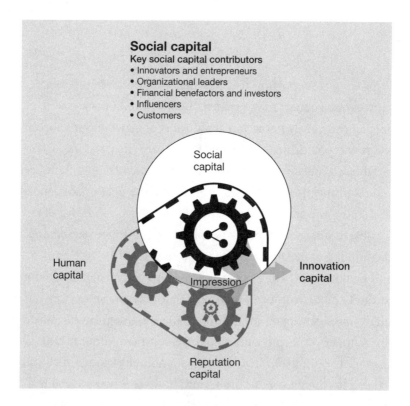

Prized Social Connection Categories

INNOVATORS AND ENTREPRENEURS: individuals who have a track record of innovation (for example, scientist or engineer inventors or entrepreneurs) and who are critical for generating ideas and participating in your projects

ORGANIZATIONAL LEADERS (e.g., C-suite executives): leaders with the authority to deploy their organization's resources

FINANCIAL BENEFACTORS OR INVESTORS (e.g., angel investors, venture capitalists, bankers): individuals who have or control financial resources

INFLUENCERS (e.g., celebrities, prominent networkers): individuals who have achieved prominence within a community and who can leverage their connections

CUSTOMERS (e.g., target customers for your innovations): key customers; could be important enterprise customers or prominent retail customers

neurs, and astute executives, your opportunities will be severely limited.

The second reason your intuition would be wrong is that your weak ties are actually much stronger than you realize. The power of weak social relationships for accessing resources and opportunities was first emphasized by Stanford economic sociologist Mark Granovetter. Granovetter decided to study a simple question: How do people find a new job? He assumed (as did most sociologists) that it's our strong-tie relationships (with family, friends, college roommates, coworkers—our Dunbar network, in other words) that are most valuable for helping us find a new job. This makes intuitive sense because we believe that the people who know us, trust us, and can endorse us will be the most willing to help us. Why would someone we hardly know be able or willing to recommend us?

But in his landmark study of how people in Boston got hired, Granovetter discovered something quite different. Rather than finding a job through their strong ties, people were much more likely to find work through their weak ties: the casual acquaintance, the old associate whom one has lost contact with, the friend of a friend, and even the chance encounter. At first, Granovetter was surprised at these results. How could weak social ties be so valuable?

The answer: scale. The scale of your weak-tie network and consequently the number of ties and the volume of resources available through your weak social ties completely dominate the resources available through our strong social ties. Although our Dunbar number may be only 150 people, the number of people with whom we may have a weak social tie can run into the hundreds or thousands. These folks can be the conduit to thousands of other individuals. For example, if you have 1,000 direct ties and they each have 1,000 direct (nonredundant) ties, then you can reach 1 million people through an introduction from someone you know. "When it comes to finding out about new jobs— or, for that matter, new information, or new ideas," Granovetter says, "weak ties are always more important than strong ties." Thus when you are trying to win support for your ideas, what really matters is the larger network of people you can access through your weak ties (figure 3-1). As an aside, because of the impact of his observation, Granovetter's groundbreaking article, "The Strength of Weak Ties," is one of the most cited articles in the social sciences.[3]

FIGURE 3-1

Why are weak ties so important to getting resources?

Answer: Scale. Because of network effects, the volume of resources available through weak social ties completely dominates the volume of resources available through strong social ties.

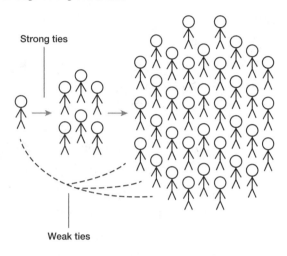

Weak Ties in Action: The Wider Social Network Created by a Smaller One

Leaders who build innovation capital learn the power of tapping into their weak ties. Take Mark Zuckerberg, for example, the well-known founder of Facebook. Most of us know that Zuckerberg started Facebook in his Harvard dorm room with college friends Dustin Moskovitz, Chris Hughes, Andrew Mc-Collum, and Eduardo Saverin, the last of which he met when the two were pledging Alpha Epsilon Pi, a selective fraternity for Jewish students. Saverin famously provided $25,000 to $30,000 in capital during the first year of Facebook. And then, after a falling out with Zuckerberg, Saverin sued him for reducing his equity share in Facebook (the stock Saverin won in his lawsuit has made him a billionaire). But what most of us don't fully appreciate is that Facebook's success relied critically on ideas and financial and human capital that were accessed through Zuckerberg's weak-tie network.

To illustrate, some of the critical ideas for Facebook probably came from Tyler and Cameron Winklevoss and Divya Narendra. The three Harvard students had heard of Zuckerberg and asked him to write code for their social networking site called Harvard Connection (later named ConnectU). The original idea for Harvard Connection was to create a social networking site to connect students and alumni of Harvard—only individuals with a harvard.edu email address. Zuckerberg used this same approach when launching Facebook. By limiting membership to Harvard and then other high-status universities, Facebook created a premium image relative to the most popular existing social networking sites, Friendster and Myspace. (The Winklevoss twins and Narendra later sued Zuckerberg for stealing some of their ideas and received a reported $64 million settlement.)

Another likely influence was Aaron Greenspan, a Harvard student who had launched houseSYSTEM, an online service at Harvard. The service had a "universal face book"—a printed book with students' photos—and provided a variety of services, including book buying and selling and course reviews. Zuckerberg invited Greenspan to partner with him on the Facebook project, but Greenspan refused, saying later, "I didn't like the idea of working for someone who had just been disciplined for ignoring privacy rights."[4] (Zuckerberg had been disciplined by the Harvard administration for hacking Facebook photos of Harvard students for FaceMash, a site he had built; it randomly pulled photos of Harvard students so that the viewer could vote on which person was more attractive.) Greenspan also later said that some of the key ideas behind Facebook came from him. While

Zuckerberg hasn't commented on what he may have learned from the Winklevoss twins, Narendra, or Greenspan, he has acknowledged the importance of connecting with others to get new ideas. "Ideas typically do not just come to you," Zuckerberg says. "They happen because you've been talking about something and talking to a lot of people about it for a long period of time."[5]

Facebook was designed to connect college students and alumni with each other. Because of its much broader appeal, it needed greater resources than Zuckerberg's earlier projects. Eventually, Zuckerberg needed substantial funds to grow Facebook. So he turned to his weak ties. One individual whom Zuckerberg met when launching Facebook was twenty-four-year-old Sean Parker, a cofounder of Napster. Parker was a consummate networker and well connected in Silicon Valley despite his young age. He was polished, spending money (when he had it) on nice meals, haircuts, and stylish clothes.[6] In fact, Parker was the one who, after seeing Facebook, first reached out to Zuckerberg to set up a meeting at a fancy restaurant in New York. (Parker reportedly had to overdraw his bank account to afford the dinner, but he believed that the meeting was worth it; his investment ultimately returned millions to him.) The two men hit it off from the beginning, and Zuckerberg eventually asked Parker to join Facebook. So when Facebook needed a large infusion of cash to keep up with growth, Zuckerberg turned to Parker.

Because Parker had a strong aversion to venture capitalists, he suggested that Zuckerberg look for an angel investor. Parker's first choice was Reid Hoffman, a cofounder of LinkedIn (also a fledgling social networking site at the time) and a friend whom he had met through Plaxo, another of Parker's startups. Hoffman saw personal and business networking as different animals, so he had invested in Friendster (a social networking site that predated Facebook) and had launched LinkedIn (designed for business networking). Given his investment in Friendster, he passed on funding Facebook. But he introduced Zuckerberg to Peter Thiel, who had worked with him at PayPal. Both Thiel and Hoffman are members of a distinct social network—wealthy former employees of PayPal—sometimes called the PayPal Mafia (which includes other successful entrepreneurs like Musk and Max Levchin). Thiel had met Parker and was impressed with both Parker and Zuckerberg. He was also impressed with the data on Facebook's growth and usage: when Facebook launched at a new university, over 80 percent of the student body joined within the first few weeks, and 80 percent of those visited Facebook daily.[7] So he agreed to lend Facebook $500,000, which would turn into 10.2 percent equity if Facebook hit a million users by the end of the year. (Thiel's investment made him a billionaire.) The real financial resources that launched Facebook came through weak-tie relationships.

Moreover, once Facebook began to expand, it needed to attract key talent. Parker's weak ties proved extremely valuable here as well. The company's first designer, Aaron Sittig, was an early Napster friend who would become Facebook's key product architect. Parker also helped recruit other influential executives to Facebook—people like Chamath Palihapitiya, who was vice president of user growth and was instrumental in growing Facebook around the globe. Parker also brought in Steve Venuto, his lawyer at Plaxo, and together they helped Zuckerberg create a corporate structure that gave Zuckerberg complete and permanent control of the company he founded. The plan fortified Zuckerberg with supervoting shares that resisted dilution during fund-raising and armed him with enough board seats to stay in power for as long as he wanted. Zuckerberg's success in launching Facebook owes much of its success to the resources that were brought to the venture through the weak-tie relationships of Parker and other early Facebook employees.

What Innovation-Specific Social Capital Is and How You Build It

Most of us underestimate the importance of building large weak-tie networks. This is not to say that strong ties are unimportant; they definitely are important (more on this later). We often overlook weak-tie networks because we feel uncomfortable reaching out to mere acquaintances to ask for something." Not so for the world's most innovative leaders. They shrewdly figure out what resources they need to accomplish an innovation initiative—and they intuitively understand, or learn along the way, that those resources are likely to be held by people outside their Dunbar number.

For example, Marc Benioff, founder, chairman, and co-CEO of Salesforce, is one of the world's truly extraordinary networkers—and this has paid big dividends for the company. His focus on networking expanded in 1999 when he was trying to raise money to fund Salesforce, which was based on the novel idea that businesses could run their apps in the cloud, the same way Amazon sold books via the internet. "We're a company that could never get venture capital," he says. "All those venture capitalists, when I went to them, would never give us capital. I was thrown out of all the names you know in the Valley—Kleiner Perkins Caufield & Byers, Sequoia, US Venture Partners, on and on. Everyone threw me out, not once, but multiple times. I had to raise money myself from individuals."[8]

Benioff's penchant for networking was critical not only for raising capital but also for building customer relationships. There have been six-month periods, Benioff told us, when he has been "mostly on the road with customers and have probably met with more than three hundred CEOs and CIOs [chief information officers]." If you're counting, that's roughly 2.5 meetings with different company CIOs *per day*. Networking with customers helps you understand their needs and challenges, which is critical to generating ideas (as described in *The Innovator's DNA*), testing and validating innovative solutions (as described in *The Innovator's Method*), and winning resources (sometimes from the customers themselves) to commercialize solutions for them.[9]

Benioff has also built his networks by launching Dreamforce, a Salesforce effort that has become the largest software conference in the world. Every fall, San Francisco is overrun by more than 170,000 salespeople, entrepreneurs, and techies. Hotels book up months in advance. Restaurants prepare for blocks-long lines. All thanks to Dreamforce. Since its humble beginnings with 1,000 attendees in 2003, Salesforce's annual conference has evolved into a one-of-a-kind spectacle, a star-studded pageant with late-night concerts—an event that makes other industry conferences look like book clubs. This event creates amazing networking opportunities for Benioff and contributes greatly to his social capital.

But it isn't just the innovation superstars who learn how to build and leverage their social connections. Leah Busque is the founder and former CEO of TaskRabbit, a transaction platform connecting people who want errands done and those willing to do them. When Busque had the idea for TaskRabbit, she had few connections and little idea of how the startup world worked. But she was willing to talk to people about her ideas wherever she went. One night, she went to dinner with some of her husband's friends from work. Although she didn't know his friends well, she went ahead and described the idea. As Busque argues, "Never worry about being afraid that someone is going to steal your idea. There is so much value in sharing your idea with as many people as possible, getting feedback early on and then developing from there."[10] As it turned out, one of the attendees at dinner was intrigued with her idea and said that her friend Scott would really love this idea. So the woman gave Busque his email. That night Busque shot off a casual email to Scott asking for an hour of his time. On Sunday morning she had a reply from Scott Griffith, the CEO of one the largest car-sharing networks in the world, Zipcar. He said he would love to talk. Over the next few months they met several times. He introduced Busque to mentors, to investors, and even provided office space at the Zipcar headquarters when she finally quit her job to start TaskRabbit. As Busque recalls, "It was so serendipitous that I got connected to him. You never know where different leads are going to take you. If you can just be really open about what you are working on, open to feedback, open to connecting to people you just never know where that is going to take you."[11] Since then, TaskRabbit has spread to forty-five cities and was acquired by IKEA, a company that is investing to expand TaskRabbit's operations worldwide.

Busque was successful at obtaining the resources for Task-Rabbit because she was constantly initiating conversations about her idea with a wide variety of social connections. As Arne Sorenson, who as CEO has led Marriott International to a tripling in market value between 2014 and 2018, told us: "Partnerships are key to the success of our business model . . . You've got to be zealous about creating the opportunity for new conversations." But who should be the target of those "new conversations"? The trick isn't just to build the largest network of connections possible; you need to build the largest network of connections possible with individuals who have the resources that can help with your innovation projects. These people fall into five prized social capital categories:

- Innovators and entrepreneurs

- Organizational leaders (e.g., C-suite executives)

- Financial benefactors or investors (e.g., angel investors, venture capitalists, bankers)

- Influencers (e.g., celebrities, prominent networkers)

- Customers (e.g., target customers for your innovations)

You can find more detail on these categories in the sidebar, "Prized Social Connection Categories," at the beginning of this chapter.

Individuals from these categories in your social network represent your *innovation-specific social capital*. Ideally, your Dunbar number will be filled with these types of individuals. In other words, you *do* need strong social ties with some individuals in each category because they represent a beachhead that will connect you to others in that category. One of the most consistent findings in research on networking and hiring is homophily—or the idea that as humans, we desire to be around, and hire, others who are like us. If you connect with inventors, they will know other inventors. CEOs will know other CEOs. And celebrities will know other celebrities.

But of course, most of us don't start with such strong connections. In fact, very few of us do. Instead, we have to build these connections first by creating weak ties with the "right" people and then, if we are lucky, eventually turning some of these connections into strong ties.

To illustrate, consider the case of David Bradford, currently CEO of FluentWorlds (Bradford has also been the CEO of HireVue, a successful firm that offers a talent interaction platform, including digital screening and video interviewing of job applicants, and Fusion-io, maker of advanced flash memory technology that had a $2.0 billion IPO in 2011). Bradford is the poster child for building innovation capital through social ties. He started out lacking any ties to people with resources. But over time, he has created an amazing network of connections that have helped him commercialize products in multiple successful companies.

Bradford says his penchant for networking wasn't ignited until he was graduating from law school and he couldn't find a job. He told us that he had been commiserating with his mother about his predicament when she said, "David, haven't I explained to you that, in life, it is not what you know but who you know?" Bradford hadn't yet learned that lesson. "I came from a small town in Montana," he says. "If there was a lawyer in that town, I did not know him. I had zero connections in the legal world. I was the least connected guy in the universe."

But Bradford took his mother's advice to heart, and since that day, he has been a networking machine. His wife calls him "the human internet." He has thirty thousand LinkedIn connections, the limit allowed by LinkedIn; he has to delete a connection to add one. "On LinkedIn, I have more than five million contacts that are only one degree of separation from me," Bradford says. "In fact, using LinkedIn, I have the power to contact over thirty million people directly or through a connection. This allows me to search, as I frequently do, for qualified resources and expertise."

Bradford has developed real relationships with individuals in all five prized innovation capital categories. During his career, he has formed connections with folks in the innovators and entrepreneurs category, like Steve Wozniak (Apple cofounder whom Bradford recruited to become chief scientist at Fusion-io); Ray Noorda (Novell founder and father of modern computer networking); Nolan Bushnell (father of the Atari and computer gaming); Gary Kildall (who wrote the first PC operating system on which MS-DOS was based); Drew Major (co-inventor of PC networking); and David Flynn (inventor of fast solid-state flash memory technology). Bradford also developed weak ties with Steve Jobs, Bill Gates, and others.

Bradford has made connections with numerous organizational leaders, including 339 CEOs and 306 company presidents currently in his LinkedIn contacts. His connections include Eric Schmidt (former CEO of Google and Novell); Dave Checketts (former CEO of the Madison Square Garden Company and Legends Hospitality Management and founder and chairman of Sports Capital Partners [SCP] Worldwide); and Scott McNealy (founder and CEO of Sun Microsystems).

Financial benefactors or investors provide another source of social capital for Bradford, who has more than a thousand of these backers as connections. Mostly angel investors or venture capitalists, the group includes many people at the top venture-capital firms like New Enterprise Associates (NEA), Lightspeed Venture Partners, Sequoia Capital, Kleiner Perkins Caufield & Byers, and Andreessen Horowitz. His connections include Marc Andreessen (cofounder of Netscape and Andreesen Horowitz); Scott Sandell (of NEA and one of only six investors to be named to the *Forbes* Midas List of top tech investors every year since 2007); Jeremy Liew (Lightspeed Venture Partners); and Doug Leone (a billionaire venture capitalist with Sequoia Capital).

Bradford has also gained social capital from influencers—prominent folks with many connections. Among his connections are National Football League hall of famer Steve Young, writer Malcolm Gladwell, politicians Mitt Romney and Orrin Hatch, talk show host Larry King, and Olympic gold medalist Peter Vidmar. And finally, Bradford has zealously networked with target customers in every business he has worked in.

Bradford readily credits his social relationships as vital to his business success. But how does someone go from being "the least connected guy in the universe" to being one of the most connected people?

Advice on Building Innovation-Specific Social Capital

So how do you get started building a network that will increase your social capital? Several methods can help you build your own capital.

Define Your Networking Objectives, and
Categorize Your Social Connections

To make the building of social connections as time-efficient as possible, we recommend investing time up front to think through your networking objectives and to categorize the contacts you already have. Leaders who apply this step and the next two steps of our networking advice can stretch the limits of their Dunbar number to well above 150 by allowing technology to stretch the natural limits imposed by their brains (the original Dunbar number range was 100 to 250, with 150 being the median; technology—and a significant time commitment—may make it possible to nearly double that number). To get started, think about what you are trying to accomplish with your social networking efforts. The following questions can serve as helpful prompts for this exercise:

- What are the top priorities and most critical needs of your current project, venture, or career? Sponsorship? Funding? Knowledge or expertise?

- In which arenas, for example, industries (telecommunications, technology, education, etc.) or technology areas (e.g., fields of expertise or knowledge domains) are you hoping to make your mark? What strong and weak connections do you have with folks in the five key categories in those arenas?

- Within those arenas, what gaps do you have in your current social capital? What type of connections would best fill those holes? Do you need connections with more organization leaders? Innovators and entrepreneurs? Influencers?

Once you have defined your objectives, you'll want to develop an approach to categorize your contacts so that you can make thoughtful efforts to build this network. "An uncategorized contact is a wasted contact," says Bradford. "Every network I create is organized by categories. This is the most efficient way to follow up with people. It is the only way to harness your people, your pool of skills, and your resources in a focused way." Bradford categorizes each new contact using LinkedIn's "network" and "tag" functions (that allow you to assign a self-generated tag to each of your contacts). His categories include *professions* (e.g., accountants, angel investors, attorneys, bankers, entrepreneurs, educators, technologists, government/politicians, venture capitalists), *positions within organizations* (CEOs, CIOs, CMOs [chief marketing officers], sales executives), and *companies* (e.g., IBM, Novell, Fusion-io, HireVue). In the *companies* category, he largely includes companies he has worked for or companies that are customers of the companies he has worked for. Bradford even uses various *friend* categories (e.g., golf friends, real estate friends, church friends, Google friends).

Other leaders we've studied used a simple Excel spreadsheet to categorize their contacts in similar fashion. It doesn't matter exactly what tools or technologies you use as long as you take the time to organize your relationships in a meaningful and useful way. The value of having these well-organized labels is that you can quickly and easily access them when you need to take action. Use these tools to track how often you interact with your connections. Strategize how you might develop stronger ties with high-priority contacts. Set weekly goals to both deepen key social ties and expand your overall network of relationships.

Invest the Time to Find Connections Through
Scrappy and Resourceful Networking

In our work with hundreds of innovators, both inside and outside large organizations, we've found that their capacity to access resources through social connections requires significant time and the scrappy approach of an entrepreneur. Most of us don't spend nearly enough time building our innovation-specific social capital. Bradford spends one or two hours *per day* (five or six days per week) on building, maintaining, and getting value from his social connections. He does this mostly using various technology platforms like LinkedIn, Facebook, and Twitter to develop weak-tie relationships that eventually, through face-to-face meetings, he can turn into stronger relationships. Over the past thirty years of his career, Bradford has spent roughly fifteen thousand hours, or over eight years of his work life, on building and maintaining relationships. How much time do you spend building and maintaining your own social connections each week?

Of course, the most effective way to build social relationships does not come through technology. You build relationships most effectively through phone conversations and face-to-face contact. But you have to make these relationships a priority. Marriott CEO Arne Sorenson understands the value of devoting time to networking, so much so that when a recent trip to China was canceled, he decided to use the three free days for face-to-face networking. "I reached out to four CEOs, names you would know, in the Bay Area whom I had met but didn't know well. I flew out and had conversations with each of them that lasted up to three hours. I just asked, 'What are you up to? What's important to you? Are there any things that we can think of that we'd like to do together? I'd love to have your advice; here are some of the things I'm wrestling with.'" Sorenson says that these kinds of conversations are invaluable. "In every one of those conversations, I left with concrete ideas that could be pursued. And I think those folks left the conversations with some useful ideas too. The key is *you have to use those conversations to listen* at least as much as, if not dramatically more than, to speak." Sorenson could have used his three free days to catch up on work or even relax, but by choosing to network instead, he opened the door to future initiatives that he might otherwise never have found.

Here are a few tools that the individuals and teams we coach have used to great effect to build their social connections. (For more resources and insights on this topic, visit www.innovators dna.com/innovation-capital.)

- We've mentioned LinkedIn a handful of times now. Two ways we like to use LinkedIn include the following:

  - Upgrade to the premium LinkedIn Sales Navigator, and use its advanced search features (you could also just do a thirty-day trial).

  - Use the "Affiliated company" feature to find similar organizations and individuals.

- One of our favorite and lesser-known resources is using the superb search options (entirely free!) provided by AngelList (https://angel.co). This social platform connects entrepreneurs, investors, and other people interested in early-stage companies. By late 2018, there were over 4.15 million startups and 7.47 million investors searchable on the site. Set the search criteria to match your interests, and start reaching out to individuals who catch your eye.

- To build your directory of potential contacts, you can identify past or upcoming conferences in your industry or in a targeted domain, search for the roster of presenters at the conference, and reach out to people on that list. You have a much higher chance of meeting high-quality individuals through this approach because they have already been vetted. Bradford met Wozniak at a conference and, after a brief meeting, invited him to join Fusion-io's advisory board the very next day. Wozniak eventually joined the company as chief science officer, bringing much-needed credibility to the startup.

- Look up popular blogs or discussion forums in your areas of interest, and send out a post describing who you are and the connections you are looking to make. You'll be surprised at who else has the same interests and desire to connect. Investors need potential startups to fund, entrepreneurs need cofounders, and everyone likes to meet and interact with proactive, respectful individuals.

This is just a short list of potential resources you can use, and new ones pop up all the time. You must think and act like an entrepreneur—continuously be on the lookout for fresh tools that can help you make new connections. Consequently, most of us have to dramatically increase the time we spend developing social connections in the five prized categories, and we need to do it using the latest channels, tools, and resources.

Develop and Maintain Relationships

Ask yourself the following question: What is the catalyst for building a meaningful, cooperative relationship? Insights into the answer were uncovered by Alvin Gouldner, a sociologist who studied the formation of norms in villages, other communities, and societies. A norm is an expectation of the "socially appropriate way" to behave within a social group. Gouldner studied numerous communities to determine which norms were identified as universal. Two norms were identified as most common across all social groups: One was the "incest taboo," the view that incest was inappropriate social behavior in all societies. The second was a "norm of reciprocity," or the expectation that people should respond favorably to each other by returning benefits for benefits.[12] According to the second norm, when someone does something positive for us, we feel an obligation to repay it (studies show that this type of tit-for-tat behavior starts at age two). Think about it. When a neighbor brings you a gift for a holiday, don't you feel an obligation to give a gift back? Indeed, Gouldner found that gift giving was the key catalyst—what he called the "starting mechanism"—for initiating a norm of reciprocity between individuals. A gift could take the form of a physical object (e.g., an electronic device, a wristwatch, jewelry), or it could be the gift of time, information, or anything that the receiver would find valuable.

Bradford has built his network by leveraging the law of reciprocity. "The law of reciprocity dictates that when we help others, help will return to us down the road in some form," he says. But ironically for the law of reciprocity to work, you have to be motivated to give *because you desire to serve, not because you expect a reward*. Ah, there's the rub.

Bradford has built an incredible network but only because he has been genuine in devoting his time and resources to help those in his network. He kindly offered free lodging to Steve Young when the hall of famer would return to visit Provo, Utah (home of his college alma mater, Brigham Young University), during the off-season. Later, Young autographed a football that Bradford sent to a Bay Area executive Bradford was recruiting to Fusion-io. The ball had the inscription "Jim. Fusion-io—Go for it! Steve Young." The executive, who was a sports enthusiast, had previously turned down the job multiple times, but the autographed football gift turned the tide. The executive joined Fusion-io and had a huge influence on the company's sales.

When radio and TV host Larry King and his wife Shawn invited Bradford to attend an event that they hosted to celebrate the life of Shawn's uncle Bobby Engemann (a member of the famous singing group the Lettermen), Bradford not only showed up but also came with his camera in tow. "He created a gorgeous photobook of the evening and gave a number of copies to our family members," King recalls. "This is a memory that we will treasure forever."[13] No wonder King was willing to write a foreword to *Up Your Game*, Bradford's book on networking.[14] Bradford's kind gestures often come early in developing a relationship because he genuinely asks the question How can I help this person achieve his or her goals?

Gifts, like the ones described above, can only be done with a smaller group of individuals with whom you are wanting to develop a strong relationship—people you want to pull into your Dunbar number. So how can you provide something of value to a large number of folks with whom you share a weak tie? Robin Chase, founder of Zipcar (a startup renting wheels by the hour), has found that a "light touch" connection every six to twelve months keeps the relationship "live." "I'll send an email at least once a year with some useful information or real news, saying, 'I just saw this article or this study and thought you might find it interesting,'" Chase told us. "Then I feel comfortable reaching out to ask them a question when I need to. They respond because I haven't proven to be a self-interested jerk who is annoying them with useless pages of information and asking for way too much. We are all so busy we don't have time for people who are sending us garbage emails. So just be respectful and find out what they want to know. What are their issues?"

Another option is to take advantage of contacts or knowledge from your company to provide value to a contact. For example, Danaher, a successful maker of industrial products that has increased its stock price threefold between 2008 and 2018, is known for its Danaher business system (DBS)—a set of execution practices based on lean principles that Danaher says are "at the heart" of its success. As we observed the work of individuals and teams at Danaher (and Fortive, a company that spun out from Danaher), we saw them use their knowledge of DBS to connect with customers, partners, and out-of-industry contacts. By simply offering to share insights from an internal set of best practices, Danaher people have gained incredible access to powerful individuals who are keen to learn about DBS.

Providing something of value to others is the key to starting, and maintaining, social connections. So think creatively about taking advantage of what you know, who you know, and what resources you can access to provide value to a contact.

Conclusion

Bradford's mother was right. In life, it is often who you know that makes all the difference to your success. But what she and others typically don't know is that learning how to access resources through weak social ties is critical to accessing the resources you will need to succeed at launching innovative projects and ventures. Moreover, the target of networking should be individuals within five prized categories: innovators and entrepreneurs, organizational leaders, financial benefactors, influencers, and customers. Building a network filled with valuable strong and weak ties with people in those categories is hard work, but it will provide you with access to resources, mentorship, and opportunities and will be an invaluable step in building your innovation capital. As you build your social network, you should also think about how you can build your credibility and personal reputation for innovation within that network—the topic of chapter 4.

Assess Your Social Capital That Contributes to Innovation Capital

To take the first step to understanding whether you are good at forward thinking, proactive problem solving, and persuading, take the following brief assessment of your social capital. (See our website www.innovatorsdna.com/innovation-capital for a full version of the social capital assessment and additional resources.)

Answer each of the following items using the numbers 1 through 7. Be honest in your assessment. In fact, when appropriate, have those who know you best assess you on these items.

1. Roughly how many people are in your LinkedIn or other professional network?
   a. less than 100
   b. 100–300
   c. 300–500
   d. 500–1,000
   e. 1,000–3,000
   f. 3,000–10,000
   g. more than 10,000

2. Roughly how many strong-tie relationships do you have with people you would classify as either successful innovators or entrepreneurs; organization leaders (vice president level and above); financial benefactors (angel investors or venture capitalists); or influencers (prominent individuals with many social connections)?
   a. 5 or fewer
   b. 6–10
   c. 11–25
   d. 26–50
   e. 51–75
   f. 76–100
   g. more than 100

3. On a scale of 1 to 7 (where 1 = one hour or less; 2 = two hours; 3 = three hours; and 7 = seven hours or more),

(continued)

how many hours per week to you spend networking to
meet new people to bring them into your network?

4. Using a scale of 1 to 7, where 1 = strongly disagree; 4 =
   neither agree nor disagree; and 7 = strongly agree, rate
   the following statement: One of my strengths is networking with others who can bring financial resources or other
   needed resource support to my innovation projects.

Add up your score. Here's how to interpret your results:

26–28: You have very strong social capital or connections.

23–25: You have strong social capital or connections.

21–22: You have adequate social capital, but it's unlikely to
have a strong impact on your career.

Below 21: Your social capital is a weakness and will not help
your career unless you improve.

4

What You Are Known For

(and Ways to Become Known)

How can you build a reputation that helps you win support for your ideas? Although we all assume we understand the idea of reputation, did you know there are actually three dimensions, or levels, of reputation? The first level is simply *general reputation*, or being known, which represents the level of awareness that someone (or something like an organization or product) has developed within a community. For example, consider whether you are known in your organization or community. Even just being known has benefits, many of which we don't fully appreciate.

For example, just being known can lead to a *mere-exposure effect*: the psychological phenomenon wherein people develop a preference for something merely because it is familiar. For example, in one study, four people with similar appearance visited a college course with differing frequency (one person visited five times, another ten, another fifteen, and the fourth didn't attend). At the end of the course, although the visitors had had no interaction with the actual students, when the students were shown photos of the visitors, they rated the people who visited the class fifteen times as much more attractive than those who visited less.[1] In other words, without realizing it, we prefer things that we have merely been exposed to. So if you can just get people to become familiar with you and know who you are, then you increase the odds that they will think positively of you.

The second reputation level is *general favorability*, or being seen in a positive (or negative) light. For example, we've all heard comments like "I've heard Sarah is really great" or "I'm glad Anup is on the team." Although Sarah and Anup may not be known for anything in particular, these favorable impressions have a more beneficial effect than does just being known. And of course, the impression can be unfavorable as well. For example,

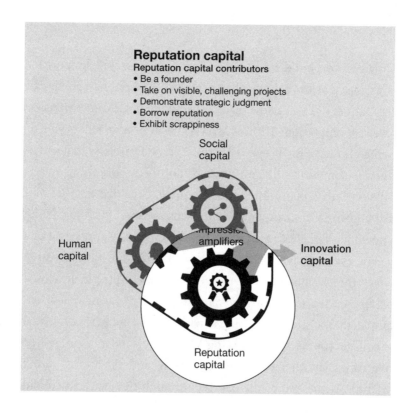

Ways to Contribute to Innovation-Specific Reputation Capital

BEING A FOUNDER: playing a central role in starting or managing an initiative that will have an impact (preferably visible and large) on an organization or the broader world; can be an internal initiative, an external project, or another activity, not just a startup

TAKING ON VISIBLE, CHALLENGING PROJECTS: raising your hand for, and then delivering, honest effort for hard projects, which typically receive more visibility and support inside large organizations; works because difficult projects have the biggest impact on the organization, the world, and, by extension, your reputation capital

DEMONSTRATING STRATEGIC JUDGMENT: showing the wisdom to clearly see a situation, make hard decisions, and proactively reallocate time, attention, and resources; builds your reputation capital

BORROWING REPUTATION: working for, or affiliating with, organizations or people with a reputation for innovation; works because reputation capital comes from our accomplishments and the people, organizations, and companies we associate with

EXHIBITING SCRAPPINESS: doing a lot with very little; if done in every situation, builds your reputation for resourcefulness and convinces supporters to give you more resources

you may have no firsthand experience with Kmart, but when you hear the name, you are likely to have an unfavorable impression because of what you've heard or read.

The third level of reputation is *being known for a specific attribute*, like innovation, execution, quality, or integrity. This is the most difficult type of reputation for you to develop, but it is also the most valuable. If someone has a problem that requires innovation, execution, or integrity (or some other attribute), the person will naturally look to you. A reputation for innovation is particularly valuable because it helps supporters reduce the inherent uncertainty they feel when taking a risk. As proof, consider the findings of a study conducted by Harvard professor Joseph Bower to understand what factors were most important for obtaining funding for a new project inside established companies. Surprisingly, Bower found that leaders did not choose projects according to whether the projects addressed the biggest market opportunity. Nor did they base their decisions on the highest projected internal rate of return or net present value. Instead, leaders chose projects primarily because of the track record and reputation of the person leading the project.[2]

Reputation has a similar impact when you are seeking funding for a startup. When weighing the benefits of who you know versus what you have done, research suggests that although knowing the right people may help you make initial contact with investors, your reputation has a much greater weight on how likely your project is to be funded.[3] As Adobe CEO Shantanu Narayen puts it: "If you look at Sandhill Road [in Silicon Valley] and the venture capital community they look more for the entrepreneur than the ideas, because ideas morph . . . but the entrepreneur is the critical person." This same principle is known among venture capitalists as betting on the jockey (the entrepreneur) and not the horse (the opportunity). Why would investors prefer to bet on the innovator than on the opportunity? Although a venture might have great financial projections, the reality is almost always different than what is expected, so innovators need to pivot and adapt to the unexpected. Experienced investors almost always prefer to bet on an entrepreneur with a reputation for being able to navigate the twisted path to success.

As it turns out, reputation for innovation also matters for public (and private) companies, not just private individuals. As described in chapter 1, our research on the S&P 500 showed that companies in the top 10 percent in terms of their reputation for innovation had three times higher market capitalization than did firms in the bottom 50 percent of innovation reputation. Moreover, the value of a reputation for innovation persisted even after we controlled for a firm's general reputation, general favorability, and actual innovation capabilities. A reputation for innovation was more valuable than other reputations we tested, such as a reputation for efficiency, execution, or quality. Remarkably, then, a *reputation* for innovation is valuable in and of itself— beyond a company's or person's actual innovation capabilities. A reputation for innovation will help you win support to pursue new ideas.

Building Your Personal Innovation Brand

So how can you build your own personal innovation brand? For most people, building a reputation is a stepwise process built through small wins over time. We first build a favorable reputation and then get known for something within our reach (efficiency, reliability, etc.). Then we slowly build up a reputation for innovation.

For example, consider how Robin Chase, cofounder of Zipcar, built her reputation for innovation. Founded in 2000, the carsharing service pioneered a new market category in a space where few people were innovating: mobility. The basic idea was to place cars around cities where people could rent the vehicles by the hour. However, given the novelty and risk associated with Zipcar's business model, Chase struggled to win the support to turn her idea into reality.

Fortunately, Chase graduated from a prestigious business school: MIT. She admits, "As a woman pioneering a new category, if I hadn't graduated from MIT, I wouldn't have had a chance." In essence, Chase's reputation of accomplishment, as represented by her graduation from an elite institution, opened the doors for a conversation with potential investors. But that only opened the door to a conversation. Chase continued to struggle to convince investors to commit. She also struggled to recruit key employees, because of the risk associated with the venture.

Chase describes her moment of awakening to the need to shape her reputation capital more actively. It was the day she attended a Harvard course discussion about Zipcar. Harvard professor Myra Hart had invited Chase to sit in the back row while the students discussed Zipcar's prospects. The plan was that at the end of the discussion, Chase could surprise the students with her insider view of what really happened. As the class discussion began, Hart drew a vertical line on the chalkboard and wrote on one half: "reasons to invest in Zipcar" and on the other half: "reasons not to invest in Zipcar." The students began debating. Chase described her disbelief as the "reasons not to invest" column began to fill up and overwhelm the few entries in the "reasons to invest" column. But what surprised her even more was the nature of the objections in the "reasons not to invest" column: most of the negative reasons related to her own qualifications!

Students pointed out that Chase had never been CEO. She had never been a founder of a startup. She had no experience in the car industry. And on and on. "I sat there stunned," Chase recalls. "I realized I hadn't communicated who I am and the things I have done. I hadn't communicated that every time a CEO or executive I worked with moved to a prestigious new role, they pulled me along as their number two. I hadn't communicated that I had a reputation for getting things done, and for precise thinking. It was an aha moment. After that, I realized I need to be more thoughtful about building and communicating my reputation." Although Chase hadn't been a founder or a CEO, she did have many experiences that could contribute to her personal innovation brand, with a bit of extra attention.

Today, after founding Zipcar (which was sold to Avis for $500 million), publishing a book on peer-to-peer platforms, and cofounding other innovative for-profit and not-for-profit ventures, Chase has established a strong reputation for innovation. But building that reputation was an incremental process. It began with building a general positive reputation (e.g., leveraging her MIT credentials), then a specific reputation (e.g., someone who gets things done), and finally a reputation for innovation (a leader in innovative startups; someone who writes about innovation). Today her reputation for innovation makes it much easier to win support for her ideas and ventures.

Advice on Building Your Reputation for Innovation

As a first step, you can exploit your present accomplishments to build a general reputation, even if it isn't specifically related to innovation (see the sidebar "How Reputation Signals Work"). For example, your education can obviously contribute to your general favorability, particularly your education level (e.g., master's degree or PhD); where you received your degree (an Ivy League school, a first-tier research school, etc.); or other distinguishing certifications (e.g., coding certification). Likewise, the companies you have worked for and the positions you have held (e.g., project leader, C-level executive, founder, member of a prestigious project) influence whether you are known favorably. Your past achievements matter as well, such as winning awards or other recognitions. For example, in a business school setting, you might

How Reputation Signals Work

What is building a reputation all about? Ultimately, you are trying to create reliable signals about your capabilities and share them with those you are trying to convince. Signaling theory proposes that the most effective signals have several characteristics. First, signals that are *hard or costly to create* are more effective than others (e.g., it is harder to get a job at Google than at the local food retailer). Second, signals are more effective when they are *easily observable* (otherwise, no one will notice).[4] Third, the more *relevant* the signal, the greater the impact on your reputation. So, for example, a PhD is a credible signal, since this degree is hard to achieve, particularly if it comes from a good university. But a PhD in autonomous vehicle technologies will give you more credit than a PhD in literature if you are trying to do a technology startup. At the core, supporters—whether they be investors, suppliers, customers, employees, or others—are looking for signals predicting future success based on your past experience and achievements.

have won a case competition or a business plan or business model competition. These factors all contribute to a generally favorable reputation, which is typically a stepping-stone to a reputation for innovation.

The challenge for most of us is that some of the more familiar reputation signals (e.g., education, degree, company positions) are hard to change. If you have already graduated from school, been working for some time, or are midcareer, you have limited latitude to change these signals. For most of us, the real question is, From where you stand today, how do you start building the kind of reputation that contributes to your innovation capital? Most of us have to get more creative! In the next few sections, we describe several of the most effective techniques the innovators we studied employed to build their reputation for innovation:

- Be a founder.

- Take on visible, challenging projects.

- Demonstrate strategic judgment.

- Borrow reputation.

- Exhibit scrappiness.

Be a Founder, but Think Creatively about How to Do It

Jeff Bezos, Elon Musk, and Mark Zuckerberg all sit atop our most innovative leaders list. Why? They are founders of successful companies doing something new and innovative—and full of impact. The most valuable thing you can do to build your reputation for innovation is to be a founder. This observation is so important that it bears repeating: To build a reputation for innovation, the most important thing you can do is to become a founder. But before you dismiss this advice as irrelevant for your situation, let us define a founder: someone who plays a central role in starting and managing an initiative that will have an impact (preferably visible and large) on an organization or the broader world. Note that being an independent startup entrepreneur is only one way to be a founder.

There are many ways to be a founder besides quitting your job to create a startup. Recent research confirms that about half of all new ventures are created by hybrid entrepreneurs—individuals who keep their day jobs and start a venture on the side.[5] Besides trying to found a hybrid venture, you can uncover many other opportunities to create a new venture—launching a new product, service, or business—inside a company as a corporate entrepreneur. Corporate entrepreneurship has a profound effect on both your reputation for innovation and your prospects for leadership opportunities. As part of our research for this book, we studied six hundred business professionals working for established companies over a five- to ten-year period. We found that those who were corporate entrepreneurs received more promotions, received these promotions faster, and were paid more money than were their colleagues.[6] Being a corporate entrepreneur gets you noticed! (However, do read the sidebar "Building a Transferable Reputation" near the end of this chapter for hints at how to take your inside-the-company status and get noticed outside your company.)

Finally, you can even just lead a project to be a founder. Indra Nooyi, former PepsiCo CEO, founded a process of identifying global megatrends and their implications for PepsiCo—a process that, as described in chapter 2, helped her engage in forward thinking. Similarly, Kate O'Keeffe created Cisco's Hyper-Innovation Living Labs (CHILL). This initiative brought Cisco together with customers and suppliers to attack big problems and start new ventures. Likewise, Kyle Nel, a former Lowe's executive, took over the concept for a Lowe's Innovation Lab and turned it into an explosive center of new ideas. All these executives built their reputation for innovation by being founders, even though they didn't quit their jobs to found a startup.

Your role as a founder has a profound impact on your career because it provides a relevant, observable, hard-to-imitate signal (the three characteristics of strong reputation signals) of your leadership capabilities. Moreover, being the founder of an innovative product or service requires holistic thinking. You must take into account all aspects of what makes a new venture successful—including its value proposition to the customer (the user), product development, technology integration, cost to deliver, performance metrics, and the resources needed for implementation. What better way to signal that you have leadership capabilities? And it's hard. "I think the most important thing that I look for [when funding a project] is, really, who's that champion?" Adobe CEO Shantanu Narayen told us. "I think ideas come from everywhere. But I think of all the great products we've developed as being characterized by somebody who is incredibly passionate about that idea." In sum, whether you are creating an external venture, an internal venture, or simply leading a new project, being a founder matches the criteria needed for a strong reputation signal: hard to imitate, observable, and relevant.

Getting Started on Your Path to Founder

How can you become a founder? Start by raising your hand for new projects. Andrew Jassy's journey to become CEO of Amazon Web Services provides an illustration. Jassy joined Amazon in the late 1990s and quickly worked his way up to be a personal technical assistant to Bezos. Because of his assignment, Jassy attended an offsite leadership event at Bezos's home, where the leadership team discussed Amazon's core competencies. At first, the conversation focused on the obvious: Amazon was good at offering customers a broad selection of products and then fulfilling their orders quickly and reliably. But the conversation quickly shifted to Amazon's technical capabilities. To support their massive retail operations and their subsidiary Merchant.com (which sold e-commerce solutions to other B2B partners), Amazon had developed deep technology infrastructure services in data storage, cloud computing, and databases. It had also become highly skilled at running reliable, scalable, cost-effective data centers. As the discussion evolved, Bezos argued that there was an opportunity to sell the technology infrastructure the company was building to other firms via the internet.

"When we thought about what Amazon was good at," Jassy recalls, "we've always been a technology company at our core. We realized we could provide all of those key components to that internet operating system." So Jassy raised his hand to be part of the team to explore the opportunity in this new space. It wasn't an easy decision, because he would have to step away from working directly with Bezos. But for Jassy, it was worth the risk to try his hand at being a founder.

To explore the opportunity, Jassy and several others put together a "vision document," one of Amazon's fast-experiment tools to think through new businesses and then test their assumptions with customers quickly (it is now called a *working-backward document*; see chapter 8). As part of their customer research, Jassy and his group discovered that other companies were experiencing the same challenges that Amazon was facing—challenges for which Amazon was building relevant technology infrastructure and solutions. Because of the depth of the customer need, the project received a green light and Jassy was tapped to lead the effort. His team had to build a suite of cloud computing services as well as new skills at selling to enterprise customers. The effort eventually evolved to become Amazon Web Services, the Amazon business unit that delivers much of Amazon's operating profits. Because Jassy raised his hand and took the risk of leaving a very comfortable and high-profile role working directly with Bezos, he became a founder of an internal venture. There was no way to predict that Amazon Web Services would become as successful as it did. But Jassy's role as a founder propelled his career and reputation forward like nothing else could.

Being a founder may also simply be a matter of thinking more creatively about what matters to you. You could, for example, create a venture on the side, while you are working; you could base it on your expertise, a hobby, or an opportunity that you see. As mentioned earlier, half of all new ventures are created by hybrid entrepreneurs who keep their day job and develop a venture on the side, but what is surprising is their success rates.[7] Although there is a stereotype that being a successful entrepreneur requires total commitment and thus the need to quit your day job and risk it all, in reality, hybrid entrepreneurs have higher survival rates than do entrepreneurs who risk it all.[8] Hybrid entrepreneurs have the chance to learn and adjust, with the cushion of their current income, before deciding to go it alone. Being a founder of a venture outside your organization not only builds your skill set but also signals to those inside the organization that you are entrepreneurial.

Finally, you can think creatively about how to be a founder centered on something you are passionate about. For example, Mary Lombardo, an executive at United Technologies Corporation (UTC), has gained prominence by founding the innovation and research group within the commercial services and Otis Elevator Company business units at UTC. Lombardo was a vice president in engineering at UTC when she saw the need to build stronger innovation capabilities within her team. Because she had a passion for innovation, she started to benchmark and study innovative organizations as a pet project. She even arranged to take her boss, John Galbraith, to visit Procter & Gamble's innovation team to help him see the potential for UTC to take a leap forward in its innovation capabilities. "That benchmarking trip helped him to see that what I was proposing was possible in a large corporation," recalls Lombardo. "That was important, and I think from there, he started to see how I was building our capability and experimenting with different things. It was right after that benchmarking trip that he said, 'Write your job description, write your vision, write your plan.'" From that starting point, Lombardo has built a successful internal innovation project and now leads the eighty members of the innovation and research group at UTC.

Even if You Try and Fail, It Can Have an Upside

As you think about becoming a founder, you may feel anxious about starting something new, because of either the risk involved or the fear of failure. In terms of risk, recall that being a founder doesn't necessarily mean leaving your work. You can lead something new inside or outside your company while still keeping your job. Think creatively about how you can start a new initiative. If you're afraid of failure, then it might help to remember that your project does not necessarily have to be a success for it to build your innovation capital. Randy Komisar, partner at legendary venture-capital firm Kleiner Perkins Caufield & Byers (which invested in Google, Amazon, and Intel), used to ask, "What do you call a failed entrepreneur in Silicon Valley?" The answer? "A serial entrepreneur."[9] Komisar tells the joke on purpose to illustrate a critical point: many of Silicon Valley's most successful companies and most successful entrepreneurs came out of the lessons learned from failure. Silicon Valley respects entrepreneurs who try, even if they fail. Trying to be a founder, even if you fail, can help build your innovation capital. Of course, continuing to found new initiatives until you have a visible success is your ultimate goal.

Take on Visible, Challenging Projects

A second way that innovators build their reputation and innovation capital is by taking on challenging and visible assignments. In chapter 2, we described how Indra Nooyi took on the difficult assignment of revamping the PepsiCo's IT system when she was chief financial officer (CFO) of the company. When she spoke with us, Nooyi reflected on how she had built her reputation and won innovation capital at PepsiCo: "If I go back to my time since I joined PepsiCo, and even before then, I was always willing to take on the most difficult assignments. I think that my credibility was built on attacking the most difficult issues; it helped me as I went forward." She offered advice for others who have high business aspirations: "I would suggest you put your hand up for the most difficult assignments. If you can prove that you can crack a difficult assignment successfully, people sort of look at you with a newfound respect."

In most companies, hard problems receive more support—and more visibility—than do easy ones. Narayen of Adobe told us how he selects which projects to support: "I look and ask, what is the harder problem to solve? If you have a harder problem to solve, it is a better problem to invest in, because someone can't compete with you long term. We are looking for hard problems to solve!" Narayen acknowledges that being a champion for a hard problem is a great way to get experience and earn a reputation at Adobe. "Championing change is hard," he says. "That's why the champions of change are so valuable."

Of course, taking on a challenging assignment presents a dilemma, since the hardest projects also often have the highest chance of failure. Should you be worried? Of course, you should carefully consider whether to volunteer for a challenging project, and you should only take on assignments for which you think you have a reasonable chance of success. You should also be careful about overpromoting your project or its success before you have actually achieved it (see the sidebar "Using, and Losing, Innovation-Specific Reputation Capital"). But we found that when people conducted themselves honorably on a challenging project, even if the project did not succeed as expected, they frequently earned some respect. Microsoft CEO Satya Nadella led the Bing project to take on Google's search function, and LinkedIn CEO Jeff Weiner had a leading role in a similar project when he was at Yahoo! Competing with Google in search is clearly a difficult assignment. While both projects realized some limited success, Yahoo! eventually left search, and Google still dominates over Bing. But both Nadella and Weiner felt that it was a valuable learning experience and that they earned respect as a result of their work on the challenging project. McDonald's CEO Steve Easterbrook

Using, and Losing, Innovation-Specific Reputation Capital

Dean Kamen was a well-known and accomplished inventor when he introduced his "game-changing" invention, the Segway, a two-wheeled, self-balancing electric vehicle. He leveraged his reputation for innovation to get attention for the product and to promote it. But Kamen, and especially the venture capitalists who supported him, were arguably too optimistic and promotional about the product (but then again, Steve Jobs also thought the vehicle would be a smash hit). The Segway was launched in 2001 in a blizzard of publicity. Yet it failed to gain market acceptance and is now something of a curiosity. As a result, Kamen's reputation as a successful inventor took a hit because of the visible failure of the Segway.

In similar fashion, Marissa Mayer left Google and took on the visible and difficult challenge of turning Yahoo! around. Given her success at Google, she promised big changes at Yahoo! and, as she had done at Google, effectively used the press to promote her

offers the following advice to business professionals who aspire to be leaders: "I'd start by suggesting you build a track record that reflects the sort of leader you want to be. And the sooner you set out that way, the better. I would encourage taking risks in your career. When in doubt, say 'yes.' Taking on new, challenging assignments gives you the opportunity to be noticed."

Demonstrate Strategic Judgment

Taking on a challenging new project can help you win positive attention that can translate into innovation capital, but so can the optimistic agenda (at Google, Mayer reportedly had a group of PR people devoted to promoting her career). But the results simply didn't materialize. Not surprisingly, her reputation as an innovative leader took a hit when her visible tenure as Yahoo!'s CEO didn't produce the desired results.

What can we learn from these examples in light of our advice to take on big, risky projects? Recognize that taking on a hard project is risky business. If you broadcast your success before you achieve it you are essentially taking a big gamble. If you succeed, it could be a massive win for your innovation capital. But if you fail, you will lose a great deal of innovation capital. An alternate approach we have seen work is to keep a low profile while you are trying to tackle the hard project. If you fail, then no one can hold you accountable for big promises you didn't fulfill. But if you succeed, you can start broadcasting (using one of the impression amplifiers described later) and reap the reputational benefits. Lesson learned? Perhaps humility goes a long way in protecting you from the downsides to your innovation capital.

courage to make hard strategic judgments. Such strategic judgment includes the hard decision to invest substantial resources to pursue a bold new initiative, but it can also be the courage to stop an initiative or redirect resources away from what had formerly been seen as a high-priority task.

Consider the experience of Scott Stephenson, CEO of data analytics firm Verisk Analytics—a $20 billion market-cap data analytics firm consistently ranked as one of the world's most innovative companies—and ranked twenty-second on our list of most innovative leaders. When telling us how he developed his reputation for leading innovation while moving up the managerial ranks at Verisk, Stephenson emphasized that he built his reputation over time by focusing resources on what he believed were the high-priority projects for the future of the company. This approach sometimes meant discontinuing activities that others saw as high priority, to put more resources on even higher-priority projects. "I would say that there were specific moments where I identified the need to accumulate resources and focus them on particular things that needed attention," Stephenson recalls, "and then you actually get a result and it's a result that everybody can see. That really makes an impression."

For example, Stephenson describes the hard decision earlier in his career to sell a growing business. As background, Verisk Analytics develops unique data sets and then applies proprietary analytics to generate insights for customers. In general, Verisk focuses on data analysis and avoids building software applications. However, there are two exceptions to the rule: whenever software is required to deliver insights for customers and whenever there are platform opportunities that can generate whole new data sets, Verisk will develop software. Previously, Verisk had entered the insurance industry with a policy administration software platform. When it entered the business, everyone was excited about the opportunity to generate new and valuable data sets with the platform. But three years later, although the business was growing, it was still struggling to become profitable. Everyone wanted the policy administration project to be successful, but Stephenson thought that the software platform business model had limitations that would be difficult to overcome. At the same time, he recognized that one piece of the project was very valuable, a set of algorithms that provided critical calculations.

Because of the business model challenge, Stephenson made the hard decision to exit the growing business. But he decided to keep the rights to the algorithms. Stephenson then focused Verisk's resources on creating a new kind of business based on the algorithms. Specifically, the team created application program interfaces that could make the algorithm reusable by other policy administration platforms. Verisk then started selling the calculation capability, not as a software platform like the old business model, but as a service to multiple platforms (think of it as kind of like the "Intel inside" approach of selling a key component for a larger system). Although in retrospect the decision made sense, at the time it wasn't easy. "It was a difficult decision to shed the revenue," Stephenson recalls, "but by concentrating on the thing that was the real difference maker, and also was the thing that was closest to our capabilities, we found a way to hook us up to everybody's policy administration system." In the end, the service became a huge success for Verisk and for Stephenson. Reflecting on how he built the reputation that led to his own innovation capital, Stephenson told us, "It's the moment when you say, 'Okay, we're going to stop doing some things and start doing other things.' Those moments get noticed."

Deprioritizing activities and reallocating resources takes courage because you will undoubtedly upset the individuals who have a stake in those activities. When people's reputation—or their continued employment—seems dependent on the continuation of a project, it can be extraordinarily difficult to help them see that the project should be stopped. How can you do it? Start with the legitimate, honest reasons for a change of course. Then consider celebrating the end! Nicolas Cudré-Mauroux, the head of innovation at the chemicals company Solvay, recalls how he used a technique in an earlier role to make it easier to exit a project. "We used to have a party to celebrate stopping a project and give some kind of reward to the project leader who stopped his own project," he says. "We wanted to incentivize and celebrate liberating resources for something more important." Having the courage to change course, to deprioritize activities to create greater impact with other initiatives, is a way to build your reputation as an influential, innovative leader.

Borrow Reputation

Although much of our reputation is built on the back of our achievements, there are ways to creatively "borrow" reputation by associating yourself with high-prestige individuals, projects, organizations, or educational institutions that lend you credibility. For example, part of Timothy "Tim" Cook's reputation for innovation comes from his association with both Jobs's and Apple's reputation. The same can be said for Sundar Pichai, Google's CEO, who now leads the business founded by Larry Page and Sergey Brin. Cook and Pichai are, no doubt, talented and innovative leaders. But a great deal of their innovation capital comes from their leadership positions at well-known innovative companies.

The idea of reputation borrowing isn't new, but few of us actively try to take advantage of it. We previously mentioned the reputation bump that Robin Chase received by attending a prestigious university (MIT). The challenge for most of us is that those big red-letter opportunities have already passed (e.g., you didn't attend Stanford). So what can you do about it now? In reputation borrowing, you try to be a bit more creative in associating yourself with prestigious institutions or people so that you can share in some of the reputation benefits.

For example, the best approach to building your reputation is to work for a prestigious company (or a fast-growing one), ideally one with a reputation for innovation (see the *Forbes* World's Most Innovative Companies list).[10] For example, even if Cook and Pichai were employees and not the CEOs of those companies, if you were introduced to them, you would naturally think more highly of them and assume they are innovative like the companies they work for.

Of course, getting a job at a company with an innovation brand is easier said than done, especially if you haven't attended a prestigious university. So what can you do? Associate yourself with a prestigious university or company through another channel. To illustrate, we have had numerous individuals volunteer to do research with us at Wharton, INSEAD, or Stanford because they want to be able to talk about "doing research at INSEAD" on their résumés and in interviews. Others volunteer to work with a center or program at the university. Doing so allows them to associate themselves with the prestige of the school, even though they may not have attended full time or graduated there. Alternatively, some executives are always telling us about their time at Harvard—not in a Harvard University degree program, but in an executive or online program. This type of reputation credential isn't as powerful as graduating from the school, but it still leaves a positive impression and may help you get a job at that prestigious company.

Another approach to building your reputation (and the skills needed to create a startup) is to work for a fast-growing midsize company. Andy Rachleff, a former Benchmark Capital partner who co-teaches entrepreneurship courses at Stanford Graduate School of Business, creates an annual list of the top fifty "career-launching companies" to work for.[11] These are companies with $20 million to 300 million in revenues and growing at more than 50 percent each year. The 2018 list includes up-and-comers like Buzzfeed (social news and entertainment), Carbon (3-D manufacturing), Health Catalyst (data organizer for health care), and Qualtrics (consumer research and experience software).

One reason to work for these companies is that while people may not have heard of one company today, it may be the star of tomorrow. Moreover, at a fast-growing company, your chances for promotion and leadership are significantly greater than at a large company. "You get more credit than you deserve for being part of a successful company," Rachleff writes. "Success will help propel your career . . . When it comes time to leave the successful company, you'll be able to write your own ticket. No one will

Building a Transferable Reputation

Reputations are created within communities. So depending on your aspirations, it's important to recognize that although you may have invested great effort into developing your reputation inside a company, the status might not transfer to other organizations or communities. Indeed, Gary Crocker, a well-known entrepreneur in the medical-device and life sciences fields, told us that "most reputational capital is specific, meaning specific to the industry, company, or even the activity." So how do you transfer your reputation beyond your organizational community?

We have found that individuals who are most successful at transferring their reputation across communities have to be their own PR firm and look for opportunities to tell their story to broader audiences. They use their activities or position inside an organization to participate in conferences as a speaker; share ideas as a thought leader or a contributor to a publication; apply for awards in their community or industry; create a video or a blogging platform; and explore other activities to tell their story.

Consider how Kyle Nel, former executive director of Lowe's Innovation Lab, thoughtfully transferred his innovation capital outside his organization. Although Nel had developed a strong reputation for innovation inside Lowe's—he led a transformation into

remember if you were employee 20 or 120. Everyone wants to recruit people from successful companies because they believe people carry the lessons of success with them . . . [Y]our choice of company trumps everything else. It's more important than your job title, your pay or your responsibilities."[12] (See the sidebar "Building a Transferable Reputation" for tips on how to take new technology areas like augmented-reality-assisted remodeling, inventory robots, and exosuits for workers—he had little status outside the company. To remedy this disadvantage, he thoughtfully explored how to transfer his reputation to the outside. He started by launching a series of videos to broadcast the innovative work he had been doing at Lowe's (more on this technique in the next chapter). The videos caught the attention of others, and he was invited to do a TEDx talk at Universidad de Navarra. Although it may not have been the biggest TEDx event in the world, the video received lots of views and soon Nel was receiving other invitations to talk about the future of retail. His appearances eventually led to an opportunity to join Singularity University as an adjunct faculty member and then as executive vice president. Over time, Nel's position at this Silicon Valley think tank led to many prestigious and reputation-building relationships. For example, he was asked to be on the advisory board of XPRIZE Innovation Board and other prominent technology companies.

All of this was achieved through a series of small steps designed to transfer his reputation to communities outside Lowe's. You can transfer your reputation to a broader audience, but you must carefully amplify who you are, who you know, and what you've done (we'll discuss amplification in chapters 5 and 6).

your inside-the-company status and get noticed outside your company.)

If you are unable to secure a full-time position with a fast-growing or prestigious company, you can still borrow reputation from a company through a part-time assignment. For example, one of our students with a modest résumé reached out to PolarityTE, a fast-growing biotechnology startup, through a social contact to express his enthusiasm for the company's technology and his willingness to do an internship for free. His enthusiasm paid off in a résumé-enhancing, even if unpaid, internship. The internship allowed him to borrow from the reputation of the startup, thereby enhancing his own reputation for future opportunities. In similar fashion, you can volunteer for programs or events—or to work with certain individuals. For example, if you are an artist, say, a screenwriter looking to win support for your ideas, you might volunteer to get involved with a visible event put on by the American Screenwriters Association. You will be surprised at your ability to borrow reputation if you use your creativity.

Exhibit Scrappiness

Perhaps you haven't had the chance to be a founder or sit in the driver's seat to make hard calls on an important project. How can you build a positive reputation that will help you win support for your ideas? The good news is that you still have a chance to build a reputation for one of the most important characteristics that smart investors and supporters look for: scrappiness. *Scrappiness*, a term commonly used in the entrepreneurial world, means a dogged spirit that enables you to get a lot done with few resources. One investor we interviewed puts it this way: "I've met many entrepreneurs, but what gets me excited is people who are getting a lot done with a little—the entrepreneurs who can take the little bit of kindling they have and they make smoke. Investors who get it look for that."

Although it's easy to tell yourself that you could do something big if you had money, the smartest entrepreneurs find ways to accomplish a lot with the little that they have. There are abundant examples, although perhaps our favorite example may be one of our most humbling moments. Shortly after graduating from Stanford, one of us (Nathan) was invited to host a television series interviewing entrepreneurs. But when the schedule listed a college entrepreneur who had started a hot dog stand as one of the first interviews, Nathan almost backed out. He was used to spending time with the top entrepreneurs and investors in Silicon Valley. What could he learn from a hot dog entrepreneur? What Nathan learned taught him both a lesson in humility and scrappiness.

Jayson Edwards, a college student who had spent time in Chicago eating the city's famous hot dogs, found that he missed the experience when he moved west. He had the idea to start a hot dog stand, but as a college student with literally no money and no investors, he knew he would have to be scrappy to be successful. To get started, he sat around campus and counted the number of students passing by at different times of the day at different locations to identify the high-traffic areas. Then he started hosting tasting parties, inviting people to try out different styles of hot dogs and sauces, and interviewing them about what they saw as a value or a deal. Finally, knowing student traffic patterns and what the students wanted the most, he scouted out locations. On the edge of campus, he found a tiny shack that had the advantages of high traffic and low fixed costs but the disadvantage of needing renovations to meet code. Rather than hire a contractor to get the work done or buying a truck to haul materials, Edwards hauled sheets of plywood, sinks, and tools from the local Home Depot on the city bus and remodeled the building himself. Then he opened for business. Starting literally from almost nothing, his business J Dawgs expanded to seven locations and provides a nice lifestyle income. Although J Dawgs isn't a tech startup transforming the world, Edwards's scrappiness in starting a successful business illustrates a more general principle: getting a lot done with a little.

We saw similar scrappiness from Jen Hyman, founder of Rent the Runway, a company that rents designer fashions to customers using a Netflix-style business model. Although today the company is valued at over $1 billion and has well over $100 million in annual revenue, when Hyman started the company, she did so with no investment. Instead, she ran fast and cheap experiments where she, for example, let students try on borrowed dresses to rent before an event on Harvard campus. Her scrappiness allowed her both to test her business model without having to invest in a website and inventory and to convince investors that she would be a good investment. As another investor told us, "A successful entrepreneur creates momentum in a petri dish. Yes, it's small. But it shows what they can do." You can build your reputation for innovation by demonstrating that you are scrappy—that you can accomplish a lot with limited resources.

How can you be scrappy? When you need resources to accomplish your goals, take every opportunity to borrow rather than buy, to trade rather than purchase, or to design and run cheap experiments to test new ideas rather than initiate expensive product development. Two of us (Nathan and Jeff) describe how to do this in more detail in *The Innovator's Method*, but the general principle is to creatively speed up the process or lower the cost of anything you are doing.[13]

Conclusion

Building a favorable reputation—and ideally a reputation for innovation—can turbocharge your leadership opportunities. "Once you establish a reputation," Gary Crocker says, "you will attract more opportunities by an order of magnitude. But it's your reputation that is the key to attracting these opportunities." Crocker built his reputation with small wins over time and has been so successful that former University of Utah president Michael Young describes him as "almost certainly one of the most imaginative entrepreneurial businessmen in the US—maybe the world." This is the type of ringing endorsement that builds your reputation. Similarly, for most of us, our reputations will be built through a series of small wins, rather than through a supernova event. So start now. As McDonald's CEO Steve Easterbrook advised, "I'd suggest you start to build a track record that reflects the sort of leader you want to be. And the sooner you set out that way, the better."

Our focus has been on explaining how you can accumulate those small wins by founding an initiative, taking on challenging assignments, deprioritizing tasks to focus on higher-priority initiatives, and borrowing from the reputation of prestigious entities. By using these techniques, you can create your own personal innovation brand that contributes to your innovation capital.

So far, we have been talking about how you can build your own personal reputation—your personal brand as an innovator. In the next two chapters, we will shift gears slightly to describe impression amplifiers, or actions that can help you win support for your ideas. Impression amplifiers differ slightly from your personal reputation capital because they are less about who you are and more about persuading others to support your ideas and projects. Thus, we now turn to describing how impression amplifiers can be a powerful way to win support for your initiatives.

Assess Your Reputation That Contributes to Innovation Capital

Rate the following five statements on a numerical scale of 1 to 7. (See our website www.innovatorsdna.com/innovation-capital for additional resources.)

1. Other people are likely to vouch for my ability to lead a successful innovation project (1 = strongly disagree; 4 = neither agree nor disagree; and 7 = strongly agree).

2. I am well known for tackling difficult problems and coming up with innovative solutions (1 = strongly disagree; 4 = neither agree nor disagree; and 7 = strongly agree).

3. I have a degree from a high-status prestigious university (7 = a degree from a highly prestigious university [e.g., an Ivy League university, Stanford, or MIT]; 5–6 = a degree from a strong university that isn't in the preceding top tier; and 4 and below = a degree from a lower-ranked state school or community college).

4. I have worked for a company (or companies) with a strong reputation for innovation (7 = worked for a company

ranked in top twenty on the *Forbes* or *Fast Company* World's Most Innovative Companies lists or *Fortune*'s Most Admired Companies list; 5–6 = worked for a company in the top hundred on those lists; and 4 and below = have not worked for a company in the top hundred on those lists).

5. I have started or cofounded a number of new businesses (products or services) using my own original idea (1 = one or zero businesses; 2 = two; and 7 = seven or more). (This could be a product or service within an existing business or in a startup.)

Add up your score. Here's how to interpret your results:

28–35: You have a very strong innovation reputation.

25–27: You have a strong innovation reputation.

22–24: Your reputation for innovation is okay but unlikely to have a strong impact on your career.

Below 22: Your reputation for innovation will not help your career unless you strengthen that reputation.

5

Personal Impression Amplifiers

Broadcasting, Signaling, and Storytelling

Do you know how to make a good impression? Most people feel they do. But what about making a good impression for your ideas? For a moment, consider what advice you would give to a friend trying to raise money for his or her idea or to win the backing of a recalcitrant manager? What would you recommend beyond "have a good idea," "have a strong business case," or "be passionate?" And would the advice be effective? Could you share any guidance that has some basis in evidence, more than what has been handed down as common wisdom?

Good impressions are important, of course, but few of us have real evidence about what makes a good impression, particularly when it comes to winning support for your ideas. Despite abundant scientific literature on first impressions and impression management between employees and bosses (and entrepreneurs and investors), most of us know little about how innovators shape impressions to win support for their ideas.[1] But effective innovators use some tactics over and over to do much more than make a good impression. They apply these tactics to get people to join their projects and obtain resources and funding to bring their ideas to life.

As we studied the world's most innovative leaders, we learned that they are very good at amplifying the signals they want others to receive. They utilize what we call *impression amplifiers*, which we define as observable actions to win support for your ideas or to multiply the perceived value of your human, social, or reputation capital. Put simply, impression amplifiers are actions taken to make you and your ideas better known and more cred-

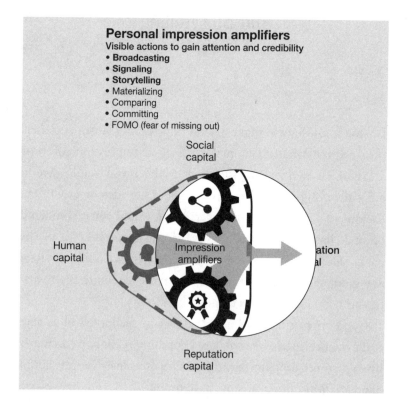

Personal impression amplifiers
Visible actions to gain attention and credibility
• Broadcasting
• Signaling
• Storytelling
• Materializing
• Comparing
• Committing
• FOMO (fear of missing out)

Social capital

Human capital

Impression amplifiers

ation al

Reputation capital

Impression Amplifiers That Strengthen Human, Social, and Reputation Capital

BROADCASTING: finding ways to visibly communicate who you are (your human capital skills), who you know (your social capital), or what you have accomplished (your innovation reputation capital) to others; works because people are more likely to believe things when they hear it from credible sources and from multiple sources

SIGNALING: securing credibility endorsements by creating visible links, other relationships, or achievements that signal an endorsement of the quality of your idea

STORYTELLING: creating an emotional connection with the audience you are trying to persuade through narratives, illustrations, or other accounts (often personal); works because an emotional connection can help listeners suspend their disbelief and motivate them to take action

ible. They are weapons in the arsenal of your personal marketing strategy. Even better, while human, social, and reputation capital take time to build, you can start using impression amplifiers more quickly to win backing for your ideas.

There are two primary categories of amplifier actions: (1) those that strengthen your human, social, and reputation capital and win support for both you and your idea, and (2) those less focused on amplifying who you are and more targeted at persuading others to provide support for a specific idea or project.

In this chapter, we examine impression amplifiers that are primarily used to get positive attention for you and your idea. In chapter 6, we focus on impression amplifiers that work mostly to persuade others to offer support and resources for your idea. As we describe each amplifier, we tell an illustrative story, explain why the amplifier works (including the psychological principle that gives it power), provide an example of how an everyday innovator has applied the technique, and recommend how you might apply it yourself.

Most of us don't spend enough time thinking about marketing ourselves or our projects. But we should. If you can master some of the impression amplifiers we describe, you will find that your personal reputation as an innovator will increase. In turn, you will dramatically increase your odds of getting the resources you need to launch a project or venture that will have positive impact—for both you and those around you.

Broadcasting

As described earlier in the book, the Netscape team members worked to carefully create an image of Marc Andreessen as a genius of the internet era. Their moment of triumph came when they landed a cover spot on *Time* magazine depicting Andreessen as the internet's barefoot genius sitting on a throne. The visibility and credibility provided by being on the cover of *Time* transformed Andreessen from a smart guy who worked on an early browser (Mosaic) to a visionary leader of the internet era. This action amplified the value of Andreessen's innovation capital at least a hundredfold. In reflecting on the purposeful effort to build the early Netscape's credibility, one of masterminds behind the *Time* cover recalled, "We really helped him [Andreessen] become a rock star. Our goal was to get him on the cover and get people excited that we had the technical capabilities to transform the internet." Even though Netscape was ultimately defeated by Microsoft's strategy of bundling Internet Explorer with its other software, Andreessen has since used the innovation capital built

through this PR campaign to start multiple ventures and investment funds, most notably Andreessen Horowitz. His story illustrates the best known of the impression amplifiers: broadcasting.

What Broadcasting Is and Why It Works

Broadcasting involves finding ways to visibly communicate who
you are, who you know, or what you have accomplished to others. Broadcasting works in part because of the familiarity principle: a psychological phenomenon by which people tend to develop a preference for things merely because they are familiar
with them.[2] People are more likely to believe information when
they hear it from *credible sources* and from *multiple sources*. Not
surprisingly, broadcasting is most credible when it doesn't come
directly from you.

One of the most effective ways to broadcast information is to
get some type of media outlet to tell a positive story about you or
your project. Kate O'Keeffe, chief innovation architect at Cisco,
recalls the moment she had her own cover-of-*Time* moment. After years of creating programs to capture and develop innovative
ideas from Cisco engineers, O'Keeffe became convinced that the
real opportunity to create disruptive new businesses lay in working more closely with external customers to cocreate industry-
transforming solutions. To address this challenge, O'Keeffe came
up with an approach she called CHILL: Cisco Hyper-Innovation
Living Labs, wherein Cisco could collaborate with uncommon
partners (the kinds of partners you might not work with) to create disruptive solutions. Although O'Keeffe found that the idea
had intuitive appeal to both internal Cisco executives and external partners, she still had to win support for the initiative. As a
strategic thinker, she naturally sought out those leaders likely to
be in a position to help her in the future, especially the executives
most likely to succeed longtime CEO John Chambers. O'Keeffe

invited these executives to be a part of CHILL and to experience multiparty innovation in spaces as divergent as retail, health care, and supply chains. As the executives experienced the power of mutually discovering and creating solutions with powerful partners like Apple, Airbus, Nike, and Costco, they quickly bought into the possibilities.

By the end of the first CHILL event, everything looked aligned to greenlight CHILL as a major internal initiative. But then Chambers stepped down as CEO and was replaced by Chuck Robbins. The succession surprised many, including O'Keeffe. Moreover, most of the senior executives who had attended CHILL and championed O'Keeffe's work suddenly left the company with the change of regime. Then, in yet another blow to her work, the business unit where O'Keeffe had been operating was abruptly disbanded.

Fortunately, O'Keeffe had been working to broadcast her activities. For example, she and her team had been creating videos of CHILL projects to show what they were doing. She also collaborated with us (as academics) to study the co-innovation process her team was applying at CHILL. This collaboration ultimately resulted in a coauthored *Harvard Business Review* article on cooperative innovation efforts between groups of firms.[3]

The article was published in the fall of 2016, just as the Cisco shakeup was happening. As support began to dry up for CHILL and the division where it was based was being shut down, O'Keeffe soon found herself starting over, trying to win new supporters for CHILL. "That *HBR* article was my *Time* magazine moment," she recalls, referring to the Marc Andreessen story. "No one in the new Cisco leadership knew me, and my division was being cut. The future was incredibly uncertain. But others inside of Cisco saw the article and began to talk about what we were doing at CHILL."

Perhaps best of all, the new CEO, with whom Kate had no relationship, independently started to hear about the CHILL program and the *HBR* article in meetings. Curious, Robbins invited O'Keeffe to speak at Cisco's annual leadership conference for the world's top CEOs. O'Keeffe recalls presenting on stage with other luminaries and then afterward bumping into Robbins. The CEO was engaged in a conversation with David Cameron, former British prime minister. When Robbins saw O'Keeffe out of the corner of his eye, he called her over and introduced her to Cameron, saying, "I keep hearing about this crazy Australian [O'Keeffe is Australian] deep in my organization, but I had no idea how amazing CHILL is and the crazy things you are doing. You cocreate startups from scratch with our partners. That's amazing."

Not only did Robbins now know who O'Keeffe was, but he was also broadcasting for her to others. At the next CHILL event, companies were brought together to look for business opportunities using blockchain technologies. Not only did Robbins attend this lab, but he also participated in the entire process. Naturally, both the *Harvard Business Review* article and O'Keeffe's conference presentation helped broadcast her work and build her reputation as an innovator inside Cisco.

To successfully broadcast your work, you have to find ways to discreetly let others know who you are and what you have accomplished (later in this chapter, we'll discuss the Goldilocks effect, the balance of just the right amount of self-promotion). Broadcasting discreetly and tastefully is important. If your broadcasts come across as overly self-promotional or even narcissistic, then much of the value is lost.

Advice for Broadcasting

Not everyone can secure a spot on the cover of *Time* or publish in *Harvard Business Review*. But there are numerous ways to discreetly broadcast who you are and what you are working on to capture others' attention.

Think Broadly about Potential Broadcast
Outlets and Your Message's Impact

Today there are more ways than ever to broadcast information about yourself and your projects. Finding ways to share information and positive news about the projects you are working on (e.g., project activities, problems solved, innovations developed, milestones achieved) can make a positive difference.

Consider these broadcast outlets and any others that would work for you:

- External traditional media (such as business, trade, and technical journals; magazines; and newspapers)

- Other external media (blogs, social media posts, tweets, and other content written by others)

- Company communications (external press releases, reports, and other media; internal newsletters, blogs, social media posts, etc.)

- Talks and presentations

- Your own press (website, videos, blogs, tweets, retweets, etc.)

The more *credible*, *visible*, and *relevant* the source, the greater the impact. But sometimes you have to start small. One innovator we interviewed got a short story about his project published in the company's annual report—and it paid big dividends for him and his project when the company faced budget cuts.

Get Surrogates to Talk Positively about You Behind Your Back

Another avenue for broadcasting is to get other people to tell stories about you and what you are working on. Research by professors Ben Galvin and Nathan Washburn shows that "stories told informally by what we call *leader surrogates*—individuals who have developed admiration and respect for you and actively share favorable information about you . . . are more powerful in helping you to inspire your people than the formal communications you crank out."[4] Getting people to tell stories about you is powerful because "there's one form of communication that [people] *don't* tune out . . . the genuine, spontaneous story about you that employees hear from a peer."[5]

So how do you get people to talk about you behind your back? First, you can develop close relationships with a variety of colleagues who have reason to support you (perhaps their ship is tied to yours in some way or you've done something to start a norm of reciprocity with them, as described in chapter 3). Also, you are more likely to develop supportive surrogates by finding time to work with others on issues and problems they care about. Hopefully you can find a way to add value to their project, thereby giving them material for a story that they might share about you. Note that surrogate support doesn't just come from oral stories. Surrogates can also be your advocate by writing positive things about you or your projects in blogs or other social media.

Strive for the Goldilocks Effect: Not Too Little or Too Much

Although broadcasting can help you become known, if you broadcast too much and it seems self-promotional or inaccurate, the practice can hurt your reputation. Thus, broadcasting is subject to the *Goldilocks effect*: too little is a problem but so is too much; you are shooting for "just right." Recent research by psychologists at Carnegie Mellon University suggests that the right balance may be more delicate than we realize: we often overestimate the positive impact of self-promotion and underestimate the negative impact on those who hear it.[6] For example, critics of Elon Musk say that he frequently broadcasts bold and ambitious goals for his ventures; these broadcasts get attention for his ventures, but he often overpromises. Indeed, the *Wall Street Journal* reported that Tesla missed twenty of Musk's broadcast goals, rarely hitting ambitious timelines.[7] As a result, the authors reported that "some analysts have begun to worry Mr. Musk's ambitious prognostications could haunt Tesla." In short, investors, customers, and other stakeholders are becoming less likely to tune into, and believe, Musk's announcements, because the statements come so often and are frequently inaccurate.

In defense of Musk, some people argue that ambitious goals keep Tesla moving forward. Musk acknowledges, "In order to have a good outcome, we must strive for a great outcome."[8] However, the *Wall Street Journal*'s and other media's discussion of Musk's "overpromising" in his public announcements suggests that he may be broadcasting a bit too much—and perhaps a bit too aggressively. On the other hand, Musk's ambitious goals for his companies help make him a compelling leader of innovation, as we will discuss in chapter 7. But reasonable minds can disagree on whether he should publicly broadcast them as frequently as he does.

In sum, broadcasting is important but it can be overdone, particularly when it is focused on you. An alternate path, and one where you are much less likely to fall prey to overpromoting, is to focus on promoting your project and what it has achieved for the company and community. The spotlight may not be shining directly on you, but you will be caught in that light as a natural byproduct, so it won't seem like you are shamelessly self-promoting.

Signaling: Securing Credibility Endorsements

If you visit the trendy eastern edge of Paris, with its hipster restaurants and bars, you might walk along Avenue Parmentier. Although the name might not mean much to you, the avenue, named after Antoine-Augustin Parmentier, honors one of the most important innovation heroes of the eighteenth century.[9]

Born in 1737, Parmentier struggled throughout his entire career to convince people of something we take for granted today: that potatoes are food. A pharmacist by training, Parmentier worked tirelessly during the Seven Years War to help injured soldiers and as a result was captured five times during the war. During his fifth imprisonment, Parmentier was forced to eat pig food, or potatoes. At first Parmentier was surprised that he hadn't died. Potatoes were supposed to be poisonous or cause leprosy. Indeed, potatoes were believed to be so dangerous that the French Parliament had outlawed their cultivation in 1748.

But after his release from prison, Parmentier wondered whether potatoes might be a solution to the problem of widespread hunger in France. So he began experimenting with potatoes, growing and eating them, and when he remained healthy, he became convinced that potatoes were safe.

To turn the tide of public opinion, Parmentier tried connecting potatoes to prestigious people, events, and places that would legitimize his claim that potatoes were safe to eat. For example, he published a book about using potatoes as food and embossed "printed by order of the King" prominently on the cover to connect it to the authority of the monarch. He also hosted parties for prestigious individuals, such as Marie Antoinette, queen of France; Benjamin Franklin, ambassador from the newly formed United States; and Antoine Lavoisier, the father of modern chemistry. At the dinners, Parmentier would serve potato dishes and gave Marie Antoinette potato flowers to wear in her hair. He even planted potatoes in a plot near where the Arc de Triomphe stands today, and he hired guards to make the crop seem valuable. But then Parmentier instructed the guards either to leave the field at night so that peasants could plunder the crops or to take bribes and look the other way.

In the end, Parmentier's actions succeeded in getting attention for potatoes as a food that was safe to eat. By 1785, during a year of particularly poor wheat harvests, potatoes saved the north of France from famine. By 1795, during one of the many sieges on Paris, potatoes grown in the Tuileries Palace garden saved the city itself. Eventually the French government declared potatoes to be food. More importantly, because of his creative actions to legitimize potatoes as a safe food, Parmentier saved millions of people from hunger. Even today, if you visit Parmentier's grave in the Père Lachaise Cemetery, you will see potatoes laid on his grave by those who remember the significance of his contribution to France. For our purposes, Parmentier's story demonstrates the use of one of the impression amplifiers you can leverage to win backing for your ideas: signaling.

What Signaling Is and Why It Works

Signaling involves creating visible links, alliances, relationships, awards, or achievements that represent an endorsement of the quality of your idea. Earlier in the book, we discussed reputation borrowing, which uses the same principles that signaling uses but is focused on borrowing reputation to support *your personal reputation*. Signaling works in part due to the social proof principle, sometimes called herding behavior. Herding behavior represents our tendency to follow or mimic the actions of others, especially those we admire or see as experts. Subconsciously we associate the positive attributes of an endorser with the target person, idea, or project. People assume that if your idea is endorsed by a prestigious institution or individual, has won a significant award, or achieved a significant milestone, then your idea must be worthwhile.

For example, when Parmentier had "printed by order of the King" stamped on all his books, he was establishing credibility for his idea through the connection to royal authority. Likewise, when he hired guards to protect the potato plot, he was trying to signal that potatoes were a valuable crop. Also, when he served potatoes to famous people like Franklin, Parmentier was making a connection between potatoes and prestigious individuals and thereby secured a "celebrity endorsement" of potatoes.

Signaling is a powerful impression amplifier that can be particularly critical in the early stages of a project, when it is difficult to objectively judge a project's potential. Recent research examining over a thousand startups across various industries found that signaling had a massive impact on whether newly created startups received any funding at all. The study found that founders with prior experience creating or leading companies had only a 5 percent chance of obtaining funding. But if the founders had prior experience, plus the endorsement of having been selected by a startup development organization (e.g., a startup accelerator), then their chances of funding jumped to 44 percent. Similarly, when startups go public, investors are more willing to invest if the startup has connections with prestigious individuals (e.g., as board members or venture capitalists) or organizations (e.g., as partners or customers) that signal their endorsement of the quality of the startup.[10]

One way the innovators we studied signaled their credibility was by forming relationships and alliances with other prestigious institutions. For example, when the XPRIZE Foundation added board members Richard Branson and Will.i.am to the prize-making committee, the foundation did so because these high-prestige individuals acted as a credible endorsement of the XPRIZE simply because they agreed to join the board. Similarly, when Mastercard Labs for Financial Inclusion formed a partnership with the Bill & Melinda Gates Foundation, the credit card company did so partly because the connection to the foundation raised the visibility and credibility of initiatives like its 2KUZE platform—an online marketplace allowing small farmers to bypass expensive intermediaries and to sell directly to larger clients.[11]

You can also gather credibility endorsements from awards or by achieving observable milestones. In fact, a recent Stanford study examined how entrepreneurs raise funds.[12] The researchers found that the entrepreneur's social ties to investors (as discussed in chapter 3) was most beneficial for smaller sums of money at the earliest stages of the venture. However, signals of quality such as awards, product launches, acceptance to incubators, customer endorsements, and other credibility endorsements quickly became more important than did social ties and had an overall greater effect on the funding received by new startups.

Advice for Signaling

Signaling involves accumulating endorsements from credible people, projects, or organizations that establish credibility for your initiative. You can create credibility signals in a couple of ways.

Create Working Relationships with High-Status People and Organizations

Endorsements are more effective when they come from high-status individuals or organizations that agree to work with your organization in some way. But getting those endorsements isn't easy—otherwise, everyone would do it. We recommend two options for getting endorsements: either find an institutional endorsement channel or make a high-status individual or organization excited about your project. An example of an institutional endorsement channel is a grant program, an award (e.g., best business plan, most innovative product), or a program you can participate in that allows you to receive a formal endorsement from a prestigious institution.

Another way to secure an endorsement is to pitch the idea in such a compelling way that the idea itself is exciting enough to acquire an endorsement from a prominent individual or organization. As described in chapter 3, David Bradford managed to bring Steve Wozniak onto the board of advisers at Fusion-io, a startup offering advanced data-storage technology. Bradford met Wozniak at a conference and got enough time with him to pitch the exciting new technology that had been developed at Fusion-io. After Bradford himself received an endorsement from a Wozniak friend who knew Bradford, Wozniak agreed to join the board because of the exciting potential of the Fusion-io technology. Within a few months, Wozniak agreed to join Fusion-io as chief scientist. Shortly after he joined as chief scientist, Fusion-io was chosen by *Red Herring* magazine as among the top one hundred startup companies in February 2009.[13] Wozniak's endorsement of Fusion-io and its technology probably contributed to the company's selection by *Red Herring* as a top startup.

Creatively Pursue Awards and Achievements

Few of us actually seek out opportunities to win awards, endorsements, or achievements. Gathering endorsements starts with being proactive about searching and applying for these awards. If there are no ways to be recognized, then perhaps you need to create them yourself or with a partner. Napoléon used this trick when he created the Legion of Honor, France's highest honor, given for merit in military or civilian service. Napoléon created it both because prior awards had been based on nobility, rather than merit, but also as a tool to win support for his ideas: "It is with baubles that men are led," he conceded. Although "baubles" sounds pejorative, Napoléon simply meant that awards and distinctions are important motivators for people, influencing their willingness to support something.

Napoléon isn't the only one who can think creatively about awards and endorsements. Many of the innovators we studied also created their own awards and endorsements. As described in chapter 1, Gavin Christensen, founder of the innovative Kickstart Seed Fund, built ties to the innovation ecosystem by running the entrepreneur award program. Marc Benioff did something similar when he created the Dreamforce conference, now one of the largest tech conferences in the world. The conference focuses on cloud-based and software-as-service solutions, with Salesforce positioned right at its center. In summary, think broadly about how to signal your credibility to your supporters.

Storytelling: Creating an Emotional Connection

Although most of the leaders we studied had a lifetime of achievement, what would you recommend to someone with a track record of failure? One leader we studied fit the latter profile exactly. He was born into a family with few connections. He struggled in school, failing his primary school exams twice, his middle school exams thrice, and his college entrance exams twice.[14] On his third attempt on the college entrance exams, he failed again but, in a stroke of sheer fortune, was admitted to university—the worst university in the city—because it had some extra slots it couldn't fill.[15] When he graduated, he applied for thirty jobs and was rejected from all of them. When he applied for a job at Kentucky Fried Chicken, KFC took twenty-four of the twenty-five applicants. He was the twenty-fifth applicant who wasn't hired. Eventually this person found a teaching job through a friend of his father. Later, he tried to start a translation business, but it struggled to turn a profit. With such limited success and reputation capital, what would be this individual's chances for winning support for a new venture idea?

Higher than you might think. As founder of Alibaba, Jack Ma is one of the wealthiest and most successful innovators in the world. Ma all but introduced the internet to China, founding the e-commerce site Alibaba when less than 1 percent of people in China had access to the internet.[16] How did he convince people to join his team, and investors to fund his efforts, when he was breaking such new territory and had such a horrible track record?

Ma is known to excel at telling a great story that creates an emotional connection and inspires those around him. When Ma pitched the idea for Alibaba, he gathered his friends around him and explained the massive opportunity that internet commerce offered for the team. He compared the Alibaba team and their mission to create China's future to the heroes in popular Kung Fu novels. He even encouraged team members to take on a heroic nickname. Ma himself took the name of Feng Qingyang, a master swordsman in Jin Yong's novels.

Ma also compared the early Alibaba team to the 108 heroes in the well-known Chinese historical novel *Outlaws in the Marsh* and told the early team members they had to fight to reach all 108 employees.[17] Today, Alibaba is much larger, but he still told the story of how Alibaba will be the company to last 102 years, spanning three centuries. According to Zhang Hong, one of Ma's early employees, Ma's ability to tell a story that inspires people is key to his success. Of his stories, Zhang recalls, "Ma can transform a hopeless situation into an exciting opportunity."[18]

Today Ma has built some of the most valuable internet properties in the world, including Alibaba (B2B e-commerce), Taobao (consumer e-commerce), Alipay (payments), Ant Financial, and dozens of related companies. When Alibaba went public in 2014, the company was valued at $150 billion, then the largest IPO valuation for a US listed company. Ma was estimated to be the richest person in China, with an estimated net worth of $40 billion, when he stepped down from leading Alibaba.[19]

What Storytelling Is and Why It Is Important

Innovators often tell stories to create an emotional connection with the listener to win support for themselves and their ideas. Numerous studies underscore the importance of emotionally connecting stories in winning support for a particular idea.[20] People buy with their hearts and justify with their brains. Psychologically, stories help create believability in the minds of potential supporters, suspending their disbelief and creating excitement about future possibilities. But what characteristics of stories win resources and support for your ideas?

Effective stories emphasize the problem or the opportunity. A long history of research in psychology links motivation and persuasion to two basic categories of emotion: threats or problems and opportunities. When it comes to threats or problems, prior research suggests that people respond more to a story: when the story depicts a severe problem, people feel a connection to the problem, the story proposes a solution, and the solution works.[21] When it comes to opportunities, people are more responsive to bigger opportunities, their ability to capture the opportunity, and the benefits they will potentially gain from participating in the opportunity. The very best stories integrate elements of the threat or the opportunity into a narrative that creates a reason to believe.[22]

Our research on the most innovative leaders revealed that they often used stories around solving big problems or pursuing exciting opportunities to drum up support for their initiatives. For example, Indra Nooyi used dramatic stories to good advantage with PepsiCo's beverage and snack foods business by introducing Performance with Purpose, a corporate mission to embed sustainability in everything it does. Performance with Purpose focuses on delivering top-tier returns, while making more nutritious products, minimizing the company's impact on the environment (including conserving water, curbing greenhouse gas emissions, and reducing waste), and supporting the people who live and work in its communities.

Nooyi then used stories to underscore the importance of this mission and to persuade people to support it. "I grew up in the city of Madras where there was no water," she says. "Every morning, my mom would get up at three or four in the morning, and she would wait for the taps to start releasing water from the central reservoir, and water would trickle in. And my mom would collect every pot and pan we had so that each of us had three containers of water, which was your quota for the day. You learned how to wash yourself, clean your uniform—everything had to be done with those three containers of water. At the same time, in the same city, I watched large corporations build plants and use a lot of water. You can't have a large corporation using excess water in a town where there is no water to eat and drink and live."

Nooyi would tell this story to engage people in her quest to "replenish the planet and leave the world a better place." Problems are more real, and seemingly more important, when conveyed through a story, particularly one that is your own. Your own personal recollections can be a powerful way to persuade others to support you.

Alternatively, innovators can tell a powerful story by focusing on big opportunities and grand visions. At the heart of Ma's ability to win support from others, despite his many failures, is his ability to inspire others about the opportunity at hand. Similarly, one of Elon Musk's core tactics is creating an emotional connection around the opportunities he is pursuing, whether they be space travel or electric cars. Musk openly admits that the Mars Oasis project, in which he intends to build a colony with plants and humans on Mars, was meant to create emotion around the opportunity: "I started with a crazy idea to spur the national will. I called it the Mars Oasis mission," Musk says.[23] The boldness and audacity of the opportunity Musk describes inspires others to support him and SpaceX. If there was one thing that impressed us most during our discussions with Musk and the teams at Tesla and SpaceX, it was how many employees at all levels of the company, from the factory floor to advanced engineering, believe they are changing the world.

Advice for Storytelling

The ability to craft and communicate a compelling story is a powerful way to influence people. Investing here will pay dividends over time. Let's look at some examples of effective storytelling.[24]

Focus on a Deep, Underlying Need, and Make It Personal

Innovators who win support for their ideas focus on a fundamental human need and then make it personal. Christensen told us about one of the most counterintuitive investment decisions he made. After entrepreneurs Vanessa and Nate Quigley presented their idea for an app that allowed families to share photos with each other, Christensen turned to the rest of the investment committee and spoke candidly: "I hate the product." Then after a moment's hesitation, he added, "But I think we should invest anyway."

How had the entrepreneurs persuaded Christensen to invest in a product he hated? When the Quigleys presented their idea to Christensen, Vanessa Quigley talked about how she had found her five-year-old son in tears over a scrapbook made by his preschool teacher. In that moment, she had a pang of deep guilt that she, the mother, hadn't created a scrapbook of photos for her son and for herself. She had taken thousands of photos, but they were effectively stuck in her phone. How could she share them?

According to Christensen, the Quigleys' solution, an app that allowed for photo sharing, had meager uptake and worked poorly. "I tried three different times to get the app to work, and it crashed every time. It was terrible," says Christensen. "But when she [Vanessa Quigley] talked about the guilt mothers feel and the deep need to capture and share memories, they convinced me there was something meaningful there." Christensen recalled, "The need was so fundamental, and they made it so personal, I knew that they would figure out how to solve it eventually." Christensen invested, and the Quigleys soon pivoted to create Chatbooks, a company that enables the automatic creation and printing of scrapbooks from photos. Within two years, the company was doing well over $30 million in revenue and expanding to become the "Netflix of memories."

Include Characters, Conflict, and Resolution in Your Stories

Too often when we talk about stories in the corporate world, we mean the chronology of events. But motivating stories have characters, conflict, and resolution. In *Leading Transformation*, one of us (Nathan) and his coauthors talk about how they used stories with characters, conflict, and resolution to motivate companies like Lowe's, PepsiCo, and IKEA to pursue transformative innovations and radical new business models.[25] For example, the Lowe's Innovation Lab, led by Kyle Nel, used science fiction writers to help the team imagine how to solve a common dilemma: envisioning and then communicating how to remodel your home. Back in 2012, before Oculus Rift virtual-reality headsets or Pokémon Go, the panel of science fiction writers imagined how customers could use virtual and augmented reality to solve the vexing dilemma of envisioning a potential remodel. The story helped the executives at Lowe's suspend their disbelief (e.g., their beliefs that Lowe's isn't a technology company and that virtual reality is too undeveloped to use with customers) and take action. They supported the development of the first retail application of augmented reality and the development of an augmented-reality phone sold in Lowe's stores. It sold out in four days with no marketing.

Conclusion

We have discussed three tactics to get positive attention for yourself and your ideas: broadcasting, signaling, and storytelling. While these amplifiers serve the primary function of drawing attention to you and your ideas, they also influence others to think positively about you and your ideas, thereby winning support. In the next chapter, we describe four amplifiers that primarily persuade others to support your innovation projects and bring resources to them.

See our website www.innovatorsdna.com/innovation-capital for additional resources for the advice provided in this chapter.

6

Idea Impression Amplifiers

Materializing, Comparing, Committing, and FOMO

Have you ever had an entrepreneur tell you about, or even ask you to invest in, his or her innovative startup? Or perhaps a colleague has asked you to support an internal initiative for a new product or service? If not, we recommend that you find an opportunity to hear a pitch from a person or two and see if you are persuaded. As you listen to the pitch, ask yourself, did they convince you? Did they do anything that was persuasive? You might recognize that they used one or more of the impression amplifiers described in chapter 5. For example, did they tell a compelling story that made an emotional connection? Did they have endorsements from credible parties or refer to a prior broadcast? If they did, they were leveraging the amplifiers described in the previous chapter to win support for themselves and their idea.

But there is another set of amplifiers that may do less to magnify your own personal qualifications but still do quite a bit to persuade others about your idea. For example, as you listened to the pitch, did they make the idea (of a new product or service) more real by creating some type of visual representation of it, like a storyboard or a working prototype? Did they compare their idea to something familiar and successful that made it easy for you to understand—and get excited about? For example, they might have said something like "This will be the Google of artificial intelligence" or "Meet the Uber of trucking." Did the presenters show an unwavering commitment to the project? And finally, did they make you feel as if the opportunity were fleeting—that a window of opportunity was closing and demanding

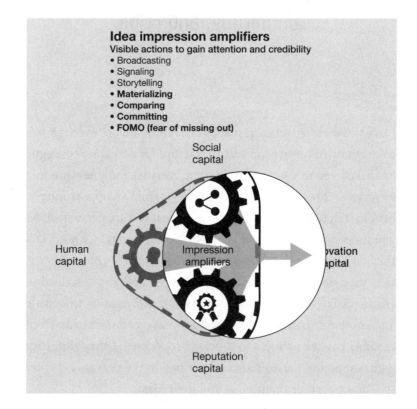

Idea impression amplifiers
Visible actions to gain attention and credibility
- Broadcasting
- Signaling
- Storytelling
- **Materializing**
- **Comparing**
- **Committing**
- **FOMO (fear of missing out)**

Social capital

Human capital

Impression amplifiers

ovation pital

Reputation capital

Impression Amplifiers That Strengthen Support for an Idea or a Project

MATERIALIZING: making abstract ideas tangible; works because people tend to believe in something more when they can see it and touch it than when it is an abstract idea

COMPARING: employing relevant analogies, namely, likening your idea to something familiar and successful; works because it gives listeners a reason to believe in your idea in light of something they already understand

COMMITTING: creating credible commitments; signals that you believe in your project so much that you are willing to put yourself at a significant, even irreversible, risk or obligation; works because supporters interpret your dedication as a signal that they can believe in your project

FOMO: generating a fear of missing out (FOMO); involves creating a sense of urgency, scarcity, or exclusivity that if someone doesn't act quickly, he or she might miss out on the opportunity; works because it switches potential supporters from a critical, evaluative mindset to an acquisitive mindset eager to capture the opportunity

action? If they did, they were leveraging the set of impression amplifiers designed to win support for a project or idea, which we describe in this chapter.

In this chapter, we describe how to use impression amplifiers that create enthusiasm for your project. (In chapter 5, we examined amplifiers that win support for both you and your idea.) We'll consider the practices of materializing, comparing, and committing and the fear of missing out (FOMO). When combined with the amplifiers from chapter 5, these techniques provide you with a full arsenal of ways to persuade others that your idea deserves their support.

Materializing: Making Ideas Tangible

Although many people think of SpaceX as the first startup to challenge the US space industry for decades, it's only because they haven't heard of Beal Aerospace. In fact, Beal Acrospace preceded SpaceX by almost a decade with the equally ambitious goal of transforming space travel by creating low-cost, disposable rockets. Founded and funded by the self-made billionaire Andrew Beal, the company made significant progress building the largest engine since the original Apollo rockets and even securing land in Guyana to build a private spaceport (the same spaceport that SpaceX later bought from Beal Aerospace).[1] But despite his advances, Beal couldn't get NASA and government officials to pay attention to his company. Ultimately, in October 2000, after spending $200 million of his own money, Beal quit. As the doors of Beal Aerospace closed, Beal issued a scathing letter to NASA and the US Congress about their failure to pay attention to private industry and companies like his own.[2]

Two years after this warning sign about entering an expensive, bureaucratic, and complex industry, Elon Musk founded SpaceX. Although there are differences between Beal Aerospace and SpaceX (primarily the focus on low-cost disposable rockets versus reusable rockets), Musk and SpaceX almost failed for precisely the same reasons: the difficulty of persuading NASA and others to buy from a private space venture. In those early days, many of the establishment decision makers at NASA, Congress, and large aerospace corporations saw SpaceX as a joke—yet another doomed effort by a rich Silicon Valley tycoon.[3] As a result, Musk's company struggled to get airtime with the decision makers who would buy its services. "At the beginning, we had to beg NASA to even pay attention," recalls Lawrence Williams, a former SpaceX executive.[4] As Musk grew increasingly frustrated with the unwillingness of the establishment to even listen to what he and his team were doing, Musk decided he would just show the doubters.

On December 4, 2003, as the National Air and Space Museum began its centenary celebration of the historic Wright brothers' first powered flight, Musk loaded the recently completed Falcon 1 rocket onto a custom-made trailer and drove it across the country. When they arrived in Washington, DC, Musk and team drove the giant rocket down Independence Avenue and along the National Mall, accompanied by flashing police lights. Then, in a moment of dramatic flair, he parked the seven-story-tall white rocket in front of the National Air and Space Museum. The rocket was so large it took up an entire lane in the road, slowing traffic and turning heads.[5]

That night, at the museum's reception, Musk told attendees—Federal Aviation Administration officials, congressional staffers, journalists, and NASA staff—that "the history of launch vehicle development has not been very successful . . . if you define success as making a difference in cost or reliability." He paused and then added, "We have a shot with SpaceX, I think, for the first time in a long time."[6] Then Musk invited the audience outside to see the giant rocket sitting in the spotlights in front of the museum. With the gargantuan rocket behind him, Musk announced that not only would the Falcon 1 fly, but they were also working on the next rocket, one with five first-stage rockets, and this new one would be "a new world record for the cost per pound access to space."[7] This bold action, which made a bold idea tangible, got NASA's attention. NASA went on to invest $140 million in SpaceX over the next decade, ultimately saving the agency hundreds of millions by using SpaceX rockets rather than developing its own.[8] By the end of 2018, SpaceX had launched more than seventy flights using low-cost, reusable rockets.[9]

Materializing: What It Is and Why It Works

To persuade a recalcitrant government to support his risky venture (one where his reputation as a Silicon Valley entrepreneur may have actually hurt rather than helped him), Musk relied on an impression amplifier we call *materializing*. Materializing involves making an abstract idea visible or tangible—especially to the target of influence. Sometimes, tangibility can mean a physical product or prototype. But ideas can also be made tangible through drawings, videos, and other graphic representations. For example, when a virtually unknown Mark Zuckerberg approached Peter Thiel to invest in a social network, the data about student adoption at Harvard and Stanford is what made the power of social networking tangible to Thiel.

Materializing an idea works because as human beings, we tend to believe in something more when we can see it for ourselves. There are deep psychological foundations for the old adage "Seeing is believing." Human brains are systematically biased to believe in tangible, visible artifacts over abstract ideas. This bias exists partly because the majority of our brain is dedicated to processing visual imagery over language, which is much more abstract.[10] Not only do we respond more readily to visual objects, but we also remember them longer.[11] Thus, materializing an abstract idea into a tangible format makes the idea not only easier to process and remember, but also more believable. The future appears closer and more realistic when it is visible.

In big companies, materializing can be an especially important tool to win support for products, initiatives, or ideas. This tool can even help a company leader change the course of prevailing opinion. For example, when Ken Smith was head of the heavy-excavator division at Caterpillar, he was tasked by the executive leadership team to build a hybrid diesel-electric excavator as part of the company's sustainability initiative. In response, Smith and the engineering team developed a best-in-class hybrid excavator and, just a few months before going into global production, took their design out to get feedback from customers.

What they heard shocked them. Although headquarters had assumed the customers wanted a sustainable solution, the contractors complained about the performance, reliability, and affordability of hybrid diesel-electric excavators in general. One contractor even said, "If you're building a hybrid excavator, don't waste my time and don't waste yours." The problem with all hybrid excavators lay in the inefficiencies of converting diesel to mechanical to electrical energy, storing that energy, and then converting it back to mechanical energy at the scale of a large excavator. After the meeting with customers, one of the engineers on the team had a radical idea: by capturing and storing mechanical energy directly, they could create a more reliable, affordable hybrid excavator that would also be a sustainable solution.

Smith and his team hurried back to headquarters with the bad news and the alternative approach, but their ideas fell on deaf ears. The executives who hadn't been in the room with the customer panel believed more in their assumptions about sustainability than they did in the reality that the hybrid didn't meet customer needs. How could Smith convince them otherwise? He turned to the engineer with the radical idea and said, "We have to show them." The team worked nights and weekends. As they sprinted, engineers bolted parts to the exterior of the machine rather than integrating them. The resulting prototype excavator was so ugly, the team called it Medusa, because of the masses of hoses and components snaking all over the frame. But it worked. Medusa proved that Caterpillar could create a mechanical hybrid excavator that met all the customer requirements and saved energy.

One by one, Smith brought members of the leadership team down to the warehouse and put them behind the controls, explaining the benefits, while they used the excavator. And one by one, the executives became convinced. This new hybrid mechanical-diesel excavator (HEX) was a much better match for customer needs. The executives approved a major change of course. The new HEX consumed 25 percent less fuel and was 50 percent to 75 percent more efficient than traditional diesel excavators. It became a major new product line at Caterpillar. Shortly after its launch, over 40 percent of all excavators sold by Caterpillar were the new HEX hybrids. Materializing had allowed Smith to change the tenor of opinion inside the company and win support for his team's idea.

Materializing can help independent entrepreneurs just as much as it helps internal innovators. For example, in 2010, while Dan Blake was a university student, he noticed the incredible sustainability challenges posed by wasted food. Roughly half of all apples and bakery items sold by major grocery stores end up as waste, and almost 70 percent of bagged salads are wasted.[12] To make matters worse, stores and restaurants are paying to haul this spoiled food to landfills, where it creates methane and other gases as it rots.

Through a series of pilots, Blake discovered that instead of paying to have the waste hauled away, retailers could give the food to his new startup, EcoScraps, which would then turn that waste into ecologically friendly compost resold to gardeners. Although Blake believed he had stumbled onto a reasonable value proposition, the real challenge soon revealed itself: how to convince big, risk-averse companies to work with an unproven startup.

Blake decided he needed to show rather than tell. Before the visit of a major retailer, Blake rented out a warehouse, filled it with rented equipment, and asked family and friends to come in and work. When the potential customer arrived, he found a large operation full of equipment and workers turning food waste into salable compost. The partner toured the facility for about five minutes and then suggested that he and Blake grab lunch to finalize a deal for national distribution. With the deal signed, Blake bought the rented equipment and scaled operations.

Today, EcoScraps works with retailers across North America, processing over fifty million pounds of food waste into compost. Every bag of compost that EcoScraps sells represents thirty-seven pounds of food that would have been in a landfill; each bag also reduces carbon dioxide emissions as much as does taking your car off the road for two weeks.[13] The company itself was acquired by Hawthorne Gardening Company, a subsidiary of Scotts Miracle-Gro Company, and continues to transform food waste for retailers like Target, Walmart, and Costco into sustainable solutions.

Advice on Materializing

Materializing involves making an idea visible, concrete, or workable. Every step you take to create a more observable, believable solution can increase your ability to win resources and support for your idea.

Think Broadly about the Tools Available to Materialize an Idea

Whenever we say the word *prototype*, people often think of finished products produced in small scale. We mean something different, however. A prototype means the fastest, cheapest way to make your idea tangible today. You can materialize a product with a drawing, video, or mock-up. You can materialize a service with a storyboard or PowerPoint presentation. You can fake software with tools like Adobe Flash, wireframe tools, or any number of prototyping applications. Even if it's a prototype, it still has immense persuasive power.

Don't Oversell What You've Materialized; Instead Ask for Help

Naturally you want to put your best foot forward when you materialize something, but a mock-up of software is still a mock-up. The point of materializing isn't to deceive people, but instead to show them what something could be. If you approach potential supporters honestly, acknowledging that something is a prototype and asking for advice or help, then they are much more likely to support you.

Comparing: Finding Relevant Analogies

A car-sharing startup is a more familiar idea in today's collaborative consumption economy. However, in the year 2000, it was a new concept. Even the internet was new: in Boston, where Robin Chase started Zipcar (see chapter 4), only 50 percent of people had internet access, and only 25 percent used mobile phones. Google was still a relatively unknown startup, Facebook wouldn't get started for four more years, and Amazon was a small business located in a sketchy part of Seattle next to a pawn shop.

So when Chase proposed using the internet to create a digital platform to create shared access to cars, which have traditionally been a highly personalized asset, most investors were extremely skeptical. Chase recalls the first time she presented Zipcar, highlighting the massive potential of the internet to unlock the value of underutilized assets. When she finished her inspiring seven-minute pitch, she half expected investors to jump out of their seats in applause. Instead, a gentleman in the front row scowled and asked, "What happens if I run out of gas?" His wasn't the first skeptical, banal question. Over and over, Chase found that investors struggled just to understand what the company did, let alone the revolutionary power of platforms. She recalls, "We were the first company in transport innovation. Most investors just kept asking me what type of business it was. When I would talk to venture capitalists, there was nothing to compare it to. They just couldn't make sense of what we were doing."

Chase realized that she needed to find a way to help others—investors, customers, suppliers, even employees—understand her idea by comparing it to something they already understood. To do so, she started by writing down her five favorite names and taglines for the company on index cards. She then carried these cards with her everywhere, testing them with everyone she met, including grocery store clerks, friends at dinner, acquaintances at swim meets, and even casual encounters on the street. She then captured people's responses on the back of the cards and, later, looking at the compiled evidence, evaluated what she had heard. What Chase learned by listening carefully to the nuances around words surprised her. For example, although *car-sharing* is the technically correct term of art to describe Zipcar, most people reacted negatively to the term. *Car-sharing* brought up images of something used, dirty, and inconvenient. Although this response might seem harsh, it's quite normal. As Chase points out, "Just imagine if we used the term *bed-sharing* to describe hotels."

Through this careful process of listening and testing, Chase began to stumble on comparisons and language that resonated more effectively. For example, she found that describing Zipcar as like an ATM—which allows you access to cash whenever you need it—seemed to resonate well with people. So she started to use the tagline "Wheels when you want them" to emphasize that, like an ATM, cars could be available wherever and whenever you needed them. As Chase began to use this new description, people began to understand Zipcar and remember it. With this new tagline, Chase was able to raise capital and build one of the first and most successful sharing startups since the turn of the 21st century. Zipcar was eventually acquired for over $500 million by Avis and operates in more than five hundred cities. Chase attributes her ability to win support from investors, suppliers, employees, and even customers in part to finding the perfect analogy to help people understand the idea and get them excited about the opportunity.

Comparing: What It Is and Why It Works

Comparing involves using mental shortcuts through analogies or metaphors to emphasize a similarity between your idea and a familiar concept (success). The psychology of mental shortcuts (or heuristics) emphasizes that analogies and metaphors are efficient mental processes that help humans learn new concepts, form judgments, and make decisions—especially when facing complex problems or incomplete information. Put simply, comparing gives listeners a reason to believe in your idea in light of something they already understand and believe in. Research examining the use of comparison has shown that startups using comparisons in their prospectus reached higher valuations during IPOs.[14] But comparisons need to be simple, accessible, and directly relevant. The same research shows that when startups use overly complicated comparisons during IPOs, their valuations decrease.[15]

Comparisons work best when you use analogies that are familiar and make intuitive sense. For example, when Chase compared Zipcar to ATMs, the analogy made intuitive sense; investors and customers could easily understand the business. Other examples include companies like Clutter, Trove, and Cubiq describing themselves as the "Uber of storage." You instantly understand the business model—a peer-to-peer approach for storage. More importantly, because Uber had a great deal of early success, the analogy probably also excites people about the opportunity.

Advice on Comparing

If done well, comparisons can strengthen your idea's or product's impression with potential supporters. A couple of techniques will help you use comparisons to your best advantage.

Pay Attention to the Comparison and the Words Used

As Chase advises, "Words really matter, and getting the comparisons right is nontrivial." Finding the right comparisons involves both finding the right analogy or metaphor and the right words to describe it through a process of testing and careful listening with potential supporters. If the comparison sounds too different or complicated, listeners won't be convinced. Consider the company Ethnamed, which is described on ProductHunt.com as "a chrome plugin—cold wallet for bitcoin (btc), litecoin (ltc), ethereum (eth.) and dash. Allows users to bind email address with crypto addresses. Extends web3 protocol to btc, ltc, dash, eth for developers." Did you get that? Do you know what Ethnamed does and why it might be valuable? If not, now listen to the tagline analogy: "Ethnamed: Like Venmo, but for cryptocurrencies." In a five-word analogy, you now better understand Ethnamed's value proposition—and probably have increased confidence in what they do.

The best comparisons try to strike a balance between familiarity and novelty.[16] So, for example, when the storage companies describe themselves as the "Uber of storage," they are emphasizing what is familiar (the Uber platform model to liberate hard-to-share assets). But as the comparison gets overused, it loses power. A better approach might be to find a new analogy or metaphor. For example, Neighbor, one of the competing storage groups, tried to emphasize a different analogy, calling themselves the "Airbnb of storage," instead of the overused "Uber of storage."

Among the Many Potential Comparisons, Choose the Best One for Your Audience

Sometimes the right comparison may vary by audience. Often, new ideas have many potential benefits, and by analyzing the benefits, you can explore the different potential anchors. Then you can select the right anchor for your audience. For example, when Andrew Kvålseth worked in group strategy for one of the world's leading telecoms in Europe and Asia, he proposed that Telenor launch startup accelerators in each of its thirteen country business units, with each business unit investing in ten startups each. This accelerator program would give the company access to the best global startup talent and an investment base of over a hundred startups per year. To convince others, Kvålseth used what seemed a rather obvious comparison: corporate venture-capital groups like those run by Intel or Microsoft ventures. Although his proposal was initially met with enthusiasm, ultimately some people inside the company felt that the exposure to so many startups would be too great a risk.

Disappointed but not deterred, Kvålseth joined one of Telenor's business units, DTAC in Thailand, as chief strategy and innovation officer. He thought that creating a start-up accelerator would benefit the company, but how could he get approval when the idea had already been rejected at the group level? Kvålseth examined the list of potential benefits from the accelerator: access to insight about the changing industry, investments in potentially valuable startups, access to human capital for the company, improved company reputation, and so forth. He astutely realized that winning support might depend less on highlighting all the benefits and more on picking the one benefit—and corresponding comparison—that would resonate most with his audience.

Kvålseth decided to use an analogy of portfolios showing spending on marketing. Most major companies look at their marketing spending as a portfolio of efforts to communicate with customers. Kvålseth argued that in terms of a portfolio of spending, allocating a small amount of the marketing budget to creating a startup accelerator would do more to improve the company's reputation for innovation, would generate free press, and would help the company attract more digital human capital than would buying a few more billboards.

The new analogy made sense to the executives, and he won approval to proceed. Now, many years later, the DTAC accelerator has enjoyed many successful years of operation. It has dramatically raised both Telenor's and DTAC's profile as an innovative company and helped it attract digital talent. Moreover, seeing the success of the program, many of Telenor's other business units have reached out and imitated the program.[17]

Committing: Making Credible Commitments

When Denver Lough (MD, PhD) and Ned Swanson (MD) handed in their resignations at the world-renowned Johns Hopkins Center for Facial Plastic and Reconstructive Surgery so that they could start their own company, the parting words from the director were, "You realize this is irreversible—right?"

Lough recalls, "It was really hard to walk away. I had put seventeen years into becoming a plastic and reconstructive surgeon and was halfway through the foremost program at the world's greatest hospital. How could I possibly justify giving that up to everyone who had sacrificed so much for me to get there?" And the sacrifice wasn't abstract. Lough had already received a request for his services on graduation—a request that would have paid well over $500,000 per year.

But on December 1, 2016, Lough and Swanson gave up their coveted plastic surgery resident positions to become the CEO and chief operating officer of a biotech startup PolarityTE. The company was formed to test and launch a revolutionary technology for regenerating new tissue—skin, bone, muscle, and other tissue. Before joining the Hopkins program, Lough conceived of an approach to grow new skin at full thickness by taking certain cells from a patient and processing them in a particular way. He had even shown, in an animal study, that his process would grow new skin in mice. But it had never been tested on humans.

Leaving Hopkins was a huge gamble for Lough and Swanson because in the medical community, leaving your residency is a one-way door; once you leave, you can't go back. But as it turns out, Lough and Swanson's willingness to take such a huge risk was crucial to their success at attracting investors and key talent. Why? Because the mere fact that they were willing to take such a huge risk and make an irreversible career commitment to the venture was one of the important factors that investors, as well as recruits to the management team considered. "These guys were at Johns Hopkins, arguably the number one institution for the plastic and reconstructive surgery work they were doing," said one major investor. "They were willing to get up and leave and lay it all on the line, even when they were so close to finishing that they could see the light at the end of the tunnel. That said a lot."

Perhaps even more important, Lough and Swanson's willingness to take this risk enabled them to recruit some amazing talent to the management team, including their former boss at Johns Hopkins, Stephen Milner (director of the Johns Hopkins Burn Center), who joined PolarityTE as chief clinical officer. "The fact that they left Hopkins without a way to return definitely influenced my decision to join PolarityTE," said Cameron Hoyler, who left a secure and highly paid position at King & Spalding to join as general counsel. "Leaving a secure position to join a fledgling startup is risky. But their willingness to leave Hopkins assured me that they had no doubts they could make this work."

Of course, Lough and Swanson's work at Johns Hopkins, a prestigious medical school, was another important consideration for both investors and management recruits (Lough and Swanson had some borrowed reputation capital, as described in chapter 4). But the doctors' resolve to walk away from lucrative medical careers spoke volumes about their belief in their tissue engineering technology.

Fortunately for Lough and Swanson—and the investors and management recruits—the technology worked as expected. PolarityTE is growing new skin on patients who suffer from severe wounds and burns.[18] Moreover, the company's stock price appreciated significantly in value after going public. But Lough and Swanson's risk could have been a career disaster because the men were taking a huge risk.

Committing: What It Is and Why It Works

Committing involves generating a signal to potential supporters that you believe in an idea or a project so much that you are willing to put your own skin in the game. When someone makes a credible commitment, it gets our attention and increases our likelihood of sponsorship. Why? Because if they do, it signals their high confidence in success. In the field of business strategy, the term *credible commitment* is defined as a commitment that is costly or irreversible—truly strategic actions are those that involve credible commitments.

Jeff Bezos and other Amazon leaders talk about the idea of irreversible commitments in terms of a "one-way door" (costly to reverse) and a "two-way door" (reversible at low cost). Because one-way-door decisions are hard to reverse, they involve much more risk. To illustrate the difference, imagine you are a real estate investor and have the option of investing in a bowling alley facility or a building configured as office space for an accounting firm. Which is the one door? If the bowling alley fails, what will you do with it? The facility is so customized to a particular use (i.e., bowling) that it can only be reconfigured at considerable cost. It is a one-way-door investment because it requires an investment in assets that cannot be redeployed without significant loss in value. By contrast, if the accounting firm goes out of business, you should be able to easily rent the office space to another firm at similar pricing. The office space is a two-way-door investment.

Walking through a one-way door doesn't make sense unless you are highly confident that walking through that door is the right decision. If others see you taking that risk, your commitment to a risky decision can influence their willingness to support you in that decision. That's why making a credible commitment can be an effective tactic to persuade others to provide resources for your project. But your commitment has to be easily verifiable by other parties.

There are a variety of ways to make credible commitments. Lough and Swanson did it by forgoing a highly valuable employment option: they stepped away from being Johns Hopkins surgeons. Another way to create a credible commitment is through monetary means. For example, in the winter of the 2008 financial meltdown, Tesla faced an existential crisis that almost ended its run to create electric vehicles. The company was struggling to manufacture its first electric vehicle, the Roadster, and cofounder Martin Eberhard had been forced out under mysterious circumstances. News then leaked that Tesla had only $9 million in the bank, not enough to even repay the down payments that customers had made on undelivered vehicles. During these dark hours, several of Tesla's prior investors suddenly backed out on funding the company (whether from lack of confidence or in an effort to grab more of the company at a lower valuation remains a debate). For some time, Tesla was in limbo and running out of cash until at the last hour, on Christmas Eve, Musk was able to secure investors, including $50 million from Daimler Chrysler. How did he manage to secure the financing in such a tough economic environment and for a company in a precarious position? He succeeded because he had made a credible, irreversible commitment. Musk convinced quavering investors by offering to fund the entire round of financing himself. This was no easy feat. It meant gambling most of the rest of his fortune, and Musk was taking a temporary loan from SpaceX to do so. But it worked. In the end, Tesla closed a round of financing that saved the company for the next decade.

Sometimes, a credible commitment can come in the form of sheer time and effort devoted to a project. Some people credit Norman Borlaug with saving an estimated billion people from starvation through his work developing hybrid wheat. For this work, he won the Nobel Peace Prize, the Presidential Medal of Freedom, and the Congressional Gold Medal. In the 1940s, Borlaug, who was trained as an agronomist, took a US government assignment in Mexico, where disease had dangerously reduced the capacity of crops to feed the population. He believed that he could create new forms of wheat that would resist disease and create higher yields. But progress was hampered because of limited government resources and the slow process of testing new wheat strains with only one growing season each year. Then Borlaug had an idea: What if he could grow wheat twice in one season, first by planting in the central highlands during the summer and then shuttling the resulting seeds to the north, where a lowland valley stayed warm in the fall?

Borlaug's supervisors were against the idea. "Everyone" knew that seeds needed a period of rest between harvest and germination. And the accelerated approach would require more plowing resources, which the supervisors were unwilling to give up. Undeterred, Borlaug pushed ahead, finding an old plow and literally harnessing himself to the plow to till the field in preparation for wheat. Seeing this middle-aged man harnessed to the plow like a mule, a neighboring Mexican farmer offered to let Borlaug use his tractor on weekends. When Borlaug's superiors learned of Borlaug's actions and saw his unwavering devotion to the project, they finally relented and provided additional resources to plow and shuttle his wheat seedlings. With the greater resources, Borlaug eventually developed a shorter-stalk wheat that could resist local disease and produced more grain in the nutrient-poor soil than did traditional wheat. His wheat turned Mexico from a starving country to a net wheat exporter. He also dispelled the common belief that seeds needed a rest between harvest and germination. His new form of wheat spread to other continents and has since fed billions.

In the end, it was Borlaug's time commitment that won the resources and support for his idea. When you work inside an organization, it may seem hard to leverage credible commitments. But as Borlaug demonstrated, sometimes a willingness to devote time and energy well beyond what others are willing to give can get leaders' attention and persuade them to support your ideas or project.

Finally, your success with a project may sometimes depend on persuading your organization to make a credible commitment to the project. For example, Kvålseth, the aforementioned chief strategy and innovation officer at DTAC, one of Thailand's leading telecoms, envisioned creating a disruptive, low-cost mobile service built around Thailand's leading social network, Line. Although both DTAC and Line expressed initial enthusiasm, anyone working in a big company knows that the winds of support can change quickly. So as Kvålseth put together the project as a joint venture between Line and DTAC, he thought carefully about what resources were needed and how to creatively get irreversible commitments. For example, he knew the venture would require a certain level of sustained spending on marketing over five years—

something that headquarters might agree to during good times but decide to cut later if times got tough. Foreseeing this unpredictable pattern of funding, he built the marketing spend commitment into the joint venture contract, with penalties for nonperformance. This and other commitments built into the contract helped Kvålseth get credible commitments from the two partners and build one of the fastest-growing mobile services in Thailand.

Advice on Making Credible Commitments

Making a credible commitment to persuade others involves significant, costly actions that signal your belief and devotion to an idea or a project. So by definition, a credible commitment is a risky action. You can take some steps to successfully use this impression amplifier.

Reduce the Uncertainty Associated with
Making a Credible Commitment

One-way doors are only risky if you want to reverse your decision. But often there are clever ways to build an *escape option*—a way to reverse the decision. For example, rather than quit your job to commit to a new venture, figure out a way to take a three- or four-month leave or sabbatical. Alternatively, you could line up another job for a few months in the future. Or make a commitment conditional, perhaps in some nonobvious way. Lough and Swanson didn't quit their positions at Johns Hopkins until they were contractually assured of not only the funding they needed but also complete control of the new venture.

Don't make a credible commitment until you have the resources you need committed as well. And you should always think through your plan B in case things don't work as expected. We certainly don't advocate risking it all without having a thoughtful plan B.

Create Credible Commitments with Your
Abundance Rather Than Your Scarcity

When Musk offered to fund Tesla himself, he was risking something of which he had an abundance, not a scarcity. Certainly he could have lost his fortune, but he had his experience, friends, and family to fall back on. For many of us, financial resources are scarce, but time, energy, or reputation are abundant. We can create credible commitments as Borlaug did, through our energy and passion.

FOMO: Creating a Fear of Missing Out

Just before the dot-com bubble transformed the scale of how we talk about success, Jerry Sanders performed what might have previously been considered impossible: he took the medical device company X-Cardia, founded a few months earlier for a few thousand dollars, and sold it for $33 million. In those brief ten months, Sanders leveraged many of the amplifiers we have discussed, such as connecting the company to prestigious investors, scientists, and institutions as well as materializing the concept—a device to measure blood flow in the heart—in a working prototype. But just before the acquisition, Sanders did something that confused many of his friends and investors: he gave away more of his own equity to raise additional funds. Why, when you have an acquisition on the near horizon, would you want to give away the very ownership you were about to cash in on?

But that wasn't all. Immediately after getting the acquisition inquiry, Sanders ran out and started conversations with other potential acquirers, juggling all the conversations in parallel. He also acquired a separate small startup that added a second product to the company's lineup. By the time the potential acquirer had to finally decide whether to acquire X-Cardia, it met an entirely different X-Cardia. Sanders said, he wanted the acquisition team to enter the room and say: "'Holy cow, these guys are really building a company. We've got to get moving because their valuation is going up and up and soon they won't want to sell the company.' We looked like a company on the cusp of an IPO. We were nowhere close. But again, appearances were everything. And if we had to, we could have built a company."[19]

FOMO: What It Is and Why It Works

FOMO involves creating a sense of urgency, scarcity, or exclusivity that if you don't act quickly, you might miss out on the opportunity. It works because of a psychological principle based on the law of scarcity: human beings crave and desire things that are scarce or difficult to obtain.[20] Think of that person you weren't sure you were interested in until they started dating someone else. Your interest may likely have risen—perhaps enough to motivate you to take action. Creating FOMO also switches potential supporters from a critical, evaluative mindset to an acquisitive one, where they focus on the opportunity that they might miss. Thus, when Sanders introduced more acquirers to the conversation, integrated a second product, and raised additional money, he put pressure on his acquirers that if they didn't act fast, they would miss the chance to purchase the company at all.

Although FOMO can be exploited to win support from investors, it can also be used to win support from others, such as potential employees. For example, when Josh Schwarzapel set out to build the technical team for his startup Cooliris, he thought the process would be easy. Cooliris had both a compelling technical vision to transform how people interact with the internet and funding from a top venture capitalist. But after almost six months of intensive recruiting effort, no new employees had joined the technical team. In response, Schwarzapel and the Cooliris leadership sat down and took a hard look at its recruiting. The members realized that they were treating recruits as if the team were buying, or picking out, the best candidate off the shelf. To win support from potential recruits, the team needed to create an environment in which it sold itself to candidates—an environment where they felt they would be missing out if they didn't join quickly.

To do this, Schwarzapel and the team redesigned their recruiting process, walking the candidate into their offices, past the desks of famous venture capitalists, and telling about legendary startups they had invested in. Then they introduced the candidate to their grand vision of how to transform how people access the internet. Finally, they created the impression that the recruit was part of a vibrant team, with a special but disappearing slot (they did this by displaying pictures of the team but with a single blank space with the candidate's picture in it). They emphasized that the Cooliris team wanted to change the world and wanted the candidate to be part of it, but that they were moving fast and the opportunity wouldn't last forever.

The technique—which created a sense of urgency and exclusivity—worked. Five of five offers extended were accepted. The Cooliris team then went on to recruit the biggest group of Stanford interns that any startup in Silicon Valley had ever recruited. Cooliris succeeded in creating 3-D imaging tools that have been downloaded more than fifty million times and have received multiple design awards. The company was later acquired by Yahoo!

Advice on Using FOMO

FOMO works by creating a sense of urgency, scarcity, or exclusivity that encourages supporters to act rather than to wait. As you try to use FOMO to win support for your ideas, several approaches can be helpful.

Make Your FOMO Strategy Credible

FOMO isn't high-pressure sales to do something unethical or a fraudulent show of scarcity. Both attempts will fall flat. FOMO is about helping supporters overcome their natural inertia and skepticism and see the value of an opportunity.

Leverage "Casual Dating" to Manage the Time Dimension

In his research on how entrepreneurs raise funds, Professor Benjamin Hallen found that entrepreneurs frequently use FOMO to raise capital.[21] He argues that the challenge, for entrepreneurs, is that investors have a strong incentive to wait rather than invest immediately. Waiting allows the investor to gather multiple data points on the entrepreneur and possibly jump in at a later date, after the entrepreneur has proven out more untested assumptions and the investment is less risky. This risk aversion by investors is the classic innovators' paradox. For the entrepreneur who needs capital, the wait-and-see approach can be devastating.

How did entrepreneurs counteract wait-and-see tendencies? First, they tried to provide investors multiple data points before the entrepreneur needed the money; Hallen labeled this process "casual dating." Specifically, entrepreneurs approached a potential supporter, seeking the person's "advice" or "feedback" in advance of when they needed funding. By the time the entrepreneurs approached the investor, that person had enough data points to take action.[22]

Try to Get Multiple Players Competing against Each Other in Parallel

The other way that entrepreneurs counteracted the wait-and-see tendency was to get multiple players moving in parallel. For example, when Sanders reached out to other potential acquirers, he was trying to get several players involved at the same time so there would be a threat of losing the deal. Similarly, in her study of how makers of low-power mobile games struck deals with high-power players like network operators and handset makers, Pinar Ozcan, professor of strategic management at Warwick Business School, observed that successful startups entertained conversations with these players in parallel.[23] So, for example, the entrepreneur might tell AT&T that he or she was in talks with Verizon and BlackBerry; this technique would signal credibility but would also create scarcity.

In Hallen's research, the entrepreneurs took it even one step further. Not only did they pitch multiple investors, but they also pitched to different kinds of investors, for example, approaching traditional venture capitalists, corporate venture capitalists, and angel investors. Because each investor group operates by a slightly different set of rules and in a slightly different social circle, investors were put off balance by not knowing whether the other investors would also wait and see. Fearing they might miss out, the investors laid their money down earlier. Likewise, entrepreneurs sometimes threatened to fund the idea themselves if investors didn't move quickly; the idea was to increase the FOMO pressure on investors.[24]

Conclusion

Impression amplifiers are the observable actions that you take to win support for your ideas. Unlike human, social, and reputation capital, which are all part of who you are, impression amplifiers are the actions you take to magnify your personal capital or stir up support for your idea. Generally they fall into two categories, those that amplify your personal capital as well as your idea, and those that help sell your idea. Although there is no particular sequence to using these amplifiers, and they can be used independently, innovators often use them in combination to win support from investors, employees, suppliers, and customers.

In chapters 2 through 6, we have discussed each of the separate components of innovation capital—human capital skills, social capital, reputation capital—and the two types of impression amplifiers. We have provided advice on how to build your innovation capital step-by-step, from your human capital skills, to your strong and weak social tie connections, and then to your track record and reputation for innovation. In chapter 7, we shift gears from your actions as an individual to proposing a pattern of innovation leadership that you can use when attempting to initiate an innovation project or entrepreneurial startup. This pattern, used by many innovative leaders, will not only build your innovation capital but will also increase the chances that your effort will succeed. Perhaps most importantly, we will teach you how visionary leadership for your project can ignite a virtuous cycle of success.

See our website www.innovatorsdna.com/innovation-capital for more resources on the material in this chapter.

7

The Virtuous Cycle of Innovation Leadership

Whatever your view of Elon Musk, one thing he did when he helped launch Tesla was articulate a lofty vision for the company. "Our goal [is] . . . to accelerate the advent of sustainable transport by bringing compelling mass market electric cars to market as soon as possible," he wrote. "In order to get to that end goal, big leaps in technology are required."[1] Musk then laid out his "master plan"—a strategy for launching desirable electric vehicles at the high end of the market followed by affordable electric vehicles for the mainstream market.

Sterling Anderson, former head of Tesla Model X and Tesla Autopilot and cofounder of Aurora Innovation (a startup that is successfully providing a full-stack self-driving solution for major automakers like Volkswagen and Hyundai), says that Musk's success as an innovative leader stems largely from a reinforcing cycle of success triggered by an exciting and inspirational vision:

> Elon understands people. He understands that a lofty
> vision, an inspirational vision, attracts world-class people,

particularly world-class engineers. With those world-class engineers, he's able to build a better product. That better product attracts customers and attracts investors, and it's self-reinforcing. As this feeds on itself, engineers are increasingly inspired to join, not only because of the lofty vision but also because of the increasingly strong brand behind it. These conditions attract increasingly strong talent; it feels good to work there and to be viewed as someone who is helping drive innovation toward that lofty goal.

Without prompting, Anderson independently has described the same virtuous cycle that we have seen many leaders utilize with positive results (figure 7-1). This cycle includes the following steps:

1. Identify an exciting, lofty, even inspirational vision. The vision needs to solve an important problem, pursue a big opportunity, or just be exciting.

2. The lofty vision attracts talented human capital (e.g., better engineers and scientists) who want to work on something exciting. It also attracts investors and/or resources from organization leaders who provide the resources and senior sponsorship needed to launch a successful innovation project.

3. The talented human capital increases the odds of developing a better product and customer experience. Put simply, talented people going after a lofty vision produces better results for the customer.

4. The better product or customer experience attracts customers. The increase in happy customers leads to the creation of a valuable, hopefully innovative, reputation. Customers of companies or brands with an innovative reputation experience

"identification"—which means their personal identity gets tied up with the products and brand which makes them much more loyal and valuable customers.

The ability to attract customers and build a valuable brand leads to a reinforcing cycle. Going back to step number two: talented human capital and investors are attracted to companies and projects with a valuable brand and loyal customers. Thus, the cycle repeats.

Musk's history of launching new ventures reveals that he has purposely ignited this cycle in many of them. For example, when

FIGURE 7-1

Virtuous cycle of innovation leadership

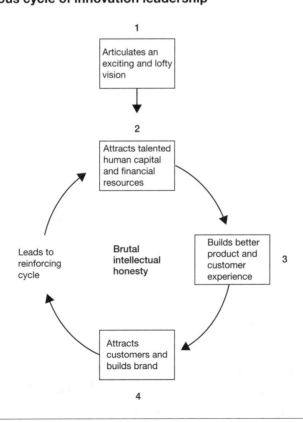

founding SpaceX, he established a mission for the company, which was "to revolutionize space technology with the ultimate goal of enabling people to live on other planets."[2] When Tesla pursued the Powerwall—a product that uses Tesla batteries to power homes and utilities (and, of course, to charge your Tesla vehicle)—Musk announced that "our goal here is to fundamentally change the way the world uses energy."[3] When he announced his idea for Boring (a transportation infrastructure company), he articulated a vision of creating a "3D transportation network of tunnel infrastructure for cars and high speed trains"[4] to relieve congestion problems in big cities (see www.boringcompany.com for a cool video on how it works). Pursuing big and important problems has been the starting mechanism for a cycle of success that Musk deftly deployed multiple times. Musk acknowledges that "I like to be involved in things that change the world."

But the cycle isn't unique to Musk. We saw a similar pattern in other innovative leaders we examined. As Jeff Bezos launched Amazon, he said, "What we want to be is something completely new. There is no physical analog for what Amazon.com is becoming."[5] When Marc Benioff launched Salesforce—one of the first enterprise software systems born in the cloud—he boldly proclaimed "The End of Software" as a tagline. Jeff Weiner of LinkedIn talks about the company's mission to connect everyone on the planet and to "create economic opportunity for the global workforce of three billion people." But it wasn't just founders of new companies. We also saw less well-known leaders deploy this strategy effectively.

Painting an exciting vision for a venture was an important first step to innovation leadership for the people we studied; the vision triggered the virtuous cycle of innovation leadership shown in figure 7-1. The leaders weren't always conscious of the cycle but seemed to intuitively understand the wide-ranging benefits of painting a vision for projects that made the ventures seem exciting and important. Of course, some of the painting involves telling stories to make an emotional connection, as described in chapter 5. Paul Polman, former CEO of food products company Unilever, talks about how one in ten people in the world lack clean water, and he describes Unilever's vision of using clean-water technologies to solve this problem. Nike's founders and current CEO Mark Parker have discovered that they can create an exciting vision out of "serving the athlete" (Nike defines everyone as an athlete) to inspire athletes to "just do it" and achieve better athletic performance.

In this chapter, we examine effective innovation leadership at the team or project level and, more specifically, the elements of the virtuous cycle of innovation leadership. (In chapter 8, we will address innovation capability and innovation capital at the organization level.) We'll start by examining *visionary leadership*, a term that you have probably heard many times before. What does it mean to provide visionary leadership? How do you avoid common mistakes that can terrify, rather than inspire, those you lead? We'll then discuss recruiting the human and financial resources you need to pursue the vision and how great leaders design the problem-solving process and culture within the team to build innovative solutions. But it all starts with "the vision thing."

Step 1: Provide Visionary Leadership

By now you've probably heard—multiple times—that great leaders provide visionary leadership. But how do great leaders actually do it? Effective visionary leadership involves three important elements: (1) vision, (2) strategic direction (setting the vectors of opportunity within that vision), and (3) stretch goals.

First, visionary leadership requires a high-level description of a problem to solve or an opportunity to pursue. This vision statement must *create emotional engagement*. It might include declarations such as "revolutionize space travel," "create economic opportunity for the global workforce," or "create sustainable food and water." But the statement could also just be the creation of something fun and exciting (e.g., a theme park that is "the happiest place on earth"). The key is emotional engagement, connecting with the emotional and social desires of supporters so that they want to bring their resources to the project because they think it is important, fun, exciting, or just interesting.

The second step in the vision is to provide the team with strategic direction, or vectors of search, about how they will achieve the vision. This strategic direction could be described as setting the vectors of opportunity within the grand vision. For example, Musk laid out a strategic direction for Tesla in the "master plan" to revolutionize transportation, notably starting by building *desirable* electric vehicles at the high end of the market before building *affordable* vehicles. This strategic direction provides a vector of search (i.e., sustainable cars, desirable vehicles, starting at the high end of the market). One of the big mistakes we see leaders make is to set a grand vision but no vectors of search. In these situations, people start out excited but then quickly become scared and confused as they ask themselves, What are we supposed to be working on? Can we really succeed?

At the same time, while the strategic direction provides just that—direction—it leaves room for exploration and modification. "One of the things that is important when leading an innovative team is to paint a vision that is clear enough that they can execute," Anderson told us. "I think one of the things that I see sometimes done poorly is, the vision is either insufficiently painted, or it's painted with such a level of detail that it's not inspiring for anyone to go and work on it. Because those who are asked to do it don't feel like they have the leeway to innovate, but instead feel like their path and deliverables—and even, in many cases, approach—are largely dictated for them."

Third, once the strategic direction is articulated, leaders need to make the direction even more concrete by establishing some measurable stretch goals that the team will work toward to achieve the strategy and vision. Stretch goals are those that appear unattainable, given current practices, skills, and knowledge; they will require some innovation to achieve. Because most people are deeply uncomfortable with uncertainty, stretch goals are important because they give people more-concrete aspirations to chase.

Nike's Mark Parker encourages stretch goals. Nike's Breaking2 project—designed to break the two-hour barrier for the marathon—offers an excellent illustration of the power of stretch goals. In the summer of 2014, Matt Nurse, head of Nike Sports Research Lab, decided that he and his colleagues were playing it too safe. Even though Nike's vision was to provide "inspiration and innovation" to every athlete, he believed that Nike wasn't taking enough risks in the strategic vector of long-distance running. During the previous year, designers within the lab had been working on a shoe that would help distance runners improve their performance by up to 3 percent. Nurse realized that although this improvement was a worthy goal, it was a safe one. He wanted to push his team members to devote themselves to an aspiration that would either succeed or fail definitively. So he asked them to imagine how they would make a two-hour marathon a reality. The fastest that the marathon had ever been run was 2:02:57; a sub-two-hour time would require a three-minute (2.4 percent) improvement, which might sound small but represents a giant leap in human performance. "We keep talking about the sub-two," Nurse recalls saying. "It's time to stop talking about it and actually do it."[6]

Sandy Bodecker, vice president of special projects, took the challenge to heart—so much so that he signaled his personal commitment to Breaking2 by having 1:59:59 tattooed across his wrist. Under Nurse's guidance, Bodecker pulled together a diverse team of experts in design, engineering, materials, nutrition, physiology, plus three of the world's fastest marathoners, including Eliud Kipchoge, winner of the Rio Olympics and the world's fastest marathoner. Then they set a deadline for the stretch goal: run a sub-two-hour marathon at the Monza auto track in Italy (chosen for its optimal running and weather conditions) in two years. The designers' goal was to develop the lightest shoes possible while providing cushioning and a design that would propel the body forward. They tested design after design with the three marathoners on the team who told them what they liked and what they disliked (one design eliminated the heel entirely to reduce weight—but the runners hated it). They finally hit on a design with a carbon-fiber plate in the midsole. The plate stores and releases energy with each stride and acts as a kind of slingshot to propel runners forward. They also designed lightweight performance clothing to minimize drag. Nutritionists and physiologists worked with the athletes to ensure that the runners' bodies were in perfect condition. Coaches provided running tips based on careful analysis of the athletes' running techniques.

Then on May 6, 2017, the team held a much-publicized running event that turned out to be a PR coup, as everyone in the running world watched to see whether Kipchoge could break the two-hour marathon. During the first fifteen, seventeen, and even twenty-two miles, Kipchoge was right behind the two-hour pace car. But during the final two miles, he slowed slightly, finishing in a world record 2:00:25. (The time was unofficial because the team had used other runners, called pacemakers, throughout the race to break the wind and push Kipchoge, but one year later, Kipchoge officially broke the world record by more than a minute.)

Ultimately, the project came up short of its goal. But the shoe that the team developed, the Nike Zoom Vaporfly 4%, and the PR that came with it were a huge success. This PR arguably contributed a great deal to Nike's innovation capital (see chapter 8). "Moments like Breaking2 are very important for our brand," Parker says. Tests of the shoes demonstrated that they reduced running times by an average of almost 4 percent, and a *New York Times* article suggested that the "shoes give runners an unfair advantage."[7] Nike couldn't buy better press than that. Not surprisingly, when the Nike Zoom Vaporfly 4% was released to the public, the shoes flew off the shelves. The results of the sub-two-hour stretch goal exceeded expectations—despite the fact that the sub-two-hour goal wasn't actually met.

"I love the ambition of trying to make history," Mark Parker told us when discussing Breaking2. "When you commit to a stretch goal like that, the whole process can be incredibly uplifting for a team. Stretch goals can also fast-track innovation. Tight timelines with a focused objective really inspire you to be creative. Through the Breaking2 journey, we came up with amazing new concepts, including the industry's first 3-D-printed performance upper. Success is never guaranteed, and sometimes, you win by just trying."

Research shows that stretch goals work best when there are clear metrics of achievement, when team members have a track record of success, and when the team is given substantial resources to remove roadblocks to achieving the goal. Moreover, when stretch goals require considerable innovation, success is more likely when the team effectively uses first principles to solve problems (see chapter 2). Of course, one challenge of stretch goals is that you can push employees so hard that they burn out or are demotivated by pursuing what they perceive as impossible targets. Musk has been criticized for setting impossible stretch goals and burning out employees. He responds by saying that he doesn't "set targets that I know can't be met" and that "in order to have a good outcome, we must strive for a great outcome."[8] Tesla cofounder and chief technical officer J. B. Straubel believes in Musk's approach, telling us, "Elon is a master at harnessing and channeling the team to do pretty amazing things that go beyond what the team even thought was possible. If you challenge people to work hard, they achieve more than they think they can. Most leaders don't want to do that."

LinkedIn's Weiner uses these three components of visionary leadership while guiding the company. As previously mentioned, his grand vision for LinkedIn is to "create economic opportunity for the global workforce of three billion people." Weiner believes that to achieve this vision, LinkedIn has articulated a strategy to "create a platform for the communication, professional development, and advancement for people around the world." Thus, the company's strategy goes well beyond simply being an effective tool for managing one's professional networks. The vision aspires to something much more inspiring: creating opportunities for anyone, anywhere, to find jobs, receive training, and anything else that might be helpful for professional communication and development.

Weiner then set stretch goals toward that mission, starting with connecting the 780 million business professionals in the world. Back in 2010, LinkedIn had a little over 50 million professionals on the site. Since then, in pursuit of its stretch goal, the LinkedIn team has grown that number to more than 590 million users. Weiner also set stretch goals around finding job opportunities through LinkedIn. At the time, around 8,000 jobs were listed on the platform. Weiner set a stretch goal of 350,000 jobs. Within a couple of years, as the team approached that hurdle, Weiner congratulated the team and then raised the ambition to 20 million jobs. Such an order-of-magnitude increase required a fundamental shift in the required resources and strategy for these operations. For example, LinkedIn acquired a company called Bright to help it achieve that objective. Today

Three components of visionary leadership

LinkedIn has more than 20 million job postings, and the number is growing.

Weiner also challenged a team to create the world's first "economic graph" (comparable to a social graph but a map of the world's interconnecting economic relationships). He told us, "This portrait of the professional world would include a profile for all three billion workers, every company in the world, a digital representation of all jobs, the skills required for those jobs (plus courses to develop those skills), profiles of all universities and schools, and a platform for people to share their knowledge." Weiner's and LinkedIn's success very much comes from developing a lofty vision, a strategic direction or vector, and stretch goals and then leading the company in its pursuit (figure 7-2).

Step 2: Attract Talented Team Members and Resources to the Project

Establishing an exciting vision is an important first step in convincing talented people to join your team. But securing talent takes more than that. Successful leaders attract people to their teams and organizations because *others want to work with them.* Think about it. Why do you want to work for a specific leader on a specific project?

We are typically drawn to work with a certain leader on a particular project for several reasons. First, we are excited by the project work itself. We like the vision and simply want the opportunity to do the work. Second, we believe we will learn important things by working for this leader. We want his or her mentorship. Third, we want to build our own reputation by doing high-profile projects and by developing a relationship with this leader or project. We want to be associated with a winning project, and we want the sponsorship of a successful leader. Fourth, the leader makes us feel as if we are uniquely suited to contribute to the project. We feel needed. And finally, we want to work with leaders that we "like." We enjoy being around them and working with them.

So there you have the recipe for attracting the best talent: Paint an exciting project vision. Credibly assure the prospects that they will learn some important things by working with you on the project. Convince them that this will be a stepping-stone to additional opportunities—and that you will proactively help them secure those opportunities. Let the prospects know that they are critical to the project. Finally, be someone who is enjoyable to work with. You just need one of these reasons to resonate with someone to persuade him or her to join your team.

As illustration, consider why Tim Cook, now CEO of Apple, left a comfortable job to take a big risk on a then-struggling company. In 1998, he was content as a senior executive at Compaq, a successful upstart that was dethroning IBM as the top dog of personal computers for businesses. Steve Jobs reached out to recruit Cook, inviting him for an interview. Cook refused at first. He was happy where he was at the helm of a rising star, and Apple had been on the decline for a decade. But Jobs persisted. Finally Cook conceded to an interview. He recalls how it went:

> Any purely rational consideration of cost and benefits lined up in Compaq's favor, and the people who knew me best advised me to stay at Compaq. On that day in early 1998 I listened to my intuition . . . [N]o more than five minutes into my initial interview with Steve, I wanted to throw caution and logic to the wind and join Apple . . . [A]ll of a sudden he's talking about his strategy and vision, and that what he was doing was going 100 percent into consumer. Everybody else in the industry had decided you couldn't make any money on consumers so they were headed to services and storage and enterprise. And I thought, I'd always thought that following the herd was not a good thing . . . And he told me a little about the design [of a new consumer computer], enough to get me really interested. And he was describing what later would be called the iMac . . . My intuition already knew that joining Apple was a once in a lifetime opportunity to work for a creative genius, and to be on the executive team that could resurrect a great American company.[9]

Jobs sold the vision, and Cook leaped in headfirst.

Of course, you have more tools at your disposal than just the vision. You can persuade others as well by using the full arsenal of impression amplifiers described in chapters 5 and 6. Tell stories to sell your vision and use broadcasting to amplify who you are and what you've done. You can use comparisons—through relevant analogies—to communicate why your project will succeed, and you can make your ideas tangible (materializing them) to show that success is possible. And if all else fails, make strong or irreversible commitments and FOMO approaches to show your deep commitment to a project that has a closing window of opportunity.

Step 3: Build a Better Product and Customer Experience

For true innovation, you must recruit talent, because you are doing something that hasn't been done before. And to have real impact, customers (or internal users) must think a new solution is not just okay, but awesome. "The balance of power is shifting toward consumers and away from companies," Bezos told us. "The right way to respond to this if you are a company is to put the vast majority of your energy, attention, and dollars into building a great product or service and put a smaller amount into shouting about it, marketing it." As the saying goes, "Build a better mousetrap, and the world will beat a path to your door."

If you are a leader, a better mousetrap requires that you carefully design the problem-solving process to enhance the probability of a breakthrough solution that customers will love. To be clear, we aren't talking about building a better solution without a deep understanding of the customer need—doing so is a recipe for failure. We are talking about how you can dramatically improve your solutions to customers' problems.

As described in chapter 2, a preferred way to increase and improve the solutions you offer is to apply first principles to solving problems. First, you identify the key constraints to achieving a breakthrough in performance, and then you test every option possible for eliminating one or more of those constraints. For example, Musk's stretch goal at the start of the Boring Company was "increasing tunneling speed and dropping costs by a factor of 10."[10] Current machine tunneling speeds are three hundred feet per week. But according to Musk's first-principles analysis, current machines are much slower than physics suggests they could be. So Musk wants to increase that speed to more than one mile per week, a tenfold improvement. Musk says that tunneling speeds have changed little in the last fifty years. "To make it a little better should be easy," he says. "To make it five times better is not crazy hard. To make it 10 times better is hard, but nobody will need to win the Nobel Prize. We don't have to change the standard model of physics."[11] The bottom line is that an important first step to building a better solution is to use first principles and identify the limiting factors that will need to be addressed with a solution.

Once the limiting factors to a breakthrough solution have been identified, the leader's role in the process of building a better mousetrap is to play the role of "chief experimenter."[12] Rather than make decisions, the leader's role shifts to coach and facilitator of experiments designed to test hypotheses about a breakthrough solution. If the manager, or anyone else on the team, says, "I think we should do X" or "I believe X," that statement is translated into a leap-of-faith assumption or hypothesis that can be tested with an experiment. Intuit founder Scott Cook (ranked nineteenth, with CEO Brad Smith, on our list) told us, "Brad Smith and I have changed the questions that we ask. We used to ask things like, 'Well, what's your answer, and what's your analysis behind it?' And now we ask, 'Okay, what's the fastest way to get an experiment to test that idea?'" Cook continued: "Brad and I have to live by the same rules. So we end up asking ourselves questions like, 'I have got a fundamental belief of what we should do. Now, what are the leap-of-faith assumptions on which it is based? And how are we going to test the leap-of-faith assumptions that are crucial to my beliefs?' We need to do this just like we would do for anyone else. Experiments will be nothing but window dressing until you change who and how decisions are made."

As a leader and the chief experimenter, you should focus on three activities:

- Forming leap-of-faith assumptions with your team

- Rapidly testing those assumptions through experiments (mostly with customers)

- Revising and retesting your assumptions as you let the data (mostly from customers) make the decisions

Of course, the ultimate goal of the experiments is to develop a solution that customers cannot resist, something awesome. The road to awesome typically begins with a minimum viable product, which is used to test assumptions and hypotheses. Although you should start with the minimum viable product and use it until you have a strong understanding of the user need, the ultimate goal is not just a viable product; it's an awesome product. We first heard the term *minimum awesome product* while observing an Intuit training session focused on a single issue: what is awesome? The goal of a minimum awesome product is to deliver a solution that is insanely great on the most important dimension that it inspires delight in your customers. As Cook explains, "You don't want to be viable in the dimension that matters. You want to be awesome in the dimension that matters, all while maintaining an uncomfortably narrow focus." In other words, you want to identify the minimum feature set possible and then relentlessly focus on making your solution awesome on those dimensions.

So how do you get to awesome? Customers describe products as awesome when the offerings inspire positive emotions. When a product or service surprises you by doing something you didn't expect—something you may not have even thought was possible—it can evoke happy surprise and prompt you to say "That is awesome!" As your team seeks to build a better mousetrap, remember that your customers are hiring your solution to do a job for them—and that every job has functional, social, and emotional dimensions. Your solution may inspire awesome by doing the unexpected on any of these three dimensions.

Step 4: Attract Customers and Build a Brand

Building a better product will not only attract customers but also build a valuable innovation brand. Companies or products with a reputation for innovation are more likely to have customers identify with them at a personal level (think of Tesla or Apple loyalists). In turn, this personal connection leads to increased customer loyalty, repeat purchases, willingness to pay higher prices, and increased tolerance for occasional product failures.[13] The power of an innovation reputation that comes from making great products, services, or experiences is frequently underestimated. This is why Bezos has argued for investing your resources and effort on building a great product rather than money and resources pushing people into thinking they are buying a great product.

Step 5: Recognize That All of the Steps Are Mutually Reinforcing

Building a valuable brand and attracting customers simply reinforces the innovation leadership and success cycle by attracting additional funding and talent. Particularly astute leaders realize that their personal innovation brand is tied to the innovations their team produces, so they use effective broadcasting to build their personal brand along with their company's brand. "I learned from Elon [Musk] that if possible, it is important to use the press to build a personal brand," Anderson says. "Having a personal brand makes people want to work with you and buy your products; in turn, those good engineers create good products and your star rises. It's all reinforcing. I think those who ignore it, or are not good at it, do so at their own peril. Some innovators do phenomenal work that doesn't get the traction it deserves, because the world never hears about it." As described in chapter 4, building a personal reputation for innovation isn't easy, but it can pay huge dividends.

A Culture of Brutal Intellectual Honesty

Even though our book isn't about creating an innovation culture, the leadership cycle works best in an environment of *brutal intellectual honesty*. We've borrowed the term from Dominic Orr, founder of Aruba Networks, a billion-dollar-plus company. Orr uses the phrase to describe how teams in dynamic environments must work together to win. He argues that brutal honesty was the secret to building one of his first unicorn companies:

> There's too many decisions to make, there's too little time . . . What you want is to get all the facts and opinions and wisdom out on the table, have a really honest debate about it, given a limited period of time. And then at the end of that period of time . . . make a decision and go. In that process, you need people to be very thick-skinned. Because I feel that if you look into a lot of situations, people get bogged down into very emotional arguments or political situations and so on . . . That is incredibly time wasting. And time is the only competitive resource that we have in our hands. We cannot allow that to happen. So what I encourage is people to be thick-skinned about it . . . and don't defend it with your ego, and let intellectual honesty dictate . . . And the brutal part is the tricky part. A lot of

people apply it to the other guy. What I really meant when I created the term is to apply it to yourself, that when you really put forward a very passionate argument, when you actually get convinced intellectually, there's a better way to do it. Be brutal to yourself, and say, "Okay. Yeah. You're right. You know, I put my best foot forward . . . [but] I've got to do it your way.[14]

In essence, Orr describes the environment that successful leaders of innovation create. In such an intellectually honest climate, leaders can challenge each other in productive ways that yield meaningful progress.

This environment goes hand-in-hand with an atmosphere of psychological safety, as espoused by Harvard professor Amy Edmonson. In psychologically safe situations, team members are willing to ask questions, express opinions, acknowledge mistakes, and have confidence that they can engage in risky, learning-related behaviors without punishment. But while you want your team members to feel comfortable saying whatever they want, when there is brutal intellectual honesty, it is impossible to avoid the discomfort that comes from real disagreement—something that is often necessary when you are pursuing truly novel outcomes.

Len Schleifer, president and CEO of Regeneron, told us that brutal honesty is fundamental to the success of his innovative organization. (Schleifer shares twenty-first place with Regeneron cofounder, president, and chief scientist George Yancopoulos on our list of most innovative leaders.) Regeneron has transformed the biopharma industry with its ability to develop new therapies at less than 20 percent of the cost of competitors. "I love this guy," Schleifer says, referring to Yancopoulos. "But we almost come to blows regularly, and we're always arguing about things. I think that leads the whole organization to just debating and challenging and questioning everything. I think that if you're going to try to break molds and if you're going to try to do new things that haven't been done before, it's almost got to start with something that you so passionately almost don't agree with."

Yancopoulos agrees: "Len and I have something like five arguments a day. We're not alone in that it is the culture here. And one of the most important things that we do is establish this notion that nothing is unchallengeable. You don't take anything for granted, and you test and pressure-test everything."

Steve Jobs was among the first to advocate for this type of environment, saying, "I'm brutally honest, because the price of admission to being in the room with me is, I get to tell you you're full of shit if you're full of shit, and you get to say to me I'm full of shit, and we have some rip-roaring fights, and that keeps the B players, the bozos, from larding the organization. Only the A players survive."[15] Depending on the leader, this type of environment can be challenging to work in. Creating an environment where individuals feel psychological safety—even while there is brutal intellectual honesty—requires creating a tricky balance. Most of us don't like confrontation and don't really like brutal honesty. Some research suggests that leaders who score high on emotional intelligence are far more successful at creating psychological safety and intellectual honesty. We've seen leaders follow three key practices to create a safe environment where team members can be brutally honest and the team can still function well.

First, legitimize the asking of any question or the challenging of any assumption. This permission to explore intellectually starts with what Bezos calls having a "beginner's mind":

> To be an inventor you have to be an expert in your domain but still have a beginner's mind because the problem with being an expert in your domain is that you become numb to all the things that are wrong, you're so used to it. We

humans quickly adapt to things that aren't as good as they could be. And if you have a beginner's mind like a child, you're not an expert, of course, so you'll ask, "Well, why does that work that way? That doesn't make any sense." But the world is so sophisticated that you also can't just be a beginner. You actually do need domain expertise . . . But they [successful inventors] can put themselves in a place where they can see it as if it's the first time they've ever seen it.

Leaders facilitate a beginner's mindset and brutal honesty by creating an atmosphere where questions and challenges to assumptions—even those of "experts"—is encouraged. People can feel uncomfortable about being challenged when they are considered experts in a particular knowledge domain.

Second, leaders must help team members know that they are trusted and valued members of the team even when they are challenged and their assumptions or position proves to be incorrect. Orr hired therapists to help his executives feel comfortable enough with themselves to be challenged. But there are other techniques you can apply. Anderson describes a technique that he learned at MIT while earning his PhD in robotics and now uses:

One of the things I actually did with various teams at MIT is, we used to tell each other, "Look, just put your ego in this little box at the door, go in and shut the door, and once we're in the conference room on the whiteboard, we don't want anyone getting their feelings hurt. We may end up saying 'No, that's not right, here's a proof as to why that's the case.' We don't want anyone feeling bad because someone else said that what they just suggested is not right. Treat it like a game if you need to, and feel like it's just a matter of seeing who ultimately prevails in presenting the evidence that makes their respective case."

Anderson goes on to describe what the leader is hoping to achieve after a working session where people disagree and are challenged. "I think you need to be able to express the appropriate degree of skepticism about someone's ideas while still making it clear that you trust the person that you're questioning," he says. "You need to trust that they came into this with a reasoned thought process, and you need to trust that they are an intelligent individual. And at the end of the day, even if you disagree on something, you still trust them to see it through and to bring the product to fruition."

Finally, building an environment of psychological safety where team members can be brutally honest requires that the leader be the cheerleader for team members' innovative behaviors (e.g., questioning, observing, networking, and experimenting) more than outcomes. Building psychological safety happens interaction by interaction, moment by moment, one-on-one as well as with the entire team. It involves being as excited about others' ideas as you are about your own. And sometimes, you might not even have the great ideas, as we discuss in the sidebar "Do You Have to Be an Innovator to Be a Great Leader of Innovation?" Research suggests that out of one hundred new products launched in the market, only about ten to twenty percent of them will succeed.[16] Failure is a common experience of teams that are trying to innovate. Thus, the leader must continually encourage and support those who try new ideas, even when they are not successful.

In the end, leaders need to make sure the collective knowledge of the team is effectively deployed to produce insights with impact. Arne Sorenson, CEO of Marriott International, emphasized the importance of creating an environment where new ideas can be brought up and successfully pursued. When he described why Marriott had bought Starwood Hotels and Resorts Worldwide,

Do You Have to Be an Innovator to Be a Great Leader of Innovation?

Can you be a great leader of innovation even if you aren't necessarily a great inventor yourself? Jeff Bezos, who sits at the top of our list of most innovative leaders, clearly is a good inventor and acknowledges his desire and penchant for innovating. "Well, that's something that, for whatever reason, I've been good at my whole life," Bezos told us. "I can't explain that I'm inventive; I come up with ideas. We could sit here and brainstorm, and I could help you fill this whiteboard in an hour with a hundred ideas. My favorite meeting is brainstorming. Really, if I have a week with no brainstorming meetings, I complain to my office staff. I'm like, 'Come on, guys, help me here,' because I love it so much."

But despite Bezos's natural talent for inventive ideas, at Amazon he preaches that you don't necessarily have to be a great inventor to be an effective leader of innovation. He uses a coaching analogy from sports: "You don't have to be the best basketball player in the world to be the best basketball coach . . . The football coach doesn't need to be able to throw, and a film director doesn't need to be able to act." But, he adds, "An inventor's mindset, I think, is incredibly important. I would say that the CEO of the company doesn't have to be the one who does that necessarily. I happen to be it, and that's my number one thing—inventing. But I don't think that would be essential for the CEO. I think the CEO would have to value it immensely, though, and find it in other people, and recognize it. So I hesitate to say that an innovative company needs to be led by an inventor, but it certainly needs to be led by somebody who makes that a gigantic priority."

he noted that a couple of Starwood's innovations helped tip the scales: the Heavenly Bed (an extremely comfortable bed covered entirely in clean linens rather than blankets) and the W Hotels Worldwide franchise. Ironically, the idea to reinvent the bed had come up much earlier at Marriott. But the idea never received the needed attention from leadership to mature. As a result, Marriott paid a great deal of money to later acquire it.

This unfortunate result would be unlikely to happen today under Sorenson's leadership. In our interview with Sorenson, he said, "My job is to make sure ideas like that get heard, that they come to the top, and that we do something about it. So we have been communicating to the organization, 'You have permission to innovate. We're going to reward you for innovating. We're not going to penalize you for mistakes, and we're going to find a way collectively to cut through the bureaucracy and allow those great ideas to be green-lighted and to be embraced.'" The organization has responded, and Marriott has successfully launched new brands in a crowded market such as EDITION, AC Hotels, and Moxy—in some cases disrupting some of the company's own existing brands. But Sorenson has green-lighted them anyway, saying, "We're much better off disrupting ourselves than having somebody else disrupt us; so let's embrace that."

Conclusion

Our examination of the world's most innovative leaders revealed that many ignited what we call the virtuous cycle of innovation leadership. It begins when a leader identifies an exciting and lofty vision that attracts others to the project, and this step ignites a reinforcing cycle of activities that increases the probability of successful innovation. As Weiner told us, "I define leadership as the ability to inspire people to achieve a shared objective. Managers tell people what to do. Leaders inspire people."

To set the virtuous cycle of innovation leadership in motion, you may need to win support for your organization to do something new. Obtaining this support may require that you build innovation capital at your organization. Not only can individuals build their personal innovation capital, but they can also take actions to develop their organization's innovation capital. Helping your organization build a reputation for innovation is often critical for launching innovation initiatives or important organizational transformations. In chapter 8, we describe how you can build your organizational innovation capital. You begin by developing organization-level innovation capabilities (bringing Silicon Valley inside) that are the foundation for innovation capital for your organization. We also examine how to transform or reposition your team or organization—when organizational innovation capital is low—to carefully build support with key supporters and stakeholders, thereby enhancing your firm's innovation capital.

See our website www.innovatorsdna.com/innovation-capital for additional resources on the topics covered in this chapter.

8

Innovation Capital as a Source of Organizational Competitive Advantage

In chapter 1, we discussed Amazon's battle with Walmart for dominance in retailing and observed that it's not a fair fight. While Walmart has to deliver consistent quarterly profits to shareholders or the company's stock price gets punished, Amazon has gotten away with delivering limited profit for two decades and then somehow has permission from stakeholders to pursue wild ideas like using drones to deliver products and suspending warehouses in the air with airships. Over this period, Amazon has launched dozens of businesses, including Amazon Prime, Amazon Fresh, Amazon Auctions, Amazon Video, Amazon Music, Amazon Publishing, Amazon Web Services, and devices like the Kindle, Fire Phone, and Echo. Many of these businesses were visible failures, and many were not even related to

Amazon's core retail business when they were launched. Skeptics could ask: What business does a consumer retail website have launching complex enterprise cloud services like Amazon Web Services or building hardware like the Kindle? Nonetheless, shareholders have supported, and rewarded, Amazon. Using a statistical analysis technique that isolates the returns to a stock because of an acquisition (the *event-study method*), we found that over the past ten years Amazon added, on average, almost $1 billion of market value with each acquisition, whereas each new Walmart acquisition did nothing to boost the company's stock price. Shareholders rewarded Amazon for doing new things, but Walmart was ignored or punished. Why?

The answer is innovation capital. Like individuals, organizations can acquire innovation capital. To illustrate, as reported in chapter 1, Amazon had almost seven times more mentions of innovations in major news publications than Walmart had (figure 8-1). Moreover, the articles describing the company as innovative do so with far greater detail and intensity. Not surprisingly, Amazon has been ranked number one (or in the top five) on numerous World's Most Innovative Company lists at *Forbes* and *Fast Company*. Moreover, Amazon's innovation capital is boosted by Jeff Bezos's personal innovation capital and the innovation capital of its other top leaders, such as Jeff Wilke, CEO of retailing; Andy Jassy, CEO of Amazon Web Services; and David Limp, head of devices. The collective reputation of Amazon leaders and employees as well as their social connections all contribute to Amazon's ability to garner the resources and support necessary to experiment and innovate. The bottom line: Amazon has an impressive reputation for innovation and has significant innovation capital. The advantages help explain why Amazon's market-to-book value ratio of 5.3 is much larger than Walmart's (1.6 multiple).

FIGURE 8-1

Amazon versus Walmart: differences in their reputation for innovation

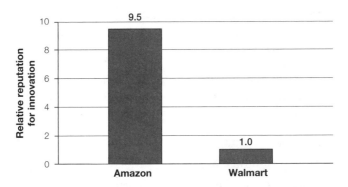

Source: Factiva database, 2013–2018.

Note: Reputation for innovation is measured as the number of media mentions of each company engaging in innovative initiatives from major news sources in the Factiva database and in Google searches.

The effect of innovation capital on the value of an organization isn't just an Amazon phenomenon. We studied the impact of a firm's reputation for innovation among the population of S&P 500 firms. We identified several factors that might influence a firm's media reputation for innovation. We then developed measures of a firm's innovation capability, such as investment in innovation (R&D intensity), innovation outputs (e.g., patents), quality of patents (e.g., patent citations), advertising spending, press releases, and even whether the CEO had a reputation for innovation. As you might predict, a company's actual innovation capability—its capability to create new knowledge and new products and services—strongly predicted both the value of the company and whether the company had a reputation for innovation. Similarly, the CEO or founder's reputation for innovation had a strong impact on the company's reputation for innovation and value. But even when accounting for the reputation of the CEO and the actual innovation capabilities of the firm, the firm's reputation for innovation had a separate and profound impact on the value of the firm (as reported in chapter 1). Companies in the top ten percent of the reputation for innovation scale had three times higher market-to-book valuations than did firms in the bottom 40 percent. In other words, innovation capabilities and innovation reputation matter a great deal to market performance.

Considering how an organization's innovation capital allows it to go after new ideas and ventures, we'll now explore how to build this type of capital. The best way to build a company's innovation capital is to increase its innovation output. We start with an in-depth analysis of how Amazon essentially replicates a Silicon Valley startup environment within a very large organization (Amazon had over 600,000 employees, 40 subsidiaries, and $177 billion in revenue in 2018).[1] This raw innovation capability allows Amazon to generate new innovations that build innovation capital. We then turn to the problem of acquiring the resources and support to transform a company from a less innovative organization to a more innovative one, and we look at how the bank ING has successfully navigated several transformations, building innovation capital over time.

Developing Innovation Capabilities in Your Organization

How has Amazon successfully launched so many new businesses? How has it absorbed many of its failures so gracefully? Visit the office of Dave Limp, Amazon's head of devices, and you may get a peek into a piece of corporate history: the original short documents drafted by an internal team in 2011 to propose the development of Alexa, the intelligent personal assistant Amazon launched in late 2014. Call it an electronic memento; Limp hasn't deleted it. And it's hardly the only memento he has stored. He can also call up dozens of other documents, amazingly similar in format, setting forth the initial visions for what would become blockbuster products and services.

And if you keep looking, you might catch a glimpse of the new proposals he's considering, again all taking the same form. Each consists of a one-page press release (for an offering that doesn't even exist and might never be commercialized); a six-page set of FAQs (frequently asked questions that customers can be anticipated to have about the offering, the straightforward answers, and sometimes a bit of additional descriptive material or even a mock-up or prototype) and a description of the expected customer response. (For details on these three parts, see the sidebar "Working Backward from the Launch.") More than a hundred of these ideas arrive in Limp's in-box every year. The same goes for leaders of other Amazon businesses, such as Wilke and Jassy. And these senior leaders see only a fraction of the total number being circulated through the company.

If you wonder how Amazon keeps up its torrid pace of launching new products and services, you're looking at the heart of it. The center of Amazon's renowned innovation prowess, *working backward*, takes its cue from Amazon's first leadership principle: "Customer obsession. Leaders start with the customer and work backward." Following that principle, these documents constitute a visualization mechanism. They force a person or team with an inventive idea to get very clear on the objective and to describe it through a written narrative in a way that others can also grasp the objective without ambiguity. If the idea wows its audience—a manager or group of managers in a position to allocate resources to develop it further—the idea receives startup funding, much as a startup does in Silicon Valley. If the idea doesn't wow its audience . . . well, the proposal hasn't necessarily failed. The "founders" of the document can revise it and pitch the updated idea to

Working Backward from the Launch

Amazon has institutionalized a working-backward process that includes three short documents that pitch the idea to leaders with resources:

1. **Press release** (one page). The press release announces something new and valuable with a name that target customers will understand. It communicates in a compelling way what the offering is and who will be well served by it. The press release evokes the problems that customers have been experiencing in the absence of such a solution, and makes clear how the new offering overcomes these difficulties. Like a real press release, it anticipates the kind of positive coverage that might appear in a media outlet impressed enough to share the news.

2. **FAQ list** (six pages). In the format of the familiar FAQ section, this document lays out details about the solution as they would be presented to customers starting to use the offering. To draft these questions and answers, a team has to put itself in the shoes of busy nonexpert users who

the same managers, or they could take it to any other manager with resources at Amazon.

Amazon: Replicating Silicon Valley
Inside an Established Company

Although Amazon isn't the only model of how to develop innovation capabilities, the company has been particularly success-are trying to solve a problem. The team must anticipate the issues customers might encounter. To help the teams draft these FAQs, Amazon provides prompts, including "What will customers be most disappointed about in version one of the offering?"

3. **A portrayal of the customer experience.** Additional material, sometimes including screen-display mock-ups or even rough prototypes, makes it easier to envision just how the customers will access and work with the new offering. The material might describe use cases, include code snippets, or describe how the product fits into broader processes or customer situations. At its best, this information tells a story about customers facing problems and having a better way to solve them.

The format creates a simple, standard interface for putting ideas in play. Once everyone becomes familiar with it, barriers to participation fall. Anyone in the ranks knows the process for proposing an idea. Wilke told us that well down into the organization, "these working-backward documents are written by individual contributors with a passion."

ful. It bears exploring how Amazon achieves this success. Bezos has consciously attempted to create an environment that replicates Silicon Valley, thereby creating a culture of entrepreneurship and innovation (see the sidebar "Amazon's Silicon Valley Model, in Brief," later in this chapter, for a quick overview of the approaches). "You need the scale and scope of a large company but with the heart and spirit of a startup company," Bezos told us. "And how do you do that? Well, you ask yourself, what are those characteristics of a startup company that make them effective?"

Amazon has attempted to replicate what it sees as several important ingredients of Silicon Valley:

- The entrepreneur or venture-capitalist funding process, in which an entrepreneur can pitch to multiple people to get funding for a new idea

- The speed of decision making possible within a small startup team

- The dispensing of additional resources dependent on hitting milestones that show the idea has promise to create significant value

- Tolerance for failure at a project and an individual level

Entrepreneur or Venture-Capitalist Funding: Multiple Paths to Yes

Most companies encourage their employees to pitch innovative ideas to corporate leaders. But pitching these ideas in most companies is constrained by a corporate hierarchy that tends to restrict and downgrade ideas from radical to incremental. Why? Bezos explains:

> A corporate hierarchy is an obstacle if you want to continue to be inventive. A corporate hierarchy is typically a path of gates. So let's say a junior executive comes up with a new idea that they want to try. They have to convince their boss, and their boss's boss, and their boss's boss's boss, and so on. And any no in that chain can kill the whole idea. Alternatively, think about the startup model that we were just mentioning. I go to Sand Hill Road [in Silicon Valley], I go to the first VC [venture capitalist]; they

say no. I go to the next VC. They say no. I can get nineteen
nos and one yes, and I'm in business. And so the VC model
is multiple paths to yes. The nineteen nos don't matter.
And so you need to also have multiple paths to yes inside
of a larger company. I'm a huge proponent of that. And
I often will disagree and commit, and I encourage other
people to do this. I'm like, "This idea doesn't make sense to
me." I'll be totally honest about it. And I'll give them all my
reasons. But I'll say, "Look, you're a high-judgment person.
Go try this." This is what multiple paths to yes means.

Amazon provides multiple paths to yes by allowing working-
backward documents to be presented to any leader who can provide seed funding for the idea. To proceed, you only need the yes
from that one leader. And the format creates a simple, standard
interface for putting ideas in play. Once everyone becomes familiar with it, barriers to participation fall. Anyone in the ranks
knows the process for proposing an idea.

Amazon also provides guidelines to help leaders decide
whether to fund proposals. First, the funding must be sufficient
to support a "single-threaded leader" for the project and a small
team. A single-threaded leader works on the project full time.
"We empower the single-threaded leader," Limp says, "to go off
and make great things." The term (coined and used exclusively at
Amazon, as far as we know) is a nod to programming and means
that the leader isn't expected to multitask. In Wilke's words, this
is "someone who wakes up and just worries about that thing."
That's "super important to how we invent," Limp insists, because
"the best way to fail at inventing something is by making it somebody's part-time job." The leader is then able to hire a team, usually beginning with one or two technical people—just enough
capacity to get started and begin building the thing.

Second, leaders with funding are taught the difference between two-way-door decisions (low risk) and one-way-door decisions (high risk), as described in chapter 6. "I'm totally happy with people saying yes and making two-way-door mistakes," Wilke says. Bezos believes that some decision makers are too timid because they mistake two-way doors for one-way doors. Wilke says that as a result, "we try to teach this distinction to everyone that can say yes."

Finally, Amazon uses some basic criteria that decision makers are taught to think about when they evaluate an idea. Does it have the potential to get big? An invention can be perfectly workable, but if you can't imagine it ever becoming a large-scale success, the idea is probably not worth the effort. Could we really manage to build it? Even without existing capabilities in-house, it should be clear that Amazon has a chance building the skills necessary for success. And the most important criterion of all: Would customers love it?

Making Fast Decisions Like a Startup Team

Besides replicating a startup funding process by creating multiple paths to yes, Amazon also attempts to imitate other basic characteristics of a startup team. As Amazon paints it, a startup is small and dedicated, focuses on meeting specific milestones (as stipulated with the funding agreement), and makes fast decisions because it is empowered. Bezos thinks that there are many advantages to small teams, but "number one is velocity"—the speed of decision making. "Startup companies make decisions very quickly," says Bezos. "There are very small numbers of people that need to be informed, and convinced, and all of those things. So the decision making process can be very streamlined." The focus and speed of decision making allows the team to rapidly test and validate whether the idea has merit. For this reason, Amazon mandates the now-famous "two-pizza team," meaning that no project should begin with a team larger than you can feed with two pizzas.

Dispensing Resources in Tranches Based on Milestones

In the corporate world, leaders typically raise and receive the full budget for a new project. But in the startup world, if an investor agrees to give you $5 million, he or she doesn't write a check for $5 million. Instead the investor gives you a small tranche—the French word for slice—to prove out a particular assumption or uncertainty. Likewise, at Amazon, teams don't receive budget-cycle funding but receive tranches based on the milestones they achieve.

As the team succeeds at demonstrating that the idea has merit, it receives greater funding to pursue the idea. And the idea only has merit if customers love the solution. "The fate of a startup is whether customers are interested in the product that they produce," says Wilke. "The customers decide. That's the same for every single-threaded team at Amazon." If the team can't get customers to love the invention, then funding is pulled and the team's resources are allocated to other projects.

Tolerating Failure at the Project and Individual Level

Finally, Amazon also replicates Silicon Valley by tolerating failure and rewarding success. In Silicon Valley, people understand that any serial entrepreneur has had failures. If a project initiative ends up falling short, the project leader doesn't suffer from that failure. "Any of us who have built things that operate for a while with any great success know that you don't usually get it right in the first iteration," Jassy notes. "It usually takes time, iterations, listening to customers, and building to have something that succeeds." And certainly, Amazon has had its share of ideas that didn't work, including Amazon Auctions, Amazon Local, and the visible Fire Phone flameout. The failure that is valued at Amazon is the kind that comes when someone takes the initiative to pursue something that is far from a sure thing. Wilke took pains to stress this point: "I've said this a couple of times and in different ways, but perhaps not emphatically enough: We work really hard to create an environment where it is completely accepted to take a risk, try hard, and fail." Of course, those who do succeed receive the financial rewards that go with promotions (and that come by owning Amazon's fast-appreciating stock) and other leadership opportunities. Moreover, "they get rewarded by being part of a growing, vibrant, innovative company," Wilke says.

Lessons Learned: More At Bats, More Home Runs, More Innovation Capital

Bezos understands that innovation is a numbers game, by which most attempts end up going nowhere but are redeemed by the few projects that pay off big. Quantity tends to yield quality. The analogy that comes to mind is the baseball player who would never expect to hit every ball out of the park, but still can become a home-run star. The key is to have a lot of at bats—repeatedly stepping up to the plate and learning with every pitch.

Amazon has created an environment with very high throughput of inventive ideas. It enjoys that extraordinary number of at bats because it achieves high engagement by employees through the working-backward process. The plethora of ideas is especially important to Bezos because the game of business differs from baseball on one important dimension: "Everybody knows if you swing for the fences, you hit more home runs, but you also

Amazon's Silicon Valley Model, in Brief

1. **Replicating the Silicon Valley entrepreneur or venture-capitalist funding process:** Amazon provides multiple paths to yes by allowing numerous leaders to provide seed funding for a new product, service, or process idea. The working-backward template creates a simple, standard interface for putting ideas in play. The company uses several criteria to evaluate an idea: Does it have the potential to get big? Could we really manage to build it? Would customers love it?

2. **Replicating the speed of decision making of a startup team:** Small two-pizza startup teams are empowered to pursue objectives to test and validate the idea. These teams are allowed to make fast decisions just like a typical startup.

3. **Dispensing resources in tranches based on milestones:** Startup teams typically don't receive budget-cycle funding but receive funds in tranches based on the milestones they achieve. But Amazon leaders have a long-term view and will continue providing funding if they believe there is a big opportunity.

4. **Tolerating failure at the project and individual level:** Individuals who take risk and fail are respected. Individuals who succeed are rewarded. Failure is accepted as part of doing new things by focusing on what you learned from the experience.

strike out more," he says. "But with baseball, no matter how well you connect with the ball, you can still only get four runs. Your success is capped at four runs. But in business, every once in a while, you step up to the plate and you hit the ball so hard you get a thousand runs. When you have that kind of asymmetric payoff, where one at bat can get you a thousand runs, it encourages you to experiment more."[2]

Amazon's innovation record speaks for itself. At Amazon's inception, Bezos announced it was "day one" for the business and started selling books via the web. By 2002, Amazon was the world's biggest online store, with revenues growing more than 50 percent per year. Over the next sixteen years, Bezos and his team have launched a dizzying array of new products and services to boost retail sales to consumers, including Fulfillment by Amazon; Amazon Auctions (an eBay-like auction site); Amazon Local (a Groupon-like service); Amazon Flex (a delivery service that uses independent businesses to provide two-hour delivery of Prime Now products and restaurant deliveries like Uber Eats); Amazon Fresh; and, perhaps most importantly, Amazon Prime. But Amazon has moved far beyond being just an internet retailer. It has entered the electronic devices business, with its Kindle, Kindle Fire (tablet), Fire Phone, Fire TV, dash buttons, and most recently Alexa and Echo.

Moving beyond consumer retailing, Amazon has entered into business services with Amazon Web Services (an on-demand cloud computing platform) and Amazon Mechanical Turk (giving businesses access to an on-demand scalable workforce for human intelligence tasks). And now Amazon has added Amazon Music, Amazon Video, Amazon Publishing, Amazon Home Services (for things like iPhone repair at home). The company now includes brick-and-mortar retail offerings such as Amazon Books, Amazon's Whole Foods Market, and Amazon Go (a new kind of store with no checkout required; shoppers simply use an app to enter the store, take the products they want, and leave with them as the goods are automatically scanned).

As the company's types of customers keep expanding and the technologies it uses keep advancing, Amazon will never lack for problems to address. And with its customer-obsessed working backward, it will continue to run hundreds of new experiments each year to find the products and services that solve customer problems. These days, it seems every company out there is looking over its shoulder, sizing up Amazon as a competitor.

Remarkably, none of the capabilities that drive Amazon's innovation capital are kept under wraps. In the recipe for managing, there is no secret sauce. Every time Bezos writes a shareholder letter or grants an interview, he takes the opportunity to give away his best thinking on how to keep a company inventing new solutions for customers. You might call it open-source-code management. It's almost as if Bezos wishes every company were full of customer-obsessed inventors. We're betting he probably does. After all, if you truly dedicated yourself to being the most customer-centric company on earth, isn't that what you would do?

Developing Innovation Capital in Your Organization

Most of us don't work for Amazon. But we can learn principles from how it has successfully built its innovation prowess, and we can take the first steps to building innovation capabilities within our own organizations. But to take that first step, we may need to win resources and support for transformational solutions from key stakeholders. This challenge can be particularly difficult in public companies whose shareholders and other key stakeholders tend to be conservative. But senior executives at companies that need a strategic reorientation, including public companies with long histories and established shareholder bases, can win support to do new things. Doing so, however, requires a thoughtful approach to both transformation and innovation capital.

For more information on how to think about transformation, we recommend *Leading Transformation* (Harvard Business Review Press, 2018). We will now use a case study of ING Group to explore how an organization builds innovation capital. ING, currently a top-thirty global bank operating in forty countries, has won support for three major strategic transformations. Under the leadership of CEO Ralph Hamers, ING has successfully evolved from a bancassurance (combination bank and insurance) company to a bank, then from a traditional bank to a digital bank, and finally from a digital bank to a technology platforms company. The ING journey provides lessons on how to build the innovation capital needed to do new things.

ING: Winning Support for Three Transformations

How did ING accomplish three major transformations? To lead each transformation, Hamers ignited the virtuous innovation leadership cycle. As described in chapter 7, this cycle begins with the vision, which can be broken down further into strategic direction (or vectors of search), and then made even more granular with stretch goals.

To determine the vision, Hamers went back to the original values of the company: "I went back to our DNA of what had made ING successful over a century," Hamers recalls. "There were two things: innovation . . . and simplicity, or low-entry barriers to banking. I just had to touch it to activate it and everyone recognized it. It was not a new story that some consultant made up."

Using these fundamental elements, Hamers crafted a story that articulated the grand vision of the bank of the future, the strategic direction, and the stretch goals the company would try to achieve.

He told us, "A good story does tell the horizon where you are going [the vision], but can be translated into milestones for a period of up to three or four years [strategic direction], which can be made even more concrete in examples [stretch goals] that can be delivered."

Although Hamers's vision ignited the innovation leadership cycle we described earlier, and helped ING make these transformations internally, Hamers still had to win support from shareholders to make these major changes. How did he go about winning the support? For the first transformation, from insurance company to traditional bank, Hamers recounted actively working to reshape shareholder expectations: "You have to actively reposition your company with shareholders." He elaborates:

> You need a new set of shareholders to make the transformation. Your existing shareholders bought your stock with certain expectations. Given the fact that you are going through a transformation, you have to take your shareholders along in that transformation with you. To begin, you need different coverage with different analysts. The first transformation required transitioning from insurance analysts to banking analysts, because they are all specialized. If banking analysts are covering you, then banking funds will buy you. Either growth or dividend funds will buy your stock.

Although this repositioning sounds easy, when we asked Hamers how he managed to convince analysts, he gave a hearty laugh and explained: "It required a lot of communication, a lot of traveling and presenting. I had to be out telling the story and repeatedly interacting with analysts." Moreover, shareholders don't change quickly; they take time to adjust to the new vision. Hamers says, "You need to be patient with your shareholders. They won't be convinced in just two quarters. You have to keep telling the story and making progress."

Hamers emphasizes that he also works hard to tell the ING story to other stakeholders and the broader community that extends well beyond active shareholders. For example, he and his team attended conferences, such as Money 20/20, to talk about the bank of the future. They also attended fintech events focused on startups transforming the industry. "In the early days, ING would be the only traditional bank at a fintech conference," Hamers recalls.

When asked why he spent precious time with non-shareholders, Hamers speaks of the value of telling ING's vision to the broader world as part of building the company's innovation capital: "You have to go to other places to tell your story. You have to get others talking about you . . . get a buzz going. Not just the financial newspapers, but get the *Economist* talking about you and saying, 'ING is really making a difference, really changing the industry.'"

In addition to communication, Hamers also changed how the company reported progress and performance. For the first transition, from insurance company to bank, ING shifted from reporting financial metrics alone to also reporting nonfinancial results. It also increased the frequency of reporting from annually to quarterly. But it did so to increase its ability to show progress on the transformation, not to increase scrutiny on the financials. "Every quarter," Hamers says, "we emphasized the nonfinancial results, for example, units sold, capital generated, and other measures of progress in our transformation. The financials came second." Figure 8-2 outlines the cycle of setting a new vision and reporting on new metrics openly.

For the second transformation, from traditional bank to digital bank (a change that Hamers suggested was more ambiguous than the prior one), Hamers says that ING had to "go even deeper" in how it reported nonfinancial metrics. Hamers first reported nonfinancial metrics showing progress on the transformation. For example, he reported how quickly the company was acquir-

FIGURE 8-2

ING's cycle of openly transforming its vision for maximum innovation capital

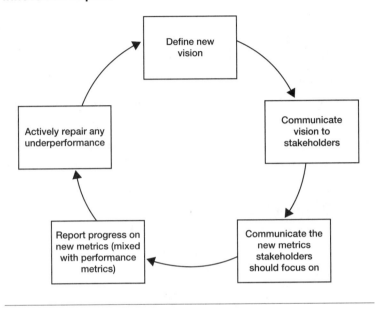

ing new customers and was cross-selling products (e.g., savings customers were becoming mortgage customers); he reported on net promoter scores and the success of ING's innovations. "When we report results," he says, "we never report financial metrics at the beginning. Instead, you have to tell a strong story and show how you are progressing. You have to teach your shareholders what metrics to pay attention to, and then you have to deliver on those metrics. Then and only then, after reporting on the non-financial metrics, did we report on the financial metrics."[3]

When we asked Hamers if the shareholders let him get away with growth metrics alone, he admitted that he always blends the metrics he wants investors to pay attention to with more-familiar metrics: "When I talk about platforms, I also emphasize the efficiency gains. That helps shareholders get on board and to understand it. And more generally, I always mix showing progress on traditional financial metrics, like return on equity, or efficiency, with our growth metrics." Using the analogy of a large ship, Hamers explains: "You can't turn a ship unless you have some speed. First you need speed, then you can set direction. For us in the early days, the cost-reductions provided the speed."

Finally, Hamers emphasizes that if you fail to deliver on the transformation metrics you have set out, you have to admit the misstep and address it: "You have to repair it. You have to admit that you failed to deliver and tell a new story or you won't be credible." As part of his transparency policy, Hamers makes a point of actively reporting on the company's failures. This practice arises from a deeper philosophy about learning from failure, he says:

> At ING, we have areas where failure is utterly unacceptable, especially when regulation and compliance are involved. Over time, we had developed a very risk-averse culture. But if you want to create the future, you are going to make mistakes. No one wants to make a mistake with regulation and compliance, but when it comes to the other parts of the business, if you want to fail fast, you have to first convince people internally that it's okay to make mistakes, as long as something can be learned from those mistakes. Then you have to celebrate it internally. Otherwise, people won't believe you. So we started by telling a story of why we needed to try and be okay with mistakes. Then we had to actually celebrate mistakes internally. But we also reported our mistakes externally. We explain to shareholders that we invested, we tried, but we failed. But we emphasize that we learned in eighteen months what a competitor might have spent twenty million and five years to understand. We emphasize how we are learning faster than our competitors about how to create the company of the future.

Today, ING is in the middle of another major transition, from digital bank to a technology platforms company (think Google or Amazon). The vision is to revolutionize the industry by developing the platform architecture to deliver both ING's own banking products and those of partners and even competitors. The vision is audacious and, if it plays out, could represent a huge opportunity to become the Amazon of banking. To make the transition, Hamers has to both educate shareholders about the value of platforms and convince them that ING can do it. "If I talk about a platform future," he says, "and I lose half the audience in terms of talking about platforms and platform economics, I go back to explaining to them what it entails to be a platform, what the power of a platform is, and why it is so valuable. I have to compare the opportunity to other platforms, like Amazon or Uber." With this explanation, Hamers is clearly employing the impression-amplifier technique of anchoring and using relevant analogies. He continues: "Then I show them what kind of platform ING could be and show them actual products we have in the market or actual apps . . . and what they do." He says that after making the new offerings tangible in this way (materializing them), the shareholders "come back to understand [that] this is what he means and how it works."

ING's Lessons for Strategic Transformations and Building Innovation Capital

There are several important lessons in the ING case study about how to build innovation capital for organizations that can be applied by others:

1. Build a credible reputation for innovation, and support the reputation with real capabilities.

2. Actively reshape your shareholder base to go along with you on your journey.

3. Communicate your vision externally, and deliver both growth and traditional metrics.

ING's approach isn't the only approach for building organizational innovation capital; not all companies transform themselves the same way (see the sidebar "Using the Leader's Reputation: Another Route to Organization Innovation Capital"). For example, some companies found sources of momentum in secret, successful innovations that they could show stakeholders, or they found other performance metrics, such as performance in a cost-cutting transformation, as evidence that they could deliver on a future innovation agenda. In contrast, less successful companies trumpeted their success before the innovations they were developing had a chance to mature, which often led to unwanted scrutiny and the loss of innovation capital if they could not deliver.

Moreover, different leaders adopted different approaches for communicating with shareholders. For example, Paul Polman, former CEO of Unilever, told us that he aggressively seeks out long-term shareholders: "If you want investors who care about social responsibility or about international development or whatever it is, then you have to go out and find them. You have to present to those funds that invest in that area, to the conferences that address those areas, and to analysts who cover those areas." Almost all our interviewees emphasized actively reshaping the shareholder base as part of winning permission to pursue new ideas. They also emphasized patience in doing so.

Finally, the leaders we interviewed said that you have to educate your stakeholders about which metrics to pay attention to. But then you have to deliver on those metrics. Part of meeting the standards you've set usually involved blending growth metrics with more familiar performance metrics. Admittedly it is a tough

Using the Leader's Reputation: Another Route to Organization Innovation Capital

An alternative approach to winning permission and support is to exploit the innovation capital of a leader. For example, earlier in this book, we told the story of how David Bradford networked his way to meet Apple cofounder Steve Wozniak at a conference to enlist his help with the startup Fusion-io. Fusion-io had developed some cutting-edge storage technology, but Wozniak's involvement created visibility for the company within the tech community. Shortly after Wozniak joined as chief scientist, Fusion-io was chosen by *Red Herring* magazine as one of the top one hundred startups in February 2009. Bradford's success connecting with Wozniak not only helped his own career (bringing Wozniak to the advisory board made Bradford a more attractive CEO candidate) but also allowed the company to borrow from Wozniak's reputation to gain needed visibility. Naturally, this association with Wozniak built Fusion-io's innovation capital.

Similarly, when Sterling Anderson, former Tesla Autopilot program director; Chris Urmson, former head of Google's self-driving car project; and Drew Bagnell, former head of self-driving cars at Uber, teamed up to form Aurora Innovation, the self-driving car startup had instant credibility. On recruiting engineers to the startup, Kirsten Korosec of *Fortune* magazine writes, "Aurora can afford to be picky. The company's three cofounders are considered to be some of the best minds in self-driving cars."[4] The pedigree of the three founders has also attracted customers. "Aurora's pedigree and technology have attracted prominent partners," Korosec writes. "In January, the company announced collaborations

(*continued*)

with Volkswagen Group and Hyundai—two of the world's largest automakers—to accelerate the development of fully autonomous vehicles for the masses."

Likewise, when Yahoo recruited Google's Marissa Mayer to be CEO, the company was clearly hoping it could leverage Mayer's Google experience and her reputation for innovation. Mayer was known to be great with the press and was well liked by the media. Google even reportedly had a group of PR people devoted to promoting her career.[5] Yahoo hoped that her reputation for innovation would allow her to recruit top engineers to the company and that her reputation might have a halo effect on the company. In fact, one Yahoo employee substituted Mayer's face for Barack Obama's on Obama's iconic "Hope" poster. While Mayer was unable to turn around a sinking ship (Yahoo was eventually sold to Verizon), her innovation capital clearly brought attention to Yahoo.

In summary, one way to bring an organization's innovation capital up to speed quickly is to bring in leaders who have already developed a high level of innovation capital themselves.

challenge to convince your stakeholders to change with you, but one well worth the rewards if you can bear them out.

Walmart versus Amazon Revisited: Building Innovation Capital from a Weak Position

Let's return to Walmart's dilemma in competing with Amazon. Does Walmart have a chance against Amazon, especially given how constrained the big-box retailer is by shareholders? It does! But even getting that chance required some dramatic moves. As described earlier, in 2015 Walmart announced that it was lowering profit expectations to reinvest in store improvements and innovation. Through an insider interview, we learned the story behind the announcement. In essence, Walmart realized that if it wanted to have a chance against Amazon, it needed to find a way to carve out the resources to pursue innovation, particularly in the online retail space. But the hour was late—Amazon had already become dominant in so many categories. Many observers had already written Walmart off as a brick-and-mortar dinosaur doomed for extinction. In desperation, the executive team adopted what might be called a fall-on-the-sword approach. The tactic included the 2015 announcement about the retailer's reinvestment in future innovation. The CFO (who was going to retire anyway) took the blame as a sacrificial scapegoat, arguing that Walmart had underinvested in the future. The stock price plummeted 30 percent while the CEO and CFO were speaking (figure 8-3).

Although the drop in stock price created pressure on the one hand, the announcement that Walmart would reduce profits to invest in innovation carved out resources to do new things in the online space. For example, Walmart acquired successful e-commerce startup Jet for $3.3 billion in 2016 and appointed Jet's founder, Marc Lore, head of e-commerce. Walmart has arguably boosted its innovation reputation through the acquisition, leveraging Jet and Lore's innovation capital to win support for its e-commerce initiatives. Walmart then expanded into other e-commerce niches, including ModCloth, Moosejaw, and Bonobos. Although small, some of these acquisitions, particularly Bonobos, have played a central role in redefining e-commerce through a new "phygital" experience—a hybrid of small physical stores that create positive experiences for customers trying products and then deliver through an e-commerce back end.[6] Walmart

FIGURE 8-3

Amazon versus Walmart: average change in company market value in response to acquisition announcements

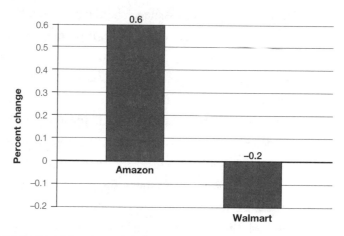

Source: Eventus database for event studies.

Note: Percent change is the average cumulative abnormal stock market response to announcements of all acquisitions above $100 million after 2005.

has borrowed these lessons both to improve its e-commerce position and to explore how to use its physical retail assets to its advantage. As it did so, e-commerce at Walmart exploded, growing 60 percent year over year. Then Walmart acquired a majority stake in Flipkart, India's largest online retailer, in the largest e-commerce deal to date.

Although Walmart clearly lags Amazon in e-commerce and in innovation capital, by 2018 many expert observers had suggested that Walmart at least had a fighting chance against Amazon, whereas before, it had had none. How the final battle plays out has yet to be determined. But by the start of 2018, not only had Walmart's stock price recovered from its 2015 trough but it had also reached an almost 50 percent premium over the price before the company had made the dramatic announcement.

Conclusion

We have argued that organizations, like individuals, can also develop innovation capital. This capital allows organizations to win the resources and support to pursue new ideas just as much as individuals can use innovation capital. There is no one way to do it right. You could actively reposition the company, as Ralph Hamers did with ING. Or you could work under the radar to deliver results that later turn into innovation capital, as Andrew Kvålseth did at DTAC (see chapter 6). A company could also announce a major reorientation or repositioning (fall on the sword), as Walmart did, or start with a grand vision that wins innovation capital from the beginning, as Tesla and Amazon did. It may also even be possible to develop a great reputation as an executor and transform that reputation into innovation capital to do new things.

Regardless of the particular approach, in each case, winning resources and support requires careful attention to building innovation capital with your stakeholders, whether they be investors or employees. In many ways, firms applied the same model we described for individuals to develop innovation capital. Although big companies may not have personal human capital, social capital, or reputation capital, they still can develop innovation capabilities and create a reputation for innovation.

In many ways, when Hamers describes the transformation at ING, he talks in organizational terms about building the organizational equivalent of human capital (i.e., organizational innovation capabilities); social capital (positioning ING among the ecosystem of fintech companies and the larger conversation about the future of banking); and reputation capital (delivering consistently and honestly on innovation initiatives). But even more importantly, Hamers applied the impression amplifiers described in chapters 5 and 6. For example, he worked aggressively to *broadcast* ING's vision and successes. He also worked to *materialize* the vision, showing off specific apps the company had already built to demonstrate the potential for ING as a platform company in the future. Hamers thoughtfully used *comparing*, by likening ING to Amazon and Uber. He also used *storytelling* with stakeholders and employees to help them understand the vision for the company.

In short, the model described in this book applies not only to people but also to organizations. The techniques only need to be modified appropriately for what these forces mean in an organizational context and for the different kinds of audiences an organization faces. Companies that pay attention to their innovation capital create a virtuous cycle that allows them to win more resources and support to pursue new ideas, which in turn increase the firms' ability to win yet more resources and support. But like individuals seeking innovation capital, companies aren't born with this kind of capital; it is accrued over time. We have shared how several leaders of established companies, including public companies, purposely built their innovation capital using the ideas described in this book. Their example provides hope that other organizations can do it as well. Innovation capital isn't built overnight. Instead it requires patience, investment, and real capability development. But leaders can transform the future of their organization, and the value of their company, by investing in innovation capital.

Conclusion: Concrete Steps for Putting It All Together

In chapter 1, we introduced innovation capital by examining the lives of Thomas Edison and Nikola Tesla, two extraordinary inventors who experienced very different outcomes with regard to commercializing innovations with impact. Their example illustrates the differences between a great inventor and a great innovator. Innovative leaders need some creative chops like those of inventors, but they also need the ability to win resources and support for their ideas by building and utilizing innovation capital. In this conclusion, we provide some advice on how to get started right away building your innovation capital. Before we do, however, we acknowledge the importance of not just innovation capital, but also a broad base of skills to commercialize innovation. "I think to drive innovation you have to do both flag planting and you have to do road building," Adobe CEO

Shantanu Narayen (number seven on our list) told us. "I think that what has become clearer to me as we've grown the company is the importance of both of these activities. There is a whole set of employees that really get motivated and excited about what's the next hill to climb. What's the vision for where we are planting the next flag? But you also have to build the road toward that next hill. Successful leadership requires both the vision setting and the execution." One thing that is clear from our research: creativity is not enough.

Tinker Hatfield, a design legend at Nike, having designed the Air Jordan, the first cross-trainer shoes, and the Nike HTM Flyknit Racer, made this observation of CEO Mark Parker: "I fall to pieces when the numbers start flying, but he is able to decipher all those things as a businessman and a marketing person and a merchandiser, yet he is equally adept at talking about design."[1] Parker, who started his career in R&D and design at Nike and designed the Flyknit Racer with Hatfield, acknowledges:

> Ideas are easy in many ways, and there's no shortage of great ideas. It's the ability to bring those to life and at scale at some point that becomes important. You need to be able to communicate with a range of people on a team, from those who are wildly creative, to pragmatic engineering problem solvers, and then eventually those in finance and manufacturing and supply chain and merchandising and all the other elements of business . . . I think the ability to bridge the gap between right brain and left brain, to live in both worlds, to get them to understand each other, to talk to each other, is critical.

One reason Parker is an effective leader of innovation is his curiosity. He is curious not only about the challenges of developing creative product designs at Nike but also about the challenges associated with engineering, manufacturing, marketing, and selling products. He is eager to develop expertise in a wide range of areas, and this greater breadth of experience is valuable in helping him spot opportunities and problems. It also helps him develop a broader network of relationships with a greater range of resources. In turn, his wide network and the accompanying resources help him build his innovation capital, which, in a virtuous cycle, helps him secure more resources to pursue new ideas.

If you really want to have impact as a leader of innovation, you must start now building the broad skill set required to succeed. If you are currently only engaged in the idea generation phase of innovation, you need to develop some knowledge and expertise in all the business fundamentals that are relevant to successful implementation of an idea (see the sidebar "How Innovative Leaders Differ from Inventors and Typical Leaders"). If acquiring business knowledge simply doesn't interest you, then you might just make peace with being an inventor or an idea person. If this is the case, recognize that either you need to find someone to complement you or your ideas may not have as much impact as they otherwise could. Many talented innovators realize the need for complementary execution skills in other arenas and wisely find others to provide that balance. There's nothing wrong with that. Many founders of companies and individuals in R&D, design, marketing, and other fields just enjoy the creation aspect of innovation. But building innovation capital and being an innovative leader requires broader interests and a broader skill set. Creativity is not enough.

How Innovative Leaders Differ from Inventors and Typical Leaders

Our research on a sample of the world's most innovative leaders confirms that innovative leaders have a broader skill set than do inventors. In particular, they engage in activities and behaviors that help them excel at both innovation and execution—they have more of a balance between imagination and pragmatism. In fact, our Innovator's DNA assessment (which one of us [Jeff] developed with coauthors when writing *The Innovator's DNA;* it can be accessed at the website www.innovatorsdna.com/innovation capital) compares an individual's propensity to engage in innovation (the discovery skills of questioning, observing, networking and experimenting) and execution (the delivery skills of organizing, analyzing, detailed implementing, and self-disciplined executing). We see that innovative leaders are strong at both innovation and execution. They have a balanced portfolio of skills that is weighted somewhat toward innovation. This distribution of skills differs from that of product inventors, whose skill set is heavily weighted toward innovation (see the figure). The assessment also sheds light on the difference between CEOs leading innovative companies (firms consistently ranked in the top one hundred of the *Forbes* World's Most Innovative Companies list) and executives leading more-typical companies (those not on the *Forbes* list). Leaders of innovative companies have skills and expertise that is more strongly weighted toward innovation than do typical CEOs, whose skills are more strongly weighted toward execution.

The skill set of a great leader of innovation differs from that of both a creative inventor and a typical leader. Effective leaders of innovation have a broader skill set and stronger execution skills than inventors do. They are better equipped to see through all the steps—all the things that need to be done—to ensure that a creative idea is implemented in a way that creates value for customers or internal users. And compared with typical leaders, they have the desire and willingness to generate and pursue novel ideas that have high risk, but also high potential returns.

Innovative leaders have a balance of innovation and execution skills

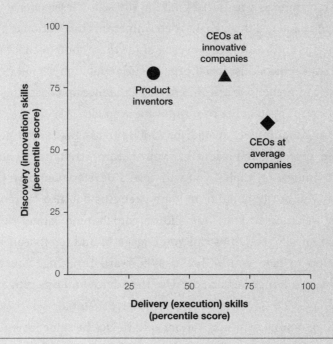

Getting Started

So how do you get started building the skill set and innovation capital needed to propel your career forward as an effective leader of innovation? We've shared many ideas in this book about how to build your innovation capital and how to be a better leader of innovation. So you might be wondering, where do I start? Let us propose the following first steps.

Step 1: Self-Assess

We recommend you start by taking the self-assessments at the end of chapters 2 through 4 to determine your innovation capital strengths and weaknesses on each of the three components: your human capital skills; social capital; and reputation capital (for a more comprehensive assessment with guidance and coaching, go to www.innovatorsdna.com/innovationcapital).

Unlike some assessments, for which you can take a strengths-based approach and just utilize your natural strengths, to build your innovation capital you will need a development plan that helps you not only build on your strengths but also overcome your weaknesses. Start by building your human capital skills. What specific activities can you engage in and habits can you develop to help you be better at forward thinking? Creative problem solving? Persuasion? Use the advice and tips provided in chapter 2 (and for more comprehensive materials, go to www .innovatorsdna.com/innovationcapital). Do the same for building your social connections with individuals in several prized categories: innovators and entrepreneurs, organizational leaders, financial benefactors, influencers, and customers. Develop a plan to build new connections, both strong and weak ties, to the social network category (or categories) that you think will provide the most resources for any new initiatives you envision. But your attempts to build relationships *must be genuine*. Remember the norm of reciprocity as described in chapter 3: you must give in order to receive. Set a goal for what you want your social network to look like one year from now, and work to meet that goal.

The last component for assessment is your reputation for innovation. What are you currently known for, and what do you want to be known for? If you want to be known for innovation, you need to look for opportunities to do your tasks creatively. Being known as an innovator means you constantly challenge the status quo and suggest novel ways of getting things done. Also, look for opportunities to work for innovative leaders or on innovative projects.

Step 2: Join an Innovation Project, or Take on a Risky, Broadening Assignment

The second step in building your innovation capital is to find and join (perhaps volunteer for) an innovation project. Or take on a new, risky assignment that will build your skill set and network of contacts. When we asked Steve Easterbrook, CEO of McDonald's, what advice he had for business professionals with aspirations to be innovative leaders, he commented, "I'd start by suggesting you build a track record that reflects the sort of leader you want to be. And the sooner you set out that way, the better. I would encourage taking risks in your career. When in doubt, say yes. Taking on new, challenging assignments gives you the opportunity to be noticed."

Easterbrook then described how, early in his career, he was trained as an accountant at Price Waterhouse and joined McDonald's in a functional role as a financial reporting manager in London. The job was secure, comfortable, and easy. But when

McDonald's asked for volunteers from the various functional areas to try their hand at an operational role, Easterbrook raised his hand. "At the time, I was thirty years old, and we were about to have our first child," Easterbrook says. "I moved from a very secure, stable, predictable lifestyle to one where I had to learn the realities of operating a business. I went through all the training courses and became an assistant manager and a manager, working from early mornings to closing at two a.m., working weekends and holidays. There were no guaranteed promotions or opportunities coming out of that experience. But it helped give me a foundation for how our business operates." The lesson: be willing to take risks with the assignments and projects you take on. Choose opportunities that will broaden your skill set and get you noticed.

Later in his career, Easterbrook volunteered to serve as a visiting fellow at the Oxford University Centre for Corporate Reputation. This experience helped him develop knowledge and expertise in corporate reputations; in turn, the additional expertise prepared and positioned him to be selected as McDonald's chief brand officer (five years later). His position as chief brand officer broadened his experience even more, further preparing him for the CEO seat at McDonald's.

But you don't have to change positions or accept new assignments to take your next step in building innovation capital. Easterbrook says young people get noticed when they "get the job done but do it more effectively, or quicker, or creatively than just doing their jobs." So even if you currently have what might seem to be a predictable or even boring job, you can get noticed if you can figure out a way to do it better—quicker, with fewer resources, more creatively. Being a scrappy innovator with every assignment can be the starting point for building your innovation capital.

Step 3: Initiate an Innovation Project

Once you have some experience working on an innovation project (and hopefully under an innovative leader who can be a mentor), it's time for you to initiate your own innovation. What does your organization need (in terms of process, product, service, or internal initiatives) that it doesn't have today? What frustrates you as a member of your organization? Use your forward-thinking skills to identify emerging problems or opportunities related to current trends and technologies. Perhaps you could organize an internal summit or external conference on a key issue that you think will influence the future. How about a new process to speed work flow? Perhaps you could help your organization with a digital transformation initiative or activity. Or you could launch a product or service that is complementary to the ones offered by your organization. It doesn't have to be just your idea. Search both inside and outside your current organization for ideas and opportunities, and collaborate with others on proposing your initiative.

Once you have identified the initiative you would like to propose, identify the stakeholders with the resources that might be important to launching your innovation project. Think of each sponsor or stakeholder as your customer—the sponsor is buying your project, and you need to sell the individual on it. Think about how you can employ your social connections, your reputation, and the impression amplifiers to convince sponsors to support your project. Start with the resource holder whom you think you have the best chance of convincing (even if it's not the final decision maker within an organization). Consider for a moment, what are that person's motivations? How could you help the individual achieve his or her goals with your efforts? Then create a campaign to convince that one person to support your initiative. Once you get that key person on board with your initiative, you can leverage the endorsement to sequentially convince others to support your initiative. This sequential approach is sometimes referred to as creating a bowling-pin social-network map of key resource holders; when you knock the first pins (sponsors) over, they help you knock the rest of the pins over. You may want to convince five or ten people who know the key resource holder and have influence on him or her to support the initiative before you approach the key person. As you convince the less important sponsors, you will learn how to refine your pitch. In this way, you build a coalition of support and endorsements that may be critical when you finally try to convince the key resource holder to support your initiative.

Finally, as you launch your project, think about how you could use the virtuous cycle of innovation leadership to your advantage. Even though you may not have the reins of a company, you can still apply the ideas behind the cycle to your project. For example, frame your project initiative to be as interesting, exciting, and lofty as possible to attract talented individuals to help make your project a reality. Use this lofty vision to start attracting talented people to your project, and from there, work to follow the innovation leadership cycle described in chapter 7. It's time to be a founder. You can do it. Even if you fail, if you operate openly and honestly, it can still build your innovation capital.

You Can Do This: Have Ambition and Dream Bigger

None of the innovative leaders we interviewed expected to have the success that they have had. Jeff Bezos, Elon Musk, Indra Nooyi, Satya Nadella, Marc Benioff, Shantanu Narayen, Mark Parker, Arne Sorenson, and the other successful leaders we studied started out just like the rest of us. But they proactively engaged in building their innovation-specific human capital skills (forward thinking, creative problem solving, and persuasion) and their social connections (willingness to reach out to their weak ties), and they gradually built their track record for innovation. The same can be said of the "everyday" innovative leaders we studied: Mary Lombardo, Kyle Nel, Gavin Christensen, Kate O'Keeffe, Denver Lough, Dan Blake, and many others. They didn't necessarily expect to have success with their founding initiatives. But these leaders proactively engaged in the same activities that the famous innovative leaders did—and achieved similar results but on a smaller scale.

You can do it too. We've provided the rough formula for how to proceed. Now it's up to you. You need to be proactive and have the ambition to do something important. You need to think, and dream, bigger.

Great leaders have ambition. They dream big. They push their teams to think big and avoid the trap of incremental thinking. Scott Stephenson, CEO of Verisk Analytics (number twenty-two in our ranking of innovative leaders), observes, "I'll call it a syndrome that I think can happen in larger companies. Even when you ask for innovation, the people that you're looking to champion the innovation will start to constrain it as they bring it forward. I don't know if . . . people don't want to be burdened with a huge expectation or [they assume] that there's only so much money the company is willing to spend. But I've seen this pattern over and over again."

Part of the innovation magic we saw at Amazon comes from how Bezos pushes people to think bigger. Andrew Jassy, CEO of Amazon Web Services, says, "A lot of times, people come to the table with very clever, inventive ideas, and Jeff will look at them and say, 'Well, this is really interesting and exciting, but have you thought about extending it this way and this way?' in a way that the team hasn't necessarily thought about. This is how he pushes them to make the idea even bigger and, again, encourages and reinforces the culture to think as big as you can imagine, even if it may take you several years to realize your vision."

Amazon Echo (Alexa) is a good example. When Amazon introduced Echo back in 2014, it was pitched primarily as a smart speaker, promising a way to ask for basic information and control your music with your voice and little else. But Bezos and David Limp, head of Amazon devices, pushed the team to think bigger. Today, the Alexa virtual voice assistant has evolved into a smart-home hub that allows you to control your appliances with your voice. Thermostats, humidifiers, sprinkler systems, IKEA light bulbs, and even salt shakers are all controllable with Alexa. And of course, you can now order whatever you want from Amazon using Alexa. The individuals who first developed the idea for the Alexa technology were willing, and were pushed, to think big and dream bigger. They simply started with a little forward thinking, and the rest unfolded as they took one step at a time.

You will achieve greater success as an organizational leader if you will proactively and ambitiously follow the advice provided here for building your innovation capital. You may just be getting your innovation capital flywheel started. But with continued skill building and focused efforts to build social connections and a track record of innovation, you can make that flywheel spin. And like the world's most innovative leaders, you too can win the needed resources to launch innovations with impact.

How We Rank the World's Most Innovative Leaders

Creating any type of ranking requires a thoughtful methodology, and none is perfect. We understand this concept quite well, having created the *Forbes* World's Most Innovative Companies ranking. We set out to create something very different with the *Forbes* list, using the wisdom of the crowd. Companies are ranked by their innovation premium: the difference between their market capitalization (value) and the net present value of cash flows from existing businesses. The difference between a company's current market value and the net present value of its existing businesses is the premium given by equity investors, betting with their wallets, that the company will generate profitable new growth. Companies with higher innovation premiums receive a higher ranking.[1]

We approached our *Forbes* World's Most Innovative Leaders ranking with similar rigor. Since we couldn't rank every leader, our sample of leaders includes the founders or CEOs (or founder-CEOs) of firms with greater than $10 billion market value plus the fifty largest private firms to go public from 2013 to 2018. We co-ranked leaders of firms if they were cofounders and if both had visible top-management positions (e.g., cofounders of Alphabet are CEO Larry Page and president Sergey Brin; cofounders of Regeneron are CEO Leonard Schleifer and president and chief science officer George Yancopoulos). We thought it was appropriate to co-rank these individuals, because their scores were identical on firm-level measures.

A leader's ability to successfully drive innovation largely boils down to something we call *innovation capital*, a multifaceted set of characteristics that allow the leader to acquire and effectively deploy the human and financial resources required to turn a risky and novel idea into an innovation with impact. The individuals we studied have innovation leadership skills that are difficult to measure; these skills are thus not a component of our ranking. However, we did use a composite of four measures that we believe represent important qualities of a leader with innovation capital: (1) a media reputation for innovation, (2) social connections and social capital related to innovation, (3) a track record of market value creation at the leader's company, and (4) investors who anticipate future growth and innovation at the firm as represented by the company's innovation premium (the same metric we use to rank the *Forbes* World's Most Innovative Companies list). These components are outlined in further detail in the following sections.

Media Reputation for Innovation

We've done research that empirically shows that a leader's media reputation for innovation has a significant positive relationship on his or her company's subsequent innovation reputation and market value. Indeed, leaders and companies with an innovation brand can attract more-talented employees and are more likely to have customers identify with them at a personal level. These benefits in turn lead to increased customer loyalty, repeat purchases, customer willingness to pay higher prices, and increased tolerance for occasional product failures.

We measure a leader's media reputation for innovation over a four-year period using the absolute number of articles and the percentage of a CEO's total coverage in the top business news sources (e.g., *Forbes*, the *Wall Street Journal*, the *Financial Times*, the *New York Times*, the *Washington Post*, and *USA Today*) that discuss the leader and mention innovation activities. The person with the highest media reputation is given a score of 100, and others are given scores below 100, according to their percentage of media attention and coverage relative to whoever is number one on the list.

Social Connections and Capital

Social capital implies a strong public following, which can translate into a leader's greater influence and persuasion when he or she is attempting to promote innovative ideas in the market. We measure social capital by using current data from LinkedIn and Twitter about the social connections of the individual CEOs. For LinkedIn, social capital was quantified using several measures or indicators, including number of followers, presence of a Newslines page (indicating extremely high level of social influence), and a simple count of contacts where neither of the other criteria were relevant. Twitter follower counts served as a second measure of social capital to augment LinkedIn. The person with the highest number of social connections from the composite of metrics is given a score of 100, and others are given scores below 100, according to their relative social connections.

Track Record for Value Creation

Value creation reflects the returns that investors in each CEO's company have realized during recent years. We measure a leader's track record for value creation through the absolute, and percentage, market value increase of the company (or companies) the person leads. We gathered year-end market capitalization data for each firm over the past three years. We also incorporated stock-price appreciation (split adjusted) over the past three years as another indicator of value creation for investors. The leader with the highest composite score on value creation is given a score of 100, and others are given scores below 100, according to their relative composite score on value creation.

Investor Expectations of Future Value Creation

We use our innovation premium metric to capture investor expectations of whether the leader's company is likely to innovate and grow new income streams in the future. This composite score measures the difference between a company's market capitalization and its net present value of cash flows from existing businesses. One of us (Jeff) and his colleague Hal Gregerson explain our methodology in more detail in a separate *Forbes* article.[2] The leader whose company has the highest innovation premium is given a score of 100, and others are scaled below 100, according to their relative innovation premium.

NOTES

Chapter 1

1. Nigel Cawthorne, *Tesla vs Edison: The Life-Long Feud That Electrified the World* (Secaucus, NJ: Chartwell Books, 2016).

2. Ibid.

3. Kevin Daum, "37 Quotes from Thomas Edison That Will Inspire Success," *Inc.*, February 11, 2016, www.inc.com/kevin-daum/37-quotes-from -thomas-edison-that-will-bring-out-your-best.html.

4. "Bubba," "Unconventional Tactics: What Thomas Edison Can Teach Us about Self-Promotion," *Branding Beat* (blog), accessed November 17, 2018, www.qualitylogoproducts.com/blog/thomas-edison-self-promotion.

5. Cawthorne, *Tesla vs Edison*, p. 23.

6. Ibid., p. 35.

7. Cawthorne, *Tesla vs Edison*, p. 39; Richard Munson, *Tesla: Inventor of the Modern* (New York: W. W. Norton & Company, 2018), p. 55.

8. Cawthorne, *Tesla vs Edison*, p. 3.

9. Ibid., p. 7.

10. Jeffrey Dyer and Nathan Furr, "How We Rank the World's Most Innovative Leaders," *Forbes*, September 4, 2018, https://www.forbes.com/sites/ nathanfurrjeffdyer/2018/09/04/how-we-rank-the-worlds-most-innovative -leaders/#884304b1139d.

11. For an explanation of simultaneous equation models, see Stephanie Glen, "Simultaneous Equations Model (SEM): Simple Definition," Sta- tistics How To, accessed November 27, 2018, www.statisticshowto.com/ simultaneous-equations-model; and Ben Lambert, "Simultaneous Equation Models: An Introduction," video, November 6, 2013, www.youtube.com/ watch?v=HfnFeJlkfZE.

12. For the logic of mutual causality, see "What Is Mutual Causality?" accessed November 27, 2018, https://thelogicofmutualcausality.weebly.com/ what-is-mutual-causality.html.

13. Kirsten Korosec, "Meet Aurora, the Ambitious (and Spunky) Self- Driving Car Startup," *Fortune*, January 25, 2018, http://fortune.com/2018/ 01/25/aurora-innovation-self-driving-car-startup.

14. We examined whether a reputation for efficiency was valuable and found that the only situation in which a reputation for efficiency was more valuable than a reputation for innovation was in low-uncertainty industries, such as basic food products and road (trucking) and rail. However, remember

our analysis was conducted from 2003 to 2018. Today, as Amazon buys Whole Foods and as Tesla is launching self-driving trucks, a reputation for innovation is becoming important even in these industries.

15. Jeffrey H. Dyer, Nathan Furr, Michael Hendron, and Eric Volmar, "Innovation Reputation and Firm Value" (working paper presented at Academy of Management Conference, August 7, 2017).

Chapter 2

1. Satya Nadella, *Hit Refresh: The Quest to Rediscover Microsoft's Soul and Imagine a Better Future for Everyone* (New York: Harper Business, 2017), p. 57.

2. Ibid., p. 47.

3. Ibid., p. 62.

4. Neil Strauss, "Elon Musk: The Architect of Tomorrow," *Rolling Stone*, November 15, 2017.

5. For more on the process, see Nathan Furr, Kyle Nel, and Thomas Zoëga Ramsøy, *Leading Transformation: How to Take Charge of Your Company's Future* (Boston: Harvard Business Review Press, 2018).

6. Ibid.

7. "The Internet Tidal Wave," Letters of Note, July 22, 2011, http://www.lettersofnote.com/2011/07/internet-tidal-wave.html.

8. Tom Kelley, "Cultivating an Attitude of Wisdom," Stanford Technology Ventures Program, 2008, video and transcript available at https://ecorner.stanford.edu/video/cultivating-an-attitude-of-wisdom. Notably, Karl Weick is first credited with the term "attitude of wisdom."

9. "Leadership Principles," Amazonjobs, accessed January 7, 2019, https://www.amazon.jobs/en/principles.

10. Matthew Herper, "How Two Guys from Queens Are Changing Drug Discovery," *Forbes*, September 2, 2013, www.forbes.com/sites/matthewherper/2013/08/14/how-two-guys-from-queens-are-changing-drug-discovery.

11. Elon Musk, interview with Kevin Rose, in John G. Johnston, "Kevin Rose Interviews Tesla Motors, SpaceX Founder Elon Musk [Video]," *The 9 Billion*, September 11, 2012, www.the9billion.com/2012/09/11/kevin-rose-interviews-elon-musk.

12. Jeffrey Dyer, Hal Gregersen, and Clayton M. Christensen, *The Innovator's DNA: Mastering the Five Skills of Disruptive Innovators* (Boston: Harvard Business Review Press, 2011), chaps. 1–6.

13. Ibid.

14. Tim Bajarin, "How Corning's Crash Project for Steve Jobs Helped Define the iPhone," *Fast Company*, November 10, 2017, https://www.fastcompany.com/40493737/how-cornings-crash-project-for-steve-jobs-helped-define-the-iphone.

15. Howard Gardner, *Frames of Mind: The Theory of Multiple Intelligences* (New York: Basic Books, 1993).

16. Barbara Minto, *The Pyramid Principle: Logic in Writing and Thinking* (London: Financial Times Prentice Hall, 2002).

Chapter 3

1. Robin Dunbar, *Grooming, Gossip, and the Evolution of Language* (Cambridge, MA: Harvard University Press, 1998), p. 77.

2. Aaron Smith, "What People Like and Dislike about Facebook," *FactTank* (Pew Research Center), February 3, 2014, www.pewresearch.org/fact-tank/2014/02/03/what-people-like-dislike-about-facebook.

3. Mark S. Granovetter, "The Strength of Weak Ties," *American Journal of Sociology* 78, no. 6 (1973): 1360–1380.

4. David Kirkpatrick, *The Facebook Effect: The Inside Story of the Company That Is Connecting the World* (New York: Simon & Schuster, 2010), p. 81; Alan Greenspan, *Authoritas: One Student's Harvard Admissions and the Founding of the Facebook Era* (Los Angeles, CA: Think Press, 2008), p. 2.

5. Timothy R. Clark, "Innovation Is a Social Process: So Oil the Gears of Collaboration," *LeaderFactor*, April 24, 2018, https://www.leaderfactor.com/single-post/2018/04/24/Innovation-is-a-Social-Process-So-Oil-the-Gears-of-Collaboration.

6. Kirkpatrick, *The Facebook Effect.*

7. Ibid.

8. Marc Benioff, "A Conversation with Marc Benioff, Founder & CEO of Salesforce.com," video and transcript, *Endeavor*, February 16, 2012, https://endeavor.org/network/marc-benioff-keynote.

9. See Jeffrey Dyer, Hal Gregersen, and Clayton M. Christensen, *The Innovator's DNA: Mastering the Five Skills of Disruptive Innovators* (Boston: Harvard Business Review Press, 2011); Nathan Furr, Jeffrey Dyer, and Clayton M. Christensen, *The Innovator's Method: Bringing the Lean Startup into Your Organization* (Boston: Harvard Business Review Press, 2014).

10. Leah Busque, "Tell Everyone About Your Idea," video, *eCorner* (Stanford University), May 21, 2014, https://ecorner.stanford.edu/in-brief/tell-everyone-about-your-idea.

11. Ibid.

12. Alvin Gouldner, "The Norm of Reciprocity: A Preliminary Statement," *American Sociological Review* 25, no. 2 (April 1960): 161–178.

13. This quote was told to us by David Bradford in an interview.

14. David Bradford, *Up Your Game: 6 Timeless Principles for Networking Your Way to the Top* (Orem, UT: Life Science Publishing, 2004).

Chapter 4

1. R. L. Moreland and S. R. Beach, "Exposure Effects in the Classroom: The Development of Affinity among Students," *Journal of Experimental Social Psychology* 28, no. 3 (1992): 255–276.

2. Joseph Bower, "Strategy Making through Resource Allocation," presentation at Wharton Management Faculty Research Symposium, Wharton School of the University of Pennsylvania, Philadelphia, October 18, 1996.

3. Benjamin L. Hallen, "The Causes and Consequences of the Initial Network Positions of New Organizations: From Whom Do Entrepreneurs Receive Investments?" *Administrative Science Quarterly* 53, no. 4 (December 2008): 685–718.

4. M. Spence, "Job Market Signaling," *Quarterly Journal of Economics* 87 (1973): 355–374; B. L. Connelly et al., "Signaling Theory: A Review and Assessment," *Journal of Management* 37 (2011): 39–67.

5. Timothy B. Folta, Frédéric Delmar, and Karl Wennberg, "Hybrid Entrepreneurship," *Management Science* 56, no. 2 (2010): 253–269.

6. Markus Baer, Jeffrey Dyer, and Zachariah Rodgers, "Career Benefits of Entrepreneurial Activity for Individuals in Paid Employment: An Application of Signaling Theory" (working paper, 2018).

7. Folta, Delmar, and Wennberg, "Hybrid Entrepreneurship."

8. Joseph Raffiee and Jie Feng, "Should I Quit My Day Job? A Hybrid Path to Entrepreneurship," *Academy of Management Journal* 57, no. 4 (2014): 936–963.

9. Randy Komisar, interview with authors, November 2007.

10. "The Word's Most Innovative Companies," *Forbes*, 2018 ranking, www.forbes.com/innovative-companies/list/#tab:rank.

11. Andy Rachleff, "The 2018 Wealthfront Career Launching Companies List," *Wealthfront* (blog), October 18, 2017, https://blog.wealthfront.com/2018-wealthfront-career-launching-companies-list.

12. Andy Rachleff, "48 Hot Tech Companies to Build a Career," *Wealthfront* (blog), October 25, 2012, https://blog.wealthfront.com/hot-mid-size-silicon-valley-companies.

13. Nathan Furr, Jeffrey Dyer, and Clayton M. Christensen, *The Innovator's Method: Bringing the Lean Startup into Your Organization* (Boston: Harvard Business Review Press, 2014).

Chapter 5

1. For a notable exception, see Christoph Zott and Quy Nguyen Huy, "How Entrepreneurs Use Symbolic Management to Acquire Resources," *Administrative Science Quarterly* 52, no. 1 (2007): 70–105.

2. Robert B. Zajonc, "Attitudinal Effects of Mere Exposure," *Journal of Personality and Social Psychology* 9, no. 2 (1968): 1–27.

3. Nathan Furr, Kate O'Keeffe, and Jeffrey Dyer, "Managing Multi-Party Innovation: How Big Companies Are Joining Forces to Seize Opportunities at Their Intersections," *Harvard Business Review*, November 2016, https://hbr .org/2016/11/managing-multiparty-innovation#article-top.

4. Nathan T. Washburn and Benjamin Galvin, "Make Sure Your Employees Have Good Things to Say about You Behind Your Back," *Harvard Business Review*, September 22, 2016, https://hbr.org/2016/09/make-sure -your-employees-have-good-things-to-say-about-you-behind-your-back. Emphasis in original.

5. Ibid.

6. I. Scopelliti, G. Loewenstein, and J. Vosgerau, "You Call It 'Self-Exuberance'; I Call It 'Bragging': Miscalibrated Predictions of Emotional Responses to Self-Promotion," *Psychological Science* 26, no. 6 (2015): 903–914.

7. Susan Pulliam, Mike Ramsey, and Ianthe Jeanne Dugan, "Elon Musk Sets Ambitious Goals at Tesla—and Often Falls Short," *Wall Street Journal*, August 15, 2016, www.wsj.com/articles/elon-musk-sets-ambitious-goals-at -teslaand-often-falls-short-1471275436.

8. Ibid.

9. Historical details in this section on Antoine-Augustin Parmentier are from Robert A. Kyle and Marc A. Shampo, "Antoine-Augustin Parmentier— Champion of the Potato," *Mayo Clinic Proceedings* 64, no. 9 (September 1989): 1133; "Antoine-Augustin Parmentier, 1737–1813," Portraits de Médecins, February 15, 2014, http://medarus.org/Medecins/MedecinsTextes/parmentieraa .html.

10. Richard Carter and Steven Manaster, "Initial Public Offerings and Underwriter Reputation," *Journal of Finance* 45, no. 4 (September 1990): 1045–1067; Timothy G. Pollock, et al. "How Much Prestige Is Enough? Assessing the Value of Multiple Types of High-Status Affiliates for Young Firms," *Journal of Business Venturing* 25, no. 1 (January 2010): 6–23.

11. Tom Groenfeldt, "Why the Gates Foundation Is Funding a Master-Card Lab," *Forbes*, December 9, 2014, www.forbes.com/sites/tomgroenfeldt/ 2014/12/09/why-the-gates-foundation-is-funding-a-mastercard-lab/ #28083a4e778f; Jake Bright, "Mastercard Launches 2KUZE Agtech Platform in East Africa," *TechCrunch*, January 18, 2017, https://techcrunch.com/ 2017/01/18/mastercard-launches-2kuze-agtech-platform-in-east-africa.

12. Benjamin L. Hallen and Kathleen M. Eisenhardt, "Catalyzing Strategies and Efficient Tie Formation: How Entrepreneurial Firms Obtain Investment Ties," *Academy of Management Journal* 55, no. 1 (February 2012): 35–70; Benjamin L. Hallen, "The Causes and Consequences of the Initial Network Positions of New Organizations: From Whom Do Entrepreneurs Receive Investments?" *Administrative Science Quarterly* 53, no. 4 (December 2008): 685–718.

13. Robert Brumfield, "Fusion-io Awarded Red Herring Top 100 Global Company," press release, February 2, 2009, http://www.fusionio.com/press/ Fusion-io-Awarded-Red-Herring-Top-100-Global-Company/.

14. Srikanth An, "Jack Ma: The Inspirational Story of Alibaba Founder," *ShoutMeLoud* (blog), December 1, 2017, www.shoutmeloud.com/jack-ma -alibaba-founder.html.

15. Duncan Clark, *Alibaba: The House That Jack Ma Built* (New York: Ecco Press, 2016).

16. Clark, *Alibaba*.

17. Retranslation of original phrase. Clark, *Alibaba*.

18. Clark, *Alibaba*.

19. Punit Prajapati, "Jack Ma: The Inspiration for All Entrepreneurs," LinkedIn, June 14, 2016, www.linkedin.com/pulse/jack-ma-inspiration-all -entrepreneur-punit-prajapati; *Forbes* Profile, "#1 Jack Ma," accessed November 27, 2018, www.forbes.com/profile/jack-ma.

20. For a review of the academic literature, see Raghu Garud, Henri A. Schildt, and Theresa K. Lant, "Entrepreneurial Storytelling, Future Expectations, and the Paradox of Legitimacy," *Organization Science* 25, no. 5 (2014): 1479–1492.

21. David R. Roskos-Ewoldsen and Jennifer L. Monahan, eds., *Communication and Social Cognition: Theories and Methods* (New York: Routledge, 2009), 378.

22. For a review of techniques to use storytelling to win support for ideas, see Nathan Furr, Kyle Nel, and Thomas Zoëga Ramsøy, *Leading Transformation: Taking Charge of Your Company's Future* (Boston: Harvard Business Review Press, 2018).

23. Chris Anderson, "Elon Musk's Mission to Mars," *Wired*, October 21, 2012, www.wired.com/2012/10/ff-elon-musk-qa.

24. To learn more about effective storytelling techniques, see the Khan Academy and Pixar storytelling course: www.khanacademy.org/ partner-content/pixar/storytelling.

25. Furr, Nel, and Ramsøy, *Leading Transformation*.

Chapter 6

1. Joe Pappalardo, "Love & Rockets," *Dallas Observer*, March 1, 2001, www.dallasobserver.com/news/love-and-rockets-6392592; Wikipedia, s.v. "Beal Aerospace," last modified May 19, 2018, https://en.wikipedia.org/wiki/ Beal_Aerospace.

2. Andrew Beal, "Statement from Andrew Beal, Chairman and Founder of Beal Aerospace Technologies, Inc.," October 23, 2000, reprinted by SpaceProjects, www.spaceprojects.com/Beal; Christian Davenport, *Space Barons: Elon Musk, Jeff Bezos, and the Quest to Colonize the Cosmos* (New York: PublicAffairs, 2018).

3. Davenport, *Space Barons*.

4. Ibid., 42.

5. The descriptions of these events are adapted from Davenport, *Space Barons*, 43–44.

6. Ibid.

7. Ibid.

8. Dom Galeon, "The NASA-SpaceX Partnership Saved NASA Hundreds of Millions," Futurism.com, November 15, 2017, https://futurism.com/nasa-spacex-partnership-saved-nasa-hundreds-millions.

9. See SpaceX's stats page at www.spacexstats.xyz for real-time count downs to the next launch.

10. M. A. McDaniel and G. O. Einstein, "Bizarre Imagery as an Effective Memory Aid: The Importance of Distinctiveness," *Journal of Experimental Psychology: Learning, Memory, and Cognition* 12, no. 1 (1986): 54–65.

11. James Bigelow and Amy Poremba, "Achilles' Ear? Inferior Human Short-Term and Recognition Memory in the Auditory Modality," *PloS One* 9, no. 2 (2014): e89914.

12. Josh Brooks, "Tesco Reveals Extent of Food Waste for Key Products," *PackagingNews*, October 21, 2013, www.packagingnews.co.uk/news/tesco-reveals-extent-of-food-waste-for-key-products-21-10-2013.

13. Wendy Gabriel, "Reuse in the Garden with EcoScraps," RecycleNation, August 25, 2014, https://recyclenation.com/2014/08/reuse-garden-ecoscraps/.

14. Martin L. Martens, Jennifer E. Jennings, and P. Devereaux Jennings, "Do the Stories They Tell Get Them the Money They Need? The Role of Entrepreneurial Narratives in Resource Acquisition," *Academy of Management Journal* 50, no. 5 (2007): 1107–1132.

15. Ibid.

16. For more on good comparisons, see Michael Lounsbury and Mary Ann Glynn, "Cultural Entrepreneurship: Stories, Legitimacy, and the Acquisition of Resources," *Strategic Management Journal* 22, no. 6–7 (2001): 545–564.

17. Andrew Kvålseth, interview with author (Nathan Furr), Bangkok, April 2018; also see Nathan Furr, Kyle Nel, and Thomas Zoëga Ramsøy, *Leading Transformation: Taking Charge of Your Company's Future* (Boston: Harvard Business Review Press, 2018), pp. 156–157.

18. Ben Lockhart, "Brand New Burn Treatment Giving Utah Family Hope 'Where There Was Absolutely None Left'" *Deseret News*, July 22, 2018.

19. M. Diane Burton and Katherine Lawrence, "Jerry Sanders," case no. 498-021 (Boston: Harvard Business School, 1998) p. 14.

20. "Secrets of Psychology 4: Law of Scarcity," Moving That Needle (podcast), https://movingthatneedle.com/legacy-video-episodes/secrets-of-psychology-4-law-of-scarcity; S. S. Brehm and M. Weinraub, "Physical Barriers and Psychological Reactance: 2-Year-Olds' Responses to Threats to Freedom," *Journal of Personality and Social Psychology* 35, no. 11 (1977): 830–836.

21. Benjamin L. Hallen, and Kathleen M. Eisenhardt, "Catalyzing Strategies and Efficient Tie Formation: How Entrepreneurial Firms Obtain

Investment Ties," *Academy of Management Journal* 55, no. 1 (February 2012): 35–70.

22. In addition to pressuring, Hallen found that entrepreneurs also purposely engaged in what he calls "casual dating." Contrary to common wisdom, investors rarely gave out money because of a single pitch. Instead, they wanted to have multiple interactions with an entrepreneur to get a better sense of who he or she is and what the individual is capable of. Recognizing this desire for more interaction with an entrepreneur, the most successful entrepreneurs in Hallen's study found ways to create these data points ahead of when they actually needed funding. Rather than approach investors and ask for funding directly, the innovators would instead ask investors for "feedback," drawing them into the cocreation of the idea and seeding the interactions that the investor would require to later make an investment decision. Then, when the entrepreneur needed the investment at a critical time, the investor was more prepared to make a decision. From Benjamin L. Hallen, "The Origin of the Network Positions of New Organizations: How Entrepreneurs Raise Funds" (PhD diss., Stanford University, 2007). Findings also reported partially in Benjamin L. Hallen and Kathleen M. Eisenhardt, "Catalyzing Strategies and Efficient Tie Formation: How Entrepreneurial Firms Obtain Investment Ties," *Academy of Management Journal* 55, no. 1 (February 2012): 35–70.

23. Pinar Ozcan and Kathleen M. Eisenhardt, "Origin of Alliance Portfolios: Entrepreneurs, Network Strategies, and Firm Performance," *Academy of Management Journal* 52, no. 2 (April 2009): 246–279.

24. Hallen, "The Origin of the Network Positions of New Organizations."

Chapter 7

1. Elon Musk, "The Mission of Tesla," Tesla website, November 18, 2013, www.tesla.com/blog/mission-tesla.

2. "About," SpaceX, https://www.spacex.com/about.

3. Alex Davies, "Elon Musk's Grand Plan to Power the World with Batteries," *Wired*, May 1, 2015, https://www.wired.com/2015/05/tesla-batteries/.

4. Max Chafkin, "Elon Musk Is Really Boring," *Bloomberg*, February 16, 2017, https://www.bloomberg.com/news/features/2017-02-16/elon-musk-is-really-boring

5. Jon Tan, "52 of the Best Jeff Bezos Quotes, Sorted by Category," *ReferralCandy* (blog), March 23, 2016, www.referralcandy.com/blog/jeff-bezos-quotes.

6. Ed Caesar, "The Epic Untold Story of Nike's (Almost) Perfect Marathon," *Wired*, June 28, 2017, www.wired.com/story/nike-breaking2-marathon-eliud-kipchoge.

7. Jere Longman, "Do Nike's New Shoes Give Runners an Unfair Advantage?" *New York Times*, March 8, 2017, www.nytimes.com/2017/03/08/sports/nikes-vivid-shoes-and-the-gray-area-of-performance-enhancement.html.

8. Susan Pulliam, Mike Ramsey, and Ianthe Jeanne Dugan, "Elon Musk Sets Ambitious Goals at Tesla—and Often Falls Short," *Wall Street Journal*, August 15, 2016, www.wsj.com/articles/elon-musk-sets-ambitious -goals-at-teslaand-often-falls-short-1471275436.

9. Alyson Shontell, "How Steve Jobs Convinced Tim Cook to Work for Apple," *Business Insider*, September 12, 2014, www.businessinsider .com/how-steve-jobs-convinced-tim-cook-to-work-for-apple-2014-9; David Pierini, "Inner Voice Saying 'Go West' Convinced Tim Cook to Join Apple," Cult of Mac, June 13, 2018, https://www.cultofmac.com/555197/ tim-cook-david-rubbenstein-interview/.

10. The Boring Company, "FAQs," accessed November 27, 2018, www .boringcompany.com/faq.

11. Chafkin, "Elon Musk Is Really Boring."

12. For a detailed description of how leaders act like chief experimenters, see Nathan Furr, Jeffrey Dyer, and Clayton M. Christensen, *The Innovator's Method: Bringing the Lean Start-up into Your Organization* (Boston: Harvard Business Review Press, 2014), chap. 2.

13. Jeffrey Dyer et al., "Innovation Reputation and Firm Value," presented at Academy of Management Meetings, Atlanta, GA, August 9, 2017.

14. Dominic Orr, "Working with and Making Decisions with Great People," video transcript, Cosmo Learning, Stanford University, lecture 6, October 17, 2007, https://cosmolearning.org/courses/entrepreneurial-thought -leaders-lectures-dominic-orr-352/video-lectures.

15. "201 Amazing Steve Jobs Quotes (That Will Motivate You)," Wisdom Quotes (blog), http://wisdomquotes.com/steve-jobs-quotes/.

16. Lonny Kochina, "What Percentage of New Products Fail and Why," MarketSmart Newsletters, May 3, 2017, https://www.publicity.com/ marketsmart-newsletters/percentage-new-products-fail/.

Chapter 8

1. Nat Levy, "Amazon Tops 600K Worldwide Employees for the 1st Time, a 13% Jump from a Year Ago," GeekWire, October 25, 2018, https:// www.geekwire.com/2018/amazon-tops-600k-worldwide-employees-1st- time-13-jump-year-ago/; "Amazon.com, Inc. Form 10-K for the Fiscal Year Ended December 31, 2017," Securities and Exchange Commission Report, https://sec.report/Document/0001018724-18-000005/amzn-20171231x10k .htm.

2. "Jeff Bezos: 'All Overnight Success Takes Ten Years,'" Consultant's Mind (blog), https://www.consultantsmind.com/2018/05/19/jeff-bezos-all -overnight-success-takes-about-10-years/.

3. As an example, see Hamers's brief video to shareholders in which he never reports hard-core financial results: https://www.youtube.com/user/ing/ videos.

4. Kirsten Korosec, "Meet Aurora, the Ambitious (and Spunky) Self-Driving Car Startup," *Fortune*, January 25, 2108, http://fortune.com/2018/01/25/aurora-innovation-self-driving-car-startup.

5. Eugene Kim, "The Rise and Fall of Marissa Mayer, the Once Beloved CEO of Yahoo," *Business Insider*, January 14, 2016, www.businessinsider.com/yahoo-marissa-mayer-rise-and-fall-2016-1.

6. Nathan Furr and Andrew Shipilov, "De-Hyping Digital: How Real Businesses Engage in Digital Transformation," *Harvard Business Review*, forthcoming.

Conclusion

1. Karl Taro Greenfeld, "How Mark Parker Keeps Nike in the Lead," *Wall Street Journal Magazine*, November 4, 2015, www.wsj.com/articles/how-mark-parker-keeps-nike-in-the-lead-1446689666.

Appendix

1. For a detailed description of our methodology, see Jeffrey Dyer and Hal Gregersen, "How We Rank the Most Innovative Companies 2018," *Forbes*, May 29, 2018, www.forbes.com/sites/innovatorsdna/2018/05/29/how-we-rank-the-most-innovative-companies-2018/#12a4bef21e3c.

2. Ibid.

INDEX

ACKNOWLEDGMENTS

From JEFF DYER

Writing a book is both exhilarating and exhausting. You learn so much from the experience and from the many individuals who help bring your ideas to life. I would first like to acknowledge and thank my coauthors, Nathan Furr and Curtis Lefrandt. Nathan and I have now written two books and several articles together, including three *Harvard Business Review* pieces. I enjoy working with Nathan because he has great ideas and also because he just gets the work done. We are great friends and have a profound mutual respect. I also want to thank Curtis, whom I've worked with for several years as he led the growth of the Innovator's DNA consultancy. Curtis has done a fabulous job building the company, and I especially appreciate his positive attitude and his friendship. I also want to acknowledge Mike Hendron, my colleague at BYU, who led the challenging task of gathering the data we needed in order to rank the world's most innovative leaders. Mike is extraordinarily capable in so many areas, but he is especially talented at understanding how to use technology to collect data that is notoriously difficult to capture. Mike is a terrific colleague to work with, and I want to thank him for his important contributions to this project.

The data collection effort for this book has been significant, and I have many research assistants to thank who worked countless hours to make the manuscript possible. I would especially like to thank Adam Pigg, Dan Wilde, Eric Volmar, Tyler Burroughs, Ryan Allen, Christopher Law, David Mella, Curtis Jensen, Kurtis Giliat, Harrison Miner, and Jordan McGee. In addition, I would like to thank the team at Innovator's DNA, especially Devin Nakama and Jerel Alvarez, for their excellent graphic design work on the figures and graphics for *Innovation Capital*. I would also like to thank all the staff members who support me at Brigham Young University. Especially deserving of my thanks are my assistants, Holly Jenkins and Krysta Whitmore, and Katy Nottingham, Marissa Tenney, Sam Tenney, and Sophie Poulsen, who helped me manage a quick turnaround on all the interview transcripts. I would also like to thank the Sorenson Legacy Foundation and BYU's Center for Entrepreneurship and Technology for providing research funding to support this project.

I'd like to offer a special thanks to the high-profile founders and executives who were willing to step away from their demanding jobs to be interviewed for this project. Special thanks to Jeff Bezos (Amazon), Elon Musk (Tesla, SpaceX), Marc Benioff (Salesforce), Shantanu Narayen (Adobe), Indra Nooyi (PepsiCo), Jeff Weiner (LinkedIn), Mark Parker (Nike), Arne Sorenson (Marriott International), Scott Stephenson (Verisk Analytics), Len Schleifer and George Yancopoulos (Regeneron), Satya Nadella (Microsoft), Sterling Anderson (Aurora Innovation), and the leaders of Amazon's three major business divisions: Jeff Wilke (Retail), Andrew Jassy (AWS), and Dave Limp (Devices). I would also like to thank Janet Christensen, who used her skills and networks to help us set up these interviews.

Finally, I would like to offer a special thanks to Melinda Merino, our editor not only on *Innovation Capital* but also on *The Innovator's DNA* and *The Innovator's Method*. Melinda is a joy to work with—she's fun, insightful, encouraging, and tactful. She knows how to help orchestrate the development of a manuscript that resonates with an audience. I would also like to thank Alicyn Zall and Anne Starr, who helped shepherd the manuscript through production, and Patricia Boyd, who did an amazing job with the copyedit.

I wish I could write a book without it taking over my life for a least a short period of time. I've said this before but, as always, I owe a deep debt of gratitude to my wife, Ronalee, who has always supported me in my work and patiently listens to me obsess about the details of whatever project I'm working on. Ronalee deserves special recognition for taking such great of our children—Aaron, Matthew, and McKenzie—and now daughter-in-law Amy and grandchildren Braze, Bradlee, and Gentri. Ronalee makes sure our family is well taken care of when I'm totally engrossed in a book project. I think she's hoping this will be my last one.

From NATHAN FURR

I want to take a moment to acknowledge Jeff and our collaboration over the years. Not only is Jeff a great thinker and great collaborator but he is also one of the finest human beings I know. It has been a pleasure to collaborate on two books and multiple articles together, and it is an honor to call Jeff a friend. My hope is that we can continue to have many fruitful collaborations.

I would also like to thank our coauthor and collaborator, Curtis Lefrandt, for his continued hard work, insights, and complementary skills in helping companies build these capabilities. We also owe a deep debt to Mike Hendron, who pulled together the research team and led the research not only for our list of the most innovative leaders but also for our study of the impact of firm reputation for innovation on market performance. In addition, Janet Christensen played a special role in this work, leveraging her expertise in business development and execution to help connect us with many of the people we interviewed in the book. I also want to add my thanks to the research assistants and the interviewees Jeff mentioned in his acknowledgments.

I would also like to thank INSEAD for financial assistance and my colleagues for their patience and support: INSEAD's entire Strategy area as well as Peter Zemsky, Mark Mortensen, Noah Askin, Michelle Rogan, Andrew Shipilov, and especially my fabulous assistant Delphine Fauché. I also want to thank Kitsune Café Palais Royal, Coutume Café, Holybelly 5, and Arabica

Beaupassage (particularly those that allowed laptops) for hosting the writing and discussion sessions that allowed the these ideas to be refined.

Finally, and most importantly, I'd like to thank my family, Susannah Adore, Jordan Elisabeth, George van Waters, Josephine Apollo, and Beatrix Cosi, for their generous support while I was writing this book.

From CURTIS LEFRANDT

Rubbing shoulders and working side by side with Jeff and Nathan has been one of the defining highlights of my professional life. I'm not sure I deserve their camaraderie and friendship, but I am grateful for their generosity and willingness to mentor me and put up with my shenanigans. It's been an absolute delight writing this book with them, building a company together, and partnering with organizations around the world that are striving to develop their innovation capital.

I echo Jeff and Nathan's appreciation for our research and support team, the founders and executives we interviewed, and the wonderful team at Harvard Business Review Press. None of this would have been possible without their collective support. I would also like to acknowledge the Innovator's DNA team for their dedication, exemplified both in their contributions to this book and in all they have done to bring our company to life. In particular, my thanks goes out to Jershon Lopez, Devin Nakama, Becca Pearson, Shane Wolcott, Jerel Alvarez, Wade Healy, Nan Abo, Robb Shirley, and Ricky Kumar. What a privilege it is to work with all of you!

Last but certainly not least, I want to express my gratitude and love for my family: to my wife, Misty, for her endless patience and support throughout the intense process of building and running a company, and to my children, Liahona Joye, Mikaela Leigh, Ezekiel Tomosue, and Cochava Zoe, for their unconditional love—no matter how many business trips or nights away there might be.

ABOUT THE AUTHORS

JEFF DYER is the Horace Beesley Professor of Strategy at Brigham Young University's Marriott School and an adjunct professor at the University of Pennsylvania's Wharton School. He earned his PhD from UCLA in 1993. He worked previously as a manager at Bain & Company and later cofounded Innovator's DNA, a consultancy designed to help companies build innovation capabilities. His previous books, *The Innovator's DNA* and *The Innovator's Method,* are bestsellers, and his first book, *Collaborative Advantage*, won the Shingo Prize Publication Award. Dyer is the only strategy scholar to have published at least six times in both *Strategic Management Journal* and *Harvard Business Review*. He was ranked the world's most influential scholar (among those completing PhDs after 1990) by the *Academy of Management Perspectives* based on citations and Google searches on his name. He has written cover stories for *Forbes*, and his research has been featured in *The Economist, Fortune,* and *Businessweek*. He regularly delivers keynote speeches and workshops on strategy and innovation to clients such as Adobe, AT&T, Dell, Intel, Johnson & Johnson, and Microsoft.

NATHAN FURR is a strategy professor at INSEAD's Paris campus and is a recognized expert in the field of innovation and technology strategy. Professor Furr earned his PhD from the Technology Ventures Program at Stanford University. He has published multiple books on how companies innovate and transform, including bestselling books *Leading Transformation, The Innovator's Method,* and *Nail It Then Scale It*, which have won multiple awards. He has also published multiple articles in leading academic and practice journals, including *Harvard Business Review, Sloan Management Review, Forbes, Inc.,* and other outlets. His research has received multiple awards, including the Kauffman Foundation Junior Faculty Fellowship. At INSEAD he leads the digital transformation and innovation teaching efforts, which have won multiple external teaching awards. He also cofounded the International Business Model Competition, which attracts more than 2,500 teams from around the world, and Innovator's DNA (with Jeff and Curtis). Professionally, Nathan delivers keynote speeches and works with many of the world's most innovative companies—and their leaders—including Google, Amazon, Citi, Intuit, Tesla, and many others.

CURTIS LEFRANDT is cofounder and CEO of the Innovator's DNA consultancy. He oversees the strategic direction and delivery of iDNA's consulting services, training programs, and product development. Under his leadership, iDNA has developed a range of innovation training offerings and tools designed to help organizations build a culture of and capability for innovation. He is a frequent keynote speaker, facilitator, and trainer of innovation for a range of industries and *Fortune* 500 organizations, including United Technologies, Unicef, Johnson & Johnson, Cisco, Philips, Danaher, Fortive, and Caterpillar. Prior to iDNA, Lefrandt worked as a consultant at Innosight, in venture capital investing, and as part of the iPod team at Apple. He also teaches innovation and entrepreneurship at Brigham Young University.

Dad, How Do I?

PART I

Dadvice

DAD JOKE

◇◇◇

The brownie told the vanilla wafer he was crazy.

"I'm not crazy," the wafer said. "I'm just a little cookie."

Dad, How Do I?

Home

Outside Your Home

CONTENTS

This book is dedicated to my family.

To my immediate family, for all you have taught me
over the years: my wife, Annelli; my children, Kyle
and Kristine; and my son-in-law, Ryan.

To my brothers and sisters, for filling voids
that needed to be filled.

To my mom and dad, for the quality traits that you
instilled in my siblings. It took me a while to forgive you, but
now I can appreciate the good that you did give me.

To my Internet kids, for your kindness,
encouragement, and support.

Dad, How Do I?

◇◇

PRACTICAL "DADVICE"
FOR EVERYDAY TASKS AND
SUCCESSFUL LIVING

◇◇

Rob Kenney

wm

WILLIAM MORROW
An Imprint of HarperCollins*Publishers*

HarperCollins books may be purchased for educational, business, or sales promotional use. For information, please email the Special Markets Department at SPsales@harpercollins.com.

FIRST EDITION

Design by Elina Cohen
Illustrations by Alexis Seabrook

Library of Congress Cataloging-in-Publication Data has been applied for.

ISBN 978-0-06-307499-6

21 22 23 24 25 LSC 10 9 8 7 6 5 4 3 2 1

Open Your Life to Awesome Goodness

Hey, kids!

Right off the bat, you might be wondering what makes me a credible person when it comes to encouraging you or giving fatherly advice. Well, I've learned a thing or two about trying to figure out life on my own. I don't know everything, and I'm still sorting out the finer points of life like everybody else. But I'm happy to share what I've learned, particularly since a lot of it was learned the hard way.

I come from a big Catholic family, eight kids in all—three girls, five boys. I really love my family, and on my fiftieth birthday we all got together to celebrate. I recognized in each person a positive character trait that I'd seen most strongly in them throughout the years and that had inspired and helped me along the way. In fact, each chapter in the first part of this book is based around attributes I learned from my siblings.

I'm the second to youngest. All my older siblings were born in Kansas, and they describe the earliest times in our family's life as really good. My parents started out so well. Dad worked for Boeing in Wichita and enjoyed his job. He loved photography as a hobby. Mom was smart and had taught school before she and Dad were married. She loved playing the piano. The earliest photos show an all-American family at its best. Everybody's smiling. Everybody's happy. Mom and Dad bought a small hobby farm south of Wichita, because that was a dream of Mom's—raising her kids in the Kansas sunshine.

Then Dad's job as an aeronautical engineer dried up, vanishing with a handshake and pink slip from the boss. Dad looked for work in Wichita, but nothing could be found. The family needed to move. But where? Mom was one of twelve siblings, and the bulk of her extended family lived near Wichita. She had always envisioned her own family settling down in that area, her kids playing with their cousins. Finally Dad found a great job working for the space program—in New Orleans.

Although excitement and relief filled the family, Mom wasn't keen on moving. She tried, however, to make the best of things. I was born in 1964, about a year after they moved to New Orleans, and my birth announcement, which Mom created by hand, read: "Our Little Space Project." She was putting on a brave face. Just like Dorothy in *The Wizard of Oz*, Mom always desired in her heart to return to Kansas. There's no place like home, and home for her was never in New Orleans, no matter how hard Mom tried.

Dad was a good worker and soon spotted another big opportunity. The Boeing 747 program was underway in Everett, Washington. They made him an offer he couldn't refuse. We moved to Bellevue, south of Everett, where Mom and Dad bought a house for under $30,000. Dad loved his new job and stayed involved with us kids. Mom did the best she could, but the stress and adjustments of the two cross-country moves were taking a bigger toll on her than she communicated to us. For years, a big pile of boxes, still packed, sat in our basement—untouched. Mom was never convinced we were staying.

In the early years of my life, I remember my dad taking us fishing and camping, and we used to play football almost every Sunday afternoon at the field at the nearby school. I was five or six then. On Sunday mornings we'd go to Mass, then head home and eat a quick lunch. We'd watch the game on TV during football season. I'm a Steelers fan today, but back then I loved the Packers since my dad loved the Packers. Quarterback Bart Starr was our favorite player. My brother Don's favorite team was always the Cowboys. He liked Roger Staubach, and there was a big rivalry in those days between the Packers and the Cowboys. Whenever those two teams played, Don would be on one side of the room, cheering for his team. Dad and I would be on the other, cheering for ours. I don't remember who everybody else in our family cheered for, but I remember that for years all we ever thought about was football. I have a vivid recollection of me, Don, and our older brother Joe, ages five, seven, and nine, respectively. We became our favorite players most Sunday mornings after Mass was finished. As we left the church building, we wove in and out of the other parishioners, cutting and faking, pretending we were aiming for the end zone. That's just how focused on football we were. We were oblivious to how that must have looked to the people we were dodging.

Generally, Sundays were good days. Once lunch was finished and the game was over on TV, we'd head up to the field at the school. There'd be maybe an hour or two of daylight left in the cool Pacific Northwest autumn afternoon. We'd divide up into teams. Dad could throw pretty well and would play quarterback for both teams, alternating sides depending on which team was playing offense.

However, over the next few years, things began to sour between my parents. Mom struggled with anxiety and turned to alcohol. She saw a therapist, but he brushed off her concerns, saying, "Oh, Barbara, just buy yourself a new hat." This was the 1970s, so there wasn't nearly the amount of mental health resources available as today. As I look back on those days from an adult's perspective, my heart goes out to my mom. She really had no support system in her life, and she did the best that she knew how.

Eventually, Mom and Dad separated. I was twelve or thirteen years old. Dad gained custody of us, but I'm not sure he really wanted us. He had become involved with another woman, who also worked at Boeing. On the weekend, he would load us kids up with groceries, then drive an hour up the freeway to Everett and stay there for the rest of the week. He would return the next weekend, stock us up again, then head back to Everett for another week with her. This pattern went on for a year or so, week after week after week. We were all alone.

When I was thirteen, my dad came home, called us all together, and announced that he was finished with fatherhood. It stunned me. "I'm done raising kids" was his exact phrase. I didn't know that was an option for a parent. (Hint: It's not!) This was cold-hearted rejection, and I was devastated. I had no stability, no sense of what was normal. The four oldest kids were out of the home by then, the four younger ones, including myself, were still at home and needed somewhere to live. Mom had slipped more into her addictions and wasn't able to take us by then. Dad told my older siblings they needed to take in the younger ones. Otherwise, he said, we'd be split up and farmed out to foster homes.

It wasn't easy for the older kids to assume responsibility for the younger kids. Joe and Don, two of the younger ones, were seventeen and sixteen, still in high school. They pooled resources and got their own apartment. Dad chipped in to help, as ordered in the divorce decree. My brother Rick, who was twenty-three, had recently gotten out of the military and was newly married. I went to live with him and his wife in their 280-square-foot trailer. The living quarters were tight, but at least I had someplace to stay.

Those were my teenage years, full of confusion, anger, and sorrow. My method of coping was to become the best kid I could be. I tried never to rock the boat. It wasn't easy to live with Rick and his wife in such tight quarters. (I am sure it wasn't easy for them, either!) But maybe, I thought, if I could just keep my nose clean and be perfect, they'd let me stay.

Trying to be flawless isn't a sustainable way of living. Yet in spite of things, a genuinely good and noble vow formed in my own soul during those years. Great pain had filled my young life—and I felt that rawness with all my being. So I vowed that when I grew up and got married and had kids, I would never cause such pain in my children's lives. At least not if I could help it. Oh sure, I knew I would make mistakes as a dad, but I would never leave my children like my dad had left us. I would never not be there for my kids. Never.

Sadly, I learned my story wasn't all that unique. At my school, I knew plenty of other kids without fathers. Those kids struggled with their own stories of pain and rejection, too. So as the years went on, my vow deepened and broadened. Someday, some way, when I grew up, I would help anybody who needed a dad. Whenever they needed direction, I would be the type of dad who offered support, who helped them along their way.

Because guidance is exactly what so many of us need. I know I needed a ton of it when I was growing up.

WE ALL NEED GUIDANCE

Here's what I mean. As a kid, I dreamed of growing up to play football. Making it all the way to the NFL was my big goal. I was a good athlete in high school. Big framed. Good hands. By the time I graduated, I was 6 feet 3 inches tall and weighed 215 pounds. I was a varsity starter and played tight end. My ticket to the pros was to play college ball first—and that meant going to a four-year university. At least that's what I figured.

Since nobody was there to guide me.

See, before I could even try out my plan of going to college, I needed to make some money to support myself. As a high school senior, I got a job where I pumped gas and washed cars. After graduation, I started working at an office supply company. The wages were okay, so I stayed at the company for three years. The longer I stayed, the more my dream slowly slipped away.

Then my mom died. Suddenly. Painfully. She had definitely not been living her dream in her last years of life. It was a wake-up call for me. I had grown resentful, and I knew I wasn't always that kind to her. I honestly was just trying to cope, and I didn't make time for my mom. Looking back, I regret that I was unable to reconcile with her before she died. That was January 1986. At the memorial service, I talked to some of my brothers and sisters about our mom's life while simultaneously taking a hard look at the road I was on. I decided that if I was ever going to pursue my dream, I needed to head in that direction as soon as possible.

By the spring of 1986, I had enrolled as a freshman at Central Washington University in Ellensburg, about a hundred miles east of Seattle. It was a small university, but it still had a powerhouse football program. I was a walk-on to the football team, which meant I wasn't recruited beforehand or offered any athletic scholarships. I simply signed up for classes, tried out for the team, and made it. I was a wide receiver for the CWU Wildcats!

Since I wasn't recruited and just showed up for spring ball, I was at a huge disadvantage. The coaches had already put in a lot of time convincing players to come there, so those players were given every opportunity to succeed. I did everything I could to take advantage of the playing time I was given, but it was still extremely tough to compete against the recruited players. As the season progressed, I didn't get much game time, no matter how hard I tried. My hope was to be discovered by an NFL scout and get a tryout with the pros. I knew it was a long shot, and so far I was struggling to get my feet on the field. Game after game, I sat and watched, mainly warming the bench. I was a wide receiver with good hands, but the limited playing time I was getting wouldn't be nearly enough to get noticed.

Imagine my surprise when late in the season a friend pulled

me aside and explained how my plan already had a flaw. If I had gone to community college first, I could have earned my associate's degree in two years and then transferred to a four-year university with two years of game time under my belt. He explained that incoming athletes can get tons more time on the field at a community college level, and that those colleges are feeder programs for university teams. If I had headed the community college route first, I could have been one of the recruited players that were given more opportunities. That would have positioned me to stand a much better chance of being noticed by a scout and making it into the pros. (Not to mention saving a bundle on tuition.)

The news hit me like a defensive lineman. If only somebody had given me some guidance before I'd enrolled, it would have saved me so much time and grief. I had taken action on my dream by myself, and that was admirable. But I didn't have all the necessary information to make the wisest choices.

MOVING PAST FRUSTRATION

Have you ever experienced frustration like I did?

You have dreams, and you want to pursue those dreams. Or maybe you are facing a problem to be solved. What you need is a guide. You want advice about how to solve your problem or follow your dream. You're looking for a blueprint. You're searching for answers about what to do next. A way forward lies somewhere, but you don't know where to turn. You might move in one of several ways. Maybe you'll charge ahead and learn things the hard way by floundering along on your own steam, or by working doubly as hard as the people around you, or by falling into pits and pulling yourself out. None of these paths is wrong—they're just difficult and often inefficient.

Maybe you'll try but fail. That can be devastating. The failure might hurt a long time. Or the failure might turn out to be an overall okay experience—if someone is there to help you grieve your losses, or show you how to grow and learn from your mistakes.

Or maybe you'll never start in the first place. You're too bewildered to begin, too overwhelmed by the countless options in front of you. It's like life is a huge puzzle that's been dumped out on the floor. You're staring at two thousand tiny pieces of blue sky. Where do you begin?

Any way you look at it, having a good guide to help you on your way can save you a heap of trouble, time, emotional energy, and expense. If you've got a problem that needs to be solved, if you've got a dream you want to pursue, one of the best ways to start is to ask someone for help.

See, around the time the guy told me I'd chosen a harder path by not playing football in community college, a light bulb came on. I realized there was plenty of advice out there, and although at the time I didn't have a strong network of people who were automatically pouring wisdom into me, I saw how I could be proactive by reading, researching, reaching out to people, finding mentors, and asking for help. I made two pledges to myself. First, I would start on a lifelong quest to ask for insight into the things I wanted to learn. And second, after I had learned something, I would pass along that insight to anyone coming up behind me, anyone needing support and guidance.

The fulfillment of those pledges hasn't always been easy. Sometimes I needed to swallow my pride. It felt a little weird to be asking someone for help. I'm a self-starter, an independent person. My natural inclination is to tear into challenges blindly and figure out solutions on my own. Years later, now on the other side of the equation and with advice to give, I've learned to respect the independent types. I've learned to give people guidance only if they ask for it. Not everybody wants advice. So if that's you, then that's okay. I'm not here to force you to do anything.

My invitation to you is to consider this a guidebook in the

pursuit of fulfilling your life's dreams. I want to pass along some nuggets of insight and knowledge that are vital for skill-building, some wisdom to help you along your way. Despite my natural independence, I've learned to see the value of having people show me how to do things, and now I want to pass that to you. I won't tell you everything you need to know about every specific question you have. But I'll give you some strong, solid advice about becoming the person you want to be, to help you on your way in any pursuit you choose.

I don't consider myself the smartest person who's ever lived. Far from it. But I'm not dumb, either. I've learned a lot over the years—not only about skills you can learn, but about actions you can take to become confident and successful. I'm interested in you developing your integrity and character, as well as practical skills such as how to change a flat tire.

I'm middle-aged, and my wife, Annelli, and I have raised two kids of our own, Kristine and Kyle. Our kids are in their mid-to-late twenties now, and both are doing well. Several years back, when Kyle graduated from high school, he wanted to play baseball at a collegiate level. So I passed on to him what I had learned. Kyle weighed his options for himself, then did exactly as I advised. He went to community college first, enjoyed a lot of game time, and made an important life decision along the way.

By the time Kyle transferred to a four-year university, he could have stood shoulder to shoulder with any player on the baseball team if he'd wanted. But in Kyle's case, he actually decided to drop sports due to a new love for computer programing he'd discovered along the way. He wanted to pour his heart and time into that, not baseball. He credits his time at community college—as well as our advice as parents—for giving him the solid foundation to help figure things out.

That's the kind of guidance and encouragement I hope this book will provide for you, too.

HUMBLE BEGINNINGS

How did these stories lead me to write this book? Well, after I grew up and finished my time in university, I worked as a drafter first, making technical drawings of electrical wiring diagrams for airplane manuals, then a lead drafter. I met my wife at work. I was the lead on the first shift; she was the lead on the second shift. Right away, I knew she was a woman of depth and character. She wasn't pretentious. She didn't play emotional games with anyone. She was the right kind of attractive. We married and had kids and started the happily-ever-after part of our story.

In my career, I changed jobs a few times, then finally returned to the office supply company I'd worked for right out of high school. This time I joined the sales department, and although I didn't know much about sales when I started, I learned and grew along the way. I never wanted to be the stereotypical used-car-salesman sort of guy, someone who promised much but delivered little. I guarded against that and instead became a liaison, an advocate for my customers, always looking out for the people I serve. Overall, my job has been a good fit, and almost thirty years later, that's where I still am.

Today, as my wife and I look back on the years when our children were growing up in our house, we do so with a sense of accomplishment. We raised them to live with integrity, smarts, and faith, to think about the long-term consequences of any action, and to become healthy, well-adjusted adults.

Yet I must admit I was feeling a bit lost when I reached my early fifties. I'd never become a professional football player. I had succeeded in my career, marriage, and parenting—the three big pillars of adult life. However, since I had so emphasized that my goal was to raise great adults, and that had been essentially accomplished, I wondered what the rest of my life would look like. I didn't want to just retire and die. Now that I was beyond the family-raising years,

I wanted to do more, something that was purposeful. I thought back to my larger vow of helping others. An idea began to form in my mind.

With my daughter's help, the plan began to unfold. She encouraged me to start a YouTube channel so I could help people. Kristine has been blessed with a gift of recognizing what people need. Since we talk all the time about managing life, she wondered what other people do when they don't have a parent to talk to. I came up with the channel's name as I pictured one of my kids calling out from the other room: "Dad, How Do I?" I started posting videos that teach people skills they need but didn't learn for various reasons, skills that in my mind are essential for everyone to have.

My channel started out small. My first videos were about how to tie a tie, change a tire, and iron a dress shirt. I wasn't trying to be anything other than who I am. In each video I'd simply say hello, tell a dad joke, then start explaining how to do a task.

I thought I might help thirty or forty people total. Each individual is important, and I certainly wasn't looking to be famous. Yet I guess I really scratched an itch that was out there. I'd hoped that my love, support, encouragement, and warmth would come through in my videos, and I guess they did, because the videos began to reach people on a level I could never have imagined. People wrote to me to say they'd watched me demonstrate how to tie a tie and they'd started to bawl. See, the videos weren't just about sharing information. They were offering a sense of care that many people had never received from their own fathers. My site went viral. I became a digital dad.

The explosive growth of the site has been ridiculous. And today, I find myself being given the opportunity to share some advice in book form. I am still trying to process it all. I didn't start my channel so you can tune in and just watch me do something. As I believe a loving dad should, I tried to have my kids help me with different tasks so they could learn and gain experience. Sure, they did a lot of watching, and maybe the job would have gone faster if I just did it alone. I included them, not merely to enjoy their company, but to instill confidence that they can take on these and other tasks. My hope is to encourage you with resources and learned skills, so you can be competent no matter the task. Go for more. Stand on other people's shoulders (their skills and experience), so you can reach higher. Be the person you were meant to be.

CONFIDENCE TO FIGURE THINGS OUT

Being a family man is a constant learning experience. Annelli and I were married at twenty-six—young, at least by today's standards—and we managed to buy our first house right before our daughter, Kristine, was born. Our son, Kyle, came along three years later. Kristine really wanted a brown-and-white dog, like she'd seen on a TV show. So we went to the pound, and she spotted an even-tempered German shepherd mix of a mutt. The dog was more gold than brown, but Kristine was convinced it was close enough. We brought the dog home, and Kristine named her Gan. None of us knew where the name came from, including Kristine, but she liked it. So that was all that mattered.

All went well with Gan until several years later when we moved into a slightly larger house. Gan was mostly a good dog, but she had one weakness. She loved to run, as wild and free as possible. We called her an escape artist. If you opened the front door, Gan was gone. And she'd mock you, letting you come just close enough so you'd think you could catch her. In an instant, she'd sprint down the street again. Our former house had a fence around it, but our new one didn't. Money was always tight, which meant that when we moved, dear old Dad needed to build a fence to contain that dog.

And I had no idea how.

Fortunately by then I'd developed a good network of people I called whenever I needed guidance. My older brother Rick worked as a cabinetmaker and was quite handy. Over the phone, he listed the materials I'd need, explained each step to take, and gave me some general pointers.

The next Saturday I took the kids down to the lumberyard and bought the materials. As I mentioned earlier, I knew the job would be easier if I built the fence myself, but I wanted my kids to help. The choice to include them was part of my pledge—I wanted to pass along what I was learning, as well as what I already knew. The three of us came home, laid out the posts and boards, and got to work. I measured and marked out the spaces. We all helped dig the holes to the right depth. One by one we centered and set the posts. Kyle and Kristine tamped down the dirt. We braced the posts. Kyle held the boards. Kristine hammered. One weekend's work stretched into two. Then three.

On a rainy Saturday in spring, we hammered up the last board, then stood back and examined our work. The fence looked terrific. All the boards were straight and sturdy. The air smelled fresh with new cedar. Kyle's chest swelled with pride. Kristine gave a big smile. I was grinning, too. We had built this fence ourselves.

The cool thing is that once you figure out how to do something for yourself, you'll have the confidence to try more things on your own. Since we built that fence, we've also installed windows, siding, roofing, flooring, and bathroom tile. All those tasks sounded hard initially, but none were very tricky after we got some advice.

That's what this book is all about. Much of life can seem difficult at first. But with a little help along the way, just like the tips I got from my big brother, you can figure things out. It won't all be easy. No matter what task lies before you, you need to plan well and think things through. Make sure your plans are solid. Get the right materials. Keep taking measurements along the way so you can evaluate your progress. You can do it. You've got what it takes.

AWESOME GOODNESS

My own kids and I speak several times each week. They're both very bright, and these days it seems that they're showing me how to do things as much as I'm offering any advice to them. My hope for this book is that I'll become to you a bit of what I am to them.

Maybe I can better explain my promise to you with another story. In 2019, my wife and I went to Rome, with side trips to Florence and Venice. This had been a lifelong dream for us. Once we got our kids through college—without debt, I might add—Annelli and I started to take trips. We didn't want to wait for retirement.

Rome was amazing. There are so many layers of history. We saw the Arch of Titus, a controversial monument that marks the sacking of Judea and the destruction of the Jewish temple in Jerusalem in 70 A.D. We walked among the ruins of the Forum, the huge rectangular-shaped area that had been home to a variety of ancient Rome's commercial, political, and religious sites. We saw the Colosseum, the largest known amphitheater of the ancient world. We saw statue after statue and ruin after ruin.

When we left Rome, I couldn't help but wonder at the power once held by this ancient civilization. At one time, Rome had been everything, and the ruins are still impressive to look at today. I considered how time changes all things, and the things that you think are so important one day might become ruins tomorrow. It really cemented in my mind how temporary this life is.

So, you need to ask yourself what really matters. What's really worth holding on to? What's really worth building? What's really worth putting time into?

People is the answer I came up with. Or to be more specific:
You.

You're important to me. What matters to me is not so much that you learn how to tie a tie. It's that you learn—and feel deeply within yourself—that somebody cares for you.

I care for you. That's why I started my YouTube channel, to help you achieve everything you're capable of achieving. And that's why I wrote this book.

I hope you fulfill your dreams and become the kind of person you want to be. I hope you discover what's truly important in life—the value of caring for others and living for what matters.

As I mentioned earlier, my parents started off extremely well in how they parented us. My siblings are a testimony to that, and they all have had a hand in shaping the man I am today. In the pages that follow, I'm going to share attributes I learned from each of them, characteristics that will help you navigate your own life.

And while you're on your journey, know that you are not alone. I'm here for you. So aim well, my friend. Your invitation is to open yourself to the awesome goodness of what comes next in your life. Big opportunities lie just around the corner. Let's walk this road together.

DAD JOKE

◇◇

Why did the outfielder phone the shortstop?

He just wanted to touch base.

Mail That Postcard

My siblings and I stayed in touch with our dad even after he left us. He remained in Everett for a while, then moved with his new wife a couple of times, finally settling in another state. He'd call occasionally. As time passed, our relationship with our dad was what I'd describe as superficial at best. None of us ever talked deeply with him. He certainly didn't talk deeply with us. He never really provided any guidance or wise counsel. I didn't feel like I could look up to him.

My older brothers and sisters seemed to take things more in stride. They'd had more time to see the best of Dad, before things unraveled in our family, so they weighed the good with the bad. But I hadn't had much opportunity to do that. Was I mad at our dad? Yes. Did I feel cheated by him? Without a doubt. Did I carry that hurt with me? For years and years.

And did I need to do something about that hurt?

Absolutely.

I'll tell you in a moment how I dealt with my own hurt. But first, let's swing the focus back to you. You're the hero of your story.

You're the one who will take action to do good. May I ask: What's your relationship like with your family members? Maybe you've got a good relationship with everybody. People love you, and you love them, and you all express your love for one another in healthy, recognizable, and reciprocal ways. If that's you, then thank heaven for what you've been given. Do you have a mom or dad who loves you? Please appreciate them. A loving family is worth its weight in gold.

But maybe you've been hurt somewhere along the line. Someone said or did the wrong thing. They ignored, forgot, harshly criticized, or abandoned you. Perhaps you've been hurt deeply by someone close to you—and the hurt is magnified because the person was in a place where they were supposed to care for you. Not long ago I received a note from a young man whose stepdad had sexually abused him when he was younger. Such great pain exists in this world. I understand that and want to acknowledge it. Deep pain might be part of your story, and if it is, then please know you're not alone. I do care if that's part of your story.

My point in this book isn't to tell you to ignore your pain, or gloss over it, or sweep it under the rug. Never. The aim of this book is to help you become successful in life no matter what has happened to you. I want to teach you skills and show you how to take action so you can live confidently. None of us can go back and change the past. What you and I can do is take control of our reactions to things in the present. We can seek advice and live wisely and make strong and solid plans for the future. The life you came from is not as important as the life you are creating for yourself today.

With that in mind, here's a very positive action you can take right now. I'll explain more in a moment why this is so powerful, so positive, and so beneficial to you and others. It's incredibly simple, yet good things almost always result from it. The action is this:

Mail a postcard.

ONE SMALL MOVE

One way we become successful in life is by moving in a good direction, even a small move, even though we might not feel like it at first. Experts tell us that action creates emotion, although that sequence can feel counterintuitive.

Why? Well, if a girlfriend loves her boyfriend, she gives him a hug, right? Or if a guy hates another guy, he might want to hit him. In both examples, the feeling comes first, and then the action follows. That sequence feels correct.

Yet experts tell us that while actions can definitely follow feelings, we can actually reverse that sequence, too. If we want to change how we're feeling, we can start acting the way we want to feel, and then a genuine emotion will be the result.[1] Act positive first. Positive feelings will follow.

For instance, a husband and wife might be arguing a lot. They feel like they hate each other, like they want a divorce. But if they deliberately start doing romantic things, even though they don't feel like doing so at first, often they can rekindle their genuine passion. If they take loving actions toward each other first, they can generate loving feelings second.[2]

Or say two people have opposing viewpoints. They might feel like they hate each other. They may want to hit each other or at least argue harshly on social media. But if they deliberately take positive, empathetic action such as listening to each other and trying to put themselves in the other person's shoes, then genuine understanding can occur. They still might not get along perfectly well, or agree about all issues, but at least they won't hate each other anymore. They can appreciate the diversity of their viewpoints and respect where the other person is coming from.

Let's go back to you and your family members. If you're not getting along, it's almost always good to initiate positive action. You can be the one who reaches out first. How? Sometimes taking positive action means confronting the person who's hurt you and working toward understanding and restoration, particularly if you do so in a nonthreatening way. Here's what that might look like. You sit down with somebody and give them an "I message." You say something like, "Hey, my birthday was yesterday, and I really wanted to be acknowledged in a good way on my birthday. When that didn't happen, I felt hurt." You describe the behavior that happened, or the need you had that wasn't met, and then the feeling that resulted. When you use an "I message" (*I felt hurt*) instead of a "you message" (*you hurt my feelings*), it prevents the other person from feeling accused.

Confrontation can be messy and complicated. Sometimes it doesn't work. What then? When I was in my early twenties and my mom died, Dad came to the memorial service in Bellevue. I was glad that he made the effort to pay his respects. We held the service in the church that our family was attending when my parents separated, so a number of people at the service knew our story. It took courage for Dad to show up, although I'm not sure how happy everyone was to see him.

After the service, several of my siblings and I were in a hotel room with Dad. My older brother, Tim, confronted Dad about some of the things that he had done. He also told our dad he should help pay for my education. That did not go over well. Dad got huffy and stormed out of the room. Everybody agreed: The confrontation hadn't worked. It also probably wasn't the best timing, with emotions running high after my mom's passing.

From that point on, an unwritten rule took shape among us. Dad wasn't to be confronted. Tim had tried to compel Dad to admit his mistakes and apologize. But Dad wasn't going there. In the ensuing years, he developed a number of health problems, including heart disease and cancer. For the last fifteen years of his life, he had a colostomy bag. With each health problem that emerged, our unspoken pledge not to confront Dad only became more resolved. Sure, we would have been justified to confront him again, but we didn't want to kill the guy by giving him a heart attack. We just wanted to get on with our lives.

But how?

IT'S NOT EASY

Your family is imperfect. Hey, *everybody's* family is imperfect, and it can be hard to love imperfect people. Yet the wise thing to do is love your family anyway. Be the person who acts first. Decide to take positive action. What action might you take?

When I was in my early forties, my older brother Rick initiated a family get-together with the specific purpose of honoring our dad on Father's Day. The plan was to hold a special breakfast at a hotel, to honor him simply because he was our dad. The Bible does say to honor your father and mother,[3] but I was struggling with that concept. Rick had thought things through carefully. He wanted to hold the gathering as an expression of a new, deeper faith he'd found. He'd been reading about the benefits of forgiveness and the need to honor your parents, simply because they're your parents. I had found a deeper faith by then, too, but I wasn't convinced about the breakfast. In my mind, Dad was my biological father who'd brought me into the world, and that was something I could thank him for. But honor him? And forgive him? After what he'd done to us? The breakfast felt like hypocrisy.

One thing that's helped me sort out problems or issues in my life is my morning practice of being an early riser. I like to get up at 5 A.M. Sometimes 6, if I sleep in. I grab my Bible, sit in the recliner in our living room, and spend time in quietness and contemplation, thinking, reading, and praying. Please understand, I do try to keep this early morning commitment every day, but there are times that I'm unable to, and I am okay with that. It's not a legalistic ritual that I have to do, but I know from personal experience it is something I need.

Early one morning, with the day of the family get-together drawing near, I was sitting in my recliner and feeling troubled. My father had genuinely hurt me, and I knew none of us could go back and change the past. My feelings were valid. My hurt was my hurt. No way could I forgive and forget, as people often say you should do. Yet I knew deep down that I should take some kind of positive action.

I thought about how Rick had decided to forgive my dad. Rick was moving on. Feelings swirled within me. I felt guilty that I couldn't forgive my dad. I believed I should forgive him, but I just didn't want to. I struggled. My spirit was in an upheaval. I wondered if I should even go to the breakfast. I tried to read. I tried to pray. Nothing felt like it was making sense.

Fortunately, at this point in my life I knew enough to ask for advice. Later in the day I talked to my wife about what was troubling me, and she was supportive. Then I called Rick and hashed things out. Rick had been there with me at my toughest times. He was the brother I had lived with when Dad had left us. Rick knew all about my hurt. Yet Rick had never allowed me to think of myself as a victim. I call these kinds of talks "coughing up hairballs." Something's stuck in your windpipe. You have to hack and hack to move it up and out. That hairball is tough coming up. Yet once it's out, you're glad. That's what our talk that day felt like.

I was hesitant to go to the breakfast, and I told him why. Rick told me he understood, but thought that maybe by going to the breakfast, I'd be taking a small action in a good direction. At least I'd be taking a step or two down the right road.

I decided to go.

When the big day came, we gathered at a hotel in Issaquah, just east of Seattle. Not everybody from our family was able to attend, but a majority of my siblings, their spouses, and their kids arrived. Dad showed up. We sat down and dined on waffles, bacon, eggs, orange juice, and coffee. After the waitstaff had cleared the dishes, Rick stood up and explained a bit about the gathering and how we were all there to honor Dad. Several people also stood and said nice things about Dad.

And me?

On the outside, I was keeping it all together. But inside, I was struggling with my emotions. Didn't people realize how much this man had hurt us? I couldn't honor this man. Yet here he was being recognized for doing good things! It felt like the hurts he had caused were being belittled or glossed over. That was almost too much for me to take.

I managed to keep it together during the speeches. I kept it together in the car on the ride home. But back at home, when it was just me with my thoughts in my recliner . . .

I sobbed.

THE FORGIVENESS MECHANISM

Forgiveness is tricky, but I was beginning to see that it's a must. When an offense is committed against you—by a family member or anyone else—you have to clearly see it for what it is. When somebody hurts you deeply, you can't shrug that off as no big deal. It's healthy—even necessary—for you to call an offense wrong. When you consider forgiving somebody, that doesn't mean you dismiss a wrong or say you weren't hurt. Forgiveness doesn't need to mean full reconciliation with a person. That may come in time as trust is built, or it may not. Just because you forgive someone, it doesn't mean you have to be best friends.

But you have to forgive.

See, if you don't forgive, then it only hurts you more.

You're the one carrying the heavy load. You're replaying the rage. Someone told me once that not forgiving someone is like drinking poison and hoping it somehow affects the other person.[4] When I heard that, it really hit home for me, because that's exactly what I was doing.

When you don't forgive, you relive that hurt again and again. It's like somebody has backed up a truckload of manure into your life and dumped it all over your front yard. When you don't forgive someone, you pitch a tent in that front yard and live in the stink. You roll around in the smell and muck and toxins. By holding tight to that pain you only succeed in experiencing more hurt.

Think of forgiveness as your shovel. Or maybe your backhoe. You have to shovel the crap off your front yard. Push it aside. Get it out of there so you can move on with your life. Some of the manure will remain, sure. You can't escape the fact that a truckload of manure has been dumped where you live. Yet after you shovel it all away, the residue that's left behind can act as fertilizer. You've been hurt? Disappointed? Absolutely. But you're going to take the residue of that fertilizer and use it for your advantage. You're going to grab that hurt and pain and turn it into a fresh green lawn. How?

Undoubtedly you'll become a more compassionate person thanks to your pain. Maybe you'll help people who have been hurt the same way you've been hurt, since you know what they're going through. Perhaps you'll simply mesh that hurt with the rest of your life and make it an integral part of who you are. You've been hurt, but you are not defeated. You'll wear your scars like medals.

It took me several years after the breakfast to forgive my dad. It's a little sad. Looking back, I wish I'd done it sooner. I was in the recliner one morning, reading and praying, when it dawned on me that it was in my own best interest to forgive my dad. I simply needed to do it. If ever I was going to move forward, I needed to lay aside the grudge I held against him. He wasn't going to come to me and ask for my forgiveness, so if I waited for him to act first, then I would have to wait another thirty years. Meanwhile, life was passing me by.

I certainly didn't *feel* like I wanted to forgive him. I still wanted a pound of his flesh. But I would no longer let my feelings dictate my life. If I continued to allow those feelings of hate to fester, then I was only damaging myself. So I decided to act positively first, believing that new, positive emotions would follow. Did I truly want to carry around a load of anger anymore? No. I wanted to be set free. So I acknowledged the hurt to myself and before God. Yes, my father hurt me. Yes, it was wrong of him to abandon us. I didn't gloss over what he did, and I didn't pretend to forget that he'd walked out on us. But I chose to forgive him anyway. I chose to extend full forgiveness toward him. What he would do with it was up to him.

Forgiveness meant that I would not hold the past against my dad. I'd stop replaying all those old conversations in my mind, the ones I'd always wanted to have with him, shouting at him for how much he hurt me. When hurtful memories surfaced in my mind, I would tell myself I was no longer looking for payment. That chapter of my life was closed. I had moved on. My life was heading forward, and I was no longer going to beat up my dad in my mind.

The choice to forgive wasn't easy. Yet that morning I consciously and deliberately released my dad from the wrongs he had done to me.

R. T. Kendall writes:

> Total forgiveness is a choice. It is not a feeling—at least at first—but is rather an act of the will. It is the choice to tear up the record of wrongs we have been keeping. We clearly see and acknowledge the evil that was done to us, but we erase it—or destroy the record—before it becomes lodged in our hearts. This way resentment does not have a chance to grow. . . . We give up the natural desire to see them "get what's coming to them."[5]

No, I didn't call my dad that morning and tell him what had happened. Maybe I should have, I don't know. I'm not sure what he would have done with the information. And anyway, to me, the action of forgiveness was more for *me* than it was for him. I simply told myself that I wasn't going to drag my hurt into my future. In the days, weeks, months, and years that followed, more than once

I've had to remind myself of my choice to forgive. Yet I did it. I forgave him.

I chose to move on.

THE FREEDOM OF FORGIVENESS

So much freedom comes to you when you forgive someone who's hurt you, even if they never acknowledge their wrong. Will the person who hurt you ever ask for your forgiveness? Perhaps they won't. That's why it's up to you to take the first step. They may not even receive your forgiveness when you articulate it to them. But then again, stranger things have happened in this world. Sometimes the people who've hurt you do ask for and accept your forgiveness. Then the transaction of forgiveness is completed. Here's how it happened to me.

Each year we still tried to include Dad in stuff we did. As adults, my brothers and I cooked up a yearly fishing trip, and Dad came with us several times. We have our favorite secret spot over in Eastern Washington, and each October we'd head over there for a three-day adventure. It was a male-bonding thing, and as our kids grew up, sometimes our sons came with us. We'd haul over our aluminum boats on Friday morning. No gas motors are allowed on the lake, so we'd bring small electric motors. We'd fish all day and play poker each night. A nine-hole golf course is nearby, so we'd usually shoot a round of golf. Late Sunday we'd go home.

Several years after I'd forgiven my dad, we were all getting ready for the annual fishing trip. Rick wrote to Dad, inviting him to come, and he challenged our dad to tell us he loved us and to ask for our forgiveness. Dad told Rick he was surprised to hear that suggestion. He loved all his kids, he said. Rick answered, "Yeah, but they don't know that. So make sure *you* tell them." Dad said he would attempt to find some alone time with each of us during the fishing trip. (As a sidelight, this was a great plan of Rick's. Kids need to be told regularly by their folks that they're loved. If you're a parent, don't assume your kids know you're proud of them, or that you love them. Tell them.)

On Saturday morning Dad and I found ourselves out in my boat, just the two of us. High cliffs surrounded the lake. A canyon opened at one end of the lake, and wind can blow through the canyon and drive the waves up quickly. But that morning the lake was peaceful. The rocks that surround the lake are white from alkaline, and everywhere we looked was beautiful and calm.

Dad was eighty-six. He was a handsome man, even into his senior years, with a full head of gray hair and a full gray beard. He had a quick sense of humor and could be fun to be around, cracking jokes. He always pulled his weight whenever we were putting the boat in the water. When we were little kids and went fishing, Dad always brought his favorite three snacks: Vienna sausages, a family-sized box of Chicken in a Biskit crackers, and Hershey's Mr. Goodbars. My older brothers had carried on the tradition on our fishing trips. So as we fished, Dad and I shared a thermos of coffee and munched on those same snacks in the boat.

I knew the talk was coming. Rick had filled me in. For a while I simply looked into my father's eyes. Brown. They looked tired. It felt rare to have this type of connection with him. After a while he shrugged, finished up the last of his candy bar, cleared his throat, and said, "Well, Rick reached out to me and said that I needed to tell you guys I love you and ask for your forgiveness." He stopped talking and looked at the cliffs.

That's all he said, those exact words. I wasn't sure how sincere or how personal his apology was. He looked a little sheepish, and he seemed unaware of the gravity of his offense, because that's as far as he went. No details. No evidence of remorse.

"I was a fourteen-year-old kid when you left me," I said quietly, "and that's a horrible time for a boy to lose his dad. Yet I do forgive you. I don't hold it against you. I just need you to understand it was a very hard time for me."

He nodded and I nodded, and we both went on with fishing. That was it. Nobody cried. Nobody hugged. No big feeling of satisfaction arrived for me. The moment felt anticlimactic in a way, almost a formality. I'm not sure if Dad ever knew how huge his decision to leave us had been. Maybe I'd envisioned something more dramatic would happen if or when he actually apologized. But the talk out in the boat didn't feel momentous. The momentous event had come years earlier, when I'd decided to forgive him. My real work had been done already, and with it came tremendous freedom for me.

I decided to accept and believe the apology. I knew my dad and I probably would never have a relationship like the one I have with my own kids, but it was kind of nice to finally clear the air with him.

The following year, when Dad was eighty-seven, he was getting ready to go on the fishing trip with us again when he fell in his garage. His wife came out and found him. He was gone.

The memorial service was held in Dad's church. Due to unavoidable scheduling, it fell on my fifty-first birthday. Funerals can be sad, but his funeral felt more like a celebration. We weren't happy that he was dead. We celebrated his life, as mixed as it was. We all acknowledged that he had tried. We chose to honor the good. My dad had found a deep faith later in life, and we had confidence we would see him again someday in a much better place. There, all things would be set right. There, all things would be made new.

LOVE THEM ANYWAY

How do postcards fit into all this?

Sending postcards was my oldest sister Mary's idea. When things were at their hardest in our family, after Dad left us and when Mom was unable to take care of us, when I—along with the rest of us kids—was feeling such a huge emptiness in my life, Mary decided to take positive action. Twelve years older than me, she had been out of the house for a few years by the time things unraveled. In Colorado, she'd met her husband, Bob, and they soon moved to South Dakota.

Mary made a habit of sending postcards to all of us. Dad. Mom. Her siblings. She sent postcards to the cousins and aunts and uncles back in Kansas. She always remembered birthdays and special occasions, and often she sent cards and letters for no specific reason. Just to reach out and tell us she was thinking of us and loved us.

Mary never looked for anything in return. For the longest time after my dad left, I was just trying to cope, wondering what my new normal would be. I received postcard after postcard from Mary. I don't think I ever wrote back. Not because I didn't love her, but because when you're fourteen you don't think those kinds of things matter a whole bunch.

But they do matter. They matter a great deal. Mary was working hard to keep us all connected. She wanted us to hold on to our roots so we understood where we came from. She wanted to remind us regularly that even though life felt rotten in this season for us, we still had people who cared about us. There was still much good in the world. She was taking positive action first, so the positive feelings would follow.

Here's my counsel to you. One of the best things you can do in life is reach out to your family members. Decide right now to take this initiative yourself. Your family is not perfect, because no one's family is perfect. Yet it's in your best interest to love and value your family anyway. Show your family members unconditional love. You won't always approve of their choices. Love them anyway. They won't always say or do the things you need them to do. Love them anyway.

I get it. If you've never been shown unconditional love, or if you haven't been shown the right kind of love, it can be hard to show unconditional love to others. In my own life, I have experienced unconditional love from God, and that love is available to anyone.

God's love has a way of flowing into your life and filling you up, so that the same love can flow out of you and on to other people. If you're searching for love, let me recommend starting with God. You don't have to get your act together or shine yourself up first. He extends love to all people unconditionally, and he's the one who said, "I will never leave you. Never will I forsake you."[6]

Dr. Gary Chapman wrote a book a while back that's become a modern classic. It's called *The Five Love Languages*, and the big idea is that there are five main ways to express and experience love: saying nice things about people, spending time with them, giving them gifts, doing kind things for them, and touching them appropriately. The action for you to take, in a nutshell, is to figure out how your family members best receive love, and then start speaking their love language to them. Maybe your mom loves it when you vacuum the living room. Or maybe your grandma loves it when you give her a hug. When it comes to your family members, be the person who proactively reaches out and shows love.

The valuable characteristic that I learned from my sister Mary was the importance of family.

Send that postcard.

Keep Your Brains from Falling Out

BALONEY   TRUTH

We called it the baloney detector.

My older brother Tim was a master at sniffing things out. (A neighbor kid, closer to my age, was also named Tim, and we affectionately called him Little Tim. My big brother, naturally, was Big Tim.) If ever there was something Big Tim disagreed with, or that didn't quite sound right to him, he would subtly puff out his nostrils. If Big Tim's nostrils were flaring, we kids knew that he was calling something baloney. He wasn't going to do what someone wanted him to do unless he believed it was right.

Maybe it was our Catholic upbringing. We kids were mostly compliant. If Dad or Mom told us to do something, seven of the eight of us almost never questioned their authority. Most of the time, we did what we were told. But Big Tim was seldom that way. He wasn't afraid of a confrontation—he was the one who confronted Dad at Mom's funeral—he was never afraid to speak his mind, and he questioned pretty much everything. It might have been a perfectly legitimate parental order, like "Hey, Tim, make your bed." Or he might have asked why our parents made us go

DAD JOKE

◇◇

Did you hear about the bald guy whose rabbit got out of the cage?

He lost his hare.

to church every week. You could look at his face and see the idea zip around in Big Tim's mind: *Should I? Or shouldn't I?* Whatever came his way, Big Tim had to develop his own opinion before he took action.

Our mother was a big music fan. We kids always liked that about her, but her passion did cause a bit of tension. I think she'd always dreamed of us becoming a musical family like the von Trapp singers from *The Sound of Music*. I know she always enjoyed *The Music Man*. Maybe she envisioned all of us being in a band. Mom had played the piano when she was young. We had a trombone, so my older brother Rick was forced to play the trombone when he was in school, and then I had to play it, too. Neither of us were good at it. I have joked that I developed my peripheral vision when I played the trombone, because I would watch my bandmate next to me out of the corner of my eye to see when I needed to move the slide back and forth. I was always a split second behind him, but fast enough to make it look like I knew what I was doing.

The girls in our family didn't have to play the trombone. Instead, they took piano lessons on the beat-up old piano in the house. None of the girls really gravitated toward music except Laurie. She was in musical theater in high school, and after graduation she toured with the production company Up with People throughout Belgium. We had a trumpet in the house, too, and when Big Tim was a kid, he was forced to play trumpet, hating it with a passion. One day he and Mom had it out. Big Tim put his foot down. They argued back and forth. He had no interest in continuing to play the trumpet. Eventually Big Tim won.

Ever been in a similar situation? A directive is given to you— maybe from a parent, a teacher, a boss, or your friends. You're told to do something, be something, believe something, or act in a certain way. Do you blindly follow that order, or do you first run it through the framework of what you know to be true?

This chapter is one of the trickier ones in this book, because in it I'm going to encourage you to be like Big Tim—at least in some ways. That might not be the advice you'd expect to hear in a book such as this, and the counsel can be tricky because the action I'm encouraging you to take can lead to either positive or negative outcomes. Sometimes it can help you. Sometimes it can hurt. So you really need to be discerning in how you take this action. The advice is this:

If you want to be successful in life, question authority.

DON'T BLINDLY FOLLOW ANYBODY

Wait! What did he just say?

That's right—it's good to question authority. When it comes to authority figures and the orders they issue, young adults are typically encouraged to toe the line. If a boss gives you an order, then it's in your best interests to do what she says, as long as it's not illegal or immoral; otherwise you could lose your job. If your professor recommends you read chapters 1 through 3 of your textbook by Monday, then it's a good practice to do what he says, if you want to pass the course. If you're still living at home, and your parents give you a curfew and tell you to honor it, then it's a good idea to respect their wishes. It is their house, after all. I agree with following these kinds of requests from authority figures.

And yet I'm still telling you to question authority. There's a negative and a positive way to do this. The negative way is to question authority from the rebel's stance. The positive way is to question authority as a searcher, a person learning to evaluate. To question authority in this positive way means you don't blindly follow anybody. These days everybody is encouraged to be open-minded, and that can be good. But it can also be dangerous if you never have an opinion of your own, or if you don't learn to think for yourself. G. K. Chesterton has been quoted as saying, "Don't be so open-minded that your brains fall out."[1]

That's what I'm getting at: I want you to develop a backbone. That means you don't just follow whatever trend comes along. You're not a sheep. You don't do something only because it's popular. You learn to be logical. You learn to think before you speak. You learn to develop your own opinions and to have good reasons to back up your beliefs and actions. I want you to have grit, mettle, resolve, and willpower. I want you to chart your own course with a high degree of fortitude. I don't want you to be at the whim of every current, tossed back and forth by the waves, blown here and there by every wind.[2]

The apostle Paul commended a group of people called the Bereans for questioning whether what he was saying was true. Acts 17:11: "[The Bereans] were more fair-minded than those in Thessalonica, in that they received the word with all readiness, and searched the Scriptures daily *to find out* [my italics] whether these things were so." They weren't blindly going to receive what Paul was telling them. They checked out what he was teaching to see if it was true. Paul applauded them for their efforts, even referring to them as "fair-minded" for doing so.

You may be familiar with the popular saying "If you don't stand for something, you'll fall for anything."[3] That's what I'm getting at here.

However, while I believe truth exists, I also know that people can use truth as a cudgel. I once heard it said that "Truth without love is brutality, and love without truth is hypocrisy."[4] I find that conclusion to be so accurate. If I know something is true and beat someone over the head with that truth, I'm acting in a brutal way. Yet if I know something to be true, but don't share it with someone I love, I would be a hypocrite. I think of the prophets in the Old Testament. Some were true prophets, and some were false prophets. The true prophets would warn of coming judgment because they loved the people. The false prophets responded to those warnings by telling the people to focus on the current peace and safety they were experiencing. Who is more loving? The one who warns people of danger, or the one who coddles people even if they're heading on a destructive path?

Here's where it gets tricky. These days, we're often expected to fall into camps, and these camps are often at odds with each other. Pro-choice versus pro-life. Democrats versus Republicans. Open borders versus closed borders. Gun control versus the Second Amendment, or the right to bear arms. People insist there's no overlap. We're urged to act in ways that are polarizing, to deepen the divide. The only way to "win" is to shout down the other side.

That's bunk. I'm not here to tell you what to believe on these issues. But what I want you to do is develop your opinions based on logic and your conscience, not simply because all your friends believe one way, or because you're expected to think a certain way, or because a professor told you so, or because a certain way of thinking has become popular or unpopular in your generation or region. For instance, if you live in the Puget Sound area, near where I live, the majority of people will tell you to vote for the Democratic party. But if you move a hundred miles east to the city of Ellensburg, Washington, the majority of people in that city will tell you to vote for the Republican party. Don't be pigeonholed into anyone's camp. Learn everything you can about both sides, then make your choice.

I have found that the more input I can get, the better the decisions that I can make. It is so helpful to listen before we speak. In my job in sales, I have learned this simple truth the hard way. If I come into a meeting prepared with all of this great information to share with the customer, and I spend the whole time talking, it's often wasted time. By far, the best meetings I have ever had are those in which I started off by asking questions, then took the time to listen to the customers' answers.

We don't have to be a polarized society. We can learn to think empathetically. It's good to learn to understand and appreciate opposing viewpoints, even if you don't hold them yourself. Learn to respectfully disagree. We need to have debate so people can make informed decisions, because we all need to coexist. More room for overlap exists than people think. Yes, it's possible to agree with someone only partially. Yes, there are nuances to issues. Yes, you can develop friends and understanding on both sides of an issue. Learn to build your own camps. Don't be forced to think, or do, or say anything you don't stand behind. Your opinions matter. Your freedom matters. Your life is yours to live. If you don't want to do or think or believe or say something, then don't.

My wife and I have always encouraged our kids to form their own opinions. We've cared enough to give them our recommendations, yet we always encourage them to make up their own minds. Sometimes as a parent it can be hard to know when to give advice and when not to, and we don't always balance this perfectly, that's for sure. When it came time for our daughter Kristine to go to college, my wife, Annelli, strongly encouraged her to become a pharmacist, since Kristine showed aptitude in that direction, and we understood this to be a marketable and stable career. Annelli is Filipino, and within the subculture of her family of origin, jobs in the medical community are considered prestigious. Annelli's brother is a doctor, and two other siblings are nurses. They've all done well for themselves. My wife has a degree in interior design, but she's always regretted not going into the medical field.

Kristine has never rocked the boat. She has respected our recommendations. She went to the University of Washington and started studying to become a pharmacist. But at the end of her freshman year she was at home one day and asked to speak to us. I remember the conversation vividly. Kristine let us know that she didn't feel called to become a pharmacist. She didn't like the chemistry requirements, and she had discovered that she wanted to become a therapist, although she wasn't sure exactly what kind.

That was a hard conversation, but a good one. Overall, we appreciated that Kristine could pivot and move to a field of study that she enjoyed more. Years have passed now since Kristine graduated from U-dub (she did it in three years). She went on to receive her master's degree, became a board-certified behavior analyst, and has started her own successful business as a tutor and behavior therapist. She works with kids with special needs, which she's very gifted at. We are so thankful that Kristine initiated that conversation with us years ago. She respected our recommendations regarding her career, yet she still developed opinions of her own. She had the backbone to head down the career path that suited her. If she hadn't done so, she would have been frustrated her whole life. When I encourage you to question authority, I hope you will keep Kristine's story in mind. You've got to live your life. So make sure it's the life *you* want to live.

REASONS TO BELIEVE

Over the course of his life, Big Tim made some healthy decisions and some not-so-healthy decisions, yet he was never afraid to stand up for what he believed in. That was a gift to me. I didn't agree with Tim about every choice he made, but I like the fact that he never blindly followed the herd. He showed grit and resolve. He had reasons for doing what he did.

His strength became a model of sorts for me. Being raised Catholic, I was taught to follow authority, particularly in my faith. But after high school, I pretty much abandoned my Catholic upbringing and lived however I wanted to live. I know now that the Bible says it is not good when everyone does what's right in their own eyes (Deuteronomy 12:8), but I was unaware of that wisdom at the time, so I definitely made some decisions that led me down a destructive path.

Shortly after Annelli and I were married, I began to come around, slowly, surely. I had already started making better moral choices, and my faith deepened in a bigger way, particularly by the time I was in my late twenties. Annelli was pregnant with Kristine by then. Due to unforeseen circumstances, I found myself out of a job. A month passed. Then another. It was near Christmas 1991, and I felt humbled by being out of work and with a child on the way. I hoped circumstances might change in the new year, but in January 1992, I was still unemployed. To top it off, Annelli was tested to determine if our baby had Down syndrome, and the results indicated a high probability. I knew that people with Down syndrome can live productive, beautiful, and happy lives, but as a family man, I felt the pressures mounting. I wasn't sure if I had what it took to raise a special needs child. My life felt like it was spiraling out of control.

Sometime in all of that turmoil I cried out to God: "If you exist, God, then please help me." It was a skeptic's prayer. I liken this to the time when the apostles were on a boat with Jesus and a massive storm came up while Jesus was sleeping. These were seasoned fishermen, mind you, but they were terrified that they were going to lose their lives. They frantically woke Jesus, amazed that he was able to sleep during such a storm. Jesus awoke, and in an instant, he calmed the storm. In this story from the Bible, we read, "then they became very afraid."[5] That's how it was for me. Storms were raging in my life. I cried out to God. Then the tempest stopped. Honestly, the sudden change of events after I prayed frightened me more than the storm, given that up to that point I had lived as if there was no God. Don't get me wrong—I was a moral person and tried to do the right thing, but I was agnostic about God.

Slowly, surely, God started opening my eyes. I landed a job. Kristine was born without Down syndrome. My questions about my faith began to be answered. I sensed that God was real, and that he was answering my prayers. He didn't give me everything I wanted or asked for, but he did care about me. I became certain of that. I knew it wasn't a coincidence that things started to fall into place, so I needed to go deeper. Right around then, I heard a pastor tell his congregation something I'd never heard before. He made a point in his sermon—I don't even remember what the point was—then said, "Don't just take my word for it. Check it out for yourself."

Wow! I had never heard that kind of suggestion before. I went home and began to do just that—I checked things out for myself. I read the Bible. I read and read and read. Gradually I came to my own conclusions about faith. I attended a Calvary Chapel for a while, a church that wasn't Catholic, then went to a nondenominational church for a season. These days, I consider myself more closely aligned with the Reformed tradition of faith, with what Martin Luther taught. Mainly, I just try to follow Jesus. I try to love God and love other people.

It felt difficult for me to break with the Catholic Church, and if you're Catholic, I'm not trying to knock your beliefs. My point is that when I decided to question things for myself, I found myself on a different spiritual path than where I'd been raised. I'm confident of my faith today, and there are logical reasons why I believe what I do. Thanks in part to Tim's influence, I developed the backbone to question things and come to answers by myself.

THE BEST KIND OF BRAVE

I love the children's story "The Emperor's New Clothes" by Hans Christian Andersen.[6] I remember hearing it when I was little and thinking, *What an odd story, and why are they telling us about a naked emperor?* But as an adult now, I'm better equipped to understand the deeper meaning that the author hoped to get across.

If you're unfamiliar with the story, it's about an emperor who believes he needs a fancy new set of clothes. One day two traveling tailors "just happen to stop by" on their way through the city. They ask if the emperor would like them to make him a sumptuous new set of duds. The emperor thinks this is a swell plan, but there's one catch, according to the tailors. The clothes can be seen by everybody who's capable, smart, and forward-thinking.

But if folks are unsophisticated or dumb, then the clothes will be invisible.

No problem. Around these parts, everyone's an Einstein.

The tailors "show" him yards and yards of beautiful fabric—the finest, most magnificent fabric anyone has ever seen. The emperor can't see anything, but he keeps his mouth shut and approves it all. Then the tailors take careful measurements and make a big show out of cutting the fabric, fitting sleeves to vests, sewing on buttons, hemming the pants, and so forth. It takes them a long while to make his clothes, and quality work doesn't come cheap. Their bill runs higher and higher.

Any number of the emperor's most trusted officials stop by to document the tailors' work. No one sees any clothes, any looms. No needles or thread or scissors or pins or thimbles or pincushions—but everybody keeps quiet. They report back on the existence of the new clothes. The clothes are provable, verifiable, checked-and-double-checked fact, they insist.

The emperor himself stops by to eyeball the situation. All he sees is a great big bunch of nothingness, but he's a genius (at least, everybody has told him he is), so he gives it a thumbs-up.

Finally the clothes are finished. The emperor comes in for a fitting. The tailors set him up before a mirror, strip him down to his birthday suit, and pantomime dressing him up.

"How do you like your new clothes?" they ask. "Aren't they terrific?"

"Wow, I look like a million bucks!" the emperor says, staring into the mirror at his flabby gut and hairy shoulders.

Now it's time to go for a walk. And since it's the emperor doing the walking, it's an occasion for a parade. The whole town turns out for the grand procession. There goes the emperor, strutting down the street in his new clothes with everybody oohing and aahing. Nobody wants to be thought of as unsophisticated or dumb. Until one townsperson—an unpretentious child—has the nerve to call it like he sees it.

"Hey, that guy's buck naked!" the kid says, and laughs his head off.

Everybody knows he's right. But the show's got to go on. It would be a huge embarrassment for the emperor to admit he's been duped all along. So there goes the emperor, red-faced and sweating, desperate to end what he's started, finishing his parade in the buff.

There are many nuggets I could pull out of this story that I believe would benefit you, such as be on the alert for people trying to fool you, or don't be too proud like the emperor. But the lesson I want you to focus on is the one modeled by the little child. I wonder if the kid had inhibitions about questioning the authority figures around him, or if he just didn't know any better. The fact that he spoke up when others didn't is an inspiration to me! There have been times in my own life when something seemed so obviously wrong, but I was scared to speak up for fear of what others would think. I want to encourage you to be like the uninhibited child. If your baloney detector is going off, then be brave and speak up. You owe it to yourself to say something.

My brother Big Tim died in 1993 at the age of thirty-nine. Unfortunately, like my mom, he left this earth way too early. I regret that I was never really able to get to know him as an adult. He was ten years older than me almost to the day, so we only ever related as big brother and little brother, and never got to the point of being peers. Before he died, we did get to have a few conversations about his newfound faith, so I know that I will see him again one day.

Bust That Logjam

The sequence swirls in my mind today: My brother Rick got married. My dad announced he was leaving for good. We celebrated the new year, 1978. What exactly happened and in what order? I don't know. What I do remember vividly is that a bunch of us were in our kitchen on an early winter afternoon when I was thirteen, and Rick asked me a question that sucked the air out of my lungs. Lots of my siblings were there in the background hubbub, although I'm not sure Dad was in the room. Probably not, because I'm sure he would have added his two cents if he was.

Half of my siblings didn't live at home by then, and I don't remember why they were over that afternoon and clustered in our chaotic kitchen. Like the rest of our house, our kitchen was cluttered, messy. Plates and pots sat unwashed in the sink. Open cereal boxes sprawled on the counter. Our kitchen reflected our lives. At least the younger kids' lives. We were trying to fend for ourselves, and we had little idea what to do. Nobody had been telling us to do our homework, to cook or clean. We'd been doing the best we

DAD JOKE

Why was the panda fired?

His coworkers found him hard to bear.

knew how, living off the cuff, haphazardly. There was no structure. No reassurance. Everything was in disarray.

Rick stood near the sink. I can still picture him there, handsome and athletic. At twenty-three, he'd just finished three years in the army, where he'd been a buck sergeant. Rick looked at me intently, took a deep breath, and said in a quiet voice: "Rob, where are you going to go?"

That was the question that caught me hard.

I shrugged, trying to be cool, weighing the options in my mind. It was a prudent question to ask, because Dad had already announced that he was done parenting us. The younger kids all needed to go somewhere. But where? I drew a blank. It was the first time I'd really faced the question, and it was far too difficult for me to process. I didn't realize that a young teen could be forced to confront such a decision.

The idea of foster care flashed through my mind. I picked up a box of cereal and scanned the back, pretending I was reading, trying to avoid Rick's question. Dad had mentioned foster care as an option, but I wasn't sure what it was or how it worked. I'd never known anyone in foster care. Maybe there were nice people who ran things there, I thought. But I wasn't consoled. My life had been turned upside down, and not much was clear in the moment, but I did know one thing for certain: I did *not* want to live with strangers.

I wanted to be with my family. With my brothers and sisters. With my parents, if only they could just be normal for a while. Four of us were too young to be on our own, and nobody was going to take four kids all at once. I knew that. So we were going to get split up somehow. Maybe I could go live with my next-door neighbors. I had a friend there. I left Rick's question hanging without an answer. We got busy with other things that afternoon. Making dinner maybe. Or trying to clean up and put things away. A couple of days passed. Or maybe a couple of weeks.

In later years, Rick confessed to me that he went into the

military to get out of the house. He'd wanted to escape, because things in our home weren't going in a good direction, even three-plus years prior to Dad's announcement. Rick also said that when he got out of the military, if the younger siblings hadn't still been at home, he would have never returned. That's how bad things were at home.

I was adrift. In those days or weeks of lag time—after Rick's question, and before the matter was settled—I wondered more than once if Dad's idea to put us in foster care was only an idle threat. Maybe he'd just said that to goad the older siblings into taking us in. He knew that none of them wanted to see their younger siblings in foster care. But then again, I considered, my older brothers and sisters were all trying to make lives of their own. None were established yet or set up to take in kids or teens. Dad had already split from Mom. He'd taken legal steps to have her declared an unfit parent. He'd been up the road in Everett with his new girlfriend for months and hadn't been living with us. So Dad had already made some decisions that were hard on us. *No,* I concluded, *the idea of foster care for us isn't an idle threat.*

I don't remember exactly how or when Rick told me the news. He and his new wife, Karen, decided to have me move in with them. They'd been married less than three months. They lived in a small trailer. I don't remember if Rick called me, or if he came over and told me face-to-face. What I remember is feeling a huge relief. I'd won the lottery. A load rolled off my narrow young shoulders. I had a home. I'd always looked up to Rick, and now I was going to get some stability. Some reassurance. Some structure. Some love.

Yet even with that decision made, tensions still ran high. Rick tried to gain physical and legal custody of me, but Dad wouldn't grant both—only physical custody. I could stay with Rick, but he couldn't make day-to-day decisions for me, such as my choice of doctor or school. Dad still wanted that authority. I never did learn why. Maybe it was one last vestige of parenting from Dad. Or maybe it was a control issue. A state attorney was assigned to my case. Every month Dad had to send Rick a bit of child support for me. If Dad didn't keep up his end of the bargain, Rick was supposed to talk to the attorney. Over the next three years, Rick talked to that attorney more than once.

And me?

I just tried to keep my nose clean.

Now, here's what I want you to understand about Rick's decision: When it came to doing what needed to be done, even the hard thing, Rick was willing. He stepped up, making sacrifices and taking on responsibility without complaint. Specifically, Rick chose the job of moving me into his home and of parenting me.

DO THE HARD THING

Want to be successful in life? Be willing to sacrifice and take on responsibility without complaint like Rick did. That might happen in your career, or in a volunteer role you accept, or with your family or sphere of friends. Whatever kind of work needs doing, do it and work hard. Do whatever it takes: The easy things, sure. The routine things, always. But especially do the hard things.

This wasn't the first time—or the last—that Rick would step up in our family. Over the years, Rick has always shown a willingness to do what few others would. As adults, we drove over to Chelan and worked on my brother Don's place. Rick was the first to pick up a tool in the morning and the last to set it down. And he did it all with a smile on his face. If we were all set to return home from a fishing trip, and everyone was bone-tired from a weekend of fun, Rick was always quick to volunteer to drive.

When I lived with Rick, he was working a day job as a cabinetmaker for a company and going to school at night to earn his journeyman's credentials. After I moved out, he started his own business on the side, a cabinetmaking company. As long as I've known him, Rick has been willing to put in a hard day's work.

He's meticulous with what he does, too. When he finishes a job, he wants to feel good about it. At the first company he worked for, they gave him the nickname O. K. Kenney—the O. K. stood for "overkill." Rick would build something better than it needed to be built. He'd never cut corners. He'd stay with a task until it was done right. He was the guy everybody wanted on their team.

Rick and Karen were married in October 1978. I moved in with them in January 1979. I wouldn't turn fifteen until May. One of the first things Rick had me do was help him build an addition on the side of their trailer. I don't know when he found the time. The trailer was nothing but a kitchenette, an extremely small bathroom, a closet, one bedroom, and a sort of living space. I slept on a small mattress on top of a shelf Rick built. I didn't really have my own room, but that was okay. I was glad to have a home.

Rick's plan was to build a 12-by-12-foot addition. There were two doors on the trailer, and the back door would be used to enter the addition. You'd have to walk through my sleeping space to enter the new room, but I didn't care. I'm not sure if Rick even knew much about construction back then. There were no YouTube videos to turn to for advice. But Rick figured it out. Building the addition was a fairly simple job, and working side by side with Rick, I learned how to frame a small building, hang Sheetrock, insulate the walls, and install flooring, lights, and electricity.

One evening Rick got into an argument with Karen. She was normally a kind and positive person, and I really liked being around her. She worked full days with Boeing as a drafter, and when she got home from work, she wanted to hang out with her new husband. But when Rick's day was done, he was either at school or working on the trailer with his kid brother. Karen wanted to know why Rick and I were working so hard on the new room, working at a pace that left them no time just to be together. It wasn't my place to step in, and I wasn't going to tell her. But I so desperately wanted her to know the news.

Karen's birthday was coming up. We wanted to get it done by

her birthday. I was sure Rick and Karen would patch things up soon, at least when she found out the addition was a present for her.

We finished the room in the nick of time. After we ushered her into the completed and well-crafted gift, Karen gave Rick a huge hug. Rick had designed the addition to be the thing he wanted us to have the most—a family room. He put a TV and a comfy couch in there. He intended the room to be full of laughter, full of fun. It was the room where we'd make lots of good memories together, he said.

Sure enough, every Thursday we gathered, munched popcorn, and watched *The Muppet Show*, which made us all laugh. We hung out in there other times, too. The room represented Rick's work ethic. He wasn't working hard simply to work. He was working hard to build something great for other people. He had a knack for creating simple pleasures. He worked to give back to others.

WHAT TO KNOW ABOUT STEPPING UP

I ended up living with Rick and Karen for two and a half years, until I was seventeen. During that time, they bought a real mobile home in the same trailer park. The new place felt so spacious. I even had my own bedroom. We lived like royalty then.

Just before I started my senior year of high school, Rick and Karen bought three and a half acres near Ravensdale, about thirty miles southeast of Seattle. Rick, Karen, and I worked together to build a fence first. There were lots of felled trees from when they had the land cleared. We limbed them, stripped the bark, and sectioned them into fence posts. After the fence was finished and the ground was leveled, they moved their mobile home onto the acreage.

I faced a new, hard choice. I'd had a great time living with them. I appreciated what they had done for me so much. But if I moved with them, I'd need to change schools, and I wanted to finish high school where I'd been going. So, with their blessing, I moved into the apartment that my two brothers shared, and I finished school while living with Don and Joe.

Rick and Karen had stepped in to help me when I'd needed help, and that speaks highly of them both. The work of caring for me inconvenienced them, yet these young newlyweds believed it was the right thing to do, even if caring for me wasn't always easy. I can tell you today that I have nothing but respect and gratitude for their decision. And they tell me that having me living with them wasn't so bad after all. It all worked out in the end.

When it comes to sacrifice, responsibility, and hard work, I modeled myself after Rick as best I could. I applied that to my decades of experience in the workforce and learned some lessons of my own along the way. Consider the following three mindsets that you can adopt to help you step up, undertake responsibility without complaint, and work well.

1. Work well for the sake of your integrity.

Integrity should be wrapped up in all our efforts and motives, no matter what we do. When you're on the job, it's easy to get caught up in working hard or smart only if your boss will see you. That's important because you want your boss to know you're a good employee. But if you're working hard or smart only when your boss is around, that's a problem.

As I am writing this, I have just put out a video on my YouTube channel in which I challenge my subscribers with this idea. We need more than a *few* good men and women. We need a *world* of good men and women. We need people everywhere who are willing to do the right thing—even when it's hard, even when it costs something, and yes, even when no one is looking.

See, you've got to work to respect your own integrity. You've got to work hard and smart when your boss isn't around, too. If you say you're going to do a job, then do the job, and do it well. Have pride in your work. Do your job with honesty, sincerity, excellence, and straightforwardness. Do your job well because it's the right thing to do.

I'm going to lay out a Bible verse for you. If you don't believe in God, I invite you simply to see the encouragement the passage offers. The verse says: "Whatever you do, work at it with all your heart, as though you were working for the Lord and not for people."[1]

That means you work with a sense of a higher calling. You aspire to work well for a reason larger than yourself. You work willingly, heartily, and enthusiastically at whatever you do, knowing that there's some kind of purpose to it, even if only to do a good day's work.

My sister Mary's husband, Bob, works a wheat farm in Yuma, Colorado. The land's been in Bob's family for a hundred years. A while back, I started wondering what it was like to work on a farm. I asked Bob and Mary if I could work with them for a week during harvest. I am so happy I had that opportunity available to me. I got to drive a combine, one of those huge machines that harvests the wheat. I wasn't very good at it, but at least I was able to have that experience. I was there when they drove the wheat we'd just harvested to the scales and had it weighed. That was cool to see. That wheat was then made available for purchase by people who would turn it into all sorts of good food. When I put my head on the pillow each night, I felt a tremendous sense of accomplishment. Each day, we really poured ourselves out, and we got to see the results of our work. Ecclesiastes 5:12 says, "The sleep of a laborer is sweet," and I have found that to be an absolute truth!

Playing football was that way to me, too. I liked the discipline of the sport. Working hard—whether on a football field, on a farm, in a sales job as I do today, or in caring for people—has been tremendously valuable to me.

2. Work well because working is better than not working.

Working is better than not working. That sounds a bit counterintuitive, doesn't it? In a couple jobs I've held over the years, I've seen people spend more time and effort trying to avoid work than doing the actual work. Now, I realize that during an economic downturn, not everybody who wants a job has one. But in a normal economy, if someone has a job but tries to avoid working while they're on the clock, it confounds me.

Comedian Brian Regan tells a story about how, when he was younger, he worked in a toy store, unloading trucks and stocking shelves. One day a coworker said, "Hey, man, I know a place to hide out and not work. Follow me." They snuck to the back of the store and ducked behind the bike racks. There, Brian spotted a hole in the drywall. Following the coworker's lead, Brian grunted and sweated to shimmy himself in sideways. It was dark inside the wall, with only about a foot and a half of space between the beams—not enough room to sit. There they stood, nose to nose, completely cramped.

"Isn't this great?!" the coworker said.

Brian shook his head. "You know what?" he said. "I'd rather be putting bikes together."[2]

Some people try to avoid work, but work can actually be a great thing. Work provides you with a sense of structure. It gives you something worthwhile to do. The money you earn from work can provide for your needs and those of the people who depend on you. I like to go on vacations and take time off from work as much as the next guy, but I also enjoy working. There's something tremendously satisfying about putting in a good day's work.

In today's casual and socially conscious workplaces, you might have a job where recharging and rest are considered part of work. Some forward-thinking workplaces have Ping-Pong tables set up for employees to enjoy during breaks. Other companies encourage midday naps. That's okay. Companies provide these perks to increase morale, alertness, and, ultimately, productivity.[3] So if it's okay for you to do these things where you work, then by all means do them.

Aside from that exception, though, consider this. If you're avoiding work while you're on the job, you're actually stealing from the company. When you took the job, you made an agreement to be paid a certain amount of money in exchange for a certain amount of time or productivity. If you're not working or being productive when you're at work, that's a breach of contract. It's theft.

In addition, if you're not giving 100 percent at your job, it may well be an indication that you are in a job that's not a good long-term fit for you. I understand that dynamic, and there's no shame in looking for a different job. As I pointed out earlier, it took me a while to find the right job for me, and even after I landed the job, it took a while for me to grow into the role. That's true for many people.

3. Work as productively, professionally, and respectfully as you can.

Over the years I've developed any number of life hacks when it comes to how I undertake responsibility and work. For instance, I love to make weekly and daily to-do lists, and then cross off each item when it's accomplished. Instead of keeping all your tasks inside your head, there's something strategic and satisfying about putting your tasks on paper, crossing things off, and seeing what you've done at the end of each day. It's simple but effective. I do this both at work and home.

I've also learned to prioritize the tasks that need to be done, and then accomplish the tasks that are deemed of higher importance first. It's not hard to prioritize tasks. Mostly, it's just common sense. Look at the tasks that need to be done, then sort out a sequence. Of course, if your boss or supervisor tells you to focus on a particular item, that task goes to the top of the list.

Learn to prioritize tasks at home, too. Maybe it's the start of your weekend. You survey your dwelling space and see that you need to change a light bulb, paint a room, fix a running toilet, and take care of a kitchen faucet because water is bursting into the air. Which task would you do first?

I'm exaggerating this example for effect, of course. Common sense tells you to take care of the faucet first. You can't have water spouting into the kitchen like a geyser. Taking care of the toilet is probably your next priority, because running water costs you money. The light bulb is next, because that's an easy fix. And painting the room is last, because it's probably not a pressing need, and if your schedule doesn't allow you to do the job this weekend, you could reschedule that task for next time.

Relationships factor into priority setting, too. That's respectful. If my wife is waiting for me to fix her sewing machine so she can hem a pair of pants, then that's a priority. If I don't complete the task she needs me to do, that affects her to-do list as well. If a co-worker is waiting for me at a job site to deliver materials before he can get to work, I'd better deliver the materials ASAP. Otherwise, he'll fall behind schedule.

A keen sense of responsiveness is key in any job. If someone reaches out to you, respond quickly and professionally. Answer your emails within twenty-four hours. Same with returning phone calls. I'm in sales, so if someone contacts me via phone or email, I try to get back to them within an hour. Even if I don't have the answer they're looking for, I will at least touch base and say, "Hey, just wanted you to know I got your email and I'm working on this." I'll usually provide them with a time line, too, by saying something like, "I'll be able to get this answer to you by Tuesday."

Put yourself in another person's shoes. If I reach out to someone but they don't get back to me, I won't know if they got my message.

I'll wonder if I should look to a competitor to have my question answered. Nobody wants to hear crickets. Being responsive is a simple skill to learn. It's respectful and professional, and it buys you time. More communication is almost always better than less communication. If no communication exists, then the other person is left to fill in the blanks.

And yes, you've got to show up on time for things. Promptness is key to any success in a workplace, volunteer situation, or relationship. If I'm meeting a colleague for lunch at noon, I'll plan ahead so I get to the restaurant on time. If I'm running late due to traffic, I'll call or text to let the person know. That builds trust. If I'm habitually late, I may think I'm being cleverly casual, but I'm really eating up other people's time and affecting their day in a negative way.

When my YouTube channel took off, a ton of media personnel reached out to me, asking for interviews, particularly around Father's Day. I was happy to do the interviews and did as many as I could. Some days, I had interviews scheduled back-to-back for hours in a row. Most of the interviews were thirty minutes, but one was scheduled for only five minutes. The interviewer sought me out, but that's all the time he allotted for me. That was fine. But when the appointed time came, the guy was two minutes late. That might not sound like much, but being two minutes late for a five-minute interview ate up a bunch of our allotted time. I tried to respond professionally, but I wasn't impressed. I had other interviews scheduled after his, and he ended up talking for fifteen minutes. The way that media representative conducted his business felt disorganized and disrespectful.

BUST THAT LOGJAM

When it comes to your responsibilities and work, you will develop a reputation whether you want to or not. You'll be known in a negative way, perhaps as a slacker or complainer. Or you may build a positive image, as a responsible, smart worker with a great attitude who gets the job done well. No company wants to be stuck with the negative guy. Learn to be the person who people want on the team, the person who can look at a logjam and figure out a way to bust it.

I've always encouraged my kids to be polite with everybody they meet on a job, and my encouragement to you is the same. Treat everybody the same. Talk to janitors, security guards, and junior-level executives. Be kind to everybody, because everybody is worth it. Also, that person might become your supervisor someday. A few years ago, I was calling on one of my customers, and I struck up a conversation with a young woman named Libby. She was part-time help, hired for the company's busy season only. I could have treated her dismissively, but I distinctly remember treating her with the same level of respect and encouragement that I'd give to anyone. The next thing I knew, she was hired full-time. Now, a few years later, she's the head of human resources.

When my son graduated as a software developer from Central Washington University in March 2018, he came home and jumped into the job search. He networked, went to job fairs, and applied everywhere, but didn't have any luck. Over and over he was told the same thing: "Your grades are good, and we like that you have a degree. But you have no experience. Sorry." It was the classic chicken-and-egg situation. Software companies like to hire developers who have experience. But of course you can't get experience unless you first work for a company. Kyle was frustrated.

I call that kind of situation the logjam, and Kyle and I had several good talks about how he might proceed. Fortunately, he decided to bust the logjam. He took matters into his own hands. About six weeks after coming home, he printed out résumés and passed them out all over, saying he'd work for free. If companies were looking for experience, then he wanted to make them an offer they couldn't refuse. He didn't want to work for free forever, but he looked at his offer as a continuing education of sorts.

Sure enough, a company took a chance on him, hired him as a contractor, and paid him some small stipend, I think about half of minimum wage. Kyle worked for them over the summer. He worked hard and smart and earned their respect. In the late fall they hired him in a full-time salaried position that was more than double minimum wage. He worked diligently, developed more experience, and soon received an offer from an East Coast company for almost twice what he was making. He took the job and made the move. He's only two years out of college now and making an above-average salary in a strong and upward-moving company.

Kyle took responsibility into his own hands and made things happen—and that's admirable. How will your story of career, volunteerism, and relationships turn out? It starts with the decision you make to work hard and smart, with integrity and positivity. Take action in that direction. Sure, you will face logjams in one area of your life or another. Everybody does. Don't resign yourself to frustration. Step up and break whatever logjams are holding you back. You've got this!

I am forever grateful to my brother Rick and his wife, Karen, for stepping up and giving me a home, even though it was a major inconvenience for them. But the work ethic I learned from Rick has served me well my whole life, and I want to pass along its benefits to you.

DAD JOKE

◇◇◇

The sun is a huge bully. The other day, it even taunted the moon.

What did it say?

"You're not very bright."

5.

Remove the Stickers

School was starting soon and I'd outgrown my clothes. It was late August, right before the start of eighth grade for me at Tillicum Junior High, and nobody was looking out for my siblings and me. At age thirteen, I wasn't giving much thought to these things, but I had a hazy feeling that something big was lacking. One morning I was sorting through my closet and dresser, and it dawned on me that I should probably wear something to school other than the ratty cutoffs and T-shirts I'd been living in all summer. Autumns in the Pacific Northwest can be chilly. I'd probably need some new pants and a couple of shirts. Socks. Underwear. A new pair of shoes that fit. A windbreaker for fall and a winter coat for colder weather. My face fell. I had no idea where these things could come from.

I needed some hope and encouragement.

Dad was staying up in Everett each week, from Monday to Friday. He came home some weekends, but he wasn't engaged with us anymore and certainly wasn't thinking about back-to-school clothes, not that I could tell. Mom was moving around from place to place. After the separation from Dad, she'd spent some time with her family in Kansas. She'd lived somewhere else after that, but I didn't know where. By this point, very little communication was happening between my mom and us younger siblings.

I don't want to paint my parents in a horrible light. Not then and not now. I was mixed up and confused by what was happening. Maybe the ramifications of their decisions hadn't completely sunk in yet with me, or it could be that the wisdom of hindsight strikes me now as I write this. But at age thirteen, when I was searching through my dresser drawer and wondering what I was going to wear to school, I didn't feel mad at my parents. I was just crestfallen and bewildered. I simply didn't know what to do.

What I needed was someone to stand alongside me and say something like: "You know, it's going to be okay, buddy. You're going to get through this. The problem of having no back-to-school clothes is just a symptom of the changes in your family right now, one symptom of many. But don't worry. We'll sort this out." My method of coping was avoidance. I hoped that if I left things alone everything would take care of itself. On the acute stress response spectrum, I'd choose flight over fight any day. I just closed my dresser drawer and thought, *Oh well*.

It's true that the effects of poor parental choices rippled through our family, and there were no excuses then or now. Dad absolutely shouldn't have left us to fend for ourselves. Yet I understand today that raising a family on your own is tough, and Mom wasn't able to give Dad much support then. Annelli and I have raised two kids, and we've enjoyed our years with Kristine and Kyle immensely. Still, it hasn't all been easy. Parenting is hard work on the best of days. And it takes money. Dad had eight kids to contend with. That had to be rough on him. I get that.

As for Mom, she had been dealing with clinical depression. She'd gone to a therapist, but he hadn't helped. Alcohol was her way to cope with feeling lousy all the time, but the mix of wine and depression hadn't been good for her. When I was a kid, I didn't know all that she was dealing with, but I knew enough to realize that she'd been unplugged from a support system. Today, I can look back on her with eyes of compassion.

So there I was, thirteen years old and no back-to-school clothes. The first day of school was fast approaching. I needed help but didn't know who to turn to.

Enter my sister Laurie. Seven years older than me, she was twenty that August when I faced my clothing dilemma. Laurie didn't live at home by then, yet she checked in on us younger kids every so often. She came in and helped, but with no big announcement. No big hoopla. She just did it because it was the right thing to do. I don't remember exactly how it happened, but the younger kids had clothes when school began. She stepped up when she didn't have to.

Today, I couldn't tell you about any single item of clothing that she bought for me. I couldn't tell you what brand of jeans she bought, or if the shirts were blue or gray. But I can tell you about how it made me feel. Her act of compassion spoke huge volumes to me.

In fact, Laurie's act of encouragement still speaks to me, more than forty years later. I'm comforted and inspired by it even now. That's how powerful encouragement can be. One small act taken or kind word offered today can have an impact *decades* later. I'm holding out hope that you can become a big encourager yourself.

THE POWER OF ENCOURAGEMENT

Laurie's good deed went further than just providing me clothes. It lent reassurance to my young life. She let me know somebody cared. Laurie's act of encouragement held tremendous power.

True, you might not get thanked for the good deed you do today. That's okay. You're not doing it to get thanked. When Laurie bought me clothes, I think my response was probably a shrug. *Oh, I guess Laurie's buying us clothes now.* Her deed didn't feel momentous to me then, and I really had no idea of what she'd sacrificed. In hindsight, now that I am an adult, her action feels momentous to me. Laurie was working her way through college, paying for her own school expenses and the rent for the apartment she shared with roommates. She had a part-time job at a department store but wasn't making much money. She was trying to spin a lot of plates at once. She gave not out of abundance, but out of her own scarcity. Laurie's act of encouragement was huge.

What does it mean to encourage someone the way Laurie encouraged me? You can help out, maybe materially, maybe in the immaterial realm. The good deed might be an action you take, such as buying something that somebody needs. Or it might be emotional. You might boost somebody's mood or spirit by saying something kind. You reassure them. You cheer them on and brighten their day. You buoy their sense of strength and confidence.

Encouraging someone involves influencing a person in a positive way. Yet your power comes with a caution, too. If you strip down the word "encouragement" to its root, what's left is "courage." You can build onto this base by adding either "en" or "dis" to the front of "courage." You have the power to *encourage* people or *discourage* them. You can give people courage, or you can take their courage away. I don't want my legacy to be that I took courage away from anybody. I want to help strengthen people and help them move forward in good ways. That's what I hope for your life, too.

These days, you're often told that the only way you can be heard is through outrage. The only way you can have power is if you let loose with anger. If you scream and shout. But that's not true. Research has shown, for instance, that high-performance business teams succeed because they receive more positive feedback than negative feedback along the way.[1] Similarly, studies show that students who are encouraged to increase their grades through studying and hard work tend to perform better than those who receive criticism or who were told that their level of intelligence was set at birth.[2] You can have a tremendous effect on people when you encourage rather than discourage them.

I saw the power of encouragement, for better or worse, when I was involved in coaching youth athletics. My son, Kyle, played Little League Baseball from ages nine to thirteen, and for those four years, I helped out his team, mostly by volunteering as an assistant coach. I liked to be there for my son and the other kids, too. When you're just entering your teen years, you need lots of encouragement. Your skills as an athlete and competitor are emerging, and you still have a lot to learn. Our league was very competitive. We always went to the state championships, so during those years I had the chance to witness parents on both sides of the encouragement-discouragement spectrum.

I'd see the dad up in the stands who was shouting his lungs hoarse, making everybody around him uncomfortable. This kind of parent was often sarcastic, and he harshly criticized or belittled his kid if he struck out or made an error. I'd see the kid's face fall, and my heart would always go out to him. I understand why parents think they need to do this. They're trying to raise tough, resilient kids who are great athletes. Maybe they're spending a lot of money on private lessons. Or maybe the parents are trying to live vicariously through the child, hoping the child will achieve something athletically that they were never able to achieve.

But it seldom works. When a child receives a lot of criticism, usually the kid ends up resenting his parents. Maybe the parent leads with discouragement because they were treated like that when they were young, and that's all they know. It's hard, but parents in this situation have to break that cycle. The worst behavior in a parent seldom brings out the best in a child. Toxic behavior usually only breeds more toxic behavior. The kid ends up hating baseball. And hating the parent.

Conversely, I'd see the dad who let the coach be the coach and trusted that the coach would handle things. When his kid struck out or made an error, this kind of dad might take the kid aside and say, "Hey, it wasn't your best day, but it's not the end of the world. We'll work on it. Bad days happen in baseball. It's going to be okay." This kind of parent is on his kid's side, not on his back. This kind of parent practiced baseball with his kid. He'd work to instill in the next generation a healthy love for and appreciation of the game.

Let's face it, not a lot of kids who play Little League ever go on to play in the majors. If you're a parent, you've got to ask yourself: What do I hope my child learns while playing the game? What is the true goal? Well, you want your children to be healthy and develop skills. You want your kids to learn good sportsmanship, courtesy, and respect. You want them to know how to resolve conflicts without being a jerk and how to become strong competitors, but they should also learn how to win and lose with class. Ultimately, you want your child to grow up to become a well-adjusted person, and deep down you know that sports (or piano recitals, spelling competitions, ballet class, drama club, or whatever extracurricular activities your child chooses) can go a long way toward achieving that goal.

Now, superimpose this sports picture onto any situation with your friends, your family, your coworkers, the students around you. Do you see that you can be the person who either encourages people or discourages them? You can shout criticisms from the stands, or you can shout support. You can help people along the way, or you can hinder people's growth. Which would you rather be known for?

WAYS TO ENCOURAGE

After reading the previous section, maybe you're saying, "Sure, I get that, but I'm not naturally an encourager. What should I do?"

The simple answer is that encouragement is a skill that can be learned. I didn't naturally start out as an encourager. In high school, there was so much chaos in my house that I couldn't spare much thought to being that way. I learned to be an encourager later on in my life. As a parent, you get to see firsthand how much it affects not only your own kids, but their friends as well.

I'm not proud of this next story, but I'm mentioning it to show that people can change, including me. In my early years of high school, a kid who rode on my bus was a bit of an outcast. I don't think he had many friends. His last named rhymed with "dodo," like the prehistoric bird. So when I got on the bus, I'd tease him by saying his last name and "dodo." He'd kind of grin, but it was to cover up his discomfort or hurt. The teasing was childish of me. Mean. To this day, I feel bad about my behavior; in fact, it makes me cringe to even write about it. So much so that I reached out to him a while back through LinkedIn and apologized. Today, I wish I had sat next to him on the bus and asked how he was doing. I wish I had tried to befriend him and help him feel less alone in the world.

What's changed between high school and today? You could say I grew up. I matured. I'd also say I learned how to be an encourager. I learned how powerful the words and actions of affirmation and support can be in a person's life. I want to be known as someone who encourages others, not discourages them. How did I change?

Baby steps. Like with everything else I've learned, I broke big tasks down into smaller bites and learned one part at a time. Back when I played college football, the coaches gave us a training regimen in June. We had to implement this regimen over the summer before practice started in the fall. For instance, we needed to be able to run three miles. I wasn't much of a runner, and in June three miles seemed impossible to accomplish. But then I broke the task up into chunks. Every day, I'd head out to the track that circled the football field. The first time, I ran only one lap. The second time I ran two. Pretty soon I was running three laps, then four. In no time at all, I was running three miles.

I didn't hit three miles overnight, and it's important to understand that few people become champion encouragers overnight, either. Start small. Decide today that you're going to encourage somebody. Tomorrow, do it again. And the next day, and the next. Keep going until encouraging others becomes automatic for you.

How do you encourage someone? Start by keeping your head up and your eyes open. Be aware. See what needs to be done. Get your focus off yourself. Then just give someone a genuine compliment. Or thank somebody for doing their job.

You can get creative. Send someone a postcard. Catch a person doing something right and let them know you saw it. Tell somebody how they helped you.

Mix encouragement in with your social interactions. When introducing two people, add in a few words of genuine praise about each person to help them get to know each other. If you're at someone's house and they're cooking, ask to help out. Be supportive of other people's initiatives. Be someone who encourages others with your actions as well as your words. Don't be the guy who's lounging around, waiting to be served.

Encouragement can take a lot of forms. See what feels most sincere for your personality. Send a friend flowers. Cheer someone up with a hug. You'd be surprised how many ways there are to encourage someone else.

One of the best ways you can encourage someone is by listening. Most of us like to talk. Far fewer like to listen. When you ask how someone's day has been, it's natural to hear a standard response in return: "Oh, fine. You?" But maybe you can ask a question that goes deeper or bring up something you remember from the last time you spoke. "Hey, you mentioned you had a big test coming up. That was this morning, wasn't it? How did that go?"

Take the time to ask questions and really listen to the answers. People love to be heard.

If you're a person of faith, one of the best ways you can encourage people is by offering to pray for them. I don't do that with every person I meet, but I have found it helpful when I have. Everyone is going through some kind of difficulty. I have heard it said that if we all gathered in a circle and laid our problems down in front of us, we would quickly take our own problems back after seeing what other people are going through. Prayer helps. I've yet to meet anyone who has turned down the offer, even if they're a person with not much faith themselves. I say something like, "Hey, how can I pray for you?" People usually like that offer. Then, of course, you actually need to pray for them. Don't just say it. Do it.

I look for examples of encouragers all the time, people I can look to for inspiration. The famous preacher Billy Graham once said, "Courage is contagious. When a brave man takes a stand, the spines of others are often stiffened."[3] I like the idea that true encouragement fosters the right sort of stand-taking.

Theodore Roosevelt's famous "Man in the Arena" speech also reflects on the topic of encouragements. I once memorized this passage.

It is not the critic who counts; not the man who points out how the strong man stumbles, or where the doer of deeds could have done them better.

The credit belongs to the man who is actually in the arena, whose face is marred by dust and sweat and blood; who strives valiantly; who errs, who comes short again and again, because there is no effort without error and shortcoming; but who does actually strive to do the deeds; who knows great enthusiasms, the great devotions; who spends himself in a worthy cause; who at the best knows in the end the triumph of high achievement, and who at the worst, if he fails, at least fails while daring greatly, so that his place shall never be with those cold and timid souls who neither know victory nor defeat.[4]

Anyone can be a discourager. Anyone can be a critic. But encouragers are much rarer and much more necessary.

THE ART OF ENCOURAGEMENT

If you disagree with someone, can you still encourage them? Yes. Absolutely. Have discernment, and be true to yourself and the situation. I'm not saying you should kowtow to anyone, or say something nice about someone that isn't true, or praise something that you disagree with. Don't call something good if it isn't good.

When my children were growing up, if my wife and I saw them straying into territory that was harmful to them, we certainly didn't encourage them to keep going in that direction. When Kristine was three and picked up a crayon and started to color on the wall, I didn't say, "Aw, make it pretty, honey. You're such a good artist." That wouldn't have been good for her—or anyone. As much as Kristine needed to be encouraged in her talents as a young artist, she also needed to learn boundaries. She needed to understand what was socially acceptable and what wasn't. If we had encouraged in a false or unhelpful way, we would have actually done her a disservice.

So, fast-forward to today, and put one of your friends or coworkers into the mix. If a buddy of yours has just been dumped by his girlfriend and wants to drown his sorrows with booze or drugs, would you encourage that kind of action? Hopefully not. Whatever pain he has right now will still be there in the morning, only then he'll have a hangover, too. My point is that we want to support people in their choices, but just as Big Tim showed me, we also want to have a backbone. We need to have the fortitude to label actions, attitudes, and behaviors helpful or harmful. It's far better to be the friend your buddy needs than to sit by idly watching him when he's hurting, or to encourage his poor choices. If his girlfriend broke up with him, listen to him. Grieve with him. Take him for a long walk. Lament with him. See a movie with him. Be there for him in his time of need, sure. Encourage him to make healthy choices, even when he's down.

In my job as an account manager, I always try to put myself in my support staff's shoes when they don't perform as I'd hoped. When I do critique a coworker, I always attempt to do so in a spirit of helpfulness, with the person's best interests in mind, as well as the company's. I try to be warmhearted but also truthful, and I often take the time to explain areas where they should improve their performance—I would be doing them a disservice if I didn't. I look for ways to genuinely praise work they've done well, and I'll mention those examples, even if the overall report isn't so great. I encourage people to step out of their comfort zones and to live with good intent in mind.

On the road to becoming an encourager, I've learned any number of hard lessons along the way. Sometimes I make mistakes, and that's okay. Once, when Kristine was in middle school, she was dealing with a bully in her classroom. I don't remember the specifics of the bully's actions, only that this student was being a genuine pain. I gave Kristine an in-depth talk and encouraged her to have compassion for bullies, because they're probably acting the way they do because they've been hurt somewhere along the line. I encouraged her to develop empathy toward the bully, even to try to befriend this person. Kristine came home from school the next day, shook her head, and said with a sigh, "It just didn't work, Dad. That person is still being a jerk."

I know now that the advice I gave to Kristine was not right for her at the time. She was just trying to live through the experience, protect herself, and move forward. It's true, in the grown-up world, that you do want to develop compassion and empathy for people. Bullies are bullies usually because they've been hurt somewhere along the line. I have heard it said that "Hurt people, hurt people,"[5] and I have found that to be true. But I know now that life isn't an ABC Afterschool Special. A happy ending isn't guaranteed. Maybe more helpful advice for Kristine at the time would have been to avoid the bully as much as possible. Sometimes your good intentions won't work out as you hoped. Sometimes you can't change the world.

In the process of learning, it's okay to make mistakes, to fail. The key is to learn from your mistakes. If you didn't handle something the best way, then ask for forgiveness and try to do better next time. Over the years, I've asked for my kids' forgiveness more than once. In marriage, I ask for it from my spouse regularly.

Just the other day, Annelli and I disagreed about something. We were both feeling stressed, and I said something to her in frustration that I shouldn't have said. Immediately, I regretted it. Annelli and I have a really good marriage overall, and it's okay to have disagreements in a marriage. Still, I'm continually learning how to be a better husband. In this instance, I needed to apologize to her. So I did. Fortunately, she forgave me. Yet what I noticed that day was that I can really hurt people with my words. Even though I apologized, and even though she forgave me, what I'd said still hung in the air. We always need to watch the power of our tongues. You can say one harsh word, or make one bad mistake, and it can damage the best of relationships.

Overall, we all need to be careful about venting. It's okay to express our feelings sometimes in safe environments to people who are willing to listen. For instance, it's okay to vent to a counselor. Or even sometimes to a good friend, when sharing our deepest feelings of frustration. But we've developed into too much of a venting culture. We've given ourselves permission as a society to rant at pretty much anything and anybody, anywhere, anytime, and we've gone too far. People vent at the woman behind the counter at the DMV. People vent at people they disagree with on social media. People vent at the waiter who gets their dinner order wrong.

What we need to realize is that once a harsh word is out there, it's out there. Period. People are people, and everyone has feelings. It's so easy to wound another person with our words. We need to be wary of a culture that prizes venting. When we feel frustrated or angry, we need to learn how to count to ten and speak from wisdom, not from rage.

REMOVE THE STICKERS

Back to my sister Laurie. Buying back-to-school clothes for me is only one way she encouraged me over the years, and she's also encouraged so many other people. After college, she became a teacher of students with special needs. Her work hasn't been easy, but she continues to be an example by encouraging the students in her classrooms. And her students love her in return. I have heard several stories from Laurie's former students and their parents about how she pushed them to achieve much more than what society expected of them. In fact, a few years ago, she was a finalist for the Teacher of the Year in the state of Washington. Encouragement is deeply engrained in Laurie's heart and mind. Consistently, she sees the possibilities in people.

I'm not the only member of my family who Laurie has encouraged. Each year my brother Don throws a Christmas party for his employees. He and his business partner, Phil, have built a very successful masonry company. Don invites family members, too, so Annelli and I try to go each year. He enjoys giving a speech to review all the accomplishments his company made the previous year. Don was gifted with a great sense of humor, so he always adds levity as he proudly talks about all of the buildings they completed. If you've ever tried your hand at telling jokes, the one thing you dread is having them fall flat. Don never has that problem, though, because Laurie never fails to attend the Christmas party. As is fitting with her being an encourager, she always has the loudest laugh.

Don is funny, so most of jokes hit, but I think it helps to know he has Laurie on his side!

Laurie's a great example of someone who bites her tongue, too. I have observed that she tries to never say anything bad about anybody. My mom used to say, "If you can't say something nice, don't say anything at all." That seems to have stuck with Laurie. She looks for opportunities to encourage people. That's her legacy— something that has changed my life, and I hope yours, too.

Laurie's influence has helped me. The other day, my wife and I were in the drive-through of a fast-food place, getting chicken sandwiches. I looked in the rearview mirror and saw a mom and her young son. They looked to be having a hard day. Their car was nothing fancy, and I didn't know their whole story, but I just felt like I wanted to encourage them. I talked to Annelli, and she said, "If you feel you need to do it, you should."

So when I pulled up to the next window, I said to the person inside, "Hey, I'd like to pay for the people behind me, too." And I did. We didn't wait around for acknowledgment or praise. We just wanted to create a true random act of kindness, one small bit of encouragement in the world. I hope to engage in small acts like this more often.

Maybe this chapter has been good for you to read, because now you're inspired to go in a good and noble direction. But maybe it's been hard for you, too. You know you have the ability to become an encourager, but you're also feeling down, like you need a boost yourself. Maybe it's tough to hear me telling you to become an encourager when what you need most of all is somebody to support and strengthen you right now.

Author Max Lucado wrote a children's book called *You Are Special*[6] about a puppet named Punchinello. The more you understand the layers of meaning within this story, the more it encourages you—and even liberates you. It reaffirms your true value.

Punchinello was a wooden toy who could walk and talk, and every other person in Punchinello's village was carved of wood, too. Each was different. Some had big noses. Others had large eyes. Some were tall, while others were short. Some were young, and some were old.

Each villager carried two boxes of stickers with them.

One box contained gold stars.

The other had gray dots.

Each day, the wooden people of the village walked around putting stickers on one another. The talented and fine-looking folks all received gold stars. But if a person's wood was rough or her paint was chipped, or if he wasn't very talented, they got a gray dot.

Punchinello wasn't very talented. He wasn't much to look at. He couldn't jump very high. His paint was peeling.

Punchinello got a lot of gray dots.

After a while, Punchinello got so many dots he started to see his identity reflected in the negative stickers. He began to believe he wasn't good enough as a result of the stickers that others had placed on him. He became really sad.

Then one day he met someone in his village who didn't have any stickers on her. She was lively and bright, and wherever she went, people tried to place stickers on her, but they'd fall right off—both the gold stars and the gray dots.

"Hmm, that's the way I want to live," Punchinello thought. "I don't want anybody's stickers on me." He asked the woman what her secret was.

"It's easy," she said. "Every day I go see the woodcarver. Go find out for yourself what happens when you see him. The stickers only stick if they matter to you. But the more you understand the woodcarver's ways, and the more you see how he values you just because of who you are, the less the stickers stick to you. He's just up the hill."

Punchinello wanted to go see the woodcarver, but he was afraid. The hill was steep and the way up was winding. It took some courage. Finally he climbed the hill to meet the woodcarver. He was surprised when the woodcarver knew his name.

"Looks like you've got lots of stickers on you, Punchinello," the woodcarver said in a deep, strong voice. "But it doesn't matter what others think of you. All that matters is what I think. And I think you are pretty special."

"Me, special? Why?"

"Because I made you," the woodcarver said. "And I don't make mistakes. The more you understand and trust my love for you, the less you care about the stickers."

"I'm not sure I understand," Punchinello said.

"You will," the woodcarver said. "But it will take time. You've got a lot of stickers. Come see me every day and let me remind you how much I care about you."

Punchinello nodded.

And with that, a gray dot fell to the ground.

Jump into the Pool

The heat beat down on us. We wanted nothing more than to get cool. It was a sweltering summer day, several years ago, and my brothers Don and Joe and I were motoring along in Don's boat on Lake Chelan in Eastern Washington. We could have just jumped over the side of the boat and gone for a swim, but we were lured by the promise of a beautiful hidden mountain pool at the base of a waterfall tucked away somewhere on the other side of the lake. Few people ever visited this pool or even knew about it, we'd been told. We were headed for what we thought would be a once-in-a-lifetime adventure.

Don located the spot on the shore that he was pretty sure would lead us to the pool. He beached the boat and tied it off on a log, and we all scrambled out. Joe lingered behind to stow a few items while Don and I forged ahead. Soon we found what looked like an old trailhead. Brush covered the path, but we managed to follow it up the side of the hill. The day was humid. Sweat poured from our bodies. A jump into the pool was going to feel so good.

DAD JOKE

◇◇◇

Did you hear about the fisherman who joined the band?

He could tuna guitar.

All his songs were catchy.

And he could really wail on the bass.

Don and I hiked up the path, every so often crossing back and forth across a creek. Joe was still back at the boat. The smell of pine trees and sage lay in the air. Before long we heard the quiet rush of a waterfall. We kept hiking. In about a quarter of a mile, the underbrush thinned out and the trail ended. Sure enough, a waterfall about twenty feet high, not huge, stood before us. Water cascaded over the lip of a high rock, and underneath lay a beautiful pool of fresh mountain water, about thirty feet across. The place was deserted. It was the perfect swimming hole. We had it all to ourselves.

"Should we jump in?" Don asked. The heat was stifling.

I shook my head. "I don't know. Maybe we should wait." The water looked so inviting.

There we stood, waiting, deliberating, and clearly overthinking the decision. A minute passed. Another. Three minutes. Four. Don and I kept discussing whether to swim or not. We wanted to experience the water. We knew it was going to feel good once we were wet. Joe wouldn't mind if we went in without him. But I didn't know. Don didn't know. Were there hidden dangers we hadn't considered? From where we stood, we could see the water from the falls crashing into the pool. It's not like either of us were chicken, but I guess the fear of the unknown was holding us back.

Then along came Joe, bustling up the trail. He reached the edge of the pool, looked at us, and raised an eyebrow. He didn't say a word, he didn't miss a step. He kicked off his shoes and hiked straight into the water. He quickly saw that the pool was deep enough for swimming and free of rocks hidden beneath the surface. In a flash he took the plunge. Joe's entire decision-making process took two seconds.

Don stared at me, still on the edge of the shore. I stared back at Don. We both laughed and followed Joe into the water, kicking ourselves that we'd deliberated so long. Joe was right. The cold mountain water felt great and maybe shocked some sense into us. I couldn't help but think what Don and I might have missed if Joe hadn't been on this adventure with us. Sure, it's wise to look before you leap. Or in this case, consider before you plunge. But you also need a balance—because he who hesitates is lost.

What I want to impart to you from this story is this: If you want to live successfully, be proactive. Take a quick look first, and then don't hesitate. Jump into the water and cool off in the pool.

THE DIFFICULTY OF DECISION-MAKING

Many people dream of doing great things but never take action. They become paralyzed by analyzing all their choices to death. Or they let fear stop them from taking the first step toward living their dream. Don and I wasted five minutes of our lives deliberating whether or not to go into the water. Yes, it was only five minutes, but still, it shows how too much deliberation can rob you of joy. What we needed to do was be more like Joe. More deliberate. More forward-thinking. If you dream of doing things, act on those dreams. Will Rogers once said, "Even if you're on the right track, you'll get run over if you just sit there."[1]

Sure, there's a time for caution. But there's also a line beyond that point where excess caution becomes a problem. Particularly if your caution stops you from ever proceeding in the good direction you want to go. You must conquer your fears. You don't want to overthink a good move. The only way to steer a car is if it's moving, so you have to be willing to go forward. If you're sitting still, it's very hard to turn that wheel. Director James Cameron said, "There are many talented people who haven't fulfilled their dreams because they overthought it, or they were too cautious, and were unwilling to make the leap of faith."[2]

I understand the tension between going forward and staying still. It's certainly okay to take a beat, think before you speak, and consider a plan of action before you take it. At times it's good to be slow, prudent, and thoughtful. Yet too much caution can be counterproductive to success. The reluctance to move forward can be a marker of a hesitant or inactive spirit, of timidity or fear. So how do you know when to proceed or not?

Dr. James Stein helps frame an answer that points to the healthy practice of discernment. "You are what you decide," Stein writes. "[So] the general rule of thumb is that you should be cautious when you have a lot to lose, and you should take a risk when you have a lot to gain."[3]

Think through the ramifications of Stein's instructions. In what areas of life do you have a lot to lose? Relationships, maybe. Finances. Your reputation. Your pride. Each person might answer in a different way.

Conversely, in what areas do you have a lot to gain? Perhaps applying for a job. Going on to get a degree. Living a fit and healthy life. Taking a risk in following a dream. Asking out the special somebody who you truly respect and admire. Making some sort of shift or change toward a better opportunity.

The key with any decision is understanding at a foundational level that you have to let go of one thing in order to gain something else. Decisions can open doors for us, yet decisions almost always close doors to us, too. We're so often told that we can have everything we want in life. But that's actually a lie. Nobody can have everything. To choose one thing is to not choose several other things. We have to accept the fact that nobody can live ten lives at once.

For instance, if you attend UCLA for your undergrad degree, it means you don't go to USC, at least not at first. You can choose one school but not the other. To become a doctor means you don't become a lawyer. If you decide to get married, you're shutting the door to intimacy with everybody else. Facing such big decisions can be frightening. Maybe you don't know if you want to go to UCLA or USC. Maybe you want to go to both. You fear that if you go to USC, you'll miss out on something good that's happening at UCLA. When it comes to what career path to head down, or who to marry, the options can seem overwhelming.

This specific anxiety has become so ubiquitous in our world today that we've actually coined a term for it: fear of missing out (FOMO). It plays out two ways. First, too many options lie before us, so instead of choosing our favorite option, we choose nothing. Or second, we have chosen one path, and it's a good one. But the grass looks greener somewhere else. We never seem satisfied with where we are and what we have. We constantly second-guess ourselves.

You have to move past FOMO. Be courageous enough to make a choice and stick with it. Decide to choose one thing and not ten things. Then, once you've made your choice, be satisfied with the decision you made.

BEYOND FOMO

I get it. FOMO is real. It's easy to wonder what the right road is or worry that you've made a wrong choice, even if you've made a good one. But you can't let FOMO stymie you from living the life you want to lead.

In 1983, I was nineteen years old and just out of high school. I worked at an office supply company, and one of our customers was a then-little-known software company located in Redmond, Washington. They'd been in business for about eight years, and they were growing in big ways. It seemed like we were sending them office supplies right and left. Some three hundred people worked for the software company at the time, all housed in three office buildings in a compound where State Route 520 intersected with Interstate 405. I developed a pretty good working friendship with the guy at the software company's loading dock.

One day he said, "Rob, you need to get a job at this company. They're hiring. The company's really growing, and they're handing out stock options to all employees along with your pay."

I shrugged. "Maybe. I'm doing okay for now."

"Seriously, think about it," he said. "This decision could change your life."

I went home and thought about it. I didn't know much about software, and the idea of working for a software company didn't really ring any bells with me. I still dreamed of playing professional football, and I was trying to figure out the best next step to take so I could head in that direction. For a while, I deliberated about the software company decision. The next time I saw my buddy at the loading dock, he asked me again if I was interested in working there. I shook my head and said, "Nah, I don't think so." My decision was final.

Can you guess what company I turned down?

Microsoft.

Today, they have more than 163,000 employees.[4] The Redmond campus currently has 125 buildings, and that's only one of the worldwide campuses. I don't know exactly how much stock the company was handing out to its employees at the start, but by 1992, as many as one in five Microsoft employees had become millionaires,[5] and stats say that if you had invested $5,000 in Microsoft on the day of its initial public offering, March 13, 1986, it would be worth more than $10 million today.[6]

Did I miss out?

Sure. But sincerely and truthfully: I don't regret that I missed out. I love the life I have today and wouldn't change it for anything. We get to live only one life. This is the life I've chosen, and I don't look back with disappointment.

My experience is an example of one of the big ways you counter FOMO. You choose wisely and choose well, and you also realize that you can't have everything. You go forward anyway. You make decisions at the time you face them, based upon the information you have at the time. In the end, you choose to be content with the paths you've walked down. I would probably be a millionaire if I had worked at Microsoft, but then again, if I had worked there, maybe I'd always be wondering if I could have made it in professional football. Or maybe I wouldn't have met and married Annelli or had our children. I probably wouldn't have created my YouTube channel. No question about it. I'd rather be doing what I'm doing today, talking to you.

You have to choose. When you come to that fork in the road, you can't simply stay there. You have to decide which path to head down. You can't stand at the base of the waterfall all day, staring at the water. You have to jump into the pool.

I've found my faith to be tremendously helpful in this area. Proverbs 3:5–6 says, "Trust in the Lord with all your heart and lean not on your own understanding; in all your ways acknowledge him, and he will make your paths straight."

That's what I'm doing in life. I want to trust that God is good and God is working things out, in his way, in his time. I have my own understanding of things, yet I acknowledge that there are things in this life I can't fully explain or understand. God knows about these things; I don't. So I lean on his understanding. I want to look to him in all my ways, and there's this promise from him that when I do, he will make my paths straight. Not crooked or tangled or devious. But clear and forward-looking. Things are going to work out okay.

TAKE THE PLUNGE

How do you make good decisions? Well, there are no black-and-white formulas to choosing the wisest options. No vending machines. No guaranteed cause-and-effect systems. For example, when you insert a dollar bill into the payment slot of a vending machine, you expect to receive a bag of potato chips in return. On the other hand, going to a university doesn't guarantee that you'll land a great job, or that you'll be happy with the one you find. You may marry a kind and loving person, but that doesn't ensure you'll always love each other or stay together, particularly if you never work at your relationship. Likewise, leading a wise life doesn't guarantee that bad things will never happen to you. Often the opposite is true. We have to expect and prepare for the unexpected.

However, there are principles we can use to help us make good decisions. What follows are five of the best decision-making strategies I've found.

1. Start with prayer.

Sometimes young people think that praying is something only their parents or grandparents do. But prayer is more widespread than you might think. According to research, some 55 percent of people pray every day,[7] and up to 80 percent of adolescents pray at least some of the time.[8]

People sometimes toss in a prayer as an afterthought to their decision-making process, but I recommend beginning with prayer. Get all your bases covered from the get-go by inquiring of God first. It's too easy to put prayer at the bottom of your list. Or to exclude it altogether. But prayer should be one of the first things we do.

I like this suggestion from James 1:5: "If any of you lacks wisdom, you should ask God, who gives generously to all without finding fault, and it will be given to you." That's a statement you can take to the bank. Need to know something? Pray for insight. Ask God to give you the wisdom to make the right choices.

If you're a person of faith, you might be tempted to pray and then wait for a lightning bolt to strike before you act. Very rarely does that happen. Learn to use the brain God gave you. Pray, seek wisdom, get as much information as you can, then make the decision and move forward. Trust that God is guiding you.

2. Get wise counsel.

Have a decision to make? Talk to others who've been down the road before. Ask the people you trust for advice, those who know you well and who have your best interests at heart. You might be too close to a situation to see it clearly, so it's useful to have someone impartial to the matter help you sort things out.

At the same time, beware of asking too many people for advice. You don't want a committee running your life, and at the end of the day, you have to live with your choices. They don't. So go ahead and poll a few trusted people, and then leave it there. Get your counsel and make your decision.

3. Gather information, make a list.

Do you need to make a decision about what school to go to? What career to pursue? Get as much data as you can. In the case of a college choice, visit the campus beforehand. Talk to professors and students. In the case of a career, do an internship first. Ask people in that particular profession what an average day looks like for them.

Next, make a pros and cons list. It's an age-old practice. Take a sheet of paper and draw a line down the middle. Write your decision at the top of the paper in the form of a question: Should I go to Central Washington University? Should I start a YouTube channel? Should I date so-and-so?

On one side of the line, list all the potential positive outcomes, and on the other list all the potential negative outcomes. Have a free-flowing brainstorming session. Ask yourself all the hard questions you can think of: What might happen? What might be accomplished? What could be damaged? What is the true cost? How might this decision affect the future? Try to fast-forward through a scenario in your mind, following all paths to their logical conclusions. What are the best and worst possible outcomes?

You might end up with a sheet that has a bunch of items in one column or the other. Good—the weight of that evidence makes the decision clearer. But you might end up with a sheet that has an even number of points in both columns. That happens in life. Most decisions are multifaceted. When making a choice, wisdom and discernment are important guiding forces.

4. Do a gut test.

Call it a hunch. Call it intuition. Call it instinct. Psychologists tell us that when it comes to decision-making, we can trust our perceptivity, particularly with practice. Intuition is often developed over time, through recognizing patterns and sequences and outcomes. We learn that if we walk into a room with a smile, people are more likely to smile back. Or we learn that when a supervisor asks us to come into their office and starts a conversation by saying, "We really appreciate the work you've done here, but . . ." a firing is imminent.

Still, at other times, your intuition will feel much less data-driven. Ask married couples how they knew when and if it was right to marry the person they were dating, and you'll often hear in reply: "Well, you know when you know."

Dr. Marcia Reynolds describes how you can force your subconscious mind to the surface: "Try the Coin Trick. Assign your options to heads or tails. Flip the coin. The moment you see the result, are you disappointed or relieved? The trick might help you uncover what you really want to do."[9]

5. Decide with integrity and selflessness.

Make your decisions with integrity and selflessness in mind. Think not only of yourself and how the decision will impact you, but how it will impact others. Success comes not only when we win, but when we help others win, too.

In a now famous cross-country footrace in 2012, a Kenyan long-distance runner named Abel Mutai was well in the lead toward the end of the race, while runner Iván Fernández Anaya of Spain was in second place. (Note: With Spanish naming customs, the first or paternal family name in this case is Fernández and the second or maternal family name is Anaya.) Mutai was a strong runner, and he'd already proven himself by winning the bronze medal at that year's London Olympics. Everybody in the crowd near the finish line could see that Mutai was going to win.

Yet with only about ten meters to go—for reasons nobody in the crowd fully understood in the moment—Mutai suddenly stopped running. The crowd uttered a collective gasp, then broke into shouts, urging him to continue. Only later would Mutai explain that he'd become confused by the signs. He thought he'd already completed the course.

Fernández came charging up behind Mutai. He was a strong competitor also, and for a split second, it looked like Fernández was going to do what many people would have done in the moment: run right on past Mutai.

Instead, Fernández chose not to exploit Mutai's mistake. The second-place runner slowed and shouted at his opponent to finish the race, but the two runners didn't speak the same language, so Fernández used gestures to urge Mutai along. Finally Mutai realized his mistake, ran to the finish, and claimed the victory.

Why didn't Fernández blaze ahead to take the lead?

"I didn't deserve to win it," Fernández told the press. "I did what I had to do. He was the rightful winner."[10]

DEVELOP YOUR PASSION

People tell you all the time to follow your passions. Do what you *want* to do. Yet so often, particularly when you're young, you find yourself working at a job you're not passionate about. Or living in a city that's not your first choice. Or maybe you're even in a relationship that you're sort of ho-hum about. What then?

It's healthy to question the whole follow-your-passions directive. Why? Because studies have shown it's lousy advice. Passions aren't as fixed as we think they are, particularly at a young age. Stanford University researchers examined the beliefs that lead people to succeed or fail at developing their interests. They concluded that "mantras like 'find your passion' carry hidden implications . . . [and] the idea that passions are found fully formed implies that the number of interests a person has is limited."[11]

For instance, you might love flying as an eighteen-year-old and believe that your life's goal is to become a pilot. The Stanford researchers would say it's fine to head in that direction, but they'd also caution that your life experiences might still be too limited to lock in a final choice. Maybe by the time you're twenty-one, you'll discover that you love architecture instead. Or working with special needs students, as my daughter did. Or developing software, as my son did. It's fine to keep options open, and it's fine to think broad-mindedly. Instead of finding your passion, the researchers would recommend developing a passion and seeing it through. Your future then becomes something you create rather than something you discover. This is particularly helpful if you don't know what your passions are yet.

Stanford psychologist Dr. Gregory Walton wrote: "If you look at something and think, 'That seems interesting, that could be an area I could make a contribution in,' you then invest yourself in it. You take some time to do it, you encounter challenges, over time you build that commitment."[12]

That's good advice, and that's certainly been my story. I'm an account manager today, but when I was young, I was never passionate about a career in sales. I entered my career much more reluctantly. I was married with a kid on the way, and I needed a job. That was my grand motivation for taking the job. When I first got into sales, I was scared of approaching people and regularly tied myself into knots. I was convinced that nobody was interested in what I was selling.

But along the way I developed a passion for my job. I saw that the world needs good salespeople. I saw areas of my job that I could thrive in, and I figured out how I could do my job and be true to myself. When it came to approaching other companies that I sold products to, I learned how to befriend the gatekeepers and not fear them. (Many of them turned out to be polite and kind.) I discovered ways of enjoying what I'm doing so I could make positive contributions to the world. Over the years, I've earned enough of a wage to support a family, which has been important to me, and my job has allowed flexibility in my schedule, so I was able to spend a lot of time with my kids, which was also important to me. Today, after being in my job for almost thirty years, I'm very grateful. I feel blessed to have this job.

In the course of your life, undoubtedly you will take jobs that aren't your passion. Or they might lie within the field of your passion, but they won't be your dream job yet. That's okay. Those jobs might be stepping stones to something better. Or they might be places to learn things. They might show you the importance of finding things you love about any job. Or you might simply work there to shine some light into that workplace for a while. Treat people fairly and with respect, and always do your best, even if your current position isn't the job of your dreams.

How does the follow-your-passions advice apply when choosing a person to date seriously? In these decisions I recommend seeking a high degree of passion, especially if you end up marrying the person. Yet you have to define what passion looks like in a close relationship. Passion can be developed as much as it's discovered. You might not see fireworks or get chills up your spine every time you're with that person, particularly at first. That person might not exactly sweep you off your feet. They might not look like a supermodel or be the funniest person. Or the most romantic. Or the most exciting. Or whatever superlative you're holding up as the benchmark.

True passion emerges when you develop respect for a person. You admire that person. You become great friends, and you enjoy being with that person on a daily basis. You can laugh together and talk together. You're kind to each other, and you work well together, even if you disagree. You have similar attitudes, beliefs, and values. You're affectionate with each other. You love that person, and they love you. I'd say we can be far too quick to overlook quality people in this age of swipe right or left.

GREEN EGGS AND YOU

Have you ever talked with a person who expressed excitement about their dreams for the future, about what could be, but then they sort of sigh and say, "Oh, but I could never do that."

Many people don't make needed decisions due to fear. They stay at the edge of the pool on a sweltering summer's day, never diving into the cool water. They think and overthink the decision, continually weighing outcomes in their mind. Forty years later, they still haven't jumped into the pool.

If you tell yourself you could never do something, then you will never do it. You're already defeated. You will get what you get, and it won't be your dream. Far better to count the costs, weigh the risks, and take the plunge, just like my brother Joe did at that swimming hole.

I've always loved the classic children's book *Green Eggs and Ham*.[13] It's a children's picture book with a few simple words repeated over and over, and the plot seems basic. But it offers strong layers of meaning, even for folks who aren't kids anymore.

Do you remember how it goes? Profound nuances fill the story. Two characters are having a discussion. One is named Sam-I-Am, and his big goal is to get the other fellow, who's never named, to eat a plate of food that's new to him. The other fellow refuses. That's the entire storyline in a nutshell. For pages and pages, Sam-I-Am tries to offer his friend what he believes is a good thing, but the other fellow keeps saying he doesn't like it. Trouble is, the other fellow has never tried the new food.

Toward the end, the unnamed fellow makes a concession. He will try one bite of the new food, just to get Sam-I-Am off his back. After tentatively tasting it, the unnamed fellow—*drumroll, please*—likes the new food! He not only likes what he eats, he becomes passionate about the new food. He's going to eat it anywhere. With a fox and in a box, and in a house and with a mouse.

Here are two thoughts that I take from this book, and which I want to leave with you. First, in the pursuit of your dreams, you will undoubtedly need to be persistent. If your job involves getting someone to try something new, you'll need to ask more than once. If you have to knock on a career door to have it opened, you might need to keep knocking for a while. If you have something good to offer that really helps people, you'll need to present it to them several times. Be persistent. Be polite. Keep your good humor. Ask twice. And again.

Second, any decision you face in life can lie before you like a big plate of unknowns. Don't be afraid to try new things. Who knows? You might just love green eggs and ham.

Hold with an Open Hand

One morning in my eighth grade shop class, a bully snuck up behind me and walloped me over the back of the head. I hadn't provoked him. He was just a jerk. I was short and chubby, maybe 5 feet 3 inches if I didn't slouch. In the harsh schoolyard currency of junior high, those physical traits made me a favorite target for bullies. When his fist hit the back of my head, I actually saw stars for the first time.

My response? I sat there and took it. Never said a word. This was the period of my life when my siblings and I were fending for ourselves at home, and I did not want to draw attention to myself. I never called the kid out. I certainly felt like whipping around and slugging him hard, but I knew better than to rock the boat. With my head smarting and my tail between my legs, I stumbled over to the shop teacher and murmured something about a headache. He pointed me to the nurse's office. That's where I spent the rest of the hour.

Bullies played into the pattern of my life for many years. I learned to be wary, to hold on tight to my sense of well-being. It

DAD JOKE

◇◇◇

The cow asked the lamb why he looked guilty.

"I'm not guilty," the lamb said. "I'm just a little sheepish."

seemed that bullies lurked around every corner: in the classroom, on the field during gym class, at the back of the bus going to and from school. I particularly hated riding the school bus. When I was younger, I walked to school. But in junior high and high school, I needed to take a bus, and every one I ever rode was noisy and crowded. Uncool at the best of times. A hotbed of bullies at the worst. I was a highly reluctant bus rider.

The year after the bullying incident in shop class everything in my life came apart. When I started ninth grade, I was still short and chubby. If I stretched as tall as I could, I was a diminutive 5 feet 4. (Back in those days in Bellevue, ninth grade was part of junior high; tenth, eleventh, and twelfth grades were at the high school.) And so I was still being picked on. Meanwhile, my home life was a mess: My parents officially split, my dad announced he was done with parenting, and chaos reigned in our lives. Overall, it was a horrible season for me, although one bright star began to shine. One singularly good and remarkable thing happened to me before that lousy year was finished.

I grew seven inches taller.

Yep, by the time I finished ninth grade, I had become a lean, muscular 5 feet 11 inches tall. The bullying stopped and I even became a bit popular, although the next fall when I started my sophomore year, I still wasn't confident. I still didn't want to draw attention to myself. I still kept an eye out for bullies. I still kept myself tightly wrapped.

A second star began to shine for me during my sophomore year. In the decades since then, I've come to see this second bright star as one of the kindest and most generous things that came my way during those unpredictable years. I needed to tell you about the bullying first so you could see the fuller context in which this generosity played out for me, because even into my sophomore year I was still feeling the sting of many unkind moments and actions. The kindness came from my brother Don, and such acts of generosity can make a ton of difference in the world today.

You already know the world is filled with its fair share of bullies and unkind people, so one of the best actions you can take to be successful in life is to go in the opposite direction from bullying. Bullies clobber others with abuse. Generous people lift others up with kind acts. Be kind. Give good things away. Inject acts of generosity into your circle of influence. Don't be like the jerk who indiscriminately walloped me upside the head in shop class. Instead, be like Don. Learn to hold things freely, with an open hand.

What did Don do that landed with so much positive force in my life? Simple.

He started giving me rides to school in his car.

FOR THE SAKE OF LOVE

At the start of my sophomore year, I was living with Rick and Karen in their tiny trailer a couple of miles southwest of Sammamish High School in Bellevue. Don was a senior at the same school, but he was living in an apartment on the other side of town with my brother Joe, who had just graduated.

To give me a ride, Don had to drive past the high school and continue on for several miles out of his way. And after he picked me up, he of course had to backtrack to the school. All that additional driving used extra gas, which he paid for. And it took extra time. He had to get up a full half hour earlier. For a high school senior, a half hour of sleep was a big deal. I understood that. It was a huge generosity on his part.

Don's rides saved me from the loud and uncool bus ride, but I appreciated him for other reasons, too. Rick and Karen lived right on the edge of the school district, and I had to walk close to a mile to reach my bus stop. Rainfall is common throughout the chilly Pacific Northwest, but no self-respecting Pacific Northwestern teen would ever be caught dead with an umbrella. So taking the bus on a rainy morning meant living with a wet head, wet shoulders, and wet shoes for much of the rest of the day. Don didn't give me a ride every morning. But he did so a couple of days a week. Particularly on mornings when it rained, Don could be a real lifesaver.

Don never held anything too tightly, including his own sense of decorum. He was a senior, sure, but he never cared about acting all dignified or broodingly cool, or like he was above me. Sometimes I wasn't sure what to think about his lack of inhibition. But from today's vantage point, I can see that Don was a hero. So much heartache was happening in our young lives. Don's zest for life encouraged me to let my hair down and have fun, if only for a couple of minutes on the drive to school. If only I could.

Let me try to paint the picture for you. Take an average morning in October 1979. Don has just picked me up. I'm fifteen; he's seventeen. We don't say much except to mumble our good mornings. He's driving his yellow 1966 Mustang, a car that originally belonged to our mother. The car doesn't have a big engine like some Mustangs, and it's more of a family model than a sports car; still, a Mustang is always cool.

We're heading toward our high school. Don throws a Led Zeppelin cassette into the player and cranks the volume to eleven. His head tilts back and his mouth opens wide, and as we roar down the road, he's free-form yelling the lyrics to "Hot Dog" while simultaneously playing air guitar on the steering wheel column. Don's air guitar showmanship is second to none. He's playing behind his back. Windmilling like Pete Townshend. Setting fire to the column like he's Jimi Hendrix.

Inwardly I'm smiling, but I'm not cool enough to pull off these antics myself. As we drive into the school parking lot, I stay quiet, not allowing myself to let go. I glance around, still on the lookout for bullies. Still feeling vulnerable. Still not wanting to rock any boats. I'm dealing with my usual bundle of tensions even on the ride to school, a bundle that keeps hold of me during this entire season of life. Don's example is pointing me in the right direction, but I'm not yet sure if I dare to fully enjoy the moment. I certainly can't bear the thought of other kids laughing at me. Maybe playing air guitar like this is sort of goofy. Don's going wild, reaching for the stars, but I'm not ready to embrace this side of myself.

At least I know this to be true: Riding to school with Don is way cooler than taking the bus. He's being more than a chauffeur to his younger brother—he is making a point to stay connected with me. Dad and Mom might not be in my life anymore to any great degree, but I've got this going for me: My sister Mary is writing me post-cards, my brother Rick is letting me live at his place, and Don is offering all sorts of generosity. He's making these sacrifices because of his love for me. Not only is he giving a ride to his little brother, he's also working to buoy me along. He's being upbeat. Optimistic. He's doing whatever he can to change the mood of our lives.

Even if that means singing like a wild man while driving me to school.

WHY IT'S GOOD TO GIVE

Have you ever thought about what it means to live generously? When it comes to being generous, we typically associate it with opening our wallets and digging deep into our pockets. The kind of generosity I'm pointing you toward may involve giving money to people, but it's broader in scope.

Living generously leads to making sacrifices for the sake of love, in whatever you do and wherever you go: school, work, home life, with your friends and extended family members, even with strangers. You give your time, talents, and treasure. You hold things freely, with an open hand. It might take the form of volunteering somewhere or giving someone a compliment. You might take the time to talk on the phone with your grandma Letty even though you'd rather play video games. It might involve something as simple as lending a friend your sweater. Or maybe, like Don on the drive to school with me, it's not caring about how you're perceived so you can cheer someone up.

When you live with generosity, it's okay to set boundaries. You can be careful in your giving so you don't squander your resources. You can hold dearly and closely the people you love, which is why you give to them. Living in the security of their close circle, you'll find you have resources—both emotional and otherwise—even to give to strangers sometimes. Maybe you live frugally and on a budget. That's good, too, but shouldn't prevent you from being charitable, because living generously is about so much more than material things. Yes, generosity means more than giving things away. You may have noticed that often when we give things away, we give with mixed motives. We might donate to a charity because we want a tax deduction. Or we might give some clothes to a shelter because the clothes are outdated or no longer fit us. Those actions might be part of your generosity, but there's an even deeper level that I'm pointing you toward.

To be truly generous you have to give to others and expect nothing in return. The truest and deepest form of giving happens as you "make the mental leap from your own vantage point to that of someone else."[1] You give simply because it's good to give. You give because it creates a kinder and more compassionate world. You give because you choose to live a life where you regularly give things away. You give because giving is part of how you define success.

See, the opposite of living generously is living like a miser. You're stingy. You're a hoarder, a tightwad. You're cheap or iron-fisted. You want every bit of goodness for yourself. It's an attitude of closedness that leads to undesirable actions. Maybe you live with pettiness and fear. You're sparing with compliments. You resist helping people out. You find it hard to lend things to your friends. You're unsure about letting go. You're even too insecure to sing along with your brother in his car. And when you don't give people basic kindness, you're in danger of giving them something else, something sinister.

That's not the type of world you want to create. I know, because that's what I was like when I was a kid. The bullying behavior was introduced to me by acts of meanness from others, especially the guy who clobbered me over the head, and you can see how it began to play out in my life. Remember I also bullied a kid on the bus? His last name rhymed with dodo, and I reminded him of that every time I saw him. The insecurity had built up in me. I had been bullied, so I had learned to become a bully myself, at least with him. I found it hard to give away love, because I was holding any love that might have come my way so tightly to my chest. I had become an emotionally stingy person. I couldn't share kindness freely, and the kid on the bus became the target of my darker impulses.

Fortunately, psychologists say we can learn to become generous, even if we've been hurt earlier. The healing begins when we understand that being generous actually makes us feel positive and uplifted. We learn to see that being generous helps us, not hinders us. The benefits come back to us as much as they go to someone else. This may not be elemental generosity, because there's self-interest at play, yet self-care is valid, too. Receiving positive feelings isn't the only reason we do something good, but those feelings can help us go in the right direction.

Dr. Elizabeth Dunn conducted an experiment at the University of British Columbia in which she instructed her researchers to dole out cash to college students. It wasn't large amounts of cash: Some students received a twenty-dollar bill. Others received five bucks. After the entire group had received money, half the participants were instructed to spend the money on whatever they wanted—just as long as whatever they bought was for their own enjoyment. The other half was told to either give their cash to charity or spend it on other people, such as buying dinner for their friends. Both groups were told to spend their cash by the end of the same day they received it.

The findings? The students who spent money on others "reported feeling happier at the end of the day than those who spent the money on themselves."[2] They described an enhanced mood, an increased sense of meaning and significance, and greater overall feelings of well-being. This was just as true for the students who gave away five bucks as those who gave twenty.

Emotional generosity follows a similar pattern. A study of adults in New York found that the act of giving someone social support contained huge benefits for the giver. Whenever you give away your time or possessions, or even take the effort to pay someone a compliment, it can positively affect your blood pressure, hearing, sleep quality, and overall mental, emotional, and physical health.[3]

What does that mean for you? Simply: It's good for you to give.

THE ART OF LIVING GENEROUSLY

When I created my YouTube channel, I did so from a place of sincere generosity. I simply wanted to help people. I believe that's one reason the channel has succeeded to a big degree. If you're focused on self-service or if you're fake, people can spot that from a mile away. But I wasn't posting to get rich or become famous. Over the years, my wife and I have planned well financially. We didn't need to start a YouTube channel to boost our bottom line. I just wanted to lend a hand.

In fact, when my channel went viral, I wasn't jumping up and down with excitement. Far from it. I was facedown on my bed, overwhelmed, praying and crying out to God, "Lord, I don't know what your plan is for this, but I can't process this so fast. So many people are reaching out, wanting to hear from me. I don't know what to do. But my eyes are on you."

It's funny that some people have great memories. They can look at a poem or a verse, read it once, and it's like their minds take a photograph. I've never been like that. Any memorization I've ever done has been difficult. Yet I can also say that whenever I've memorized any scripture, it's been a good thing for me. I can look back on a lot of seasons in my life when I've wasted time. But I've never looked back on any time that I've spent memorizing scripture and regretted it.

So when I was facedown on my bed, feeling so overwhelmed, a couple of verses that I'd memorized in the past came to mind. One was Luke 6:38: "Give, and it will be given to you. A good measure, pressed down, shaken together and running over, will be poured into your lap. For with the measure you use, it will be measured to you."

Jesus said those words during what's known as the Sermon on the Mount, when he was encouraging people to love others indiscriminately. Love those who do good to you, and love those who don't do good to you. Bless those who curse you. Give freely and generously and treat others in a way you'd like to be treated yourself. Whenever you give good things away, Jesus said, those good things have a habit of returning to you in good ways also. I was starting the YouTube channel to help others, yet much good was going to come back to me from it.

I also recalled what the apostle Paul said in 2 Corinthians 9:6. "Remember this: Whoever sows sparingly will also reap sparingly, and whoever sows generously will also reap generously." It was going to take time and energy to create videos for the YouTube channel, but I didn't need to feel overwhelmed by the extra work. God loves a cheerful giver, and that verse encouraged me to feel good about the time and energy and information I was giving away. There was a freedom to the giving, since I wasn't trying to hang on to anything. I just wanted to let go and see helpfulness spread out into the world at random. I had no idea who might be helped, but God knew.

The cool thing about giving is that we're able to truly participate in what we believe is important. You might not be called to start a YouTube channel, and that's perfectly okay. Just ask yourself:

What do I value? Are you a father who values his children? Then invest time in your kids. Give your time and energy generously to them. Are you someone who wants to see every person in the world eat nutritious meals each day? Then sponsor a child through an international relief organization. Give your money direction.

Generosity is about action, not just talk. Hey, anybody can wear a T-shirt with a cool altruistic slogan on the front. Anybody can stick a sign in their yard that advocates today's politically correct codes of conduct. Anybody can rant about the latest cause on Twitter. But show me your wallet. Show me your calendar. Show me where you volunteer and where you give money. Those things are the truer indications of what you value. If you care for something, then it's good to actually invest in it. Enough with the bumper-sticker living. It's far more noble—and helpful to the world—to actually give.

NUTS AND BOLTS OF CASH

Okay, let's talk about cash. That's where generosity is truly tested, isn't it? Volunteerism is good and needful. But it's too easy to volunteer somewhere without ever giving away any money. I say go ahead and care, yes. Volunteer, yes. And then give money, too. Don't forget to give money. And don't use your other good acts as an excuse not to give money.

Sometimes people will tell me, "Well, I'd like to give. But I just don't make enough money to give." Actually, I've discovered that that's the best time to give. When you're broke. If you're a billionaire and you give away a hundred thousand dollars, that might sound like something huge and important, yet for a billionaire, that is only 1/10,000 of their net worth. I am not knocking the donation; it just isn't really that much of a sacrifice for a billionaire in comparison to their wealth.

What about if you have, say, seventy-five bucks in your bank account, and you give away fifty to a worthy cause? That's a pretty big deal, but not because the money is a huge amount. It's big because it reflects the sincerity of your heart.

Jesus told a story along those lines. One day in ancient Jerusalem, Jesus was sitting with his closest followers in a place where they could see people putting money into the temple treasury. Plenty of rich folks threw in large amounts of cash. Then along came an impoverished widow, a person in that day and age who was hard-pressed to find employment or have enough money to live. She gave two small copper coins, worth only a few cents.

Jesus turned to his followers and said, "Truly I tell you, this poor widow has put more into the treasury than all the others. They all gave out of their wealth; but she, out of her poverty, put in everything—all she had to live on."[4]

What's the point of that story? It's not that God would stress you out by asking for a donation. The point is that the amount you give is sometimes less important than the heart behind it. The widow's gift was a true sacrifice. She gave from true devotion.

A few years back, I went through a big shift in my own life. I'd always been hesitant to give sacrificially to charities or to my church. When we went to the Catholic church when I was young, I think my folks donated some money here and there, but it was always a minimum, at least as far as I was aware. As adults, my wife and I never gave money off the top; instead we gave from what was left over, which never seemed to amount to much.

In my job as an account manager today, I'm paid on a commission basis only. My income fluctuates from month to month depending on my sales performance. Annelli and I have always tried to live below our means and with margin in mind. Yet my lack of a consistent salary has been one of our big excuses for not giving before we pay our bills. We think: *Well, next month we might have a poor month. So we need to save.*

Annelli and I discovered that if our fists are closed, then that's all we'd have—whatever was in our fists. But if our fists are open, new things can get in. New opportunities can come our way. We started studying about living generously. We saw how it would be good for us to give more and give regularly—and to give money, too, not just our time volunteering. So we made a pledge to each other and to God. We adjusted our budget and started giving away 10 percent of our earnings, each and every month. It seemed a good place to start.

Immediately our resolve was tested. One of my largest accounts was bought by another company, so it looked like I was going to lose the account along with the commission. Then a few days later, I received a phone call from my largest account, and they told me they wanted to work with a national company to service them across the United States. We were mainly a local company, so it was a long shot at best if we would be able to keep that account. The potential loss of income from both of these accounts scared us. Annelli and I prayed. We had promised to God that we were going to give off the top, so now we needed to trust that God would provide.

And things worked out. Sure enough, I was able to keep the account that was bought out, and I ended up winning the other account nationally. It went from being my largest account to the largest account at our company. Soon after, I landed two more accounts with different companies, both really big. Everything fell into place. At the end of the year that we had decided to give regularly, I had earned one and a half times more than what I'd made the year before.

Many people think that God is a killjoy, out to ruin your life. But that's the opposite of the truth. God wants you to live abundantly, and he knows that one of the ways you live that way is by being a generous person. We're actually happier when we give things away. We're living abundantly when we hold things loosely. We can't out-give God.

One TV show I absolutely love is *American Pickers*. Ever seen it? Two partners, Mike Wolfe and Frank Fritz, travel around the backroads of the United States looking for antiques and other collectibles. Those guys have a great job. They sift through old barns. They stop at people's houses if the folks have a bunch of stuff lying around in the front yard. With people's permission, Mike and Frank look through garages and sheds and outbuildings, wherever people have stored stuff that they might want to sell.

Plenty of the folks Mike and Frank meet are self-described hoarders, and I'm always fascinated by them. Hoarders typically spend their lives acquiring a bunch of stuff, but then they're unwilling to do anything with it or get rid of it, even when they become elderly. For example, Mike and Frank will meet some old guy who's ninety-five and has a beat-up motorcycle in his barn. He's always planned to restore it—someday. He knows his time is short, and he knows he'll never get around to restoring that bike. But nope, he won't sell it, either. Whenever I watch situations like that, I think: *What's the point? You can't take it with you. Ever see a hearse towing a U-Haul trailer?*

I'm guilty of this myself. I'm a hoarder of books. Once I get a great book, I love to hold on to it. It might be ten years since I last read it, but I have to work really hard to get rid of that book. Who knows? I loved the book once, so I might love it again. Surely I'll get around to reading it again soon. But will I really?

We—myself included—have to realize that life is short. A vapor. There's no point spending your life amassing a bunch of belongings that you're just going to leave behind. Far better for me to read a book, enjoy it, and then give it away to someone else who can appreciate it. You might keep building bigger barns so you can store stuff, but to what end? Ever go to an estate sale? Strangers pay pennies on the dollar to buy items that other people once highly cherished. Things lose their value. I say the older you get, give more of your possessions away, while you're still here to do so. Hey, give it *all* away. It's not going with you to your funeral. It'll be fun, and you'll be able to see other people enjoying your things, too.

Being generous is a freeing way to live. Giving away is rewarding. It truly is better to give than receive.

ALLOWING YOURSELF TO LET GO

My brother Don grew up to become an incredibly generous person. Today he's a busy guy who runs his own masonry company. But if ever you need help, Don will fit you into his schedule. Don gives of his time. Over the years, he's done such things as building me a retaining wall and helping me construct a fireplace. He's built a successful business, and he treats his employees well. People love working for Don. He's a generous boss, and all his employees speak highly of him.

Don was one of the first examples of generosity that I encountered, and he served as a model for me to learn to give away things freely, from a kind heart, with an open hand. With generosity comes confidence. Peace. Trust. You're not bound to the stuff you think is so important. You're not bound to a certain image of decorum. You don't even care so much if people laugh at you. You don't even care so much if people laugh when they see you playing air guitar in your car.

Last year when it came time for our annual fishing trip to Lake Chelan, Don and his son, Ian, picked up me and my son, Kyle, to drive us to the lake. Don wasn't driving a Mustang anymore. He pulled into my driveway in his Toyota Tundra work truck, a four-seater. Kyle and Ian sat in the back while Don drove and I sat beside him in the front.

We weren't even out of Seattle before Don flipped through his iPhone, found some classic Zeppelin, and cranked the volume. The tunes blasted through the speakers of his truck, and just like old times, Don tilted his head back, opened his mouth wide, and started to shout along as if he was Robert Plant himself. A verse and a chorus went by, another verse and another chorus, then the song blistered into a guitar solo. Don let rip his air guitar on the steering wheel column. Man, Don was really wailing. A true rock legend in his own mind.

This time, I glanced at our sons in the back seat. They were grooving to the music. Grinning. It felt impossible not to join in.

These days, my soul isn't filled with the angst it once was. Undoubtedly, I'm still not cool enough to pull off the same antics as Don. But I know more what it feels like to live generously. It means you allow yourself to let go. To share joy. To give yourself permission to live freely. You hold all things—even your insecurities about what others might think of you—with an open hand.

This time, I looked ahead toward the road we were on, and I played the drums on the dashboard and sang along.

Live Your Wild and Precious Life

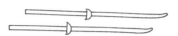

When I was twelve, my mom signed me up for ski school. We were still trying to function normally as a family, and I was grateful for her initiative and the gift, but I felt apprehensive, too. The plan called for me to ride a bus each Saturday morning for the next four weeks up the mountain to the Snoqualmie ski area. A bunch of kids would meet with an instructor, and she'd give us lessons. One of my brothers had some old ski equipment that I used, even though the skis were too long for me. A new world of fun and adventure awaited.

The bus was full of strangers. On the first bus ride I started talking to the kid next to me. He was friendly, and I thought, *Oh good, at least I have one friend.* Two hours later on the slopes, my new friend crashed and broke his leg. He was out for the remainder of the season. As he was being carted off the mountain, I made a simple mental note: "Whatever you do, Rob, keep your balance. Don't crash."

I hoped our instructor would become my new best friend, but I wasn't having much luck there. She was sixteen, maybe seventeen,

DAD JOKE

<><><><><><><><><><><><><><><><><><><><><><><><><><><><>

A manicurist was really troubled. Kept taking her work home with her.

Poor woman. She slept on a bed of nails.

a whiz at skiing, and more gorgeous than Farrah Fawcett. To-day, I've forgotten my instructor's name, but I remember how she showed us the snowplow: the beginners' way to ski. With Farrah looking on, I maneuvered my ski tips into a V shape and inched my way down the mountain, one cautious turn after another at a sleepwalker's pace. That snaillike speed was fine by me. I'd just seen my buddy bust his leg, and I wanted none of that. I became a very cautious and timid skier.

The four lessons passed without further incident. I mastered the snowplow. A few weeks later, Don and Joe and their friends took me skiing. No instructors this time. Don was a better skier than me, and Joe looked amazing with his twists and turns. At the top of our first run together, I assumed the snowplow posi-tion. Joe chuckled and jetted down the mountain with his buddies. I watched for a moment as Joe bounced in and out of the moguls on the edge of the slope. While Don was a better skier than me, he couldn't quite keep up with Joe, and he stayed behind with me. I'm not sure if it was because he felt compassion toward me, or because he wasn't quite ready to push himself to keep up with Joe and his friends. On Joe's next run he caught up with us. We still hadn't reached the bottom yet.

"Enough with the snowplow, Rob," Joe called. "That's not how you want to ski forever."

Joe showed me how to bring my skis together, lean forward to gain a bit of speed, and drop my ski tips down the mountain in the direction I wanted to go. That way I could initiate a turn in one smooth motion by transferring my weight on either ski. The parallel turn seemed so easy when Joe did it. He showed me the move again, then he and his friends took off and swooped down the mountain.

I tried to do a parallel turn, but my skis crossed and I fell on my face. I tried again but crashed hard onto my behind. The snow-plow seemed so much simpler. I switched back to what I knew and slowly maneuvered across the face of the slope in one long, slow skid. Carefully I inched my way around so I pointed in the other direction, still in a snowplow position, and made another long boring skid toward the other edge of the run. Again, Joe made it down the mountain long before us. He and his friends caught the chair lift up and met Don and me on the same slope before we even reached the bottom.

"Hey, Rob, when you push yourself, it's more fun," Joe said. "Don't be afraid to gain a bit of speed. You hafta move. You can't be afraid to fall."

And that, right there, is the final lesson I want to share with you. It isn't locked into any particular sport and certainly doesn't apply exclusively to what you learned at age twelve. Rather, the lesson points to the whole gamut of moments and seasons any person faces in life. My buddy had fallen and broken his leg, and his example had charted me onto an ultra-safe tack. But if I was ever going to learn how to fully enjoy the mountain, I needed to follow the advice my brothers gave me. I needed to stay safe, sure. But I also needed to point my skis down the mountain, gain a bit of speed, and not be afraid to fall. My final lesson for success in life is summed up like this: Go and live your one wild and precious life.

THE HIGHS AND LOWS

Mary Oliver (1935–2019) ended her famous poem "The Summer Day" by asking a powerful question. "Tell me, what is it you plan to do with your one wild and precious life?"[1]

I don't know everything she was trying to express in that question, but I gather she was describing how life is two opposite things at once. Life is *precious*, which means it is valuable, even a bit fragile—like an expensive vase that could be knocked off a table and shatter into a million pieces at any moment. Yet life is also *wild*. It's free and fierce and bursting with possibilities. Life is meant to be lived to the fullest.

You and I need to hold both of those truths in the same hand. We should not live too delicately. And we should not live too dangerously. Life is short, and we should always keep the limits of life in mind. Yet life is also huge. We're given boundless opportunities to make something great out of life. Either way, what we must do is truly live. How we truly live lies somewhere in between.

This lesson sounds similar to what we discussed in chapter 6, when I described the hike and the plunge into the pool that my brothers and I had taken near Chelan. The lesson there was simple: Don't hesitate. Make decisions and make them well. This chapter's lesson takes decision-making another step. Life is full of ups and downs that result from your decisions—or from whatever life throws at you. You experience good and bad seasons, highs and lows, successes and failures, pleasure and pain, wins and losses. This further step is about our need to learn how to relish both the wildness and the preciousness. Why? Because some people want the ups without the downs. They do everything they can to avoid pain. They consistently choose the safe pathway, the easy way out. Maybe they inoculate themselves against ever feeling anything awful or dreadful or difficult or painful. They constantly fill their calendars with activities so they don't have to think. They've always got a TV on in the background, or a smartphone in front of their eyes, or a bottle in their hands, so they don't have to face the inevitable reality of life.

If you want to be successful, you need to traverse—and even learn to appreciate—the lows as well as the highs. The lows can be tremendously important in teaching you to recognize the bad along with the good, the difficult with the smooth. It's not the easiest lesson to learn. Most of us have no problem appreciating life's highs. But how do we ever appreciate life's lows?

Sheldon Vanauken (1914–1996) wrote a classic book titled *A Severe Mercy,* in which he described how as a young man he experienced great love for a young woman named Jean "Davy" Davis. He and Davy married, and she loved him just as intensely as he loved her. They pledged to put their love before all else, and as part of their vow, they promised to share everything in life—all their interests, friendships, and work. In the years that followed, they aimed to weave their lives so closely together that nothing could ever pull them apart.

But time passed, and they developed new and differing interests. Their relationship cooled. Their braided cord of love wasn't as tightly wound as they'd hoped. They both wondered if they would ever experience that deepness in their love again.

Then Davy became sick. In the summer of 1954, when they were both forty years old, she contracted an unnamed virus that destroyed her liver. The prognosis looked bleak, and Sheldon couldn't bear the news. Now they had no time to lose. They had to love each other, and love intensely. The clock was ticking. Strangely enough, in this season of their dismay, their great love once again kindled brightly. In their pain, the couple pulled closer together than ever before.

Sadly, Davy died on January 17, 1955. They'd been married for seventeen years. Out of intense devotion to Davy, Sheldon never remarried. Many years later, after he died of cancer at age eighty-two, his body was cremated, and his ashes were scattered in the same churchyard that Davy's ashes had been scattered. Several years before his death, Sheldon wrote the following about himself and his quest to live a meaningful life:

Great joy through love always seemed to go hand in hand with frightful pain. Still, he thought, looking out across the meadow, the joy would be worth the pain—if indeed, they went together. If there were a choice—and he suspected there was—a choice between, on the one hand, the heights and the depths, and, on the other hand, some sort of safe, cautious middle way, he, for one, here and now chose the heights and the depths.

Since then the years have gone by and he—had he not had what he chose that day in the meadow? He had had the love.

And the joy—what joy it had been! And the sorrow. He had had—was having—all the sorrow there was. And yet, the joy was worth the pain.[2]

Did you catch the last line? "The joy was worth the pain." There's preciousness and wildness served up on the same tray for you. Sheldon had experienced great highs and great lows, and they mixed together to form a great richness. Davy's sickness had brought them back together. That's why Sheldon titled his book *A Severe Mercy*. The severity of the sickness had saved their deep love.

USE YOUR PAIN FOR GOOD

How can you appreciate your lows as important parts of your life? The temptation is to stay focused on the lows, to let your past lows dictate your future. But that's not part of the pathway to success. I've experienced any number of lows in my life, and I've told you about some of them in this book. It would be easy for me to live the rest of my life with my mind and heart glued to the lows. My parents left me at a young age. Surely that gives me license to view the rest of my life through pain. I could have used my pain as an excuse not to develop new dreams or to pursue those dreams. How easy would it have been for me, for instance, to say as a young man: "Well, my parents' marriage was a failure. Therefore, all marriages are doomed to failure. I certainly won't be getting married. And I certainly won't be having any children. I'd just mess it all up."

Nope. I went in the other direction. I didn't ignore the reality of my parents' shortcomings or the pain those shortcomings had caused me. Instead of concluding that my life was permanently broken, I chose to put my energies into creating a great marriage of my own. I wanted to be the husband who didn't leave his wife. I wanted to become the father who never walked out on his kids.

And I did become a husband and father who was there for his family through hard times as well as good. I used the pain in my life as motivation to heal and change and grow.

It wasn't all easy. Annelli's family of origin had seen its share of difficulties, too. So she and I needed to learn how to become loving, committed spouses to each other. We had to learn how to become devoted parents. We made mistakes along the way. But we didn't stay in our pain. We accepted that hard times had happened to us. We didn't gloss over our pain or pretend they didn't happen. Instead, we used them as a teacher. We used our pasts to propel us toward a better future.

How about you?

Life gets hard for everybody. We all have difficult experiences. Many people, when they feel pain, walk out the door, abandoning the people or pursuits they associate with that pain. Or they stay stuck in their pain. They see the rest of their lives through the grid of that pain. But neither of those paths is the way to wisdom. If you want to be successful, you can't run from your pain and you can't stay stuck in your difficulties. Life is short, so you want to live it well. You have to learn to do so at every stage of life—and during the good and the not-so-good times. When you're in pain, it's helpful to talk about it with a trusted friend. Cough up that hairball, get the hurt up and out and onto the table. The hurt can be tough coming up, but you'll be glad to get it out. Then you can go forward. You can use your pain to make positive changes. You don't want to let your past determine your future.

I've found that having an eternal perspective on my life has helped me tremendously. My focus isn't here on temporary things, but on the eternal. I think of the movie *Toy Story,* near the end when Buzz and Woody are strapped to the rocket flying above the moving truck and the car that Andy is riding in. As they dive-bomb toward earth, Woody says, "Buzz, you missed the truck!" Buzz answers: "We're not aiming for the truck!" They proceed to land in the car with Andy.

That's an important picture for all of us. If your focus is on the correct place, the temporary trials and struggles of this life will be kept in their proper perspective. C. S. Lewis captured this sentiment when he wrote: "We are half-hearted creatures, fooling about with drink and sex and ambition when infinite joy is offered us, like an ignorant child who wants to go on making mud pies in a slum because he cannot imagine what is meant by the offer of a holiday at the sea. We are far too easily pleased."[3]

The apostle Paul describes in 2 Corinthians 1:3–4 how our trials can be used to help others: "God . . . the Father of compassion and the God of all comfort . . . comforts us in all our troubles, so that we can comfort those in any trouble with the comfort we ourselves receive from God." Whatever difficulty you have gone through can help you to become an amazing person. A compassionate person. A person who uses your pain to understand other people in pain. And not only to understand them, but to help them. You can use your pain to help you live with increased purpose.

You can use your pain to help you live a great life.

YOUR PAST DOESN'T DETERMINE YOUR FUTURE

It will be hard for you to progress forward successfully unless you become willing to accept pain along with pleasure as two of life's inevitabilities. Any professional skier will fall hundreds of times before she reaches a high level of accomplishment. You have to get up again after you fall. You can't stay stuck forever doing the snowplow on the bunny hills.

The idea of falling can be scary for anyone. I know it was for me. Hey, I didn't want to risk a broken leg. I liked the idea of playing it safe on the bunny slopes, snowplowing my way down the mountain each time. I didn't mind missing the thrills people talked about. But eventually I learned how to deal with my fears. Today,

I'm an accomplished skier. I'm not an expert, but I've mastered the parallel turn, and I know enough about skiing to have a great day on the slopes with my family and friends. What did I do along the way that changed me? I kept going forward. It was as simple—and as complex—as that. Maybe I can illustrate the idea of progression better by using a different example. Public speaking is the single most common phobia that people identify, affecting some three out of four people everywhere.[4] If you've ever seen my videos on You-Tube, you might think I have no problem with public speaking. But I do. I've struggled with a lot of anxiety in my life. I think it stems from the PTSD I've experienced because of what happened in my childhood. Ask me to speak somewhere, and I hate the idea right away. I clam up.

One Sunday morning when my kids were little, the children's ministry coordinator at our church took me aside and asked if I'd like to teach Sunday school. My first inclination was to flee. It would have been so easy to say, "Oh, somebody else will be better at that than me."

And maybe they would have been. But I told the coordinator I'd think about it, and I went home and wrestled with the idea. I knew that volunteering would be a good way for me to plug in more deeply at the church. When you just attend church, but don't participate further, it's super easy to sit in the back and hear a rousing message, then peel out in the parking lot and head home, like my family did when I was a kid. This treats churchgoing as a consumer activity, the same way you'd stop in at a Walmart. You glance around, pick up what you like, pay your dues, then head home without another thought. I didn't want to be a consumer when it came to church. I wanted to belong. I thought maybe teaching a class would help, because I would be giving something back. Plus, I didn't want the anxiety I'd felt for so many years to keep me from a good thing. I didn't want my past to determine my future.

So I said yes.

I wasn't any sort of polished public speaker. The idea of talking to eight second graders put a knot in my gut. That's how bad the monster of anxiety had become for me. For safety's sake, the coordinator assigned a helper to each room, so no teacher would be in a room alone with little kids. I was fine with that, but on my first day of teaching I discovered that the helper assigned to me was none other than the pastor's wife, Miss Charlotte. That made me quake. Annelli and I were fairly new to the church, and we didn't know anyone well. Miss Charlotte was about a decade older than me, and I was certain she was a brainiac about all things church-related. Surely she'd be sitting there with her arms crossed, grading me with a red pen, thinking, *My goodness, who is this heretic teaching our children?*

The church met in a converted strip mall. The kids and I sat around a table on cold, hardbacked chairs. That first Sunday, they stared at me with huge unblinking eyes. The pastor's wife sat in the corner with her notebook. I had no idea what I was going to say. I'm sure the coordinator had given me some teaching notes and a text to teach from, which I must have looked at beforehand. I probably figured that if I ad-libbed, everything would turn out okay.

I started out my talk by presenting a quotation from Blaise Pascal, the famous seventeenth-century mathematician, physicist, and theologian. Hey, I figured every smart seven-year-old should know some Pascal, right? The quote was "There is a God-shaped vacuum in the heart of each man which cannot be satisfied by any created thing but only by God the Creator, made known through Jesus Christ."[5]

I let the words sink in while preparing my next thought. But before I could speak, a girl raised her hand and asked, "Uh, teacher. You mean a vacuum like my mom uses to clean our house?" All the kids laughed. I gulped and thought fast. I explained that it wasn't the same type of vacuum, but maybe if they saw an image of a vacuum along with the quotation, they would remember better what it meant. I turned to the whiteboard and quickly sketched a Hoover upright. "That's sort of like the vacuum your mom uses, right?" I said, pointing to my sketch. "Or maybe your dad. But the vacuum in that quote is different. It's like a big empty space. Pascal is saying that all of us have a big empty space in our lives that only God can fill."

The students nodded. Even a seven-year-old could understand that. A boy raised his hand and told me he liked my picture. A girl raised her hand and said she liked Sunday school this morning. The pastor's wife said something gracious and encouraging. We were off and running.

The idea of public speaking, even to a classroom of children, never became completely comfortable for me, but I stuck with it. I stayed with that same group of kids for the next several years, rotating between my daughter's and son's classes, and the kids all told me over time that they liked the way I taught. I never overcomplicated things. I taught lessons in a way that made them easy to remember.

I came to see the students in a different light, too. I tried to picture myself in their shoes. Some children looked just as shy as I was. I tried to encourage them along. I wanted them to think of Sunday school as a fun place to be. So whenever I asked questions of the group, I encouraged the students to offer answers, but I never pushed them to talk. If they didn't want to speak up in class, that was fine with me. I could relate.

Fast-forward a number of years, and today I've been asked several times at my work to do presentations for the sales teams, but I still try every way I possibly can to say no. Once I was asked to speak at our regional sales training conference. I'd been the top sales rep for the previous year, so they wanted me to encourage the group. Frankly, the idea scared me silly, and it took me a couple of days to think through the request. Other than teaching Sunday school, I hadn't done much public speaking. At the conference, I'd have to present to adults, my colleagues and peers. My gut immediately felt tied in knots. I could avoid pain if I said no. But I also wanted to move forward, and I knew God didn't want me to be mastered by this irrational struggle I had in my own head. I wanted to conquer my fears. Or maybe not conquer those fears entirely, but at least I didn't want to give in to them. So I said yes.

It was a two-day conference. Not huge. Maybe forty or fifty people came to the event, which was held at a hotel conference center in Seattle. I was scheduled to speak at the very end. The first day consisted of a variety of seminars, and I sat through them with my hands clammy and my knees knocking. All I could think about was the talk I was supposed to give the next day. More than once I regretted that I'd said yes. In my mind I kept going through what I planned to say. My thoughts churned. That night I hardly slept.

The next day passed slowly. I was a wreck. Finally it came time for the last event of the conference. A fancy dinner was served, and I tried to choke down a few bites. The host took the stage, recognized people for their sales accomplishments, and handed out awards. He called up the top five sales people, and I took the stage along with four others. He recognized us, and the four others sat down. I took the microphone. I looked over the people in the crowd and coughed nervously.

My time had come.

But you know what happened? Once I started speaking, things went pretty smoothly. All the nervous anticipation I'd felt had drained out of me by then. I spoke carefully and conversationally and bravely and realistically, working from material I'd prepared beforehand. In the end, everybody applauded, and I sat down, feeling okay with what I'd said. My sales manager, Will, came up to me afterward, clapped me on the back, and said, "Rob, wow, you did great! We're going to have to get you to speak more." He laughed and added, "It's like we have a prize-winning horse in our barn, and we don't let him out enough."

That's what I needed to hear. I didn't want to allow my fear of public speaking to hold me back in life. I didn't want to let my past determine my future. I had to go forward.

I've been doing more public speaking since then. Just last week, I received a request to fly out and speak at a camp in Tennessee for children of military personnel who've died. I know that request is for a good cause, so I said yes. I'll be the headliner and will speak twice in front of their main group, and teach four breakout sessions. I feel a bit nervous, but I know that's okay, too. This is my one wild and precious life, and I'm going to keep living it well.

LIVE IT WELL

A famous old story called "The Magic Thread"[6] has spoken to me greatly over the years. In it a boy named Peter found it hard to enjoy whatever he was doing in the moment. In winter, he longed for hot days, so he could go to the beach. In summer, he longed for winter, so he could go skating and sledding. He particularly hated going through hard times. Each day in school, he longed for the day to be over so he could go home again and play. Each fall, he wished the school year would hurry up and be over so he could have a vacation again. He longed to be older so he could marry his girlfriend, Liese. He dreamed of the career he would someday have and the life they'd one day live.

One day Peter wandered into the forest, dreaming of the future. He lay down on the soft forest floor and grew sleepy. Suddenly he heard a voice calling him. He opened his eyes and saw an elderly woman, perhaps his fairy godmother. She held out a gift to him, a magic silver ball. From the ball dangled a golden thread made out of silk.

"It's your life thread," the woman explained. "If you want time to pass more quickly, just pull the thread. An hour will pass like a second. Pull harder and a year will pass like a minute. But watch out—because once you pull the thread, it can't be pushed back in again."

Peter figured the gift was just what he wanted. The following day in school, the teacher scolded him for not concentrating on his work. Peter pulled the magic thread. Instantly the day was over. He could go home again. He grinned. Life was going to be a breeze.

The next day he saw his girlfriend. How he wished they were older. He gave the thread another tug. Suddenly they were young adults. He was apprenticed to a carpenter, a career he looked forward to, and was engaged to Liese. How happy they were.

Years went by in that manner. Whenever a difficulty came his way, Peter tugged the magic thread. Time sped up, and every difficulty disappeared. His compulsory military service was over in a wink. A dry season at work was done in a flash. Problems in child-rearing passed in an instant. And on and on life went, until at last Peter neared the end.

He very quickly found himself a gray-haired old man, stooped and frail. His children were grown and living in distant lands. He and Liese lived all alone, and she was often ill. In her infirmity, Liese had better days and worse days, and during her darkest moments, Peter pulled on the thread, wishing to speed her toward another good day again. But the more he pulled, the more his beloved came closer to death. He couldn't bear the thought of being apart from her. He decided to go for a walk in the forest to think. There, he met the elderly woman again. She asked if he'd had a good life.

"Maybe," Peter said. "I've never had to suffer or wait for anything. Yet life has passed so quickly. Now there's so little time left. I dare not pull the thread again. Sorry, but I don't think your gift has brought me much happiness."

"How would you want things to be different?" the woman asked.

"I want to live my life again, this time without the magic thread," Peter said. "Then I'll experience the bad things as well as the good without cutting short my days."

The old woman snapped her fingers. Peter awoke from a dream. He was a boy again, but this time did not have a magic thread to pull. He had only one life to live, facing the richness of all its ups and downs.

That's the image I want you to remember, my friends. You each have been given one wild and precious life, so live it well.

My invitation to you at the start of this book was to consider this a guidebook for the pursuit of fulfilling your life's dreams. Do you want to be successful? Do you want to live a good and full life? If so, open yourself to goodness. Reach out to family members. Have a backbone. Be willing to do the hard and necessary thing. Become an encourager—both of yourself and others. Be proactive. Be generous and hold things freely, with an open hand. And lastly, embrace both the easy and the hard, because both are part of a rich life.

Please know this—and never forget it: I believe in you absolutely. You are loved. You are cherished. You are respected. And you are not alone in this world.

You are going to go far!

How-Tos

◇◇◇

It's been a great privilege to be a resource for dadvice for viewers of my YouTube channel. While Part I of this book dealt with advice for living a fuller and more meaningful life, in Part II I provide the kind of helpful instructions you might find on the channel. I've collected a variety of how-tos in the following pages, from how to open a bank account to how to mow your lawn—and everything in between. I hope you find these how-tos helpful and that they make life a little more manageable. And remember, the process doesn't end when you've learned how to perform a task. You can always share the knowledge with a neighbor, friend, or family member, or perhaps even help them jump-start their car or whatever else they need help with. Lending a hand, as with any act of kindness, will resonate far beyond the time spent spackling a wall or sending a Tupperware container of Christmas cookies.

Personal Finance

BILLS

1. How to Organize Your Bills

Set up a file to hold all of your bills and receipts, perhaps an accordion file. I prefer to use a letter-size filing box, hanging files, and file folders. This system makes it easy to transfer files to a filing cabinet when you have more materials to organize.

Write the name of the bill category on the hanging folder's label tab. For example: Insurance.

Label each file folder that you put in  a hanging folder. For example, label a file folder Health Insurance and place it in the Insurance hanging folder.

Keep all of your receipts. You will need them if you have to return any purchases or to refer to when you do your taxes.

2. How to Pay Your Bills

As soon as you receive a bill in the mail, go to the vendor's website and sign up for online bill paying. Enter your payment details (have your banking information handy when you do this) and set the payment to be made on the due date. Paying bills online is so easy; there really is no excuse to be late making payments.

If you don't have online bill paying set up or prefer to pay by check, write out a check, making sure to date the check for the bill's due date. Make a note on the outside of the envelope, or use a sticky note, of the date to mail the payment so you don't send it late.

Don't allow a stack of unopened bills or letters to pile up. You will be surprised how quickly mail can get away from you if you don't stay on top of it. I set up automatic payments for several of my bills directly from my bank account. Some of the billers send helpful payment reminders that include the due date. For all other bills, I pay them as soon as I receive my paycheck.

It's very important to pay your bills on time for several reasons

- *Creating a track record of paying your bills on time will help you build credit. If you don't pay your bills on time, you can hurt your credit score.*

- *Bad credit can also hurt your chances of being hired. Yep, some employers will look at your credit history before they hire you.*

It can make sense if you think about it, because this record—
assuming it's accurate—shows whether you are responsible or
not.

- *If you don't pay your rent on time, you could possibly get evicted.*
  The same goes for paying your utility and cable bills, and so on—
  these services can be cut off due to lack of payment.

BANKING

3. How to Open a Bank Account

I prefer a local credit union for opening a first account. To start, you'll have to make some calls and:

- *Ask if you can pay bills online with this account.*

- *Look for no or low fees to minimize expenses.*

- *Set up direct deposit of your paycheck if available.*

- *Pay attention to how your call is treated.*

- *Set up an appointment to visit the bank in person.*

Remember to bring two forms of identification. A Social Security card, driver's license, state ID, passport, and/or birth certificate are commonly used. You will also need to bring proof of address and an opening deposit; usually $25 or $50 is adequate. It's wise to open both a checking and a savings account. Note: These accounts will be used to pay your bills and keep some money in savings for easy access. Later I will explain how to set up an account with a broker to handle larger amounts of money.

4. How to Write a Check

1. **DATE:** Use today's date.

2. **PAY TO THE ORDER OF:** Name of the person or company or organization you are paying.

3. **$ AND FILL-IN BOX:** The amount to be paid written in numerals.

4. **FILL-IN RULE IN FRONT OF THE WORD "DOLLARS":** The amount to be paid expressed in words.

5. **FOR/MEMO FILL-IN RULE:** A short note explaining what the check is for.

6. **SIGNATURE RULE:** Where you sign the check.

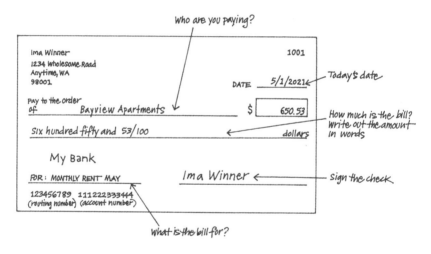

At the bottom of the check are two sets of numbers. The first set is the routing number that identifies your bank. The second set you should recognize: It's your checking account number.

5. How to Reconcile Your Checkbook

When you write a check, or make a deposit, you should reconcile your checkbook. This involves keeping a record of the check you wrote or the deposit you made, so you can update your balance. The word "balance" refers to the amount of money in your account.

RECORD ALL CHARGES OR CREDITS THAT AFFECT YOUR ACCOUNT

DATE	CHECK#	DESCRIPTION	PAYMENT	DEPOSIT	BALANCE $	
					$347	62
4/22/21		Payday		$887.55	$1,235	17
MEMO LINE	Yay!		EXPENSE CODE			
5/1/21	1001	Bayview Apartments	$650.53		$584	64
MEMO LINE	Monthly rent May		EXPENSE CODE			
MEMO LINE			EXPENSE CODE			

- *When you make a deposit, you add it to the balance.*

- *When you make a payment, you subtract it from the balance.*

Any automatic or direct deposits or online payments have to be recorded, too.

When you receive a box of blank checks, a register to be filled in by hand is included. Alternatively, you can create your own spreadsheet online. No matter the format, you need to keep track of your account balance somewhere. If you don't pay attention to it, you may cause checks to bounce. A check bounces when you don't have money in your account to cover the amount you wrote the check for. This will be a painful lesson for you, with several repercussions:

- *You may have to pay nonsufficient funds fees from your bank as well as the bank of the person or company you tried to pay.*

- *Bouncing checks can also affect your credit in a roundabout way. The bill you are trying to pay with the bounced check obviously won't get paid on time, which hurts your credit.*

- *Bouncing checks is a huge red flag that makes you look irresponsible to future lenders and even employers who look at your credit history.*

6. How to Open a Credit Card Account

Credit cards can be extremely dangerous, so please proceed with caution. I would compare them to a fire: A controlled fire can be very useful and powerful, but if you let it get out of control it can be extremely destructive and overwhelm you.

When you pay with a credit card, you don't feel the pain of pulling money out of your wallet, so it is much easier to spend more money. However, a credit card does allow you to build a credit history, which you'll need if you want to buy a house.

My biggest rule: Pay it off every month! Compare the benefits and fees of credit cards online. I am not overly concerned with a card's interest rate because I pay off the balance each month. You can apply for a card online and get approved instantly. I would start with a credit card with a very low limit, like $1,000. This limit will keep you from getting too far into debt until you prove that you can handle a larger credit limit responsibly.

SAVINGS

7. How to Budget

It's good to set up a budget for several reasons, but the main one is summed up in a quote by Dave Ramsey: "A budget is telling your money where to go, instead of wondering where it went."

Let's look at a very basic budget to get you started. Say you bring home $4,000 per month (not gross pay; this is your net pay after taxes are taken out). You can break that amount down as follows:

CHARITY: $400

SAVINGS: $100 (Remember: Pay yourself first, to get out of the rat race.)

RENT: $1,200

FOOD: $600

CLOTHING: $200

ALLOWANCES: $200 (Fun money to spend on anything.)

UTILITIES: $400

  Electricity/Gas: $100

  Water/Sewer: $40

  Internet: $50

  Phone: $100

  TV: $50

  Other: $60

ENTERTAINMENT: $100

CARS: $500

INSURANCE: $200

GIFTS: $100

If your numbers are higher or lower than what I've listed or you have different expenses to account for, fill in your own numbers and categories appropriately.

The purpose of a budget is to help you to better understand where your money is going. Don't get too stressed the first time you track it; you just need to start somewhere to better understand your spending. Your numbers should add up, though, so every dollar—or at least very close to every dollar—is accounted for.

8. How to Get Out of Debt

I recommend the resources of radio host and author Dave Ramsey, especially if you are deeply in debt. Dave can come across a little harsh, but please consider following his advice.

Some key points:

- *Save $1,000 for a starter emergency fund*

- *Pay off all of your debt using the debt "snowball" method*

To paint a clear picture of your situation, start by listing all of your debts except your mortgage. Put your debts in order from smallest to largest regardless of interest rate. Include car loans, credit cards, student loans, and any other major purchases, even those you maybe shouldn't have bought.

Ramsey's "debt snowball" method recommends paying off the smallest bill first. Once it's paid, redirect the money you were paying toward that bill each month to the next smallest remaining bill, and so on until you pay off the biggest debt. You may need to make some tough decisions, like selling an expensive car that you shouldn't have bought and downgrading to one that you can afford.

As I mentioned earlier, I think having a credit card is not a problem as long as you pay it off every month. If you don't have the discipline to do so, you should not be using credit cards. There is something painful that happens when you pay with cash, but paying with a credit card doesn't inflict that same pain.

9. How to Get Out of the Rat Race

As I am writing this book, 78 percent of Americans are living paycheck to paycheck.[1] That is four out of every five people. With a little discipline, you can build up some savings that you can draw on during a financial emergency.

If you're living paycheck to paycheck, you may have had to use a payday lender to make ends meet. These lenders have a reputation for taking advantage of people in vulnerable situations, so if you have had to turn to them, I want to offer some advice to make sure you can avoid them in the future.

Step number one in building up savings is to pay yourself first—set aside some money in an account that you don't touch. This will become your emergency fund. Note that an emergency is not that pair of shoes that you absolutely must have!

To start, aim to deposit $100 into this account, then build the balance to $500, then $1,000. To get to the $100 starting point, save $25 each month for four months. Once you have that $100 in your account it, I promise you it will feel good to know you have that money set aside. If I had suggested starting with $1,000, that number may have seemed like an impossibility. Instead, $100 may be more within your reach, and you can add on from there. If possible, increase your monthly deposit; it is exciting to see that money grow.

Once your emergency fund is established, you should have enough saved to cover an extra month of expenses should an emergency arise. Paying your bills with money you already have that's earmarked for those expenses, instead of having to wait to get paid to cover your bills, will help you move away from living paycheck to paycheck.

INVESTING

10. How to Invest

Here is where the fun starts! A typical bank or credit union account, as of the writing of this book, is paying less than 1 percent on your money. With the rate of inflation around 2 percent, your money is losing value faster than it's growing.

When I was in my late twenties, I used to listen to a radio show called *Money Matters, with Don MacDonald*. At that time, he gave advice on no-load mutual funds, something I had never heard of, but I am glad that I listened. Investing was a lot more complicated then: I used to have to go to the library to research what funds to invest in. It's much easier now. Here's how to do it:

- *Set up an online account with a respected broker. You can do this online or over the phone.*

- *Go online and search Best Online Stock Brokers for Beginners. I personally use Fidelity, because I have found their site easy to navigate, but I am sure there are other good options that you can use.*
    - For this example, go to www.Fidelity.com
    - Click on News & Research, click on Mutual Funds, choose Fund type
    - Choose All Asset Classes, then View Results
    - I like to look for funds that have a track record of at least ten years, so sort the columns by Rate of Return/10 years.
    - Wowsa, as I am looking at this right now there are over thirty funds with a return over 20 percent/year, over a ten-year period. If you invested $1,000, after ten years, it would be worth over $5,000. If you left that same $1,000 in a traditional savings account making 1 percent (that's being generous, my bank is paying less than that), you would have less than $1,100.

A penny saved is a penny earned, but a penny invested wisely is a dime! You will have to pay taxes on your earnings, but don't let that stop you from investing. You pay taxes on your paycheck—does that mean you'd want to make less per hour, to pay less in taxes?

1 PERCENT RETURN YEARLY OVER 10 YEARS

1	2	3	4	5	6	7	8	9	10
$1,000	$1,010	$1,020	$1,030	$1,041	$1,051	$1,062	$1,072	$1,083	$1,094

20 PERCENT RETURN YEARLY OVER 10 YEARS

1	2	3	4	5	6	7	8	9	10
$1,000	$1,200	$1,440	$1,728	$2,074	$2,488	$2,986	$3,583	$4,300	$5,160

11. How to Invest for Retirement

Saving for retirement is different from investing, because you won't touch this money until you retire. Start early even if it is a small amount every month. Remember: Compound interest is your friend.

If you have a 401(k) at work, invest as much as you can as long as you get some sort of match. For example, your employer may match 25 percent of the first 5 percent that you contribute. So before your money is even invested, you will already have a 25 percent return on your money. Some companies match more, some less.

If you want to invest more than the percentage your company matches, I recommend an individual retirement account, or IRA. Set up an IRA with a broker like Fidelity or Vanguard. There are two basic types of IRA accounts: traditional IRAs and Roth IRAs. To decide between a traditional IRA and a Roth IRA, consider the following: While you'll receive an immediate tax break on your money with a traditional IRA, you will be better off in the long run with a Roth IRA (which has some additional benefits such as easy early withdrawals and tax-free money in retirement). Most 401(k)s now have Roth as an option. When you're young, I recommend being more aggressive with your investments, but as you get older, I advise taking on less risk.

12. How to Invest for College

A 529 plan is a great tool for investing for college and can be set up through your broker, similar to what I showed you at the beginning of this section. This plan is an investment account that offers tax-free earnings growth and tax-free withdrawals when the funds are used to pay for qualified education expenses. For colleges and universities and other eligible postsecondary educational institutions, expenses include tuition, fees, books, supplies, equipment, computers, and sometimes room and board.

The IRS also allows tax-free withdrawals of up to $10,000 per year, per beneficiary, to pay for tuition expenses at private, public, and religious K–12 schools. The 529 plan is a great way to save for education expenses, while cutting down on the amount of taxes you pay on the investments. Another way to save for college is through a prepaid college plan. This plan allows you to pay today's rates for college. In Washington state it's called the GET program.

INSURANCE

13. How, Why, and When to Get Insurance

Insurance is almost as inevitable as taxes. The general rule is, if you can't afford to replace something—or someone—insure it. Emergencies and unexpected events happen, and the unfortunate truth is that many Americans don't have enough money saved to cover a $500 emergency. Knowing you have insurance to fall back on during a crisis can provide some relief during an otherwise challenging time.

There are several types of insurance you should consider having:

HOMEOWNER'S INSURANCE: If you own a home, you must have homeowner's insurance; most mortgage companies require it as part of the lending process. Most policies are relatively inexpensive and cover your assets in the event of a burglary, fire, or leak. If you have expensive electronics, lawn equipment, or jewelry, you may want to consider adding a rider that covers these items to a standard homeowner's insurance policy.

RENTER'S INSURANCE: Rental insurance covers you as a renter, rather than the structure where you are renting a place to live. Your policy should cover both yourself and your things.

CAR INSURANCE: A car insurance policy that includes comprehensive coverage is required when financing a car purchase with a loan. After you pay off the loan and own the car, you still need to have liability coverage, which pays for the other driver's property or medical expenses if you're in an accident.

LIFE INSURANCE: In the next section I go into more detail on this topic, which I think a lot of people find confusing.

PROFESSIONAL INSURANCE: If you own your own business, you may be required to have a minimum amount of general liability insurance to protect you in the event of a lawsuit.

14. How to Choose Life Insurance

You should have life insurance if:

- *You have a home.*

- *You have kids.*

- *Your savings and investments don't contain enough money to cover your debts and continue to take care of your loved ones upon your death.*

Life insurance salespeople make their money by selling whole life or universal life policies, because they cost more than term life policies, which leads to larger sales commissions. However, I recommend buying only a term life policy because it's very straightforward versus a whole life or universal policy, which has an investment component. Whole or universal policies are generally more expensive, and I believe that the amount you pay into these policies will never equal the benefit you receive.

A smart thing to do would be to buy term life insurance and invest the difference from what a whole life policy would have cost. Remember that life insurance itself, though, should not be treated like a regular investment.

Here's an example to help explain the policies offered: Let's say you're 30 years old and in decent shape. An insurance company might offer a $500,000 whole life policy for $150 per month. The salesperson will tell you about all the policy's other benefits, but you should just ignore them; they aren't worth it.

In contrast, a similar 30-year term life insurance policy costs around $30 per month.

Be aware that this policy will last only 30 years. However, in that time, your mortgage will be paid down and your kids will probably no longer be living in your house, so you should no longer need life insurance. And, if you invest the $120 difference in cost between a whole life policy and a term life policy into your retirement plan at an 8 percent rate, over that 30 years it will grow to around $175,000—and no one needs to die to access it!

You don't need life insurance if:

- *You're single and renting.*

- *You're newly married, have no kids, and you don't own your home.*

CREDIT AND TAXES

15. How to Build Credit

The ability to make major purchases in our society, for good or bad, is built around your credit rating. When you are ready to buy a house, the first piece of information a mortgage company will want to know is your credit score.

Using credit cards responsibly is one way to build good credit, but I feel strongly that you must pay off the balance each month. If you don't, the interest added to your outstanding balance can become overwhelming, and you can find yourself spinning your wheels trying to get out from under this debt. Credit card companies see college students and young adults as a big marketing opportunity. Be careful of any student credit cards you apply for; their interest rates can sometimes be steep.

Other options to build your credit are credit-builder loans, secured loans, or cosigned loans. Becoming an authorized user on a family member's credit card can also help you build credit, but use this option wisely. Making your rent, phone, and utility payments on time also helps build your credit history.

It's important to be responsible with your money and not become overly reliant on credit cards. Also, get in the habit of checking your credit score each quarter to ensure there are no errors to report to one of the credit bureaus. Be organized, pay your bills on time, watch your credit score, and build up a credit history so you will be ready when it comes time for a big purchase.

16. How to Get a Loan

Before you set out to get a loan, you need to be aware of your personal budget and know what sort of payment you can afford as well as how much of a loan you'll need for your purposes.

Consider your local banks and credit institutions, compare their lending options, and shop around for the best interest rate. Not all loans are equal. Also, some lenders are better at certain types of loans. Mortgage lenders are an example of a specialized lender; many of these organizations only loan for purchases or refinancing.

Once you've shopped and compared, you're ready to choose your lender and complete the application process. Be aware that every time you apply for a loan, the lender will run a credit check. Too many lenders accessing your credit file in a small window of time can be a red flag to the credit bureaus. These multiple credit checks are called hard inquiries and can result in a lower credit score, which may raise your potential interest rate.

Once you've accepted the loan, the funds will be yours to spend, and the payments will begin soon thereafter.

17. How to Do Your Taxes

We're taxed when we earn, when we buy, and when we die. And yet most adults don't even understand their W2s. And it doesn't end there. While most Americans accept dealing with taxes as something they can't change, there are ways to lower one's tax burden. Kids also need to have a good understanding of how all of this works. At a minimum, school curricula should include a basic overview of the different kinds of taxes.

Here are a few tips for tax time:

- *Keep all receipts filed in the same place throughout the year.*

- *If you are self-employed, don't comingle personal receipts with business receipts.*

- *Review last year's return before you start the current year's return.*

- *Review withholding for any advantageous adjustments for next year.*

- *Keep copies of all tax returns together. Consider a small fire safe for important documents like this.*

- *Don't overlook common deductions like charitable donations.*

- *Be sure you've evaluated any medical or dental expenses for deductibility.*

- *Likewise, some education expenses, especially if they're work-related, might be deductible.*

- *Remember to think about state and/or local taxes that may be deductible.*

- *Depending on how complex your return is, use an online source like TurboTax for preparing a simple return or find a local accountant for a more in-depth return that involves multiple streams of income or complex tax situations.*

The Big Decisions

18. How to Choose a College

Most kids coming out of high school get infatuated with a four-year college. I believe this is one of the reasons our young people are so deeply in debt. Please at least consider a community college or perhaps even a trade school. You can usually attend a community college close to your home to save on housing costs.

Most universities accept transfers who've earned an associate's degree (two-year degree). Enrolling in a community college for the first two years allows you to get all the basic classes out of the way and gives you more time to figure out your major. Then, when you transfer to a university, you can focus on the courses in your declared field of study.

Please, please stay disciplined while you are at the community college—or at least long enough to earn a two-year degree. If you go there and mess around and leave with lots of credits, but no degree, the university you want to transfer to might not accept some of the credits you earned.

A program in my state called Running Start is a great option depending on your circumstances. It allows you to attend a community college while simultaneously finishing high school credits. I know many people that have come out of high school with a two-year degree. What an advantage they have had on other kids coming out of high school!

The steps I advise when trying to pick a college are:

1. Make a list of the priorities you want from a college.

2. Research online to find schools that fit those overall priorities.

3. Create a list of the chosen schools along with their yearly all-in costs.

4. Request information from each of the schools. Many have great websites, but most still send out prospective student packets.

5. Narrow the list down to four to six schools, and plan school visits for each.

6. Make a list of scholarship or financial aid deadlines and stay on top of submitting your applications.

7. Many college-bound students apply to three to five schools, including a stretch goal and a safety school. A stretch goal would be a college you think may be a stretch to get into. A safety school would be one you are sure you can get into.

19. How to Rent an Apartment

Steps for renting an apartment:

- *You can do a lot of research online. Make phone calls to see how the landlord treats you.*

- *Visit more than one apartment. Check faucets, open cabinets, and inspect in general to find any issues.*

- *While visiting, try to start a conversation with a tenant. Ask them how long they have lived there, and what their experience has been like.*

- *Check online and see if there's a lot of crime in the neighborhood.*

Questions to ask a potential landlord include: How much is a deposit or upfront payment? Do you need first and last month's rent in addition to a deposit? Is the deposit refundable?

When you move in, pay careful attention to the move-in form and note any damage you might get charged for later. Move-in forms are pretty standard in my experience. If the landlord doesn't provide one, it would be in your best interest to create one before moving in.

If the apartment has carpet, take a quick video with your phone before you move in and note any problems so that later you can provide proof of any issues that were already there. Carpet damage is a primary reason renters don't receive their deposits back.

Purchase enough renter's insurance—some apartments require it. Before making any changes to the apartment such as hanging a picture, painting, or other cosmetic improvements, make sure to check with the landlord first.

Finally, get a copy of the lease agreement in advance and read it thoroughly before you sign anything. Make sure you understand what you're responsible for and what the landlord is responsible for and how to address any problems that may arise.

20. How to Furnish an Apartment

There are a few essential items you will need for your first apartment, which I've gathered in the following list to help you prepare for your new home. If you're on a tight budget, thrift stores are a great place to pick up gently used items.

Basic Kitchen Items

Blender

Coffee maker

Cookie sheet

Dishware set (plates, bowls)

Frying pan

Glasses

Large pot

Measuring cups and spoons

Mixing bowl

Mugs

Plastic storage containers

Set of knives

Silverware

Small pot

Spatula (wood or silicone)

Toaster

Basic Household Items

Fire extinguisher

Iron

Ironing board

Mop

Plunger

Smoke detector

Vacuum

Cleaning Supplies

Broom and dustpan

Laundry detergent

Trash bags

21. How to Buy a House

Work with a real estate agent who is an expert in the area where you'd like to live. This is a no-brainer, because coordinating with a buyer representative doesn't cost you anything—they get paid by splitting the commission with the agent selling the house.

Get preapproved with a lender before house hunting so you have a good idea of what size mortgage you qualify for. Don't overextend yourself and become house poor. Instead, be patient and stay within your budgetary constraints. If you can put down a 20 percent mortgage deposit, you should be able to get a better interest rate than with a lower or no deposit, and you can avoid an extra private mortgage insurance (PMI) fee. Note that first-time home buyers can buy a house with less than 20 percent down. This is a good way to get into a house if you are worried about "throwing away" money on rent.

Once you are in the house, pay extra on the principal. After a couple of years of your house appreciating, and your paying the debt down, you may own 20 percent of your house. You can refinance at that time to get the PMI removed.

As I mentioned in the earlier section on insurance, you must have homeowner's insurance when you buy a house. The policy won't cost that much compared to the expense of replacing your house or belongings if something catastrophic happens.

I have never made a claim on my homeowner's insurance, and I encourage you to think twice before making one. Let's say your dishwasher leaks and ruins your kitchen floor. I would rather fix the floor myself than make a claim, because every time you make a claim, your rates go up. Also, know that if your insurance deductible is high, it might be cheaper to pay for the repair yourself.

Home

TOOLS

22. How to Build a Tool Kit

The following are the essential tools you should have in your home tool kit. When using any and all tools always read and follow the safety precautions of the tool manufacturer.

Hammer

Pliers

Slip joint

Needle nose

Channel locks

Wrenches

Adjustable Wrench

Wrench set

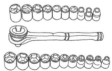

Socket set

Screwdrivers

Flat head

Philips head

Tape measure and level

23. How to Use a Tape Measure

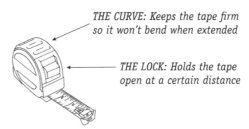

THE CURVE: *Keeps the tape firm so it won't bend when extended*

THE LOCK: *Holds the tape open at a certain distance*

The black numbers indicate inches and millimeters.

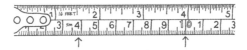

Red numbers appear every 16 inches to use as a guide for stud spacing.

The black diamonds that appear every 19³⁄₁₆ inches on metal tape measures are for spacing engineered floor joists.

There are three different elements to the hooked end of your tape measure.

The nail grab allows you to hook the end of your tape measure to a nail so you can use it for leverage if you're measuring on your own but need an extra hand.

Top hook

Nail grab

The top hook lets you attach the tape measure to the bottom of objects so you can read measurements without ducking down to hold the tape in place.

The scribing tool can be used to mark measurements if you don't have a pencil handy.

Make sure the hooked end is flush against whatever you're measuring so that you get an accurate measurement.

Scribing tool

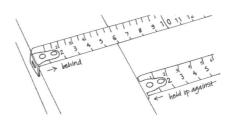

The outside of the tape measure with the belt clip is called the housing. If you look under the belt clip, you'll see a measurement indicated there, which is the length of the tape measure itself. If you're measuring the interior of a drawer or cabinet, you can place

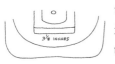

the tape measure at one end and add the length from the housing section to your measurement to get an accurate number.

24. How to Use a Cordless Drill

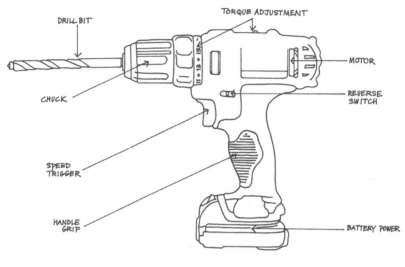

PARTS OF A DRILL

A cordless drill is a tool kit must-have. It can help you in so many ways—drilling holes is only a small part of this tool's usefulness.

Drills usually have two speeds:

Setting 1 is for torque and for general purpose.
Setting 2 is for speed.

To replace a drill bit:

1. There is a clutch setting next to the chuck, which is the part on the end of the drill that tightens and loosens to hold the bit. Set it to 5.

2. Hold the chuck, put the drill in reverse, pull the trigger, and open the jaws.

3. To put in a new bit, insert the bit inside the jaws, hold the chuck, put the drill in forward, pull the trigger, and close the jaws.

4. Now change the clutch setting to whatever is appropriate for the job.

The most common attachment I use is this  Phillips head driver.

The attachments seem to be endless, though.

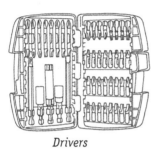

Drivers

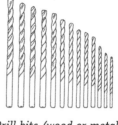

Drill bits (wood or metal)

Speed bits

Sockets (Includes the adapter.)

25. How to Use a Circular Saw

Note: Please be extremely careful around saws! If they can cut through wood, they can also cut through you. Never wear loose clothing when operating a saw, as it can get caught in the blade, which can be an extremely dangerous situation. And always wear protective glasses. Use a firm grip and beware of kickback. Kickback happens when you are cutting and the blade gets pinched by the wood. It can be a little scary the first time it happens and can cause injury if you're not paying attention.

A circular saw can be very handy for several kinds of tasks until you're able to get a table saw and or a chop (miter) saw. Understand that the finished cut will be rough and not as accurate as those made on a table or miter saw, but close enough will work for a fence or other construction projects.

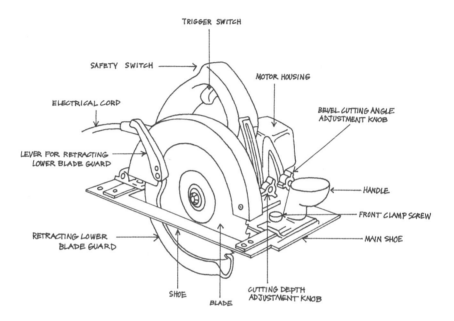

The main adjustment to pay attention to is the depth—how deep the saw will cut.

A circular saw also has an adjustment for the angle, but for most applications you will set it to 0.

To use the saw:

1. Make a mark on your board where you want to cut.

2. Secure the wood properly so it is stable as you cut.

Short lengths

3. Push the trigger and start to cut. Pay attention to your mark and stay just to the side of it.

DAD TIP: **Circular saws cut upward, so face the good side down.**

Long lengths

26. How to Use a Fire Extinguisher

Being familiar with a fire extinguisher can allow you to quickly prevent a small fire from becoming a large fire. You should have at least one fire extinguisher at home.

Remember the PASS acronym:

PULL THE PIN: You have to remove the pin to use the extinguisher.

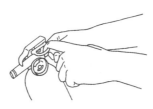

AIM: Point the nozzle at the base of the fire from about six feet away.

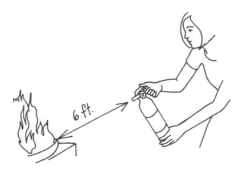

SQUEEZE: Squeeze the trigger to activate the spray.

SWEEP: Move the nozzle back and forth across the base of the fire to spread the spray.

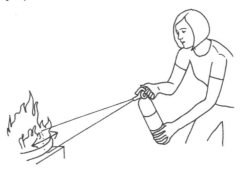

REPAIRS

27. How to Unclog a Toilet

If the level of the water in the bowl looks like it might overflow out of the toilet, you have a couple of options:

1. Cut off the water at the source (this doesn't work for all toilets).

2. Remove the lid from the tank and close the flapper.

Before you attempt to unclog a toilet, make sure you have the correct plunger, one with a flange to create a good seal.

If your plunger is cold and stiff, run it under hot water to soften the rubber to get a better seal.

Work the plunger around to ensure it is sealed. Then push the handle up and down to force the clog out.

Adding add some dish soap and hot water to the toilet bowl can help the clog on its way.

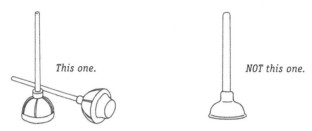

This one.   NOT this one.

28. How to Repair a Hole in the Wall

For a small hole left by a nail or screw, you should be able to patch it with some joint compound or spackle applied with a putty knife. Put a small amount of the joint compound on the end of the putty knife and run it across the hole. Don't apply too much; you just want enough to fill the hole.

To repair a larger hole, you will need the following tools:

Drywall knife
Small piece of Sheetrock
 (hardware stores sell 2-by-2-foot pieces)
Small pieces of wood for backing
1-inch drywall screws
Self-adhesive mesh joint tape
Joint compound
Putty knife
Fine sandpaper
Orange peel texture (if necessary,
 to blend in the joint compound)

1. Cut away the damage, leaving a
   rectangular hole. Then cut out a piece
   of the new Sheetrock similar in size
   to the hole.

2. Using the Sheetrock screws, attach the
   wood inside the hole for backing.

3. Cut a piece of Sheetrock roughly the size of
   the hole and screw it to the wood backing.

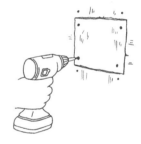

4. Cut four pieces of the joint tape and apply
   them to each seam of the patch.

5. Apply one coat of joint compound with
   the putty knife over the entire hole,
   paying close attention to the seams. Let
   it dry, then lightly sand it before adding
   another coat of joint compound. Repeat
   these steps until you have a smooth
   surface where the hole was.

6. Lightly spray on the orange peel texture
   (you might want to test this material first
   on a spare piece of Sheetrock to get the
   hang of using it before spraying your wall).
   If it doesn't look right the first time, don't
   worry—let it dry, sand it down, and try
   again until you are satisfied with how the
   patch looks.

THE BASICS

29. How to Polish Your Shoes

Believe it or not, your shoes say a lot about you. I was totally unaware that my shoes were important, until my wife (before we were married) pointed this detail out to me. When you walk into a room, even though your clothes may be pressed and you're well groomed, if your shoes aren't shining, they will stand out. Now I like to have at least one pair of nice dress shoes, and I make sure to take care of them.

The general steps to shining shoes are:

1. Remove the laces.

2. Wipe off any dirt with a damp cloth.

3. Rub on a tiny bit of polish that's the same color as your shoe, using a small brush if necessary to get into the small areas around the lace holes and where the tongue meets the rest of the shoe.

4. Buff with a cloth or brush to remove any streaks or unevenness.

5. Create a nice shine with a gentle once-over with a clean cloth.

30. How to Use an Iron

First tip to ironing: Buy clothes made
of wrinkle-free fabric as often as pos-
sible to avoid having to iron in the
first place. I use the steam setting on
an iron whenever possible, as I have
found it the best way to remove wrin-
kles. (Be sure the iron's water reservoir is full so the steam is produced for use of that function.) However, when ironing delicate
fabrics, you may not be able to use a setting hot enough for the
steam function.

When ironing linen or a heavy button-down shirt, using spray
starch is a must. It will help the garment stay nicely pressed for a
longer period of time than ironing alone.

To iron a shirt, start with the collar. Lay it out flat on an ironing
board. Run the heated iron over the surface in quick, even motions,
pressing down if necessary (the type of fabric will determine how
much heat and pressure to use).

Sleeves are next, followed by the body. Remember that setting
each part of the shirt on the ironing board with the fabric flat en-
sures a smooth result.

Ironing pants follows similar steps. I start with pulling the
pants over the narrow end of the ironing board and ironing out
wrinkles between the waist and the leg. Then I take each leg and
lay it out, paying attention to
the crease I want to create down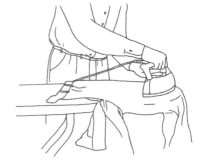
the front and back of the pant
leg. On some pants you may not
want a crease, so pay attention
to how you iron the legs.

Be sure to unplug your iron
when done!

31. How to Wash Clothes

Before washing, separate clothes by color.

- *Reds should be washed separately in cold water.*

- *All other colors should be washed together in cold water.*

- *Whites should be washed separately in hot water. Add bleach if you like.*

If you wash whites with colors, they will turn gray. If you wash whites with reds, they will turn pink. Always refer to the washing instruction tags if you are concerned about a particular garment.

Now look at the settings options on the washing machine—they will vary depending on the model.

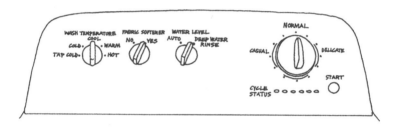

After selecting the water temperature, pick the speed of the agitation.

- *The delicate cycle agitates clothes slowly and has a short wash cycle. Use this setting for nicer clothes to ensure they are washed gently.*

- *The heavy cycle has a high-speed agitation and long wash cycle. This setting is for towels and jeans or clothes that are especially dirty.*

- *The normal cycle is the setting you'll probably use for most of your washing. It has a high-speed wash and spin that are suitable for most clothing.*

There are generally two types of washing machine models: a top-load model and front-load model.

How to use a top-load model:

1. Turn the washer on and let the water start to fill.

2. Add detergent while the water is filling the washer to help it dissolve in the water.

3. Now add your clothes, but don't overfill the machine. Close the lid.

How to use a front-load model:

1. Put your clothes in the washer and close the door.

2. Add the detergent and optional fabric softener and bleach (for whites).

Be careful not to pack items to be washed into the machine too tightly—leave wiggle room for them to move around. Otherwise, the washing machine will have to work extra hard to clean the clothes, which shortens the machine's life.

32. How to Dry Clothes

Before you get started, always refer to the instruction tags if you are concerned about the garment.

Be sure to clean the lint filter before you load your clothes. Every time you dry your clothes, some of the fibers

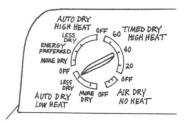

come off and are caught by this filter. If you don't clean it, your dryer won't work properly because it isn't able to breathe. Sometimes the lint filter is accessed from the top, and sometimes it's inside the front door of the dryer.

A dryer is a little simpler to use than a washer because there are fewer settings. You mainly need to be concerned about time and temperature, but as mentioned above, always refer to the tags on your clothes if you're uncertain about the settings to use.

Hint: When the clothes are done drying, remove and fold them immediately. Doing so cuts down on wrinkles.

FOOD

33. How to Shop for Groceries

You should have a set budget for groceries. Make a list before you go to the grocery store. Ideally, the list should correspond to your weekly budget.

Pay attention to grocery store labels. If you read the fine print, you might find that an item on sale is not as great a deal as it first seems!

Grocery shopping tips:

- *Don't shop when you're hungry.*

- *Plan out a weekly menu.*

- *Try to grocery shop at a nonpeak time.*

- *Discount grocery stores, like Aldi, often have the same quality of products as other grocery stores but at much lower prices.*

- *Clip coupons—you'll be surprised how much you can save, especially on nonperishable items and paper goods.*

- *Don't overbuy perishable items.*

- *If you're busy, plan to make enough of your recipe to have leftovers that can be warmed up. Shop accordingly.*

- *Try the store brands—the products they make are usually just as good as name-brand items.*

34. How to Fry an Egg

1. Use a nonstick ceramic frying pan and a silicone spatula.

2. Turn the stove on to medium heat.

3. Pour about 1 tablespoon of oil (preferably olive oil) into the pan.

4. Let the pan heat up before adding the egg.

5. Gently crack the middle of the egg against the side of the pan.

6. Break open the shell where it's cracked and gently pour the egg into the hot oil.

There are generally three types of fried egg:

- *Over easy: The yolk is supposed to be served runny; don't flip the egg to cook on the other side.*

- *Over medium: The yolk is partly cooked; flip the egg over to cook briefly on the other side.*

- *Over hard: The yolk is cooked all the way through; flip the egg and cook thoroughly from the other side.*

35. How to Bake

Baking might seem easy, but there are a few subtle things you need to know.

When a recipe calls for dry ingredients like flour and baking soda, you almost always combine these ingredients together before adding them to the liquid ingredients. If you don't, you can end up with clumps of baking soda instead of it being evenly mixed in the batter.

It's good to read through the recipe before you begin, for several reasons:

- *To become familiar with the process of baking.*

- *To make sure you have all of the ingredients on hand.*

- *To check that you have the necessary pans and utensils.*

If you bake more than one tray of a recipe you will have to adjust the cooking time and/or the temperature. For example, a recipe may call for baking one tray of cookies for 12 minutes at 350 degrees; if you decide to bake two trays at once to save time, you may need to increase the baking time to 14 minutes. If one tray is set on the oven's top rack, and one is on a lower rack, you may need to swap them halfway through the baking; otherwise the top tray's cookies will have gooey bottoms, and the bottom ones will have overcooked bottoms.

Finally, follow the recipe directions in the order that they are given. This might seem like a no-brainer, but you'd be surprised at how often a recipe doesn't turn out properly because someone decides to do the steps out of order.

Outside Your Home

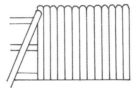

36. How to Mow Your Lawn

The best time to mow your lawn is early evening. This allows the grass to recover overnight. Mowing damages the blades of the grass. If you mow in the morning, for the rest of the day the sun will beat down on the freshly cut lawn, drying it out and making it more prone to look scorched—especially in the hotter months.

I like to use a weed eater around the edges of the lawn before I mow so the mower can further chop up the clippings. After trimming all of the edges, it's time to fire up the mower. Lawn mowers have come a long way since I was a young boy pulling and pulling to crank the engine. A variety of mowers can do the job, depending on your situation. Some small yards are easily done with a push mower. Larger lawns are better served with a walk-behind or ride-on mower. As with any job, it's important to have the right tools; if you're not sure about what you need, visit your local lawn care center and ask.

Before you start cutting, make sure you have enough fuel in the mower and that its blades are sharp. Next, think about how you want the yard to look when you're done. One of my friends is particular about his lawn and insists on cutting it in a precise grid pattern, which does look really nice when finished. Most people find a cutting pattern over time that suits their preferences.

DAD TIP: **Don't cut your grass too short. A mower deck set too low can leave bare spots in the yard and make it more prone to weeds.**

37. How to Change a Propane Tank on a Barbecue

If you have never changed a propane tank, doing so can be a little intimidating. Like anything else, as long as you pay attention and think safety first, you should be able to handle the task without too much stress.

1. Make sure the knob on the top of the tank is closed.

2. Unscrew the line that is attached to the propane tank. Set the old tank aside.

3. Attach the line to the new tank.

4. Turn the knob on the top of the new tank to open it.

Happy grilling!

38. How to Build a Cedar Fence

LAYING OUT THE FENCE AND SETTING THE POSTS

Materials:

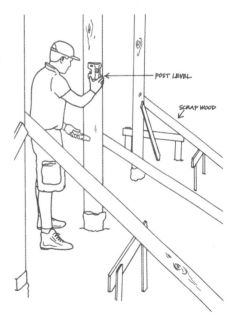

Post hole digger

2 stakes
String
Post hole digger
8-foot-long pressure-treated posts (amount
  depends on the size of the area you are fencing in)
Level
Scrap pieces of wood

1. Before you begin: Make sure it is okay to dig in the area you want the fence. You don't want to start digging and hit a water line, for example. A little planning goes a long way!

2. First, pound one stake at one end of your fence, and the second stake at the other end. Run a string between the stakes.

POST LEVEL

SCRAP WOOD

3. Now figure out the spacing of your posts. Hint: They should be just under 8 feet apart. With the post hole digger, dig holes 24 inches deep (for most applications). Make a mark on your post hole digger at 24 inches for easy reference.

4. Once the holes are ready, drop a post into each hole. Make sure the posts are level and straight; use some scrap pieces of wood to brace the posts.

5. After the posts are straight, you can move on to the next step: preparing the cement.

MIXING AND POURING THE CEMENT

Materials:

Concrete mix
Wheelbarrow or cement trough
Flat shovel or hoe
Five-gallon bucket of water or
  hose with a nozzle

1. Pour the cement into the wheelbarrow or cement trough.

2. Using the shovel or hoe, create a hole in the middle of the cement. Pour some water into the hole and then begin mixing. Repeat this step: add water, mix, add more water, and then mix again. Don't make the cement soupy. It should be the consistency of a thick milkshake.

3. Pour the cement into the post holes and let it cure overnight.

4. When you are all done pouring the cement, make sure you clean your tools completely. If you don't, the next time you try to use the wheelbarrow or the mixing tool, it will have cement stuck to it.

ATTACHING THE FENCE RAILS

Materials (each section of fencing between two posts requires a set of the following supplies):

Metal braces and deck screws

Cordless drill
4 metal fence braces
4 deck screws
Two 8-foot-long pressure-treated
  2-by-4-inch fence rails
Post caps

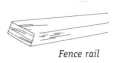
Fence rail

1. Make sure the cement in the post holes has set. Then, using your drill and the braces and deck screws, attach one of the rails 6 inches from the top of the post and the other 6 inches from the bottom of the post.

2. You'll recall that earlier I said to set the posts just under 8 feet apart. This distance allows for a little wiggle room when attaching the rails. You can always trim off any excess, but you can't add length. Use a chop saw or a circular saw to trim the rails if needed.

3. Top the posts off with a post cap to prevent the posts from rotting.

Post cap

ATTACHING FENCING TO THE RAILS

Materials:

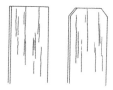

Straight-top and dog-ear planks

6-foot cedar planks (These planks are roughly 5½ inches wide, so you will need to do some math to figure out how many your fence will use. They come in two styles: straight-top or dog-ear.)

Two 1½-inch coated deck screws for every cedar plank (I prefer deck screws, but you can use your preference.)

Deck screw

Cordless drill

1. Start at one end of the section of fencing and begin attaching the planks using the deck screws and drill. Some people add spaces between the planks, but I don't. Over time the planks will shrink, creating space naturally.

2. At the end of a section, you may need to cut one of the planks lengthwise if the space it has to cover is narrower than the full width of a whole plank. A table saw works best for this task, but you can also use a circular saw. Please be extremely careful around saws! If they can cut through wood, they can also cut through you.

Your Car

39. How to Get a Driver's License

Most states allow you to get a driver's license at age sixteen and a learner's permit at fifteen. Check with your state's Department of Motor Vehicles website to confirm the local requirements in your area for obtaining a driver's license.

You will likely need two forms of identification and will be required to take some sort of test: written, road, or both. To prepare, read your state's driver safety handbook and put in plenty of hours of driving practice with an experienced driver. If you fail the test, some states have a mandatory waiting period before you can retake it. So go into the testing as prepared as possible.

DAD TIP: Expect not to like your photo on your license—nobody likes theirs!

40. How to Buy a Vehicle

My best advice about buying a car is to buy used and pay for it without taking out a loan. A vehicle is the largest investment you'll make that goes down in value. Never lease a vehicle! A lease seems like a good idea because it offers a smaller payment but there are often mileage restrictions that carry heavy penalties, and at the end of the lease, you don't own anything. It's like renting a car but with a lot of rules that aren't in your favor.

When searching for a used car or truck, many websites can be helpful. But, word to the wise, be careful about buying a vehicle from popular online classified ads. People trying to pass off previously totaled vehicles or cars with significant issues often list these cars online, where unsuspecting buyers are looking.

Here's a checklist to keep in mind:

- *Always ask if the car has a clean title. A rebuilt title means the car was totaled at one time.*

- *Inspect the body and windows, wheels and tires, and the interior.*

- *If the car has a manual transmission, can you drive a stick shift?*

- *Mileage: I usually try to buy a vehicle with fewer than 100,000 miles.*

- *Look under the car for leaks, damage, and/or signs of an accident.*

- *A mechanic will do an inspection for approximately $100.*

- *Check the Kelley Blue Book for pricing based on a vehicle's mileage, year, conditions, and features.*

DAD TIP: **If you see a vehicle for sale on the side of the road, don't bother to call if there is no price listed on the For Sale sign.**

41. How to Look under the Hood

Many people who look under their car's hood have no idea what they are looking at. Before I go on any trips, I always check these things. A good way to remember which fluids to check is by remembering the acronym WASH BOATS.

WASHER FLUID: Check to make sure that your windshield washer fluid reservoir is full. If you're driving and mud flies onto your windshield, you'll be thankful that you did so. Turning on your wipers without the fluid will only smear the mud, making it even harder to see.

BRAKE FLUID: Check your brake fluid container to make sure it is full. Brakes work through hydraulics. When you push on the brake pedal and the fluid level is low, you'll have to push the pedal down further before your brakes engage, which can be scary!

OIL: Check your car's oil to make sure it is clean and full. Oil keeps the engine lubricated so that it runs properly. If you let the oil level get too low, the engine has to work harder, the parts can get damaged, and your engine may seize up. Park your car on a flat surface and turn off your engine. The oil reading will be most accurate if the engine has been off for ten minutes, so all of the oil has time to run down into the pan.

ANTIFREEZE: Check the antifreeze level to make sure it is full of engine coolant. Never check this when the engine is hot because the fluid could scald you. The "cool"ant is necessary to keep your engine cool so it won't overheat.

TRANSMISSION FLUID: Check the transmission fluid. Your car's transmission is what transmits the power of the engine to the wheels to move the vehicle. It needs to stay lubricated so that the gears shift properly. The engine should be running while checking this fluid.

STEERING FLUID: If the power steering fluid level is low, steering will be difficult.

A few other items to check besides the fluids are:

BATTERY: Take a look at the battery to make sure the connection is good and there isn't a lot of corrosion.

AIR FILTER: Look at the air filter to make sure it isn't overly dirty. Change it periodically so your engine can breathe.

TIRES: Keep an eye on your tires and the recommended air pressure. They can often change due to the change in the weather. It's also a good idea to keep an eye on your spare tire to make sure it is in usable condition in case you need it. To decide if your car's tires are still roadworthy, stick a penny between the treads with the Lincoln side facing you. If you can see the top of Lincoln's head, it's time to change your tires.

Self-Improvement

42. How to Start a Conversation (and Keep It Going)

One of the most helpful skills in life is being a good conversationalist. However, we often make getting the conversation started the hardest part. If you're like me and you wait until you have the "perfect line," you will probably never even begin. Don't overthink this part; once you get past it, things should move pretty naturally. The main rule to remember is to be genuinely interested in the other person, and the conversation will almost always flow. Other tips I've learned over the years to start, or carry on, a conversation are:

- *Think about what you may have in common.*

- *Try to challenge yourself to avoid asking "How are you?" Instead, try to use what you may have in common to come up with something a little more thoughtful.*

- *Remember their name and use it once or twice naturally in the conversation to help it stick in your mind long-term. Don't overuse their name or it will look like you're trying to sell them something.*

- *Ask the other person open-ended questions instead of ones that will elicit only yes or no replies. For instance, a query such as "Tell me about your hometown" is going to require a longer response than "Where are you from?"*

- *If a sensitive subject comes up, tread lightly. Focus on the positive.*

- *It's okay to have an opinion; just make sure the other person feels like they can safely share theirs.*

- *Listen to learn, not to reply.*

- *Know when to be silent, and don't overshare.*

- *Last but not least, be present in the moment. Don't check your phone or your watch!*

43. How to Be Loving

It's easy to love the loveable; it's much harder to love the unlovable. This very practical list comes from 1 Corinthians 13:4–8.

LOVE IS PATIENT. It's easy to be impatient. It takes effort to have patience.

LOVE IS KIND. Choose kindness.

LOVE DOES NOT ENVY. When others are successful in an area that we wish we were, it's easy to feel envious rather than rejoice with them for their success.

LOVE DOES NOT BOAST. No one likes a bragger.

LOVE IS NOT PROUD. Lay aside your pride so you can love well.

LOVE DOES NOT DISHONOR OTHERS. Be aware of other people's feelings.

LOVE IS NOT SELF-SEEKING. Put others before yourself.

LOVE IS NOT EASILY ANGERED. Don't be quick-tempered; if you are, look for help in this area.

LOVE KEEPS NO RECORD OF WRONGS. If the scab has healed, don't keep picking it.

LOVE DOES NOT DELIGHT IN EVIL. Don't participate in evil, flee from it!

LOVE REJOICES WITH THE TRUTH. The truth will set you free.

LOVE ALWAYS PROTECTS. Look out for others whenever possible.

LOVE ALWAYS TRUSTS. Be trusting, but also verify.

LOVE ALWAYS HOPES. Never give up hope.

LOVE ALWAYS PERSEVERES. Keep on loving, and love will win.

LOVE NEVER FAILS. Love will never let you down.

Choose love!

44. How to Be a Good Friend

The best advice I have on this topic is to remember the golden rule: "Do unto others as you would have them do unto you" (Luke 6:31). To be a good friend, keep these tips in mind:

- *Life is short, don't hold a grudge. If it's in your power to forgive, do it.*

- *Admit when you're wrong, and ask for forgiveness.*

- *Don't allow things to fester.*

- *Don't let the sun go down on your anger.*

- *Be loyal as long as it doesn't compromise your own convictions.*

- *Make sure to initiate contact with them. Don't make them always have to reach out to you.*

45. How to Be a Good Parent

My friend Justin Batt sums up my personal philosophy on parenting well: "The days are long, but the years are short." Your kids are little for such a short window of time—enjoy it. If you get off track, readjust and try again.

Parenting is a rewarding experience, but it isn't easy. You have to balance helping your child feel loved while still helping them to learn the difference between right and wrong.

Here are a few of my tips on parenting:

- *Set clear boundaries with defined consequences in advance.*

- *Be consistent with punishment.*

- *Create a loving environment.*

- *Give plenty of affection. Make an effort to bond with your child.*

- *Love your children unconditionally.*

- *Emphasize the importance of experiences over things. Toys might be entertaining for a while but sharing an experience with you makes children feel loved and cared for.*

- *Praise them for their accomplishments.*

- *Don't compare your children to others, especially their siblings.*

- *Pay full attention to your kids when they're talking to you. Put away your phone, turn off the TV. Be fully present.*

- *Make one-on-one time for each child.*

- *Respect your child's privacy.*

- *Be there—especially for the milestones. Your boss may not remember if you missed that meeting, but your child will certainly remember if you didn't attend that game, that play, or that event.*

Work Life

46. How to Write a Résumé

First, pick the right résumé template based on what others in your field have used. A quick Google search will send you in the right direction. Note that a résumé is used more often than a curriculum vitae, which is the preference in academic or scholarly circles.

Most résumés follow a general structure: name and contact information at the top, then pertinent experience listed in chronological order followed by education information and achievements. Some résumés include names and contact details for personal references and relevant skills, where applicable.

It's easy to overcomplicate a résumé with fancy fonts and graphics, but please resist doing so. Employers are not looking for the prettiest or most cleverly designed résumé (unless you're in the graphic arts field). They're looking for a summary of information that tells them if you are a candidate with the right experience for their position.

The most important thing is to communicate your experience and skills in a concise, one-page format with *no* typos. Be sure to have multiple people proofread your résumé.

DAD TIP: **Always include a personalized cover letter with your résumé—make sure to proofread it as well.**

47. How to Interview for a Job

Here are some key points that I believe are helpful in putting your best foot forward during job interviews.

- *Dress appropriately. It's better to be a little overdressed than underdressed; just don't overdo it.*

- *For men, it's usually safe to wear a button-down dress shirt with a tie and slacks. For women, dress pants and a blouse can carry you almost anywhere.*

- *Pay attention to your shoes. They can tell people a lot about you whether you know it or not.*

- *Be on time! Arrive a few minutes early if possible.*

- *Shake hands firmly but not too firmly and look the person in the eye.*

- *Bring a copy of your résumé and portfolio, if applicable.*

- *Always send a thank-you email—a handwritten note is polite, but may be a bit too formal depending on your situation.*

- *If you haven't heard anything back after a week, follow up politely to inquire about the status of the job.*

It can be useful to do a practice walk-through with a parent or good friend to help you become familiar with the interviewing process. Role-playing might not exactly match the real thing, but it can ease your nerves a little bit.

You got this!

AT WORK

48. How to Be Productive

I owe thanks to my son for showing me the Pomodoro Technique. It's a great way to structure your time so you get things done. And it's probably one of the simplest productivity methods to implement: All you need is a timer. It's called the Pomodoro Technique because the inventor used a tomato-shaped timer in developing the method, and *pomodoro* means "tomato" in Italian.

Choose a task to be accomplished. Then:

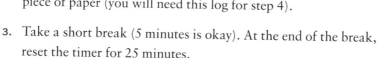

1. Set the pomodoro to 25 minutes (the pomodoro is the timer).

2. Work on the task until the pomodoro rings; if you like, keep track of each work session by making a checkmark on a piece of paper (you will need this log for step 4).

3. Take a short break (5 minutes is okay). At the end of the break, reset the timer for 25 minutes.

4. Every four pomodoros (or after you've logged four checkmarks on your list), take a longer break, up to 30 minutes.

Each is usually 15 to 30 minutes—however long it takes to make you feel recharged and ready to start another 25-minute work session. Repeat the process a few times over the course of a workday to get a lot accomplished.

It's important to note that a pomodoro is an indivisible unit of work—if you're distracted partway by a coworker, meeting, or emergency, you either have to end the pomodoro at the point of interruption (save your work and start a new session later), or you have to postpone the distraction until the pomodoro is complete. If you can do the latter, all the better.

49. How to Prioritize

It's a learned skill to be able to prioritize. Learn as early as possible in your life how to decide what is important; otherwise you may spend too much time on things that don't really matter and not enough on things that do. When it comes to my family, I have always put them at the top of my list. What that meant, especially when my children were young, was that I had to pass on things that were a lower priority. As you make decisions in your life, it's a good practice to make a list of your priorities, especially the top several. For example, my list of relationship priorities looks like this:

God
Family
Myself
My friends
Others

I personally start with God, because I have found that if my relationship with him is good, everything else falls into place. I can love my wife and kids properly when I have his love flowing through me.

To help prioritize your time, follow the 80/20 rule, also known as the Pareto Principle, named after Italian economist Vilfredo Pareto. The principle states that roughly 80 percent of the effects come from 20 percent of the causes; that is, 80 percent of the results come from 20 percent of the work.

Being able to prioritize is an often overlooked skill, and one that I would highly recommend you learn sooner rather than later.

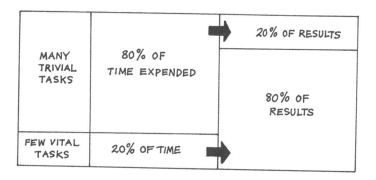

50. How to Give a Speech

Anyone who knows me would be surprised that I decided to include a how-to on public speaking in this book. However, as I look back on my life, I wish I would have taken the opportunities presented to give speeches.

It's easy to say this now because public speaking has by far always been my biggest fear. However, because I constantly avoided it, the monster was able to grow and take on a life of its own. It honestly got so debilitating for me that I would do literally anything to get out of having to speak in front of a group. A few years ago, I was able to reel this fear back in. It wasn't easy, and I went through several fight-or-flight episodes, but now it's at least manageable. I still don't necessarily seek out the opportunity to give a speech, but if an offer comes my way, I don't immediately turn it down.

According to the National Institute of Mental Health, the fear of public speaking affects roughly 73 percent of the population.[1]

Comedian Jerry Seinfeld has joked, "According to most studies, people's number one fear is public speaking. Number two is death. Death is number two. Does that sound right? This means to the average person, if you go to a funeral, you're better off in the casket than doing the eulogy."[2]

The following tips are based on what I've learned from giving speeches over the years.

- PREPARE BEFOREHAND. *Write down some cues to refer to, but don't read straight from them. Only read directly from your notes when quoting someone else, so you get the wording right. Don't write out and then read your entire speech. You might be tempted to do so, and you obviously will get through it, but that isn't the point of public speaking, and your audience will just be waiting to get through it, too!*

- VISUALIZE A SUCCESSFUL SPEECH. *See yourself performing well in your mind.*

- IT'S NORMAL TO BE NERVOUS, SO EMBRACE THE FEELING. *Be kind to yourself.*

- WHEN YOU'RE INTRODUCED, WALK QUICKLY *to the podium so you look excited to be there.*

- PAUSE *for a second, take a breath, and look at everyone before you start.*

- SPEAK LOUD AND CLEAR, *don't rush.*

- WAIT FOR APPLAUSE *when appropriate. Don't step on your success.*

- MAKE EYE CONTACT. *It's funny, but I used to think that looking over the audience's heads would help me relax. However, that made me more nervous because I had no idea how they were reacting, and all I could picture was an angry mob. When I began to make eye contact, I would see familiar faces and think, Oh,* that's my friend Jim, and There is my sister Laurie. *Connecting with the audience really took the fear of public speaking out of me.*

- THANK YOUR AUDIENCE WHEN YOU'RE DONE.

- WAIT FOR THE FINAL APPLAUSE.

You've got this!

Bonus Section

1. How to Read the Bible

Many people reject the Bible without ever reading it for themselves. My challenge to you is to look at it for yourself, then make your choice. Like I shared with you in chapter 3, it's smart and healthy to question authority and to consider something from your own perspective. If you choose to reject an idea or experience, at least you'll know what it is you're rejecting.

Most people want to start at the beginning of the Bible, which seems like the logical place to start. However, I would encourage you to start with the Gospel of John and to ask God to open your eyes to understanding it. If you do start at the beginning, you have my permission to skip Leviticus, Numbers, and Deuteronomy, and jump to Joshua after Exodus. I have known many people with the best intentions of finally reading the Bible who've given up after Exodus.

The following is an extremely brief outline of the Bible that hopefully will help you understand how it is laid out. If you have watched my YouTube channel, you know I try to keep things as simple as I possibly can.

OLD TESTAMENT

GENESIS, EXODUS, LEVITICUS, NUMBERS, DEUTERONOMY: The books of the law. Genesis and Exodus are mainly history, and the next three cover the law as well as some history.

JOSHUA, JUDGES, RUTH, 1 AND 2 SAMUEL, 1 AND 2 KINGS, 1 AND 2 CHRONICLES, EZRA, NEHEMIAH, ESTHER: The historical books that pick up where Exodus leaves off.

JOB, PSALMS, PROVERBS, ECCLESIASTES, SONG OF SOLOMON: The books of poetry.

ISAIAH, JEREMIAH, LAMENTATIONS, EZEKIEL, DANIEL: The major prophets (called major only because of their size).

HOSEA, JOEL, AMOS, OBADIAH, JONAH, MICAH, NAHUM, HABAKKUK, ZEPHANIAH, HAGGAI, ZECHARIAH, MALACHI: The minor prophets (called minor only because of their size).

NEW TESTAMENT

MATTHEW, MARK, LUKE, JOHN: The gospels. These books tell the story of Jesus's life from four different perspectives.

ACTS: Written by Luke, this book tells of the early church. It includes the tale of the conversion of Saul, who is renamed Paul.

ROMANS, 1 AND 2 CORINTHIANS, GALATIANS, EPHESIANS, PHILIPPIANS, COLOSSIANS, 1 AND 2 THESSALONIANS, 1 AND 2 TIMOTHY, TITUS,

PHILEMON: Letters (called epistles) written by Paul to the various churches.

HEBREWS, JAMES, 1 AND 2 PETER, 1, 2, AND 3 JOHN, JUDE: General letters written by various authors.

REVELATION: The last book of the Bible, a book of prophecy, written by John.

I hope you take the time to read the Bible for yourself. I am praying for you.

2. How to Remember

I use acronyms and mnemonics all of the time to help me remember things, like grocery lists or other similar lists of items.

Here's how I use an acronym to remember the order of the planets, starting with those closest to the sun.

M-VEM-J-SUN-P

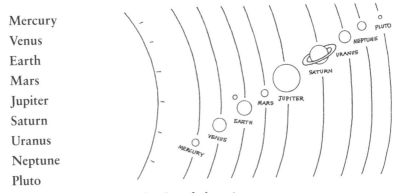

Mercury
Venus
Earth
Mars
Jupiter
Saturn
Uranus
Neptune
Pluto
(Pluto is now considered a dwarf planet)

3. How Addresses Work

Most city addresses are laid out on a grid. Let's take a look at a simple layout in a city close to me. Notice four things:

1. The streets running horizontally (east to west) have "NE" and "SE" before street number.

Ave.- North & South
Streets- East & West

105th Ave NE 106th Ave NE 107th Ave NE 108th Ave NE

N ⬆

NE 2nd

NE 1st

Main St

SE 1st

SE 2nd

105th Ave SE 106th Ave SE 107th Ave SE 108th Ave SE

2. The streets running vertically (north to south) have "Ave." after the street number.

3. The streets running horizontally change from SE to NE when they cross Main Street.

4. The streets running vertically change from "Ave. SE" to "Ave. NE" when they cross Main Street.

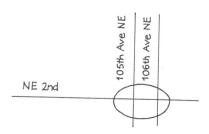

NE 2nd

105th Ave NE   106th Ave NE

Now let's zoom in on a portion of the map. Notice four more things:

1. The addresses on the north side are all even numbers.

2. The addresses on the south side are all odd numbers.

3. The addresses between 105th and 106th all start with 105.

4. As you move from 105th Ave. SE to 106th Ave. SE, the address numbers gradually get larger.

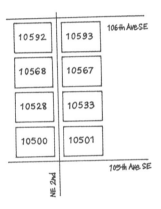

4. How to Determine Your Net Worth

Your net worth is based on how much money you keep, not how much you earn. There are plenty of people who make six figures, and have for some time, but who still aren't millionaires. Your net worth is how much you have minus how much you owe, otherwise known as assets and liabilities. Assets are the things you own. Liabilities are what you owe.

Let's use the following examples to understand how assets and liabilities work in relation to net worth:

IF YOUR HOUSE IS WORTH $300,000, AND YOU OWE $200,000 YOU CAN ADD $100,000 TO YOUR NET WORTH.

IF YOUR CARS ARE WORTH $20,000, AND YOU OWE $25,000, SUBTRACT $5,000 FROM YOUR NET WORTH.

IF YOU HAVE $20,000 IN RETIREMENT FUNDS ADD THAT NUMBER TO YOUR NET WORTH.

IF YOU HAVE STUDENT LOANS OF $50,000 SUBTRACT THAT NUMBER FROM YOUR NET WORTH.

Tally up these numbers:

HOUSE: + $100,000
RETIREMENT: + $20,000
CARS: − $5,000
STUDENT LOANS: − $50,000

And your net worth in this scenario would be $65,000.

Several years ago, I started tracking our net worth in a spreadsheet, and honestly it has been fun to watch it grow. It has also encouraged us to want to make it grow faster, by adding more to our investments and savings. Try it, you'll see what I mean!

5. How to Double Your Money

Now that we've covered investing, I want you to learn about the power of compound interest. Albert Einstein has been rumored to have said: "Compound interest is the most powerful force in the universe." No matter the source of this comment, I understand the sentiment behind it. Compound interest is your friend!

Take a look at the chart below.

KNOW THE RULE OF 72

The Rule of 72 tells you how long it will take for your money to double: Multiply the interest rate by the years. For example, at a 6 percent interest rate, your money will double in 12 years (6 × 12 = 72). It will double in 9 years at an interest rate of 8 percent (8 × 9 = 72), and so on.

THE RULE OF 72
It's not exact, but it's a good rule to know

6%

Year	1	2	3	4	5	6	7	8	9	10	11	12
$1,000	$1,060	$1,124	$1,191	$1,262	$1,338	$1,419	$1,504	$1,594	$1,689	$1,791	$1,898	$2,012

8%

Year	1	2	3	4	5	6	7	8	9
$1,000	$1,080	$1,166	$1,260	$1,360	$1,469	$1,587	$1,714	$1,851	$1,999

12%

Year	1	2	3	4	5	6
$1,000	$1,120	$1,254	$1,405	$1,574	$1,762	$1,974

6. How to Negotiate

In my opinion, negotiation tactics are important life skills to obtain as soon as you possibly can. You will find them helpful not only in the business arena, but in personal and financial areas as well. If you don't ask for something you want, how will you know you can't have it? However, it is important to always be respectful in how you ask.

Here are my steps for good negotiations.

- RESEARCH. *Before entering negotiations, do your research. It's always better to be overprepared rather than caught off guard.*

- AIM HIGH. *It's not really much of a negotiation if what you want is too easily attained.*

- **ASK LEADING QUESTIONS.** *Try to get the other side talking.*

- **BE QUIET.** *Once they're talking, close your mouth and listen.*

- **BE COOL.** *Never be in a rush, and always know that you can walk away. When I was in Florence, Italy, at their public market, I got the best deals when I simply began to walk away.*

- **FLIP SIDES.** *Try to see things from the other person's perspective. As much as you can, put yourself in their shoes. Then paint a picture for the other side, so they can see how what you want benefits them. Also, consider what pressure(s) they may have on them in this deal.*

- **STAY FOCUSED.** *Always keep in mind what you're negotiating, and don't get distracted by personal issues you may have with the other person. Remember, it's not personal.*

- **GET SOMETHING IF YOU GIVE SOMETHING.** *Never give something away without getting something in return. You might be surprised, but the other side will actually feel better about the deal if they give you something than they would if they gave you nothing.*

7. How to Travel

Traveling has certainly changed while I've been writing this book. However, knowing how to travel when it is again safe to do so is certainly a skill I want to pass along.

Traveling domestically is pretty easy. Obviously, having a photo ID is essential when you travel by plane. Here are the general how-tos that I keep in mind.

BOOKING TRAVEL

- *Book at least two weeks in advance to get the lowest fare. Using one of the popular travel sites, like Trivago or Expedia, is a great way to compare fares.*

- *If your dates are flexible, you might be able to save a little bit on your fare by shifting around your departure and return schedules.*

- *Be aware that you can earn points from airlines and some credit cards; do some research on this to get the most value from any travel you book.*

- *Booking a hotel room at the same time that you book your airfare on one of the travel websites often can save money.*

- *Be aware that if you're traveling during a holiday or a high season it's best to book as far in advance as possible to get your preferred flight and hotel.*

- *Don't prepay for a hotel room unless you have to. Rather, a room can be secured with a credit card. Cancel at least twenty-four hours in advance—or according to the hotel's cancellation policy—to avoid your card being charged.*

- *Decide whether you'll require a rental car while making your other reservations and book if needed. Note that most car rental companies require renters to be twenty-five or older. It's possible to find one that doesn't have this age minimum, but they will generally charge more.*

AIRPORT PROTOCOL

- *Research what size luggage your airline allows to be carried on. Carrying on is by far the easiest way to travel because it keeps you from having to wait for luggage to be unloaded once you arrive.*

- *Note the FAA's guidelines on what you can and can't pack in carry-on luggage. Pay special attention to the size of certain toiletries allowed.*

- *Arrive two hours early to ensure you can be processed through the security line in time for your flight.*

- *Check your luggage at the curb if you're not carrying on. Tip the luggage handler.*

- *Have a photo ID ready to present along with either a hard copy of your boarding pass or an electronic copy on your smartphone.*

- *Make your way to the concourse and stay in your gate area. Be alert for any announcements that affect your flight.*

INTERNATIONAL TRAVEL

- *Visit the State Department website, www.travel.state.gov, for information on how to get a passport for international travel.*

- *In some cases, you may need to apply for a passport in person. The State Department travel website explains these instances.*

- *You must have proof of U.S. citizenship, such as a birth certificate.*

- *At the time of this writing, passports routinely take ten to twelve weeks to be processed.*

8. How to Make Christmas Cookies

My mom used to make these cookies every Christmas when I was little, and they were always a favorite!

Mom's Christmas Cookies

MAKES **8** DOZEN COOKIES

1½ cups margarine
1½ cups salted butter, softened
2 eggs
2 teaspoons vanilla
8 cups flour, plus extra for rolling the dough
2 cups sugar
2 teaspoons baking powder
Icing (recipe follows)
Sprinkles

1. In a large bowl, beat the margarine and butter together with an electric mixer on high for 30 seconds.
2. Add the eggs and the vanilla and beat until combined.
3. In a separate bowl, combine 2 cups of the flour, the sugar, and the baking powder.
4. Add the dry ingredients to the margarine mixture. Beat until thoroughly combined.
5. Add the remaining 6 cups of flour, 1 cup at a time.
6. Form the dough into a ball and wrap it in plastic wrap. Chill in the refrigerator for 2 hours (this makes it easier to work with).
7. Preheat the oven to 375°F. Line baking sheets with parchment paper.
8. Sprinkle some flour on a flat surface and roll the dough out evenly until it is about ¼-inch thick. Cut the dough into shapes using cookie cutters.
9. Place the cookies on the prepared baking sheets and bake for 12 minutes, or until the cookies are just starting to brown around the edges. If you're cooking two trays at a time,

increase the time to 14 minutes, and swap the trays on the oven racks halfway through baking.

10. Cool the cookies on a wire rack.

11. When the cookies are completely cool, decorate with the icing and sprinkles. The icing will harden in a few hours.

ICING

2 cups powdered sugar, sifted
½ teaspoon vanilla
1 tablespoon milk, plus more as needed for desired consistency

In a medium bowl, mix together the powdered sugar, vanilla, and 1 tablespoon of milk. Add more milk, 1 teaspoon at a time, until you reach the desired consistency.

ACKNOWLEDGMENTS

I first want to thank my Lord and Savior, Jesus Christ. The hope and unconditional love he lavishly pours out upon me is beyond all human wisdom.

Thank you to my wife of thirty years, Annelli, for your ongoing support and help with everything. Our lives were unexpectedly turned upside down last year, and I am glad I had you to go through it with me. I love you, Honey Honey.

Thanks to my daughter, Kristine, for believing in me, and encouraging (prodding?) me to put myself out there. Also, for all of the "behind the scenes" help that you are constantly providing. You are an unsung hero to your dad.

Huge thanks to Mauro DiPreta and the team at William Morrow for believing in me and giving me the opportunity to write this book.

Thanks to my team at EPIC Agency with not only this book, but also for helping me navigate my chaotic schedule when my YouTube channel went viral.

Thanks to my collaborative writer and newfound friend, Marcus Brotherton.

A special thanks to my brother Rick and his wife, Karen, for always being there for me and helping me yet again with their well-needed suggestions in the writing of this book.

NOTES

2. Mail That Postcard

1. See, for instance, Noam Shpancer, "Action Creates Emotion," *Psychology Today,* October 25, 2010, https://www.psychologytoday.com/us/blog/insight-therapy/201010/action-creates-emotion.

2. For an extended discussion of how the principle of positive proactivity works in marriage, see the book *Cherish* by Gary Thomas (Grand Rapids, Michigan: Zondervan, 2017).

3. See Exodus 20:12, Deuteronomy 5:16, Matthew 15:4, Ephesians 6:2.

4. Quote has been modified over the years and attributed in different forms to Carrie Fisher, Nelson Mandela, and others. The earliest strong match appeared in 1980, in *The Angry Christian* by Bert Ghezzi (Ann Arbor, MI: Servant Books, 1980), 99. See https://quoteinvestigator.com/2017/08/19/resentment/.

5. R. T. Kendall, *Total Forgiveness,* rev. ed. (Lake Mary, FL: Charisma House, 2007), 33.

6. See Deuteronomy 31:6 and Hebrews 13:5.

3. Keep Your Brains from Falling Out

1. See https://quoteinvestigator.com/2014/04/13/open-mind/.

2. See Ephesians 4:14.

3. A modern proverb with unknown authorship. A precursor was in circulation by 1926, and the earliest known close match occurred in an article by Gordon A. Eadie in 1945. See https://quoteinvestigator2 .com/2014/02/18/stand-fall/.

4. Warren Wiersbe, *Be Loyal: Following the King of Kings; NT Commentary: Matthew,* 2nd ed. (Colorado Springs: David C. Cook, 2008), chap. 15, Kindle.

5. See Mark 4:35–41.

6. See the story at the Hans Christian Andersen Centre, https://andersen .sdu.dk/vaerk/hersholt/TheEmperorsNewClothes_e.html.

4. Bust That Logjam

1. Colossians 3:23.

2. Greg Ukuhara, "Brian Regan Keeps It Clean While Delivering Laughs," *Houston Chronicle,* October 21, 2009, https://blog.chron.com/ peep/2009/10/brian-regan-keeps-it-clean-while-delivering-laughs/.

3. Tim Herrerra, "Take Naps at Work. Apologize to No One," *New York Times,* June 23, 2017, https://www.nytimes.com/2017/06/23/smarter-living/take-naps-at-work-apologize-to-no-one.html.

5. Remove the Stickers

1. Belle Beth Cooper, "Why Positive Encouragement Works Better Than Criticism, According to Science," Buffer, January 13, 2014, https://buffer .com/resources/why-positive-encouragement-works-better-than-criticism-according-to-science/.

2. "Words of Encouragement and Inspiration: The Science Behind How They Work," Fact Goods, September 22, 2019, https://www.factgoods .com/blogs/fg/words-of-encouragement-and-inspiration.

3. Billy Graham, "A Time for Moral Courage," *Reader's Digest*, July 1964, https://www.quotes.net/quote/37210.

4. Teddy Roosevelt, from the speech "Citizenship in a Republic," given on April 23, 1910. See the text of the speech at Theodore Roosevelt Center at Dickinson State University, https://www.theodorerooseveltcenter.org/ Learn-About-TR/TR-Encyclopedia/Culture-and-Society/Man-in-the- Arena.aspx.

5. Attributed to Charles Eads. See https://quoteinvestigator .com/2019/09/15/hurt/.

6. Max Lucado, *You Are Special* (Wheaton, IL: Crossway Books, 1997).

6. Jump into the Pool

1. See https://en.wikiquote.org/wiki/Talk:Will_Rogers. Note: This quote is sometimes attributed to Mother Teresa.

2. See https://www.quoteslyfe.com/quote/ There-are-many-talented-people-who-haven-284200.

3. James Stein, "The Calculus of Caution," *Psychology Today,* May 29, 2010, https://www.psychologytoday.com/us/blog/ you-are-what-you-decide/201005/the-calculus-caution.

4. "Number of Employees at the Microsoft Corporation from 2005 to 2020," Statista, https://www.statista.com/statistics/273475/ number-of-employees-at-the-microsoft-corporation-since-2005/.

5. Timothy Egan, "Microsoft's Unlikely Millionaires," *New York Times,* June 28, 1992, https://www.nytimes.com/1992/06/28/business/ microsoft-s-unlikely-millionaires.html.

6. John Ballard, "If You Invested $5,000 in Microsoft's IPO, This Is How Much Money You'd Have Now," Motley Fool, December 15, 2019, https://www.fool.com/investing/2019/12/15/if-you-invested-5000-in-microsofts-ipo-this-is-how.aspx.

7. "Frequency of Prayer," Pew Research Center, https://www.pewforum.org/religious-landscape-study/frequency-of-prayer/.

8. National Study of Youth & Religion, "Do Teens Pray? How Often?" University of Notre Dame, https://youthandreligion.nd.edu/related-resources/preliminary-research-findings/do-teens-pray-how-often/.

9. Marcia Reynolds, "How to Determine if a Risk Is Worth Taking," *Psychology Today,* January 6, 2019, https://www.psychologytoday.com/us/blog/wander-woman/201901/how-determine-if-risk-is-worth-taking.

10. Carlos Arribas, "Honesty of the Long-Distance Runner," *El Pais,* February 24, 2013, https://english.elpais.com/elpais/2012/12/19/inenglish/1355928581_856388.html.

11. Melissa De Witte, "Instead of 'Finding Your Passion,' Try Developing It, Stanford Scholars Say," Stanford News, June 18, 2018, https://news.stanford.edu/2018/06/18/find-passion-may-bad-advice/.

12. Ibid.

13. Dr. Seuss, *Green Eggs and Ham* (New York: Random House, 1960).

7. Hold with an Open Hand

1. Maria Konnikova, "The Psychology Behind Gift-Giving and Generosity," *Literally Psyched* (blog), *Scientific American,* January 4, 2012, https://blogs.scientificamerican.com/literally-psyched/the-psychology-behind-gift-giving-and-generosity/.

2. Jenna Bryner, "Key to Happiness: Give Away Money," Live Science, March 20, 2008, https://www.livescience.com/2376-key-happiness-give-money.html.

3. W. M. Brown, N. S. Consedine, & C. Magai (2005). "Altruism relates to health in an ethnically diverse sample of older adults," *Journals of Gerontology Series B-Psychological Sciences and Social Sciences*, 60(3), P143–P152. Cited in Summer Allen, *The Science of Generosity*, a white paper prepared for the John Templeton Foundation by the Greater Good Science Center at UC Berkley, page 19, https://ggsc.berkeley.edu/images/uploads/GGSC-JTF_White_Paper-Generosity-FINAL.pdf.

4. Mark 12:38–44.

8. Live Your Wild and Precious Life

1. Mary Oliver, *House of Light* (Boston: Beacon Press, 1992).

2. Sheldon Vanauken, *A Severe Mercy*, rev. ed. (New York: HarperCollins, 2011).

3. C. S. Lewis, "The Weight of Glory" in *The Weight of Glory and Other Essays*, ed. Walter Hooper (New York: Macmillan, 1980), 3–4.

4. John Montopoli, "Public Speaking Anxiety and Fear of Brain Freezes," National Social Anxiety Center, February 20, 2017, https://nationalsocialanxietycenter.com/2017/02/20/public-speaking-and-fear-of-brain-freezes/.

5. Blaise Pascal, *Pensees* (New York: Penguin Books, 1966), 75.

6. "The Magic Thread" is told in William J. Bennett, *The Book of Virtues* (New York: Simon and Schuster, 1996), 59–63.

Personal Finance

1. Zack Friedman, "78% of Workers Live Paycheck to Paycheck," *Forbes,* January 11, 2019, https://www.forbes.com/sites/zackfriedman/2019/01/11/live-paycheck-to-paycheck-government-shutdown/sh=ed82f824f10b.

Work Life

1. John Montopoli, "Public Speaking Anxiety and Fear of Brain Freezes," National Social Anxiety Center, February 20, 2017, https://nationalsocialanxietycenter.com/2017/02/20/ public-speaking-and-fear-of-brain-freezes/.

2. Jerry Seinfeld, "Seinfeld on Public Speaking," *I'm Telling You for the Last Time*. Directed by Marty Callner. New York: Live at Broadhurst Theater. HBO, August 9, 1998. Archived at https://www.youtube.com/ watch?v=yQ6giVKp9ec.

ABOUT THE AUTHOR

Rob Kenney has been married for thirty years. He and his wife have two adult children in their twenties. Rob lives near Seattle and hosts the popular YouTube channel *Dad, How Do I?* He is affably referred to, the world over, as the Internet's Favorite Dad.